Architecture of Schools

Architecture of Schools

THE NEW LEARNING ENVIRONMENTS

Mark Dudek

Architectural Press

OXFORD   AMSTERDAM   BOSTON   LONDON   NEW YORK   PARIS
SAN DIEGO   SAN FRANCISCO   SINGAPORE   SYDNEY   TOKYO

Architectural Press is an imprint of Elsevier
Linacre House, Jordan Hill, Oxford OX2 8DP, UK
30 Corporate Drive, Suite 400, Burlington, MA 01803, USA

First edition 2000
Reprinted 2002, 2006, 2007

British Library Cataloguing in Publication Data
Dudek, Mark
    Architecture of schools: the new learning environments
    1. School buildings   2. School buildings – History
    I. Title
    727

Library of Congress Cataloguing in Publication Data
Dudek, Mark
    Architecture of schools: the new learning environment/Mark
    Dudek.
    p. cm.
    Includes index.
    ISBN 0 7506 3585 1
    1. School buildings – Great Britain – Case studies.   2. Schools
    – Great Britain – Sociological aspects – Case studies.   I. Title.
    LB3219.g& D83
    727.0941-dc21

ISBN–13: 978-0-7506-3585-1
ISBN–10: 0-7506-3585-1

For information on all Architectural Press publications
visit our website at www.architecturalpress.com

Printed and bound in *China*

07 08 09 10   10 09 08 07 06 05 04

Contents

Foreword by Bryan Lawson   vii

Preface   ix

Acknowledgements   xi

Introduction   xiii

Part A Education and the Environment

    1   Origins and significant historical developments   1

    2   The educational curriculum and its implications   41

    3   Making the case for architecture in schools   72

    4   The community in school and the school in the community   101

Part B Case Studies

    1   The Speech and Learning Centre, Christopher Place, London   133
        Troughton and McAslam

    2   Seabird Island School, Agassiz, British Columbia   138
        Patkau Associates

    3   Strawberry Vale School, Victoria, British Columbia   141
        Patkau Associates

    4   Westborough Primary School, Westcliff-on-Sea, Essex   145
        Cottrell and Vermeulen

    5   Woodlea Primary School, Bordon, Hampshire   148
        Hampshire County Architects

    6   Anne Frank School, Papendrecht, The Netherlands   153
        Architectuurstudio Herman Hertzberger

    7   The Bombardon School, Almere, The Netherlands   159
        Architectuurstudio Herman Hertzberger

    8   Pokesdown Primary School, Bournemouth   163
        Format Milton

Contents

9   Ranelagh Multi-Denominational School, Ranelagh, Dublin   168
    O'Donnell and Tuomey

10 Little Village Academy, Chicago, Illinois   172
    Ross, Barney and Jankowski

11 Saint Benno Catholic Secondary School, Dresden   178
    Behnisch and Behnisch

12 Haute Vallée School, Jersey   184
    Architecture PLB

13 Elementary School, Morella, Spain   189
    Carme Pinõs

14 Admiral Lord Nelson Secondary School, Portsmouth, Hampshire   193
    Hampshire County Architects

15 Heinz Galinski School, Berlin   200
    Zvi Hecker

16 North Fort Myers High School, Florida   209
    Perkins and Will

17 Albert Einstein Oberschule, Berlin   214
    Stefan Scholz

18 Barnim Gymnasium, Berlin   220
    Stefan Scholz

19 Odenwaldschule, Frankfurt   224
    Peter Hübner

20 Waldorf School, Chorweiler, Cologne   226
    Peter Hübner

Index   235

Foreword

Professor Bryan Lawson

Of all the projects an architect can be asked to design, none can be more interesting and challenging than the school – in which the most important of all human activities, the education and development of our children, takes place. That activity is simultaneously purposive, planned and controlled, and yet also subtle, delicate and easily disturbed. We know precisely what we want to achieve in a school and yet we are clearly uncertain as to how it should be realized. Critically, the success of education depends so much on the quality of the pupil/teacher relationship. This then requires an architect who is sensitive to human relationships and aware of how to promote and foster them through the built environment.

Schools have many stakeholders, from the pupil to the teacher, from the caretaker to the head, from the parent to the governor. These various participants tend to have different levels of involvement in the briefing and design process and to have unequal influence. Characteristically those furthest removed from the architect during design may be the most vulnerable to bad design. The great Dutch architect Herman Hertzberger has a reputation for a very humane approach to architecture and for taking at least as much of an interest in the occupants of his architecture as the buildings themselves. He is known for his Apollo schools in Amsterdam and it must have been the experience of working on these that led him to tell me: '... *I prefer for instance to make a school over making a house, because the house I feel has too much of a constraint to just follow the particularity and idiosyncrasy of just one person or a couple. I prefer to have a school where you have a board, you have teachers, you have parents and you have the children, and the users are all of them.*'

Recently a group of my students have been trying to extend and re-order an existing inner city school. On the site were buildings constructed over a period extending from the Victorian era to the 1960s. These buildings revealed not only changing architectural styles, but also, more fundamentally, changing values about the school itself. The Victorians with their pride in the institution and their obsession with natural light and fresh air built classrooms now too formal, large and high for modern needs.

By contrast the 1960s was a period in which flexibility was thought to be important, but the architectural result was placeless and uninspiring. So there are many ways to get a school wrong. Of course my students found even more ways of being wrong, but also some ways of being right too! For each of us, the school is such an important part of our own personal history that it may be difficult to imagine a school any other way. It is of course the job of architects to do just that, and yet also to understand what is good about what has gone before and to interpret this good practice in a contemporary way.

This is only likely to happen if we first establish some sound theories about the building type. Mark Dudek has studied the children's environment now for many years. He has shown us how important the environment, and specifically the architectural environment, is to the child's development. His previous book on the Kindergarten has become widely read and recognized as a major contribution to the field. Mark combines design practice with research and teaching and has used all three activities to develop both scholarship and sensibility about this complex area. This book, then, continues that combination in a rather special way. It provides a scholarly account of the history and changing values about education and how these have been reflected in the architecture of schools. It shows the development of the school as a building type. It provides ideas and guidance for the practising architect.

Recently there has been some debate about the nature of architectural research and what specifically constitutes architectural knowledge. Mark Dudek demonstrates here just how design can contribute to our understanding and knowledge. He shows, evaluates and compares many innovative and progressive pieces of school design. He tests them against theories of education and developmental psychology, as well as against more generic architectural ideas. Most importantly he also shows us how, through the practice of architecture, we can imagine places and ways of relating adults to children. It seems to me that architectural knowledge has to advance by just this sort of work.

University of Sheffield

Preface

The role of education within society has always been important. Today, the function of school architecture in that process is less obvious. Successive governments have failed in this area. Now, at the beginning of the new millennium, the evidence of this neglect can be seen in numerous badly maintained buildings, so-called 'reception classes' for the rising fours accommodated in lofty Victorian classrooms, inner city secondary schools with little or no external recreation space, and generally overcrowded, noisy classrooms. These and other anomalies are the result of a sustained period of neglect of the state education system.

One is almost tempted to describe it as wanton neglect by successive UK governments. And who is to say that this wasn't a deliberate policy of 'dumbing down'? In the immediate post-war years, many viewed education as a bridge between relative poverty to material and intellectual well-being. During the 1980s it is possible that the aim had been to allow or even to encourage the fabric of the state education system to run down. If the sons and daughters of cabinet ministers in charge of education policy were catered for in the well-funded private sector, why should the state make any more than adequate provision for the rest?

Apart from the obvious need to provide guidance on the design of environments for education, why embark upon such a lengthy exploration of school architecture? The answer lies partly in my own personal experience, which in hindsight is worth relating; the first school I knew comprised a series of temporary wooden huts built just after the Second World War. The transmission of noise from adjacent rooms, the unpleasant aroma of lunchtime cooking emanating from the galley kitchen, the hard exposed playground areas were a sudden, chaotic transformation from the relative order of my home environment. My senses became so heightened to the atmosphere that developing a critical response to any new environment became easy from a very early age. Trying to learn how to read and write in such an environment was another matter.

Perhaps the most disturbing effect of this was a sense of impermanence. If this was the message communicated by the spaces we were to inhabit for over a third of our waking lives, how could we develop our own innate sense of esteem and security? What brought this home even more profoundly was the change of school environment experienced around about the age of seven. A new purpose-built school was provided to replace the ageing huts. The effect this was to have on my sense of well-being was inestimable.

The new school within its own secure site had classrooms with solid walls and large openable windows, providing views onto the playing fields beyond. Each classroom had its own lavatories and cloakrooms. There was a multi-purpose hall with a sprung beech floor. The sign which read 'No Stiletto Heels' added an exotic touch which lent to that space a symbolic significance in my mind; it asserted the value of the architecture placing the needs of children over and above those of adults. Perhaps as a direct effect of those bright, spacious classrooms and the green spaces in which to run around at break times, my academic performance and my health improved in equal measure; the effect of a truly therapeutic environment.

That school had a particular architectural form which, on the evidence of a recent return visit, has endured the thirty or so years since it first opened. More about that aspect later in the text. For the moment it is interesting to speculate on the effect that new building may have had on me and its other alumni. Of course the staff in that new school must have been responsible for much of my newly discovered sense of well-being. However, for this particular old-boy, it was the architectural qualities which made all the difference. The quality of that school environment, its aromas, textures and colours, the ordered rituals it reinforced, all fixed within me a measure of my own value.

Despite this, different priorities now apply. Colleagues comment on my professional interests and the way in which they appear to follow my own children's progress through the education system. In this respect my motivations are clear. This interest reflects the crucial importance to me of my family and their well-being. Today the role children play in the lives of many people is accentuated in a similar way. Part of the reason for this is explained I believe by Ulrich Beck, when she talks of children as the focus of stability, *'the port in the storm'* which the stresses of contemporary family life cry out for: '... *Doting on children, pushing them on to the centre of the stage – the poor over-pampered creatures – and fighting for custody during and after divorce are all symptoms of this. The child becomes the final alternative to loneliness, a bastion against the vanishing chances of loving and being loved. It is a private way of "putting the magic back" into life to make up for general disenchantment. The birth rate may be declining but children have never been more important.'*

Perhaps it was always thus. However, it seems that we are living in times of great social change, where for large sections of the community the nuclear family of my youth is no longer the norm. People can easily become isolated and disconnected from their family roots. For various reasons, many parents, particularly fathers, spend extended periods apart from their children. The care and education they receive from others can quite rightly become an obsession.

Quotation from The Normal Chaos of Love
Ulrich Beck and Elizabeth Beck-Gernsheim,
Polity Press, 1995, p. 37

Acknowledgements

This project has been directly supported by the School of Architecture, University of Sheffield. Latterly, much of the research work was carried out with, and by, diploma students in Studio Three. This enabled a deeper understanding of school architecture to emerge. I would like to thank all who assisted in its difficult gestation and belated delivery, particularly Marie Milmore at Architectural Press.

My thanks also to those schools which allowed me to observe and learn whilst visiting, especially the following: The Good Shepherd Primary and Eskdale Primary, Nottingham; Cleves Fully Inclusive School, London; The Admiral Lord Nelson, Portsmouth; Wisewood Secondary, King Eckbert's Specialist School and Mosborough Primary, Sheffield; and the Albert Einstein Oberschule, Berlin.

I would also like to acknowledge the help of the following people, without whom this publication would not have been possible: Andy Thompson at the Architects and Buildings Branch, Department for Education and Employment, London; John Waldron at Architecture PLB, Winchester; Richard Jobson of Whitby Bird and Partners; Andrew Beard, Sheffield City Architect and Hilary Cottam, Architecture Foundation (see Chapter 4); Melanie Evans; Annabel Yonge and Andrew Mortimer; and all the architects who have provided material both for chapters one to four and the featured case studies.

My special thanks to Kenneth Macdonald, who once again gave me the wisdom of his architectural insights, and Dr Helen Penn who provided a similar and often critical appraisal with regards educational theory. Finally I would like to mention my mother who died suddenly during its research in October 1997. She taught diligently for 25 years at the same primary school in Nottingham. She dedicated great care and attention to the well-being of countless children. It is to her that I dedicate this book with great love.

Mark Dudek

Introduction

Education and its exemplification in buildings and environments has always been concerned with radical ideas set in new and stimulating settings. It had to be radical because it was a system of mass education, constantly reinventing itself to provide more and more educational places of an ever-improving quality.

The roots of an architecture for mass education can be traced back to the mid-nineteenth century, represented by Arts and Crafts movement board schools. In Europe a similar, albeit more monastic, route can be discerned going back even earlier. The original church-based models which comprised children surrounding, and by definition subservient to, a master, gave shape to today's private and grammar schools both within the UK and further afield.[1] Other educational milieux such as the domestic home environment (explored in the introduction to Chapter 1), the institutional workhouse, or even the prison, helped to provide the pattern for state schools during their early development.

Where the public school tradition suggests architectural forms which were solid, dependable and largely uninspiring to the pupils, the new school buildings for mass education in the twentieth century would be light, airy and practical. Thus right up to the 1970s, two opposing styles continued to be used side-by-side in the design of new school buildings: traditionalist schools in a reduced neo-classical style and the modernist inventions of the Bauhaus pioneers. For a time, the blossoming of exciting new forms of school architecture not only transformed the image of education but also affected the perceptions of all who inhabited those new structures.

Inevitably, these developments carried with them some of those earlier influences to create hybrid forms combining new and traditional ideas. Both the radically new and the hybrid form of twentieth century school building will be explored in terms of the experimental technologies employed and the educational systems they reflected. I will pose the question, how far did the planning and conceptualization of the 'hybrid' school buildings dictate the pedagogy? How did the evolution of the modern school bring about more humane environments for learning? What lessons do these precedents hold for the current generation of school architects, as the educational curriculum moves away from the child-centred approach?

The design of school buildings is viewed here as a particularly specialized field encompassing ever-changing educational theories; I will illustrate in the historical sections how the best early school architecture was often a close representation of the pedagogic needs of educators of the time supporting their chosen educational curriculum. Similarly the role of the contemporary school designer should go some way towards interpreting and anticipating the specific needs of new learning methods. Therefore I include an extended section on the curriculum, focusing on current educational debates taking place particularly within the UK. It is of fundamental importance that any school designer should anticipate the evolving nature of education within society and make provision for it in their architecture.

During recent years progressive or modernist educational methods have been questioned in Japan, the United States and Europe. This process is currently taking place vigorously within the UK. With it comes the need for new and refurbished school premises. It is evident that school building comes about as political and economic transformations force change and modernization in roughly 35-year cycles. The last such phase, again precipitated by a reforming Labour government, encapsulated an ideologically driven political climate. In 1964, Harold Wilson referred to *the white hot heat of technological change* which celebrated experimentation. This spirit was implemented through the adoption of new building techniques and educational practices, with the consequent construction of thousands of new schools; ultimately, some would say, with mixed results.

There is a parallel to be drawn between the great modern movement architects and twentieth century progressive educationalists in that their theories are currently subject to radical re-appraisal. In architectural terms, this is due to an evident failure of these lightweight modernist structures to modify and control the external environment and maintain comfortable teaching conditions even within, let alone beyond, their expected life span. However, the diminution of radical technologies is also due to a devaluation of progressive ideas generally. For a number of years, this was manifested by an approach to teaching which emphasized the process and the experience of education over and above the acquisition of knowledge and practical skills for their own sake. This is gradually being replaced by a more factual content-based system, as exemplified by the 1988 Education Reform Act. This is perhaps more market driven, demanding constant evaluation of pupil and teacher performance, and the buildings which go with it.

The need for school architecture to respond in a progressive way to social transformations is accentuated during times of political change. The challenge is to prevent radical ideas from derailing the evolutionary process which guides the development of design for education. Nevertheless, this constant quest for modernization can be seen in almost every industrialized country. For example, the requirement to provide support for working women is perceived as a relatively recent phenomenon. It is widely agreed as being a necessity and implies an extension of care and education downwards and sideways. Downwards to provide for young children and even babies within universally understood quality thresholds. Sideways to provide breakfast clubs and after-school facilities for school-age children to support family conditions which currently prevail.

The radical nature of these changes and the effect they will have upon the development of young people should not be underestimated. They are potentially cataclysmic. The prospect of such change sends many commentators rushing for the safety of bygone times and their outmoded ways exemplified by more traditional teaching methods. This is a mistake. To borrow an image from Max Weber, talking about this reactionary quest to return to the mythical ideals of the 1950s nuclear family '... *modernization is not a carriage you can climb out of at the next corner if you don't like it. Any one really meaning to restore family conditions as they were in the 1950s would have to turn the clock back. This would entail not just indirectly keeping women away from jobs by subsidizing motherhood or polishing up the image of housework, but openly denying them opportunities and education.*'[2]

Profound transformations can be anticipated in areas such as the use of information and communications technology and its effect on staffing levels in schools, building ecology, the classroom environment and many other areas of the agenda. At times of change such as these, teachers, carers and their voluntary helpers become particularly stretched. The need for supportive multi-functioning environments of the highest quality become essential constituents in the smooth implementation of new practice. I approach this project with a belief in this progressive philosophy and the significance of the environment in the educative process. I direct the case study section towards state of the art design, across a range of international contexts.

*

This publication focuses particularly on the primary and pre-school sector, although the subtle spatial and psychological requirements of growing children up to, and beyond, the age of sixteen is broadly considered. Chapter 1 focuses on history, origins and significant historical developments, and incorporates a general overview which illustrates the link between progressive educational ideas and experimental architecture. This tendency can be seen particularly during the early post-war years when architects such as Alvar Aalto, Denys Lasdun and the Smithsons first made their mark as designers of new school buildings, reflecting social and educational transformations of the period.

Chapter 2 is largely devoted to the classroom environment. This area of the school is often referred to as the 'home base'. It is where most time is spent, particularly during the early primary years. The concept of an 'ideal classroom' and its relationship to the UK national curriculum is explored. A format where the teachers can contribute to its form and functional make-up prior to its interpretation by a design architect is explained. This process enables an educational and architectural convergence to emerge.

In addition I take the view that the comparatively recent discipline of environmental psychology is important in its encouragement of spaces which themselves further the development and learning of the child through his or her comprehension of space. Therefore a consideration of more esoteric factors such as the effects on behaviour of colour, light and texture will be woven into the more practical aspects of designing for comfort, health and education. Debates about the philosophical role of the school environment are touched upon. Should school environments for children serve certain common functions with respect to children's development, to foster personal identity, to provide opportunities for growth, to promote a sense of security and trust and to allow both social interaction and privacy? If so, how?

In Chapter 3, I consider the design of schools within a wider architectural and political context. Within the UK the whole subject of education has taken on a new significance, and some of the best new examples of school architecture are analysed and discussed within the context of the contemporary debate. It is hoped that educationalists as well as designers coming to this subject afresh will gain a deeper understanding of the theories which dictate the sometimes baffling moves architects make within the privacy of their drawing studios.

Chapter 4 concentrates on issues which come outside the confines of the classroom. This includes a consideration of environmental factors defining healthy comfortable buildings for education. The functional differentiation of spaces such as the assembly hall is analysed so that readers can make up their own minds as to the most appropriate form and type. It is also considered how best to optimize the external environment in order to improve the educational opportunities. Finally, the structure of school funding within the UK is set out, to provide architects and their clients with the knowledge to initiate improvements to their own buildings, as the concept of the *local management of schools* becomes a reality.

Part B of this book analyses a series of school or educational buildings in diagrammatic and visual terms. Although the content of the Case Studies is structured pragmatically, with comparative analysis on different technical aspects, the selection of the twenty examples featured is based on my own subjective view; namely those buildings that I consider combine the highest aesthetic and technical qualities. It is true that the size and material nature of new school buildings, particularly in the state sector, is increasingly dictated by limited budgets and public accountability, which largely negates the possibility of architectural experimentation. However, it will be seen how wit and imagination applied in a discerning manner can be every bit as inspiring as the cutting-edge technologies which were adopted in previous eras.

Equally, architectural aspirations can sometimes be blunted by the involvement of community groups, who play an increasingly significant role in the designation of new school buildings. However, the work of architects such as: Cotrell and Vermeulen; Nev Churcher and Michael Keys working at Hampshire County Architects; and Richard Jobson at Architecture PLB show that by adopting an inclusive approach to consultation with teachers and involved parents, inspiring educational buildings can be created which do not step outside the prescribed economic and legislative framework. Indeed, it will be seen how the consultation process can be a positive and binding factor in the creation of new educational environments.

One architect I spoke to during the course of this research expressed frustration at the redundancy of the special water feature she had designed. Considering the distinct ages and varying sizes of the children, she had set three washing-up sinks side-by-side at varying heights within a common area, the lowest sink being for the youngest children. She had imagined how appealing it would be to see three differently sized children together using appropriately positioned sinks. Unfortunately, from the outset even the smallest children refused to use the lower sinks. Instead, no matter what their height, they all opted to use the highest, and therefore the most adult installation.

This anecdote is not recounted to dissuade architects from adopting novel approaches to the design of children's environments; merely to stress that easy sentiment should be avoided. Overly playful ideas may merely patronize the natural aspirations of children to behave in a grown-up way within the school setting. In Disneyland, anthropomorphic references are in the form of teddy bear door handles and plastic animals. Children relate to these forms instantly. They may feel totally at home in Disney-esque and other proscriptively childlike settings outside of school times. However it leaves little to the imagination. The shapes are too obvious and direct ... whereas animal shapes can be represented in a more abstracted way, thus open to imaginative interpretation. In the best new learning environments, children recognize education to be a serious business, relating themselves to the group dynamic in a complex series of self-conscious social interactions. New learning environments should reflect the studious aspirations of pupils and teachers.

Architecture of Schools is intended to be a celebration of imagination and diversity within the framework of a rigorous understanding of children and their developmental needs. I do not set out to produce a 'design guide'; rather I feel that good school design evolves out of a complex set of variables which are in the main unique to each regional and social setting. For example, the section on designing the ideal classroom applies specifically to its own staff and its particular east London context. However, I believe that the process which helped to bring this design to fruition is broadly applicable. The quest is how best to respond to these conditions and create an architecture which optimizes creativity and deepens understanding within each child.

To paraphrase Newton's Second Law of Mechanics, every action promotes an equal and opposite reaction.[3] Architects are usually the final arbiters in the choice between different – often competing – priorities when designing school buildings, providing realistic guidance to assist in this complex ordering process. I illustrate that the high aspirations of the community, working with ambitious and knowledgeable design teams, can produce enchanting environments, within existing budgets. I hope to disclose the factors which help to encourage this symbiosis, and provide a framework to interpret creatively the rules and regulations which must guide the contemporary architect.

*

The intention of this book is to present an international survey of the best in contemporary school design. Naturally I touch upon aspects of the debate in regions throughout Europe and the USA. It becomes apparent, however, that the primary focus within the text (Chapters 1–4) is the UK scenario. This is an inevitable response to a political climate which has brought the condition of schools, and the state education system, to the forefront. I believe the debate holds valuable lessons for anyone designing or commissioning new schools, wherever they may be.

Although the theoretical chapters focus in the main on the UK education debate, the case studies are international in scope, exploring the 'state of the art' in current new school design. It is accepted that, in reality, most school development within the UK will take place in and around existing school sites. The case studies, therefore, focus on both new schools built over the past decade and significant new extensions to existing premises.

The word 'environment' is used to define the total space within which children learn, not just architecture and landscape architecture. This implies an integration between equipment and furniture, buildings and the urban, suburban or rural context within which schools are located.

Throughout the text I am concerned with provision for mass education within the state sector. However, I make reference to some private provision, as relevant exemplars.

Notes

1 It is important to recognize how early educational ideas spread beyond the present somewhat parochial regional or national systems. The ideas of early educators such as Froebel, Pestalozzi and Dewey had a profound influence on the developing practice of education throughout the world. Today educational theory is disseminated within academic circles by way of the Internet, publications and international conferences. However this elevated academic sphere appears to have little direct impact upon the everyday practice of education, which is driven by a more pragmatic ethos. This often focuses upon health and safety legislation at the expense of imagination and experimentation.

2 As quoted in Beck, U. and Beck-Gernsheim, E., *The Normal Chaos of Love* Polity Press, 1995, pp. 143–144.

3 To every action there is always opposed an equal reaction: or the mutual actions of two bodies upon each other are always equal and directed to contrary parts. Isaac Newton, *Principia Mathematica.*

Part A

1

Origins and significant historical developments

Introduction

The naturalistic settings sought for education at the beginning of the century, seen in early examples such as the open-air, Steiner and Montessori schools, all carried within them themes which run throughout the history of twentieth century school architecture. Initially viewed as an issue relating merely to hygiene and the spiritual well-being of underprivileged children in the newly industrialized cities, the desire to make the experience of education more suitable to young children broadened to encompass other concerns. From the 1920s these included a growing interest in child psychology and a more enlightened approach to the educational needs of large pupil numbers within the expanding cities.

To balance these radical impulses, it can be said that the more privileged private education systems tended to maintain an approach to buildings for education which deliberately set out to make them institutionalizing in their own right. This could be seen particularly in the English public school tradition, where strict hierarchies were reflected by an architecture which changed little within the intervening decades of the nineteenth and twentieth centuries. How to de-institutionalize the institution can be seen as a significant topic within the evolving theory of school design elsewhere.

Within this chapter I explore some of the more enduring themes represented by both the radical and the traditional wings, viewed through the most influential buildings and architects. I do not set out to present a detailed account of the history of school architecture. Rather, I describe some of the recurring educational and social concepts which enabled architects to respond in specific and distinctive ways to the needs of children in mass education.

To begin I consider briefly the roots of an architecture for education, not by way of the first dedicated school buildings, but within the framework of an anthropological view of space as defined by Edward T. Hall and his analysis of the house:

> People who 'live in a mess' or a 'constant state of confusion' are those who fail to classify activities and artefacts according to a uniform, consistent or predictable spatial plan. At the opposite end of the scale is the assembly line, a precise organization of objects in **time** and **space**.[1]

Hall's dialectical arguments may quite easily refer to contemporary school design, which has reached a point where rooms and spaces are intended to meet precise functional needs, and the function of school is framed in neat periods of time, dedicated to specific subject areas. If a modern secondary school comprises as many as twenty specific areas for teaching (aside from numerous smaller ancillary areas), although the outcome of education may be predictable, it also suggests that the range of activities is encouraging a broad and interesting form of education, which nevertheless encompasses large measures of control. It is, however, far removed from the mono-functional spaces of the factory floor or, as we will see, the first schools with their provision of large schoolrooms in which hundreds of children could assemble for instruction at one time.

The implication of Hall's analysis of function relating to the house, where there are special rooms for special functions, does however determine a modernist conception of how people should live their lives. Rooms in the house are allocated specifically to cooking, eating, lounging/entertaining, rest, recuperation/procreation and sanitation. These are functions so precise that they might set the agenda for life. They can impose mental straitjackets. Life is framed by the environments within which it is set; an order is established levelling and stultifying the possibility for wider social interaction, the source from which education springs. Seen in these terms, there is little or no possibility for the form to be interpreted imaginatively. If the

Figure 1.1a
Tehtaanmäki Elementary School, Anvalankoski (formerly the County of Inkeroinen), Finland. Designed by Alvar Aalto in 1938, view of the double height entrance hall with second floor balcony. The foyer level is in fact a raised ground floor due to the sloping site with a gym and changing facilities at the ground/basement level. The architect was absent from the construction, overseeing the development of Villa Mairea and the Finnish Pavilion; however, it is an important example of school design in the early modernist style which subsequently became very influential. (Photograph courtesy of Anjalankosken Sanomat. The plans were drawn by Susanna Salmela.)

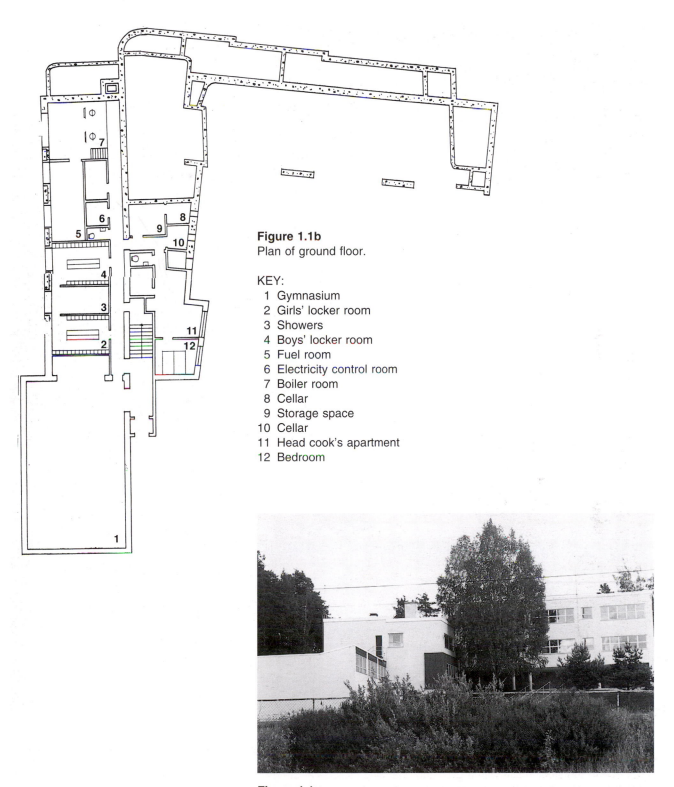

Figure 1.1b
Plan of ground floor.

KEY:
1 Gymnasium
2 Girls' locker room
3 Showers
4 Boys' locker room
5 Fuel room
6 Electricity control room
7 Boiler room
8 Cellar
9 Storage space
10 Cellar
11 Head cook's apartment
12 Bedroom

Figure 1.1c
View towards double height entrance hall with the main classroom block on the right.

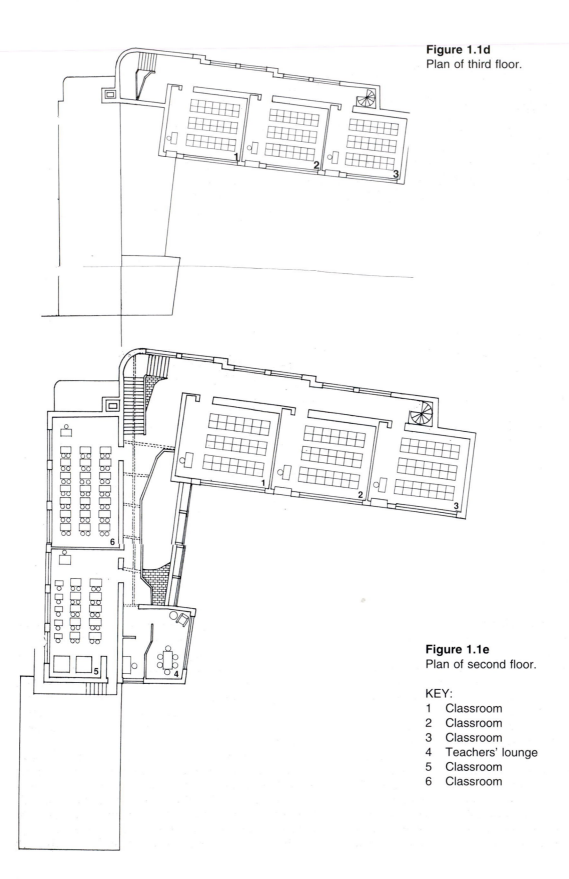

Figure 1.1d
Plan of third floor.

Figure 1.1e
Plan of second floor.

KEY:
1   Classroom
2   Classroom
3   Classroom
4   Teachers' lounge
5   Classroom
6   Classroom

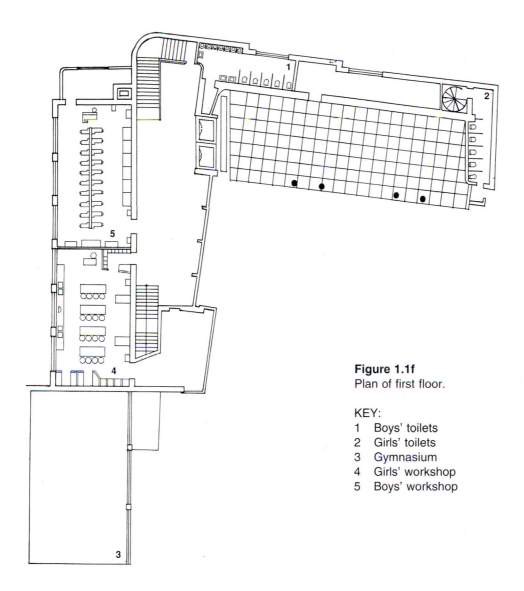

Figure 1.1f
Plan of first floor.

KEY:
1   Boys' toilets
2   Girls' toilets
3   Gymnasium
4   Girls' workshop
5   Boys' workshop

school is based upon a similar mono-functional model to the house, it may also have a negative effect on the personal development of the child.

Dutch architect Herman Hertzberger, who has made a significant contribution to the architecture of schools, puts it this way: '... *a thing exclusively made for one purpose, suppresses the individual because it tells him exactly how it is to be used. If the object provokes a person to determine in what way he wants to use it, it will strengthen his self identity. Merely the act of discovery elicits greater awareness. Therefore a form must be interpretable – in the sense that it must be conditioned to play a changing role.*[2] This defines the essential dialectic at work within the history of school design during the nineteenth and the early part of the twentieth century: on the one hand, the urge to impose discipline and control through a resolute set of spaces; on

the other, the emerging desire to encourage individual creativity by the production of buildings which were not enclosing and confining. Rather they opened themselves up to the surrounding context, its gardens and external areas, which themselves became a fundamental part of the 'learning environment'. Social interaction, rather than autonomous isolation, became the educational strategy embodied in Hertzberger's influential school buildings of the 1980s.

As with the school, the house as a functional layout with a deterministic programme, which is now taken for granted, is a relatively recent interpretation. Philippe Aries' *Centuries of Childhood* points out that rooms in European houses had no fixed function until the eighteenth century. He asserts that, before this time, people came and went relatively freely within dwelling

Figure 1.2
Geography lesson at Alma School, 1908. (© GLC.)

houses. Beds were set up whenever they were needed. There were no spaces that were specialized or sacred. Certainly there were no rooms or buildings dedicated to the education and development of younger children. The 'school', for most children of the middle ages, was the everyday world they inhabited.

Nevertheless, in eighteenth century western societies the home began to take on characteristics of its present form. Rooms were identified as being bedrooms, dining rooms and kitchens, each having their own function. Furthermore, the concept of the corridor came into being. This was a rationalization of the communal meeting place (around the entrance) or hall, which had been the original all-purpose living/sleeping/eating area. The corridor enabled private activities to evolve and the house took on the form of an internal street, with rooms arranged in an orderly form along either side. The children's playroom or nursery would often double as their sleeping area,

enabling children's games to develop and evolve over extended periods of time.

Often it would be treated as a private territory, a little house in its own right. The room was a secure microcosm of the home itself, with its own social hierarchies played out between brothers, sisters and childhood friends. It would become an important mechanism in the development of social competence, safe from the outside world yet capable of replicating some of its difficulties and complexities. According to Hall, man's knowledge and control of space, which he describes as being 'orientated' is a fundamental characteristic of this social development. Without this sense of control of one's environment, to be disorientated in space, is the distinction between survival and sanity: *'To be disorientated in space is to be psychotic.'*

Hall describes this conception as *fixed feature space*. There is no denying the effect this has upon the psychology of the child, indeed on our society as a whole. Winston

6

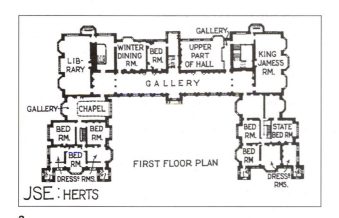

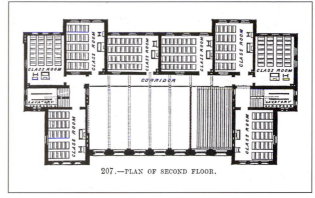

a

b

Figure 1.3a and b
First floor plan of Hatfield House, Herts, 1607–11, taken from *A History of Architecture* by Banister Fletcher (Figure 1.3a). Compare this with the plan of a typical Robson School, 1911. (*School Architecture*, E.R. Robson.)

Figure 1.3c
Bonner Street Primary School, Hackney, London, designed by Robson in 1875. An early example which is still in use today. Although added to and extended on a number of occasions in the years after it opened, the building adapted well to curriculum needs, providing a robust workable environment. Despite the contextual additions, the most significant losses are the tall chimney stacks and bell tower which gave the original composition a romantic castelated quality.

Figure 1.3d
Detail of the giant gable ends protruding up towards the pitched roof.

Figure 1.4
Whiteley Woods
Open Air School,
Sheffield, 1911. (*The
English School,
1870–1970*,
Seaborne and Lowe.)
Both settings show
the school master
and mistresses
positioned to control
and supervise;
however, the
Whiteley Woods
image suggests a
more spacious
approach to the
environment. (*The
English School,
1370–1870*, Malcolm
Seaborne.)

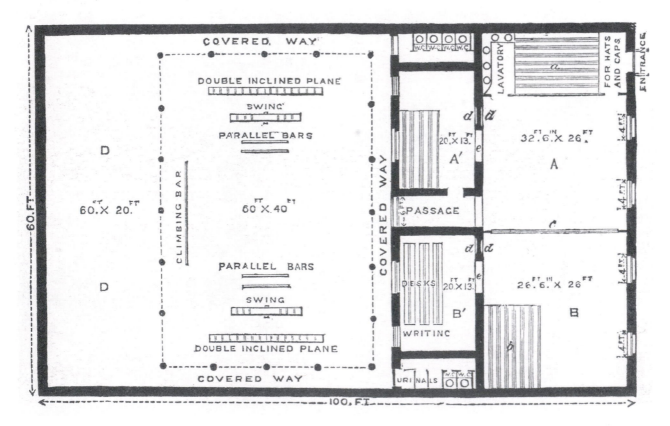

Figure 1.5
Plan of school playground suggested by the Home and Colonial Society. Each of five types of apparatus (four shown), are prescribed for different aged children in this highly ordered layout.

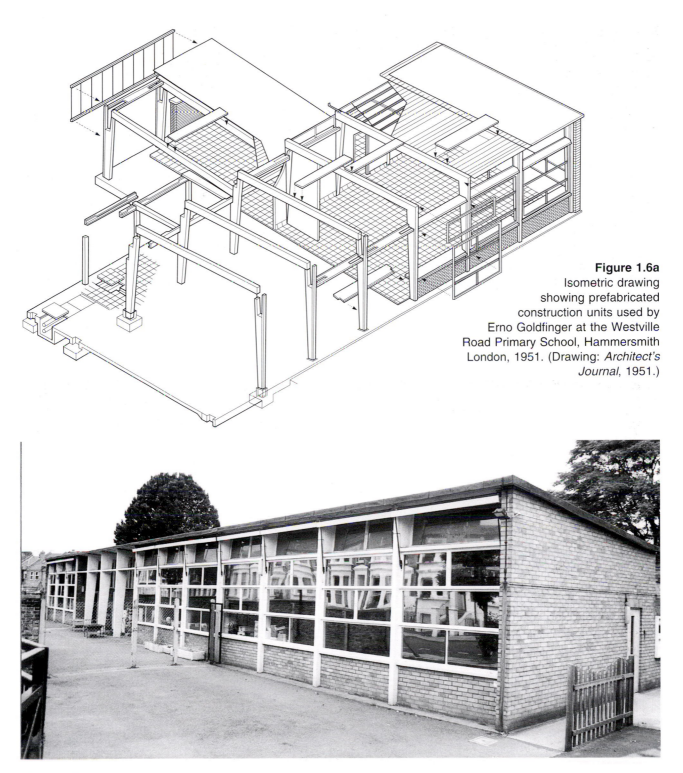

Figure 1.6a
Isometric drawing showing prefabricated construction units used by Erno Goldfinger at the Westville Road Primary School, Hammersmith London, 1951. (Drawing: *Architect's Journal*, 1951.)

Figure 1.6b
The school as it is today. With its draughty single-glazed windows and poorly insulated roof, the fabric does not meet modern environmental standards; its prefabricated form of construction makes it difficult to refurbish, however its organization and internal scale works well. (Photo: © Mark Dudek.)

Churchill's oft repeated dictum, *'We shape our buildings and they shape us'* is never more apposite than when it is applied to the first schools.[3] Austere they may have been, but the first board schools designed by E.R. Robson inadvertently adopted a model based around the form of the eighteenth century house, with individual (class) rooms, clearly articulated circulation routes and a large assembly hall at its heart. They had an ordered configuration which was an essential characteristic of the educational process itself, establishing a framework for both. Many aspects of this conjunction prevail to this time.

This interpretation can also be applied to the wider urban environment. For example, the ways in which civic buildings such as town halls, churches, prisons and recreational buildings assumed a particular architectural language, which helped to impose a social hierarchy upon the nineteenth century city. This could be seen particularly in the architectural styles adopted for the earliest elementary schools in England at that time, with the use of Tudor gothic for the Anglican Proprietary schools in towns such as Sheffield, Liverpool and Leicester. This was often countered by nonconformist schools in the same towns adopting italianate or Palladian styles. Whatever the style, the end result was one of calm, slightly overbearing order, a reflection perhaps of the existing social hierarchy.

Although the styles reflected an interdenominational rivalry, the school spaces themselves were essentially similar, exhibiting the primary characteristics of that most essential example of fixed feature space, the nineteenth century schoolroom. For urban children, exuberance and pure unadulterated play were the domain of the pre-school, the home environment and the street. The school house was intended to be a sober antidote to this, with a single school master imposing strict discipline. The extent to which it is appropriate to determine the form of a classroom on the basis of control is a debate which will be developed in more detail in Chapter 2. However, the notion of a fixed feature space as deterministic as the early schoolroom was, I will argue, central to the actual form of the education.

If the school is essentially concerned with imposing discipline, this conjures up the notion of children being moulded through education to be factory fodder, which would clearly neutralize the potential for school to develop creativity and freedom of expression as part of the educative process. Relating a specific range of functions to a particular space, such as a classroom, in too precise a structure is analogous to the architectural design guide complete with its so-called 'generic plans'. It can smother creativity for both the architect designing the space and the teacher who must use it as the context for teaching, since the plans can be copied to create a single model which takes no account of the context, the physical and social particularities of the site or the creative aspirations of its designer.

To reiterate, the overriding need to provide for large numbers in education is and remains the prevailing requirement throughout the first two hundred years of school design. The constructional technology adopted ranged between two extremes: on the one hand, heavy traditional structures, which were robust but inflexible. On the other extreme, lightweight modernist conceptions which were quick and relatively cheap to build, but had all kinds of constructional and environmental shortcomings. A similar educational dichotomy can be discerned, which pitched traditional teaching methods against more progressive experimental approaches. The relationship between the educational experience and the architectural context was, and is to this day, understated. As I will argue, it was a reciprocal partnership – one feeding off the other in both negative and positive ways.

The notion of designing a children's environment, such as a school, which does not facilitate a degree of imaginative interpretation, or one which does not allow children to develop their own spontaneity, chance meetings and interactions with their peers, may fail to engender interest in education amongst the pupil body. Child-only spaces, which can be seen in many of the case studies, show children that they too have their own identity and value. These spaces are complementary to the more traditional fixed feature spaces such as the classroom, the gym or the school yard.

The development of the urban school during the nineteenth century

Lighthouses, my boy! Beacons of the future! Capsules, with hundreds of bright little seeds in each, out of which will spring the wiser, better England of the future.[4]

Sherlock Holmes' view of the (then) new London Board Schools, looming up above the London skyline like 'beacons' of hope for a bright new future, is a recurrent theme. This metaphor interprets education as a radical and evolving social phenomenon which requires the vision of a strong light shining and illuminating the way forward but also reflecting back to maintain the best of what has gone before. This enlightened view was reinforced by a concern for many aspects of the internal environment prescribed for these new buildings, which set the tone for elementary education in Britain during the early years of the twentieth century.

England had been the first country to experience industrialization and sought educational provision for the so-called industrial classes from the beginning of the nineteenth century. However, the early facilities were patchy, comprising church or factory schools paid for by subscription. Nevertheless, radical educators such as Johan Pestalozzi in Switzerland, Samuel Wilderspin in England and Friedrich Froebel in Germany, developed progressive theories regarding the education of poor

Figure 1.7
This Board School of 1910 has larger and smaller entrance doors for infants and juniors. (Photo: © Mark Dudek.)

children. These were concerned not just with spiritual well-being of children, but were also a response to the insanitary, overcrowded cities where children were often forced to work in factories from a young age.

From the implementation of the 1833 Factory Act, which enforced two hours instruction daily on factory children, reform developed as an all-too-evident response to the plight of the exploited masses. However, the level of government grants allocated to erect school houses in Great Britain seems paltry when compared with similar developments in other European countries at that time. For example, the Irish government provided a £2.5 million subsidy to assist education in Ireland between 1821 and 1828. It was not until the implementation of the UK Elementary Education Act in 1870 that similar sums were invested in England. The Act made education compulsory for all children between the ages of 6 and 11, so that the need to construct large schools within the urban areas became an overriding necessity. At this time, the London School Board advertised for an architect and surveyor to direct the massive expansion anticipated throughout the mainly working class areas of the capital. It was their great fortune that they appointed to the position the then architect surveyor to the Liverpool Corporation, E.R. Robson.

Whilst school systems in some shape or form had been developing throughout the world from the earliest part of the enlightenment, there was no coherent idea as to the educational needs of teachers and the school environment. The schools were usually part of church or commercial institutions. Spaces for education, whilst necessary, were

seen as being secondary to the delivery of 'instruction', which tended to concentrate on discipline and correct moral teaching as exemplified by Dr Thomas Arnold, a headmaster at Rugby School during the nineteenth century: '... *what we must look for here is first religious and moral principles, second gentlemanly conduct, thirdly intellectual ability.*'

Nevertheless, the first half of the nineteenth century had seen the publication of a number of treatises purporting to be about the design of schools. These were written either from a purely architectural perspective (with an emphasis upon the external style of the building), or from an educational point of view *per se*. Most notable of these was *Designs for Schools and School Houses*, published in 1847 by Henry Kendall, which urged the use of the gothic style, with little or no reference to the interior function of the building.

On the other hand, *School Architecture*, published by Henry Barnard a year later, was mainly concerned with the pragmatic health and safety needs of the children during their time in school. As Secretary of the Board of Commissioners of Common Schools in Connecticut, his concern was almost solely educational: '... *so that his book, like many manuals of the time, was little concerned with the external architectural style chosen for schools. Kendall and [others] were architects but not educationists and showed themselves only marginally concerned with matters of internal school organization. Robson's great achievement was to make himself proficient in both the architectural and educational aspects of school design and to integrate the two ...*[5]

Figure 1.8
Design for a school in the Early English style by H.E. Kendall, 1847, a form which became typical for many English village schools built at the time. (*The English School, 1370–1870*, Malcolm Seaborne.)

The new Education Act assumed that the existing voluntary schools had sufficient resources to provide education to the required standard. This was often not the case, since most of them did not have prerequisite separate classrooms. Rather, they were comprised of single-volume spaces for the instruction of the whole school simultaneously. Nevertheless, the new state schools would be regulated by school boards and funded in areas of extreme poverty where gaps in provision needed to be filled. The gaps proved to be greater than anticipated, providing architectural opportunities for Robson and his contemporaries over the next thirty years.

Robson had travelled widely following his appointment in 1872. His view of overseas systems, particularly those he viewed in the USA, Switzerland and Germany, led him to the conclusion that although there was a tradition of secondary school education in these countries, upon which England could draw, there was no such tradition in elementary schooling. Ironically, the elementary schools designed by Robson hardly related to the smaller scale and magnified perceptions of most infants, many of the buildings later having been readily transformed into colleges of higher education. Nevertheless, observing the best systems of education the world had to offer proved to be a valuable experience in balancing his professional background in architecture.

His theories were set out in a book published in 1874 called *School Architecture: Practical Remarks on the Planning, Designing, Building and Furnishing of School Houses*. The book was in reality something of an eclectic mix including chapters on the layout of schools, the planning of classrooms, the interior environment, 'warming and ventilation', school furniture and architectural style. Robson's ideas were widely implemented in London and subsequently adopted by other metropolitan boroughs throughout the country, largely as a result of this influential publication. These austere buildings were to have a profound effect not just on the educational aspirations of subsequent generations but also on the way in which those inner city communities evolved socially.

Views on the classroom set out in *School Architecture* were important in their practical response to the health concerns for the poor working classes. The children were to be kept well ventilated in lofty spaces proportionately relating plan width to height. Robson stated that the lighting of classrooms was all-important. Direct sunshine should never be from the south or south-west, although some sunny windows may be provided. He concluded that the coolest steadiest light was from the north and recommended that there should be a minimum of 30 square inches of glass to every square foot of floor space. This he asserted had been partly based upon previously unpublished German research. The tone of this publication had a reassuringly scientific clarity for other school designers of the time: '*... in this sunless climate of ours it is difficult to make a school room too sunny; yet this may be done if the sun be admitted at the wrong places, as, for instance, right in the eyes either of teacher or children, and without most absolute power of control.*'[6]

Figure 1.9
French rural school at
Saint Pardoux Les Cars
where a small population
is serviced in this
decorative timber
pavilion. (*School
Architecture*, E.R.
Robson.)

The overall shape of these new schools was largely determined on the basis of two key criteria: firstly the layout of the classrooms and secondly the number of pupils to be accommodated. Robson introduced the Prussian system of separate classrooms organized around a communal hall. Previously, lessons had taken place within vast communal halls. For example, the plan of the Southwark Central School of 1816 showed benches in rows with children sitting side-by-side in lines of 16, eighteen rows deep. Robson felt this to be too inflexible and arranged the classrooms to accommodate five rows of double desks ranged from front to back, a dimension of approximately 11 feet, (rather unscientifically) determined it seems by the distance a teacher's voice would carry. The desks had enough circulation space for the master to inspect the academic progress of each child. Crucially the arrangement allowed each child to leave their desk during the lesson. The classrooms would also include a generous area at the front for display, presentation and general circulation.

The second criterion established class sizes on the basis of a predetermined schedule of accommodation, with an optimum number of 40–60 pupils in each. This was based upon the numbers which could be comfortably serviced by a single school master. The recommended format for these board or elementary schools was an infant department of 400 children and a junior department with separate boys and girls sections comprising 320 pupils in each. Generous circulation, latrines and the school keeper's house were crucial aspects of the programme. Thus a recommended size of 80 cubic feet per child was prescribed.

The style of these buildings is often described as 'Queen Anne'. They are mainly constructed of light yellow London stock brick with red brick dressings. Robson and his assistants avoided fashionable terracotta details, utilizing instead a little external ornamentation of carved title panels over entrance gates usually cut into the brickwork. The buildings were functionally rather than stylistically determined, with Robson's analysis of use patterns and efficient circulation largely setting the form. Although the contexts for many of Robson's schools were confined urban ones, the building was effectively an object, the form being largely dictated by functions of size (the schools were often three or four storeys high in order to accommodate

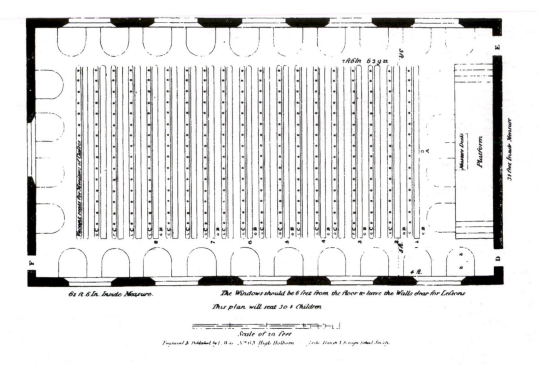

Figure 1.10
Plan of a British school for 304 children. (*The English School, 1370–1870*, Malcolm Seaborne.)
The inscription suggests that views outside would be restricted with windows starting six feet above the ground.

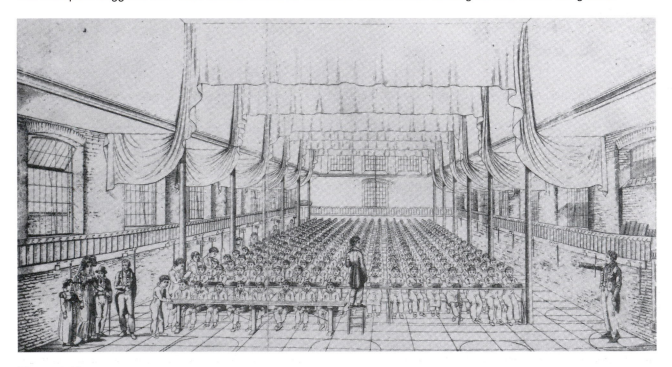

Figure 1.11
A class at Southwark Central School, early nineteenth century, with drapes introduced to soften and break up the large volume. (*The English School, 1370–1870*, Malcolm Seaborne.)

Figure 1.12
Robson's ideal can be seen in this early classroom layout with two desks for each teacher and a dividing curtain, a configuration reminiscent of more recent paired classroom arrangements. (*School Architecture*, E.R. Robson.)

all the local children onto a single site), orientation, and the designer's predilection for romantic variegated skylines; thus pitched roofs with gable ends, and by structural necessity, heavily buttressed brick walls with a prodigious number of chimney stacks established a 'recognizable architectural vocabulary, if not a coherent style.

As a consequence of these site exigencies, the external areas were often problematic. They were secondary to the constructional economics of the buildings themselves, leaving tight overshadowed pockets of 'play' space sandwiched between the high school walls and the boundary walls to the street. Within these bleak overshadowed conditions the children were expected to spend their play-periods. The needs of society were exemplified by the scale of the provision. The uniformity of the environment was reminiscent of the factory floor, where most of the incumbents were destined to end up. Nevertheless, the buildings were robust (many being still in use today) with an environmental strategy which to some degree countered the unsanitary London slum conditions. The schools became a symbol of enlightened progress which combined some aspects of the eighteenth century manor

house layout with a reassuringly sturdy fortified image. Most importantly, Robson was the first designer to marry educational theory to architectural practice in any meaningful way.

Meanwhile, developments in Scotland, particularly in infant education, had been advancing slightly ahead of England. Robert Owen had established his first model infant school at his New Lanark industrial community in 1816 and David Stow founded the Glasgow Infant School Society in 1827, and in 1828 its first school. The single-storey building focused much of its activity on the garden: '... *the uncovered schoolroom ... a little world of real life where mental, moral and physical character are best developed and consequently where moral habits can best be formed.'*[7] However, the children were not permitted to touch the fruit on the trees. Stow interpreted this as a vital act of self-discipline within the vice-laden world of the industrial city. Indeed, the flowers and shrubs in the garden were viewed as the antithesis to the cramped environment of the Glasgow tenements, a symbolic assertion of innocence, an invocation of the mythical Garden of Eden prior to the fall from grace.

Figure 1.13
Stow's model infant school interior, 1836; the arrangement was quickly superseded as the UK school population rose by individual classrooms for age- or ability-related children. (*School Architecture*, E.R. Robson.)

Stow was involved with the founding of the Glasgow Education Society in 1834, and subsequently oversaw the construction of a seminary for teacher training purposes. It had four model schools: an infants, a junior, a commercial school for fee-paying boys and a female school of industry. The key to the teacher training programme was, according to Thomas Markus, that of control. As a consequence, the space within which the ritual was enacted was precise and focused towards that end: '... *everything is designed for surveillance* ...'[8] The school was housed in a single volume where the master taught simultaneously to all ages; there was a gallery which had to be large enough to accommodate the whole school so that all the children received the same message. For writing, the children sat at desks around the edge of the school room, facing the wall.

Within a period of thirty years, Stow's negative view of the city had evolved into school organizations which reflected a more sophisticated approach. Robson's archetypal plan for the Jonson Street Board School in Stepney of 1873 shows eight classrooms organized around a central hall. Although the hall was still used by the master or headteacher for rotating class groups and whole-school assembly, the classrooms, which were accessed off the hall, were intended for a single teacher working in isolation. There were windows for observation from the hall to the classrooms; however, the (head) master was no longer the sole source of instruction. Not only would it

have been impossible logistically for the simultaneous system to continue, it was pedagogically inappropriate. The newly trained teachers had their own vocational message to add to the standard curriculum which provided a varied and therefore more balanced education for children moving through the school system.

In 1872 an Education Act was passed in Scotland requiring a school board to be established in each district. The committees were given statutory legislation to supervise the building of schools and to provide an acceptable standard of education for all of their children from the age of 5 to 13. Many of the new schools were designed on the principles set out in Robson's book. In 1895, Charles Rennie Mackintosh, the emerging star of the Scottish Arts and Crafts Movement, designed his first school, the Martyr's Public School in Parson Street, Glasgow. The Martyr's had a formal plan very much in the Robson style with tall staircase windows, three storeys of accommodation, and the usual separate entrances for girls and boys. Each floor included two master's rooms.

The form was a Scottish vernacular stretched and adapted to fit its institutional function and its slightly inappropriate site. The style reflects Mackintosh's deeply absorbing study of old Scottish baronial buildings. Although of a higher architectural order, the scale of the building fitted in with the surrounding urban grain of Glasgow tenement blocks, in contrast to the overpowering

Figure 1.14a
Scotland Street School.
(Photo: © Eric Thorburn.)

Figure 1.14b
The interior stairwell,
looking up. (Photo: © Eric
Thorburn.)

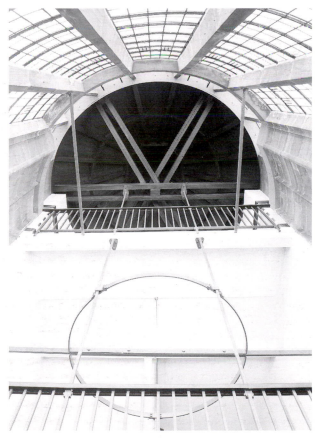

effect most of Robson's schools had on their surroundings. The hall, which was annotated as a 'Drill Hall', was surrounded by four classrooms and two staircases. There was no lift and the staff and pupils may have spent much of their time between lessons running up and down the staircases. Although the plan was compact, the building feels too tall for its site and purpose.

In 1902, Mackintosh was asked to design a board school in Scotland Street. Although the programme of accommodation had generally been settled by 1903, the building was not completed until 1906. Cost limitations and the Scottish School Board's fixed ideas about its design emanating from Robson's *School Architecture* caused disagreements and delays. By this stage of his career, however, Mackintosh was an independent practitioner with a growing reputation. After much argument the architect got his own way and succeeded in increasing the budget. This enabled the inclusion of crucial spatial and decorative additions which were intended to raise the architectural quality above that of the typical Robson board school.

The three-storey building was constructed of red sandstone with a plan which was based on the standard Glasgow School Board type. It had mirrored entrances with separate staircases for boys and girls. The staircases were articulated as semi-circular towers, with flat protruding entrance porches at ground floor. There was an assembly hall at the centre of the plan, one side of an enclosed corridor running down the middle. There were six classrooms and attached staff/cloakrooms. Above the hall at first floor there were a further three classrooms, and at second floor, six south-facing classrooms with a north-facing cookery/demonstration room. In total the building had 21 classrooms designed to accommodate 1250 children.

Decorative detail was limited to door and window surrounds. However, the effect of the powerful abstracted organic forms, which appeared on the upper stair towers, combined with the light airy quality of the staircases and other circulation areas, elevated its spatial ambience above the austerity of Robson's proto-functionalism. Robert Macleoud observed: *'Perhaps not surprisingly, in trying to exploit what Mackintosh called "the spirit of the old" without slavishly emulating its details, he produced a building with "the spirit of the new".'*[9]

The elegant spatial ambience of the interiors illustrated the manner in which good architectural design could raise the quality of the educational experience. Mackintosh achieved a masterly relationship of the elements translated into a building form which in plan terms was similar to the London Board Schools, but a million miles away architecturally. For example, the proportions and forms of the windows largely respond to the internal functions, making the building's various rooms and spaces legible from the street. With its refined symmetry and articulate façade treatment, Scotland Street School heralded the beginnings of an architectural typology, the urban school. To some extent this straddled the educational attitudes of the nineteenth and twentieth centuries, maintaining some of the worthwhile traditions of the past whilst looking forward towards more advanced spatial relationships.

John Dewey and the Frank Lloyd Wright connection

In the years immediately following the establishment of a widespread compulsory education system throughout Europe and North America, a number of key educators emerged who influenced the architecture of schools in a profound way. For example, Margaret MacMillan in London who addressed the needs of the working poor and Maria Montessori in Rome who pioneered the first apparatus scaled to the size of young children, amongst other innovations. The effects of the First World War, as well as depleting the teaching profession, caused a hiatus in the ongoing development of mass education. Many school buildings were requisitioned by the military. After the carnage of the trenches, an understandable wish to look forward rather than backwards prevailed, which heralded modernist movements in the arts generally and education in particular.

In Britain, there was a realization that the understanding and knowledge of ordinary German soldiers in the trenches had been greater than their British counterparts,

especially in relation to science subjects. A further concern had been the recognition that many of the revolutionary cadres of the Russian Revolution of 1917 had been led by teachers. The new post-war president of the board of education, H.A.L. Fisher, former vice-chancellor of Sheffield University, sought to pay additional grants to serving teachers and where possible to give them what they wanted in the form of buildings and equipment. However, as a result of the obliteration of a generation of men, more and more women entered the profession.

Many conservative educationalists were unhappy about this development, believing that boys should be taught by men. Indeed, they believed that education was primarily to service the needs of industry and was more important for male children anyway. However, after the loss of so many, there was really no alternative and they were powerless to stem the feminist influx. This supplanting of the master with the school mistress was a universal phenomenon which carried the new spirit in education further and more quickly than would have occurred with an exclusively male-dominated profession. Many believe that it promoted a deeper, more questioning, approach to teaching and the environments within which it should take place. Novice teachers now looked for radical new approaches. At the same time, new generations of architects were turning their backs on the stylistic concerns of the nineteenth century, in search of a more meaningful social role for themselves, through their work.

John Dewey (1859–1952), who had influenced those schools designed by Frank Lloyd Wright between 1900 and 1908, had a particular approach to education. It captured the imagination of this new generation of educators during the immediate post-war years. Although the schools designed by Wright were not for mass education – rather 'one offs' commissioned for middle class children – nevertheless they became paradigms in the history of school architecture and in the wider work of the great man. They encompassed a more advanced approach to education than Robson's. Most importantly, they incorporated many of Dewey's radical educational ideas, in new architectural forms of real sophistication.

Born in 1859, Dewey taught philosophy at a number of North American universities before settling at Chicago University where as director of the school of education he remained from 1894 to 1904. During this time Dewey established an experimental school which explored new ways of teaching. He came to formulate democratic (as opposed to autocratic) principles and occupational hands-on instruction which revolutionized educational practice in the USA, Europe and Asia for the next thirty or so years. The primary focus was the desire to create schools which were cooperative communities helping individual pupils to fulfil their true potential. He recognized the importance of stimulating children's senses as part of the educative process: '*... The boy flying a kite has to keep his eye on the* *kite, and has to note the various pressures of the string on his hand. His senses are avenues of knowledge not because external facts are 'conveyed' to the brain, but because they are used in doing something with a purpose.'*[10]

Robson and his precursors were largely concerned with the educative process as one of control, where the school environment was relatively autonomous and closed to the outside world. Dewey promoted a more open approach, seeking to replicate the ordered diversity of the real world, through an enriched educational curriculum. Administration within the school community, the selection of subject matter, methods of learning, teaching and discipline, reinforced the idea that there was one reality rather than a duality between school and home life. Writing in *School and Society*, published in 1899, he stated: '... *[we must] make each one of our schools an embryonic community life, active with types of occupations that reflect the life of the larger society, and permeated throughout with the spirit of art, history and science.'*[11]

The accommodation of these experimental schools would henceforth not just include classrooms, but also laboratories, workshops, a gymnasium and drawing studios to furnish the pupils with broader more questioning skills.

His strongly held views on architecture showed the important relationship which he felt existed between the two disciplines. From the outset, Dewey equated the dated educational methods of the nineteenth century to a similar spirit in architecture of that period, with its stylistic as opposed to social concerns. It was, he believed, an approach which was overly academic and therefore irrelevant to the needs of everyday life. Just as the single controlling message of the early nineteenth century educators was largely obsolete, so too was its architecture, with its similar hectoring stylistic obsessions. The use of history and tradition in itself was not a problem, but '... *the latter have not entered into his [the architect's] mind; into the structure of his own ways of seeing and making. They remain upon the surface as tricks of technique or as extraneous suggestions and conventions as to the proper thing to do.'*[12]

This philosophy initially reflected the authentic spirit of the new pluralistic architecture exemplified by the work of Frank Lloyd Wright and C.R. Mackintosh during the early years of the twentieth century. Good planning and sound construction were graced with a genuine concern for visual delight and variety exemplified by Arts and Crafts embellishments. During the post-First World War years, Dewey's brand of philosophical pragmatism, including practical as well as academic learning together in the same educational package, quickly infiltrated architecture. This lasted for twenty years until, in the spirit of the machine aesthetic, such visual enrichment became suspect. Nevertheless, he continued to assert the importance of architecture, drawing subtle analogies between educational practice and architectural theory.

He recognized the chasm opening up between the modern practice of architecture which was as he understood it, new and authentic, and the ideas of the past. In his view, the theoretical tricks of the academic architect created a pompous, largely irrelevant form. The best new architecture carried in it a quality which brought it closer to nature than any other artistic medium such as painting, sculpture or poetry: '... *Compare buildings with other artistic products and you are at once struck by the indefinitely wide range of materials it adopts to its ends – wood, stone, steel, cement, burnt clay, glass, rushes, cement, as compared with the relatively restricted number of materials available in painting, sculpture, poetry. But equally important is the fact that it takes these materials, so to speak, neat. It employs materials not only on a grand scale but at first hand – not that steel and bricks are furnished directly by nature but that they are closer to nature than are pigments and musical instruments.'*[13]

Dewey hoped to bring about a similar transformation in the way children were educated, making it more various and natural. Buildings for the new education were to have complementary qualities. Frank Lloyd Wright almost certainly picked-up on this philosophy, mixing as he did with the major figures of Chicago's intellectual life. In 1887, when he was only 18, Wright had designed the first building for Hillside Home School at Spring Green, Wisconsin. This had been for his maiden aunts, Jane and Nell Lloyd-Jones. The manner of the building was shingle in style with roofs and gables of a picturesque, vernacular form reflecting the Queen Ann revival emanating from England. By 1900, having been much altered, the buildings had become outmoded spatially.

In 1902 Wright gained a second commission, for a group of buildings for Hillside Home School. This was the first major building he designed independently and the precursor to his masterpiece, Taliesin North. It was constructed of local sandstone formed in rough ashlar blocks. Architectural critic Grant Manson suggests that the rugged effect of the architecture, which came about through an integrated approach to structure, materials and landscape, reflected the client Lloyd Jones' own earnest hard-working spirit. In his view, the strength and primitive lines of Hillside Home School 2 responded to the crags and gorges of the Wisconsin River Valley. This is much more appropriate than the shingle style of the first school. Manson asserts that the second school building has a simple majesty more emphatic than that of its Illinois prairie setting. However, it is more appropriate because it competes and contrasts with the bluffs and ravines of the Wisconsin Valley.

The plan of Hillside Home School 2 is based on a brief from Wright's client which in turn was almost certainly influenced by the ideas of John Dewey. This is evidenced in the provision of classrooms served by a gallery with manual training below, a gymnasium at one end and an

Figure 1.15
Hillside Home School, designed by Frank Lloyd Wright. (© Kenneth Macdonald.)

assembly hall at the other. The school entrance was adjacent to the assembly hall, which was linked to the science laboratory and the drawing studio by a bridge. The pragmatism of John Dewey's thinking is demonstrated in this layout with its deterministic allocation of spaces each for a particular range of vocational skills. The bridge link suggests a more tentative connection between traditional and new curriculum activities.

Horizontality is emphasized by roofs and the mullioned screen windows fixed in the vertical with oversized chimneys. Internally the building was an exploration of complex volumetrics. There was a sophisticated modulation of daylight, with walls which no longer appeared to enclose space in a conventional manner. Screens and other flexible elements largely replaced fixed solid walls. The whole building appeared to be 'spread' across an undulating landscape. Changes in profile externally and stepped floor levels internally added variety, the latter putting into question contemporary thinking that schools should all be on a single uniform level. It can be argued that the spatial awareness of able-bodied children is heightened by this effect. The various forms are complemented with flattened overhanging hipped roofs which are neatly coordinated and bring about a real sense of unity to disparate parts of the plan.

The Prairie House formula applied Dewey's views on flexible multi-functional spaces and harmony with the natural environment for the first time. It demonstrated the suitability of such thinking in education and, in 1902, was widely recognized as the most advanced school form of its type. Built at a time when most school design was essentially based on historicism, Wright's interpretation of the Dewey philosophy illustrated a flowering of architecture for schools in its integration of two radical new philosophies, one educational, the other spatial. Subsequently it was much copied, but never with such architectural dexterity.

It was only thirty years after Robson's first schools opened, but light years away in terms of advanced school design. It could be said that like Robson forty years previously, Wright, with the aid of Dewey's prompting, had invented a new form of school architecture; one which was not confined to a restricted urban site. Rather, it opened itself up to the surrounding green spaces illustrating the positive benefits of rural settings or what in later years might be characterized as suburban. The classroom vista was no longer restricted by high window sills with children stiffly focused on the teacher sitting on a raised dais. Instead they were encouraged to use the surrounding context as a catalyst to creative thought and activity, all on the same physical and social level as the teacher. Furthermore, the architecture developed in response to its setting, which was used to complement and inspire its design.

Susan Isaacs and the Free Schools

Immediately after the First World War, translations of Freud's writings on psychoanalysis were published for the first time in England and North America. A little later Percy Nunn, professor of education at the University of London, produced the influential *Education: Its Data and First Principles* (1920) which dealt with natural selection and the physical inheritance of the child. As a liberal idealist, Nunn believed in enabling '... *each child to realize his potential more completely and he called upon knowledge of human psychology and educational practice for this purpose.*'[14] Educational theory picked up on the ideas of Dewey, Bergson, Freud, Jung and Adler, distilling concepts which emphasized the importance of freedom rather than restraint, stressing the primacy of the emotions over and above the intellect. A truly radical spirit of experimentation was transforming the thinking of key educationalists, which would be disseminated into some mainstream practice, within the space of thirty years. Perhaps most importantly, the functioning and processes of the unconscious mind were promoted as having a significant effect on development and well-being, the educational significance of which was keenly felt within these circles.

In 1924, inspired by the writing of Dewey and enthused with this new radical spirit, Susan Isaacs became the principal of the Malting House School and developed her own educational philosophy. This focused on the natural environment, encouraging freedom of expression and a spirit of communality. She allowed, even encouraged, children to behave in free and unrestrained ways, which contradicted much traditional thinking on education. She recognized the radical nature of the Montessori system, which challenged children in their learning. The importance of sensory material to promote understanding was also stressed, as well as the benefits of group and social interaction. The school was an attempt to recreate the 'embryonic community' in its formulation of scaled-down adult activities. This was very much in the mould of Dewey, but applied in a more radical context, the free school as a laboratory of new educational practices.

Children of university-educated parents, with a high level of mental capacity, comprised the majority of the pupil intake throughout the three-year life of the project. The Malting House School, which initially opened with 10 boys, had expanded to a maximum of 20 boys and girls aged 2.8 to 10 years of age by its second year. In the first year it was a day school only, and in the second year

weekly boarders became part of the intake. By the end of Susan Isaacs' reign, one-third of the pupils were accommodated as boarders in two converted houses annexed to the main school. Observation of their activities was to provide data for research, which produced the influential publications *Intellectual Growth in Young Children* (1930) and *Social Development in Young Children* (1933), both written by Susan Isaacs.

Each child had his or her own brightly painted bed sitting room scaled to an appropriate size, with a lock on the door to encourage a sense of independence. As part of the educational curriculum, the children were encouraged to cook, bake and make drinks, using the facilities provided. Furniture was made to the scale of the children, echoing the principles of Maria Montessori. Beneath the observation gallery within the hall, climbing bars and swings provided for indoor physical activity. This was the first such apparatus and a radical transformation from the disciplinarian 'drill halls' of the late nineteenth century schools. The gallery itself was strategically positioned to facilitate discreet viewing by numerous visiting academics engaged in research. There was direct access to a large garden with sandpits, water pools and the first 'jungle gym'. Beyond were trees and wilder shrubbery which provided the opportunity for children to lose themselves.

A complete kit of tools, including saws for wood cutting, were provided as well as more conventional building blocks and craft equipment. The use of practical teaching methods, such as animal dissection, prefaced the introduction of a science curriculum in secondary schools. Mary Field, who made a film about the school's activities, recounted this story of her first visit for filming purposes: '... *the children were dissecting Susan Isaacs' cat which had just died, when normally they worked with frogs or dogfish. They all seemed to be enjoying themselves immensely, digging away at the carcass ... Then there was the bonfire. It was supposed to be an exercise in free play, but it got a bit out of hand. The fire spread and spread and reached the apple trees, and then destroyed a very nice boat. Even Geoffrey Pyke was a little upset about that, and he seemed a very calm man.*'[15]

Unfortunately the film made by Field has been lost. However, we can surmise that the school buildings themselves were unremarkable, comprising of a malting house barn converted for the use of the children, two existing houses and a large garden. Since there were a maximum of twenty boys and girls, only one or two dedicated teaching spaces were required. However, the curriculum was to have a profound effect. The children were encouraged to be curious about everything, and there was no formal class teaching and no fixed lessons. The permissive informality of the Malting House routine was prescribed by Dewey, whilst experimentation in teaching techniques was inherited from Montessori and others. Freud brought the most shocking of the innovations in his perceptions on infantile sexuality. Isaacs was anxious to study the less attractive aspects of children's behaviour as well as the more acceptable areas, and there were few behavioural taboos.

Evelyn Lawrence started teaching at the Malting House School in 1926 and commented on the uninhibited crudity, savagery and sexual interest displayed by the children, obviously with some concern. She had doubts about the future manners and habits this approach would develop within the incumbents. According to Stewart, her worries were unfounded as later acquaintance showed that Malting House alumni generally possessed easy manners and deep social consciences. However, the school was not dealing with poor children. These were the children of the wealthy intelligentsia, and the highly educated parents reinforced the pedagogy at almost every level. Where such parental support was less understanding of the liberal ethos, such freedoms proved unworkable (see reference to the William Tyndale School in Chapter 3).

The influence of the Malting House School has been out of all proportion to its three-year life span and the limited numbers of pupils with which it dealt. The Russells, Susan Isaacs, Curry and Rudolph Steiner were concerned about a form of education which went beyond the enabling ladders of achievement, lessons being learnt and examinations being successfully passed. Their experimental spirit exemplified by this, the first free school, was akin to those prevalent within the fields of art and architecture. Much of this utopian thinking was to be put to the test in the years leading up to, and following, the Second World War, with the construction of dramatic new school buildings which paid scant regard to the architectural forms of the past. Due to the 'found' nature of its buildings, the environment of the Malting House School was never believed to be of great significance. Its lack of an overt architectural stance was a weakness which was not addressed by Isaacs. She said nothing in her books about architecture and the environment. However, with its focus on child-friendly details and equipment, and its open aspect to the garden, its environment was a vital element of the educational process and an early example of architecture for childhood. The quest to de-institutionalize the institution had reached its nadir.

In a similar spirit to the Malting House School, an experimental educational community was established in Dartington as part of a larger social and economic experiment. In 1931, Leonard and Dorothy Whitney-Elmhirst had established a trust for this purpose. They invested all the land, buildings and services both inside and outside the Devon estate which they owned. The principal aim of the Elmhirsts was to develop its natural resources, and this included the educational potential of the local people. The commercial enterprises owned by the Trust included farms, a textile mill, saw mills and 2000 acres of forest. These provided funds for the development of non-commercial activities which included an art centre, an adult education centre, research projects, the general upkeep of the garden and grounds, and the establishment of an experimental school.

William Burnley Curry served the school from 1932 to 1957 as its first head and was pivotal in the development of new approaches to teaching during this time. He had first taught at Gresham School Holt and in 1922 went to Bedales where he taught physics until 1926. There he began to experiment with a radical new approach to education which encouraged the independence of the pupils within a traditional educational framework. In Curry's words: '... *a modern school is one which recognizes that the social order must be radically changed if civilization is to advance at all and which also recognizes that education will have perhaps the most difficult and the most important part to play in the changes which must come about.*'[16]

Curry went from Bedales to Oak Lane County Day School in Philadelphia, which had been founded in 1916 by a group of businessmen who wished to apply John Dewey's educational theories. Curry became head of school at Oak Lane in 1927, where he remained until in 1931 he became Director of Education at Dartington on the basis of his progressive educational ideas. These could be summarized firstly as an enhanced concern for individual children and their way of learning, secondly the need for pupil participation in school governance, thirdly a resistance to uninformed parents forcing their views of education upon teachers. Instead, parents and other adults should be friends to the pupils in their care. These three tenets became the somewhat unusual principles of education around which Dartington was founded.

Leopold Stokowski asked architect William Lescaze to design a nursery school for the Oak Lane County day school near Philadelphia. After Curry was appointed director of Dartington, he in turn asked Lescaze to design his house. The Trustees of Dartford were so impressed with High Cross that they commissioned him to design a series of projects including a gymnasium addition to the existing school and three boarding house/classroom block combinations. The Dartington Hall work which Lescaze undertook was influenced by his fascination with the Dessau Bauhaus. He designed three buildings for the lower school. Perhaps the most significant architectural loss in the history of twentieth century school architecture was the progressive school project, which would have encapsulated many tenets of the new educational theory in its rejection of past styles. By way of consolation, one might have predicted that the damp Devon weather would not have treated its light planar construction kindly.

The new spirit of functionalism was becoming more and more influential, particularly within modernist housing developments such as the Karl Marx Hof in Vienna. This massive municipal housing scheme was humanized by the incorporation of shops, clinics and, most importantly,

Figure 1.16
A progressive junior school proposed by Howe and Lescaze in 1931 but which was not built in this form because it was too expensive. (William Lescaze Catalogue 16, Rizzoli.)

schools, which created a distinctly European form of social housing. However, many education officers in England viewed this radicalism as being too politically extreme. The village school movement had emerged partly as an anti-European response to this radicalism. Amongst others, Raymond Unwin's conservative theories became highly influential. Unwin and his partner Barry Parker had strong ideas about social amelioration which influenced the wealthy Rowntree family. A site three miles outside York owned by the family was to become the village of New Earswick. This was in direct response to the appalling statistics of overcrowding and ill health identified by one of Joseph Rowntree's sons.

The new development was to include good economic housing, sound healthy education and recreation for its inhabitants. Built from 1910, schools, churches and shops were constructed around a large village green.

Everywhere, children's facilities were given a special emphasis. A paddling pool was included together with an open-air swimming pool next to the main school buildings. In addition to conventional schools, an open-air school was provided with large folding classroom windows and two open verandas on the East and West, to provide additional shaded teaching spaces. The plan of New Earswick was illustrated initially with only the streets and major institutions set out. Although something of an experiment, the development adopted a traditional architectural language, and provided a clear framework for the subsequent housing development.

Around the same time, Henry Morris, the newly installed Director of Education for Cambridgeshire, adopted a less circumspect view in community developments under his jurisdiction. He divided the county into nine areas, each with its own senior elementary school or college. The programme

Figure 1.17
Walter Gropius with Max Fry, School and Community College at Impington, Cambridgeshire, double aspect classroom along the west courtyard. (Photo: © Mark Dudek.)

for these new schools would include a cultural centre for adults on the same site. The first college was opened in Sawston in 1930. It coordinated traditional and eighteenth century forms into a modern unified composition. S.E. Urwin, the architect for the second college at Bottisham and Luton, abandoned the neo-Georgian style in favour of a modernist approach. During the course of its construction, Morris met Walter Gropius and became excited by his architectural ideas and charismatic enthusiasm for the new architecture. He awarded the fourth college commission to Gropius working in partnership with Max Fry.

The first scheme was too costly and, much to Gropius' frustration, was modified. However, the building proved to be his finest work of the 1930s. During the day it worked extremely well as a primary school for 240 pupils, and later in the day and during the evenings, it doubled as a regional centre for adult education. The building was planned around a central promenade walkway, which provided an informal social focus, hosting school exhibitions and meetings; this important element of the design also acted as a spill-over area during intervals when evening concerts and plays were being performed in the school hall. The warden's office and staff rooms occupied one side of the promenade, children's entrances and changing rooms the other. The wing on the right of the assembly hall was used for adult education evening classes. The curriculum included courses in the arts and sciences, handicrafts, agricultural and physical training. This sophisticated functional mix was in perfect harmony with the architectural aesthetic, suggesting a progressive and enlightened view of education. It was much imitated by the school designers of the post-war years.

In the years prior to the First World War, the Ecole des Beaux Arts in Paris hosted a radical strain of committed staff and students which led to the emergence of international talents such as Tony Garnier and August Perret and his students Le Corbusier and Erno Goldfinger amongst others. Having won the Prix de Rome (1898), Garnier developed his ideas on urban planning away from Paris. In 1901 he returned with his first study of the Cité Industriel to the Ecole. In it he devised a plan for an ideal city based on mixed functions. Perhaps most significant were his plans for the residential areas, which had an advanced form of tertiary schooling, located close to the dwelling units.

Garnier adopted an undecorated form of architecture for these schools based on geometry and an unprepossessing 'hole in wall' aesthetic. Children were separated in terms of age and advancement in learning. The schools were coeducational, which was another significant advance. Primary schools were dedicated to children from the age of 6 to 14 years. Adjoining infant schools were provided for children from 2 to 4 and from 4 to 6 years. Although unbuilt, Garnier's plans had advanced features such as age-related classrooms and special streets landscaped as safe child-friendly gardens separating younger from older children – usually older and younger children would all play in the same schoolyard, whereas here they were given separate playgrounds so there was less bullying. They also incorporated covered and open play yards, dining facilities with kitchens, covered play areas, and assembly halls laid out with individual chairs and projection facilities. The primary schools were to have gymnasia. His thinking on secondary schools included compulsory attendance for all young people up to the age of 18 or 20. The education system was to be designed for the needs of an industrial city, which included administration and commercial vocations, and, for a small number, professional and artistic education. Those who were recognized as having an extraordinary talent would go to a special school for higher education elsewhere.

Unwin's school in New Earswick had been designed in a typical arts and crafts idiom, with sharp gables, half timbering and barn-like tiled roofs, where the visual character of old England was recalled. Between the wars, many new schools were designed to a similar conservative formula, incorporating retro arts and crafts embellishments. The Nazis in Germany responded in a similar way, rejecting any form of modernist references, clothing their new school buildings with ornate bavarian fachwerk dressings. For a time the garden city idea became a popular alternative to the traditional city, with more green open spaces and a comprehensive education system central to the planning.

Garnier's was a garden city idea, but conceived on a far larger scale than Unwin's 'folksy' village idiom. More importantly, it adopted a modern architectural form as opposed to a sentimental arts and crafts style. However, education and the role of children within the city were central to both developments. For Garnier, education commenced at the age of 2, and for the brightest children would continue up to the age of 20 years. These principles, along with the open-air philosophy, were helping to formulate a new architecture of schools which emerged and flourished.

Educating the architects – the post-war years

Education is the result of experience. The wider and more complex the experience, the deeper and more intense the education. The field of experience widens in direct relation to the frequency of contacts, and its complexity grows with the increase in their variety ... institutions limit both contacts and education.[17]

Accommodating new generations of schoolchildren in the 1930s and 1940s would require large institutional buildings with multi-functional spaces to match complex social and academic aspirations. The architecture, like the pedagogic philosophy, was seen as an instrument for social change rather than solidification (of the existing social status) as had been the Victorian vision for mass education. The buildings were to be democratic and open reflections of the new societies aspired to by British politicians and educationalists such as Henry Morris, Secretary for Education at Cambridge County Council. He rejected all aspects of the past, including *'the magical view of man and the universe'*, which had seeped down into the work of certain educational designers, such as those pursuing the Steiner philosophy.[18]

Schools were to be based on scientific principles as befitted the age, with a democratic philosophy which (in principle) held that within the context of the school, children developed best through social interaction with their peers, both inside and outside the classroom. In short, the new buildings for education were to be 'cities of childhood' encompassing all the variety and richness implied in Giancarlo's opening quotation, yet adopting the new spirit of modern architecture. They were certainly institutions, yet their pedagogic emphasis shifted away from authoritarianism *per se* towards a freer more balanced approach, adopting many principles of the more extreme educators such as Susan Isaacs.

This could be seen in less self-conscious spatial hierarchies which did away with segregation of the genders as initiated in Garnier's school designs. However, the two to three stage structure comprising pre-school, primary and secondary schools which had developed as a response to the 1870 Act remained remarkably intact within the UK and elsewhere. This, one suspects, was due in no small measure to the traditional urban school environments inherited by the new educators. The architect's desire to lift the nineteenth century institutional weight of the building to reflect a more modern visionary spirit is caught by Summerson's *'... profound desire to escape from the remorseless discipline of gravity, a desire to dissolve the heavy prose of building into ... a multiple, imponderable pile of heavenly mansions.'*[19] This was exemplified by the move towards lightweight building technologies away from traditional masonry construction.

Pre-First World War health concerns continued to be applied during the inter-war years. This had been seen first in the early open-air school movements. Major conferences on school hygiene were held at Nuremberg in 1905, in London in 1907 and in Paris in 1910. They were attended by a large percentage of the medical profession. A special deputation from the BMA was made to the president of the board of education on the necessity for the teaching of hygiene in schools. An open-air school required a garden site and the adaptability of classrooms which could be opened completely on one side. This enabled teaching to be carried out virtually outdoors for much of the year. The lightness of touch and inside/outside themes were prefaced by Margaret MacMillan when she had referred to the new schools as 'cities of childhood':

The idea of a large and strongly built edifice as a school for children went by the board long ago. To hold such a conception (and it was long held) as if one, escaping from a cave dwelling, insisted on living in a large prison ... The school of tomorrow will be a garden city of children; that is to say a place of many shelters – a township, if you will, of small schools built as one community but with every shelter organized as a separate unit designed to meet the needs of children of specific age or stage of life ... every shelter is in effect a small school, it is also a self contained unit or school home ... [20]

A very early example of this thinking was applied to the Whiteley Woods School in Sheffield. Provided for the sickly children living in the centre of the city, it comprised a series of timber pavilion type classroom buildings each with a retractable wall on one side. Within the framework of the curriculum, hygiene was taught for two hours per day. A rest period was obligatory. Ralph Williams, the Sheffield Medical Officer, alluded to the importance of the garden spaces when he said: *'More space should be made of the playgrounds of the ordinary elementary schools during the summer months, classes should be held in the open air, and nature study walks in the country for children attending schools in the centre of the city should be frequently undertaken.'* [21]

In later years, the importance of a hygienic environment was emphasized in the form of numerous hybrid designs, with classrooms articulated as pavilions which were linked together by 'marching' corridors, colonnades or open courtyards. These combined the advantages of cross-ventilation and all-round natural light within classrooms, without children having to get wet when moving around the school. In 1911, George Widows designed a school at Highfields, Long Eaton, which comprised a tripartite plan bisected centrally by a broad corridor, which was to be used for drill lessons. It had an open veranda on both sides. There were six classrooms, one for each standard, with two central classrooms linked by folding wall/doors which could be thrown open to provide a single assembly hall. The form was considered highly experimental by the Board of Education, and only six examples were ever built. Seaborne and Lowe assert that whilst establishing the principles of much twentieth century school design, these buildings paid little attention to architectural style: *'They were among the most hygienic and ugliest of English school buildings.'* [22]

The 1931 Hadow Report on the primary school recommended that the full use of the environment should be made and that school design be influenced by the open-air principles. Consequently, primary schools built just before and immediately after the war incorporated classrooms, halls and corridors which were generally more spacious than their predecessors. Furthermore, they were located wherever possible on open greenfield sites with southerly aspects. Many retained the open-air feel with window/door partitions which could be opened fully. This set the pattern for a large proportion of the new schools commissioned after the Second World War; they were often located around the edges of the expanding suburbs, rather than in urban locations within the city centres. There was a concern for health, fresh air and ventilation. In later years, the best new architecture which was at the cutting edge of

technological innovation incorporated these health features.

The Architects and Buildings Branch of the UK government's Education Department also had a key role to play in the development of new and innovative ideas. Established in 1949, they produced guidance for the LEAs which was based on research and considerable in-house expertise. They became the intermediaries between the Ministry of Education, dictating policy to the communities in receipt of funding for the construction of new schools. As a result of material and labour shortages one of their concerns was to produce good quality schools at a fraction of the traditional build cost. They took many of the lessons on prefabrication learnt in Hertfordshire, where the local aircraft industry had acted as the catalyst to new methods of construction and procurement.

Stirrat Johnson-Marshall, the Chief Architect at the Ministry of Education from 1948, was a keen advocate of prefabrication. He was concerned with two key issues: choice and control. Choice meant that that there would be several independent competitive systems available. Control meant that they should all use the same module such that components were interchangeable between systems. This in theory meant that an infinite number of variations was possible. The strategy was to develop proprietary products with existing manufacturers for use in schools designed by the Ministry. Between 1949 and 1957 the development group devised five complete systems, all of which were lightweight constructions designed for buildings up to three or four storeys in height. They economized on wet trades and all but one used the 3 ft 4 inch Hertfordshire module. The commitment of the manufacturers had to go beyond purely financial considerations and they explored new ways of dealing with social and educational concerns. One of the first such schools to be constructed in this way was St Crispin's Secondary Modern in Wokingham, which opened in 1953.

The well funded A & B Branch were able to take a longer term strategic view of educational buildings than the LEAs, responding to the needs of communities up and down the country. For example, during the early 1950s, activity focused predominantly on urban and suburban facilities, at the expense of small village schools which often lay at the heart of the areas they served, acting as surrogate community centres. A programme to regenerate village schools, many of which had small cellular spaces, heavy pre-war furniture and dangerous open stoves, was instigated. The Ministry of Education Building Bulletin No. 3, which appeared in June 1961, took two typical examples of village schools and provided information on appropriate modifications. The bulletin included detailed building specifications. Such guidance was used to great effect over the following twenty years on other village schools.

The closeness of government architects to education policy enabled the new school buildings to be tailored more to the needs of the evolving educational curricula. The Plowden Report directed classroom activities away from work in large groups, towards smaller group activities. The basis of the proposals came from similar American prototypes which had adopted an open, zoned approach to the organization of the school. It was not exactly a return to the single volume school room, but in terms of its general openness, it came close. The success of the system would very much depend on the way in which the teacher could organize and control space, to provide three clear zones: a generous outside covered space, a messy practical zone, and a zone for reading, writing and arithmetic which maintained the discipline of children interacting with each other.

Such was the fluid movement of educational ideas that similar thinking infused other countries of the developed world in their own new buildings for mass education. Sophisticated modern architecture first appeared in European state schools designed in the early 1930s – Dudok in Hilversum, André Lurcat in Villejuif near Paris and Duiker in Amsterdam. This work was in strong contrast to the hygiene-obsessed utilitarianism of many schools built at that time within the UK. One of the foremost examples of the new school architecture was a project designed by Jan Duiker and Bernard Bijboet in 1927. The commission was for an open-air school 'for the healthy child' in a suburb of Amsterdam. As Jan Molema described it at the time, the work would create: '... *one of his most outstanding and characteristic buildings. Like a transparent sparkling crystal the school expressed Duiker's desire for a healthier society.'*[23]

Duiker's first plan was for a T-shaped building with a smaller one-storey rectangular block connected by a covered way. The main part was on four floors with staircases which had projecting landings at each end, reminiscent of a Le Corbusier balcony detail. However, the indoor and outdoor classroom arrangements were unsatisfactory so modifications were made to achieve an improved relationship. Unfortunately, negotiations by the local authority and the client for the original site proposed for the new school were abandoned because of a lack of funds. The building was relocated from an expansive green field site to a more urban setting within the centre of a perimeter block. Modifications were made to Duiker's earlier scheme, incorporating a new entrance block, an entrance gateway, a handicraft room and a cycle shed. The building fitted its new site remarkably well.

The greatest design modification was the rotation of the main block in order to introduce a diagonal axis into the plan. The structural columns at the corners were then displaced to the centre of the external walls, and the classrooms were interchanged. This produced a refined building with a slender concrete frame, a maximum amount of openness and free-standing siting, all of which gave the school a delightfully light quality. The plan on the upper floor comprised three truncated squares on a diagonal rotation, served by a central staircase and lifts. Two of the stairs on each floor were glazed, lending an airy transparency to the circulation routes. The gymnasium was formed by an extended leg on the diagonal. Classrooms were accommodated on four storeys, with the gymnasium beneath provided within an extra half level, dug out from the basement. Duiker's inspiring school was strongly influenced by Russian constructivism, the concretization of a revolutionary ideology.

The Italian Rationalists, of which Giuseppe Terragni (1904–1943) was at the forefront, incorporated the structural discipline of the machine age with nationalist values of Italian Classicism. According to Mimica and Shannon, the Sant'Elia nursery school in Como designed by Terragni was a 'canonical' representation of the school type in its synthesis of tradition and innovation.[24] All furniture and fittings were designed in lightweight materials at child scales. Classrooms had opening partitions for flexibility yet the whole building was integrated and solid in its architectural composition. Inspired by Duiker's open-air school, each classroom had its own outdoor terrace with canvas awnings, defined and supported by a bold concrete screen wall. Boundaries between indoors and outdoors were dissolved, an effect which was enhanced by external night lighting reflected up onto the bright concrete surfaces, to accentuate the rhythmic verticals of the entrance porches.

Six years later, Eugene Beaudouin and Marcel Lods, who had collaborated on Cité de la Muette à Drancy, designed an open-air school located at Suresnes, six kilometres to the west of Paris. It was designed for children whose fragile health prevented them from attending the normal schools of the commune, and integrated the special needs sections into the structure of an ordinary school. Sited on the south slopes of Mont Valerien, its natural east–west orientation strongly influenced the layout of the school spaces. The main block was two storeys in height and 75 metres in length. Boys were accommodated in the west wing and girls in the east with the kindergarten occupying the centre block. An octagonal classroom was rather self-consciously placed in the garden adjacent to the kindergarten for children with learning difficulties. The eight 'pavilion' classrooms were arrow-headed in layout, connected to the main block only by lightweight covered arcades. The roofs of these arcades acted as access points to sun-decks on top of the classrooms. The medical unit was at the intersection of these covered ways. Each classroom was surrounded by grass and was openable on one side, to provide the best possible environment for learning.

The school accommodated up to 350 children arranged in the form of eight ordinary classes, a special class and two kindergarten classes. The intake was to be thirty pupils per year, selected on medical grounds from other schools around the commune. There were thirty children to each class, which were sex segregated. In the main school, children aged 6–14 years were accommodated, whilst the kindergarten had spaces for forty children aged 4–6 years. The isolated class system was developed as the best answer to the needs of health and teaching. Boys and girls had separate entrances into the main block. On the ground floor, children reached classrooms from exercise spaces by means of covered ways. Both girls and boys each had their own communal dining rooms, service pantries and rest rooms.

The rest period was intended to take place on the sun-decks, weather permitting. The constructional system was similar to that used at Cité de la Mette à Drancy near Paris by the same architects. It consisted of standardized wall and floor units supported on a steel frame. Floor units were of reinforced concrete frames with infill concrete slabs. External wall slabs were of concrete finished with white pebbles set in. These were used for north walls of classrooms and north and side walls of the main block. All other external walls were glazed, with horizontally sliding doors and windows, or infilled panels of sheet steel. It was an example of an advanced open-air school laid out as a city of childhood. It is conceivable that this influenced a generation of school designers who were developing similar green field sites.

Willem Marinus Dudok was born in Amsterdam in 1884 and moved to Hilversum in 1915. His early work was influenced by Berlage and his attraction to the massive grandeur of the Romanesque. Later work appeared to derive its style from both the expressionist Amsterdam school of Kramer and De Klerk, and the De Stijl movement, where giant horizontal and vertical elements dominated. When Dudok was appointed director of public works in 1915, the town was in the process of rapid growth, from what had been merely a large farming village. Textile mills and farming were flourishing and the new railway passing through Hilversum linked it directly to Amsterdam. This produced growth in local industries and, as a consequence, a substantial increase of the residential population. During the course of his professional career, Dudok designed and built eighteen schools, eight of which were built at the heart of new housing districts in Hilversum.

Between 1916 and 1918 Dudok produced a programme for the town's growth, and planned to achieve an urban architecture with an overall system of space whereby groups of basic urban units could be utilized in a variety of ways. Following Raymond Unwin's ideas, the working class districts of Hilversum were designed to provide adaptable relationships between, on the one hand, the house and garden, and on the other, groups of buildings and urban spaces. Dudok used this urban vocabulary primarily on low-cost housing projects and schools. Public buildings, such as theatres, swimming baths and schools, were to have an urban presence acting as focal points for the local community. Sometimes, as was the case with the Hedenschool of 1926, with its double L-shaped plan, the gymnasium itself doubled as a community centre.

Many critics believe that Dudok's was a rather indulgent pluralistic approach. The evolution of his designs for schools neither developed chronologically, nor did they demonstrate a maturing language of architecture. Sometimes they recalled tradition, sometimes the buildings stressed function and user needs; alternatively, historicism was evoked, and even new fashionable trends in architectural language. Dudok was a latter-day eclectic, choosing a style on the basis of his personal taste at that time. These divergent preoccupations are exemplified by the Berlage-influenced Geranium School of 1916–18, followed in 1921–22 by the Bavinck School, a stereometric play of geometry very much in the manner of De Stijl, and subsequently in the 1926 Fabritius School. There, Dudok exploited the vocabulary of vernacular architecture, mixing traditional materials, under a thatched roof, with continuous industrial-style glazing, set on rendered walls. Tiny staircase towers and the heating chimney helped to articulate the composition.

Dudok never embraced, nor was he embraced by, the ideas of the new international movements in architecture and design. Fifty years ago in *Space, Time and Architecture*, the myopic Siegfried Gideon dismissed Dudok with a single line, describing his work as merely romantic. However, the school work was copied in some quarters, particularly during the 1930s, as it combined elements of tradition with the expressive mass and volume of the constructivists and De Stijl. For example, the Burlington Secondary School (1935) by Burnet Tait and Lorne was highly derivative of Snelliusschool School in Hilversum and others of the early 1930s. Designed for a long narrow site next to Wormwood Scrubs, it is articulated with ponderous deliberation in its horizontal and vertical massing. It is self-consciously asymmetrical to break with classical tradition and has strip windows with brick cladding. However, it incorporates the flexibility of a concrete structural frame. The classrooms are all south-facing, onto the playground areas, with the school hall and entrance block placed as a barrier between the classrooms and the busy main road. Despite its ambivalence, it has outlasted much of the later modernist work, in providing environmentally workable and pragmatic accommodation, in a form with which many ordinary people can relate. This hybrid building is still in a very usable condition today, having accommodated the vicissitudes of generations of noisy teenagers.

Modernism in mainstream school design

Many of the ideas which influenced two generations of school architects in the UK were included in a special issue

Figure 1.18
Burlington Secondary
School (1935), London,
by Burnet Tait and Lorne.
(Photo: © Mark Dudek.)

of the *Architectural Review* published in July 1940. What was not discussed were the fascinating architectural precedents which largely dictated the style of these new buildings. There appears to be strong de Stijl influence at work, seen in the intersecting planes of Rietveld's work, and in the use of ashlar as a cladding material. Le Corbusier's Swiss Pavilion and the Villa at Toulon were similarly of great significance. Rubble walls were not used in their traditional way, but as single wall planes offset by large infill glazing panels, all supported by a separate structural frame. These buildings incorporated new spatial relationships and geometric principles which appealed to young designers as truly vintage modern buildings paralleled in the 1930s only by the work of Breuer and Lubetkin in the UK, Lurcat in France and Neutra in the USA.

A little-known precursor to all of this was one of Alvar Aalto's earliest buildings. In June 1938 the county council of Inkeroinen (in the region of Anjalankoski) bought an area of 6000 sq. m on which to build a new elementary school. The following month Aalto was commissioned to produce a design which was to be as economic as possible. His drawings were approved unanimously; however, after September of that year Aalto was not involved on the site works due to commitments elsewhere.

The school was to accommodate 200 pupils. The entrance hall, which was two storeys high, contained an expressive staircase and a free-form gallery which suggests that it was contemporaneous with his other work of the time, such as Villa Mairea and the Finnish Pavilion in New York. The building was sited on a slope and stepped down in three elegant stages. It included a house for the headteacher. On the ground floor there was an apartment for the head cook, a gymnasium, storage, a boiler room and girls' and boys' locker rooms. The first floor included the entrance space, the school kitchen, the boys' workshop and lavatories. There was a teachers' lounge on the first floor with a girls' workshop and classrooms. On the third floor there were three more classrooms.

The overall effect of strip windows, piloti and spiral stairs referred back to Aalto's early rationalist period; however, it was still considered to be very modern and it is hard to believe how early it was conceived and built. It used rendered brick painted white, concrete beams and some timber framing. The building displays many of the features developed and refined by Aalto in his later work, such as a sophisticated response to the site with integrated horizontal and planar massing. The school exhibits for the first time many of the qualities which were to make Aalto famous in later years.

In 1937, adopting a similar form of elegant modernity, the young architect Denis Clarke Hall entered the influential *News Chronicle* competition and won the main section for the design of a larger school. The competition was held during a period of much new school commissioning and research. Other competition entries included those from Marcel Breuer and FRS Yorke, Erno Goldfinger, Denys Lasdun with Wells Coates, amongst others. Clearly they found the design of schools a new and exciting proposition well suited to the technologies promised by the modernist ethos. Mass repetitive construction allied to a pure abstract aesthetic seemed appropriate to the needs of education. Clarke Hall's success in this ideas competition led to a real commission from Frank Barraclough, a progressive education officer in Yorkshire. The project was for a new secondary school with a plan based largely on research Clarke Hall had carried out for his *News Chronicle* scheme.

Richmond High School for Girls had accommodation for 160 pupils. It was completed in 1940. The site, which was located on high ground with a south east orientation towards the Cleveland Hills, lay approximately half a mile from the centre of Richmond, Yorkshire. Local stone was used as a walling material with stone cobbles as paving for the forecourts. Paths were of smooth concrete with rough pebbles laid out in a geometrical form reflecting the rhythms of the whole building. Solid rubble walls were adopted for those parts of the construction which were small enough to be spanned by stone lintels. Concrete frame construction was used for walls which had larger openings. Each pair of classrooms had glazing on one side, set into concrete frames. The building was generally one storey throughout with the exception of a two-storey block of staff and library accommodation.

The free development of the plan on its green-field site gave Clarke Hall the opportunity to organize nearly everything on a single level. The two major environmental concerns were firstly the need for even light and ventilation and secondly acoustic isolation for the quiet areas intended for study. Classrooms were isolated in pairs, and articulated as independent pavilions with open terraces between. A wide central corridor connected the pavilions with short enclosed glazed links. This was the spine of the building and it accommodated all the book lockers and floor ducts carrying mains services. In its general principles, it was a development of the competition-winning scheme, with pavilions sitting in the landscape enclosing neat open courtyards internal to the plan.

In subsequent years it was much criticized because it treated education as a process with little concern for the diverse needs of people working and being taught within the building. Like many of its type, the environment was often cold in winter and hot in summer, and it was difficult to find spaces which fulfilled the need for more private contemplative activities; the acoustics of the quiet spaces were far from perfect. Most crucially, the extent to which Richmond became a model to be plagiarized in less appropriate settings by less accomplished designers became one of the main reasons for its widespread condemnation in later years; it set the wrong example. However, for its time this was a spirited building incorporating new spatial relationships which expressed modernism in its raw uncompromising state. It must have been an inspiring building to grow up in during its early years, whilst new and pristine.

The extent to which schools became the testing ground for later, grander projects by key architects of the twentieth century could be seen in a number of projects of this time. One can cite the work of Aalvar Aalto, as previously mentioned, the Smithsons, Karl Ehn, Aldo Rossi and most importantly Denys Lasdun, who designed his first and most successful project for a school in Paddington, before going on to design London's National Theatre, amongst numerous other high profile public buildings. Whereas Karl Ehn's Karl Marx Hof housing scheme of 1930 included an infant school within the enclosed space of a large island of housing, and Le Corbusier's nursery school was located on the roof of the Unite d'habitation at Marseilles (1947–52), Lasdun's Hallfield School was a dynamic composition in a ville radieuse layout, which nevertheless related well to its traditional urban context.

Initially designed as a Tecton commission with Lasdun as the partner in charge, it was completed after the dissolution of that practice in 1948. Lasdun dismissed the diagrammatic approach to design, eschewing modernist devices such as grids, boxes and stilts. Standardization for its own symbolic purpose, which dismissed the human element, was rejected perhaps as a response to Richmond. Instead an integration into its 2.75 acre urban site was sought, retaining most of the existing trees in a similar manner to Nev Churcher's Woodlea School, 45 years later (see Figures 3.11a–c, page 91, conceptual sketches of Woodlea and Hallfield Schools). Lasdun's concerns with the site ultimately forced on him the curvilinear block and the fragmented position of the various elements to produce its poetic and appealing form. When compared to the adjacent high rise housing blocks it appears humane and of a fitting scale: '... *an approach is favoured in which individual human activities are enhanced by the articulation of spaces of different character, in which a building's unity of form and idea is considered paramount, and in which technique is made the servant of the controlling form. The humanism of this approach and the departure from mechanistic modern architecture are underlined by the biological analogies of the plan, especially the resemblance to the unfurling form of a plant, with stem, leaves and petals.*'[25]

The scheme included a long, twisting sinuous block, which houses junior school classrooms and staff rooms, all of which are east facing and on two floors. At the east end of the block there are dining facilities. Halfway down, the block is bisected by a cross route. This links two identical assembly halls, one above the other on the north side, and on the south, a group of four pentagonal pods, each divided in half to provide eight infant classrooms in a hybrid pavilion form. Thus the building develops a fragmented appearance when catering for infants, and a more conventional linear shape at junior school level. The main entrance is from the north and is organized as a connecting extension of the Hallfield housing scheme.

Administration, assembly and dining halls are stacked for structural economy. Close collaboration between the architect and the structural engineer ensured that load-bearing elements would be fully exploited for reasons of economy and to provide column-free space as necessary. In the junior classroom block, nine-inch brickwork is employed to form load-bearing cross walls at 24 ft centres providing optimum noise reduction. Deep reinforced concrete beams create a solid framework for the walls which enclose the classrooms. A series of large-scale reinforced concrete mullions at 4 ft centres transfer loads from the first floor and roof levels only. The rhythm of the façade is emphasized by these elegant tapering vertical elements. The continuous glazing is set back slightly. All structural members are of pre-cast concrete faced with Portland Stone or in-situ reinforced concrete with natural and splatter dash coloured finishes, which lend a humane texture in a contemporary idiom.

Interior finishes continue in this solid, authentic vein. Pink sandlime bricks are used for the load-bearing cross walls and staircases. Internal panels of the junior school corridors are constructed in black bricks, and in the children's lavatory white glazed bricks are used. Bright colours are restricted to focal points at the end of vistas. Between the mullions in the dining halls, interior panels are available for mural paintings. In total the school comprises eight infant classes and ten junior school classes providing accommodation for 540 pupils. It is a building which, perhaps more than any of Lasdun's later projects, remains as fresh and appealing as the day it was opened; it is arguably his best work. The constraints of the difficult site place restraints on the extremes of modernist ideology, to create a school which is human in scale and detail. Almost 50 years after it first opened, with its robust structure and finishes Hallfield is still perfectly serviceable. Assembly halls and classrooms are used after school and at weekends for adult activities making it a building of immense value to the community.

By contrast, the infamous Hunstanton School in Norfolk, designed by Allison and Peter Smithson in 1949 (completed in 1954), has proved less durable. It possessed an even more mechanistic architectural image than Richmond, and unlike Hallfield, it had no site or client constraints. Influenced by Mies van der Rohe's work in Illinois and by the Palladian tracts in Wittkower's *The Principles of Architecture in the Age of Humanism*, the building caught the flavour of the times. Although the Smithsons said in 1953 that the form of the school was not arrived at through precedent, but by a careful study of educational needs, it seems more likely that the economic compactness of the planning was the main determining factor in its layout. The construction was similarly cheap, yet in a form which was 'radically chic' for its time.

Light and air was still seen as being very important in the 1940s, as a foil perhaps to the Victorian and Edwardian school interiors of Robson. In addition, the use of steel framing which allowed for maximum areas of glazing, fast track construction and an air of advanced purposeful technology in use, was the potent mix. However, the windows were detailed without sub-frames, so the glass was fixed straight onto the steel structure. Even under initial construction, 50 out of the thousand odd panes of glass had to be trimmed to fit, the tolerances required being too demanding for the manufacturing process. In 1984, after many years of piecemeal repair, hundreds of panels were condemned for replacement. Tony Twiggs, Norfolk's deputy county architect at the time, said: '... *after a clear frosty November night, I have watched panels shatter one by one as the sun has come up and heated them.*'[26]

In a similar vein, Douglas Little, headteacher in 1984, described how he would sit at his desk and watch the changing reflections in the windows as the sun moved round; the panes becoming concave or convex and then flat again. No wonder the architecture of schools was held in such low esteem in subsequent years. On the one hand, it was lauded by the architectural establishment winning prestigious awards, on the other the building contained extremes of technical incompetence integral to the design aesthetic. Recently, new glass panes have been fixed with timber sub-frames, a design compromise to the original minimalist concept at which the puritanical Smithsons would probably have been appalled.

Extensive repairs have also been made to the flat roofs. Acoustic problems have been attended to internally; however, the building plan is so geometrically complete that it is almost impossible to extend. One of its major problems is the need to accommodate 900 pupils, twice the number for which it was originally intended. As an echo of the Richmond School experience, the current headteacher suggests that it is '... *a bit of a nightmare because the building is too cold in winter, hot in summer, the interior is too noisy and open and creates teaching difficulties, maintenance costs are high.*'[27]

However, the building was more economical than the Mies' Illinois example, with its specially designed windows and expensive broad flanged steel members. The Smithsons' building used an assembly of readily available components which they described as 'found'. The competition of 1949 was judged by only one assessor. This had been Denis Clarke Hall, architect for Richmond, which had been visited by the Smithsons in 1945. Despite the functional and performance shortcomings, it was an attempt to produce an exciting alternative to the more conventional approaches to school design at that time. In a certain light it appears Mondrianesque and contains perhaps unconscious allusions to de Stijl. The A & B Branch, however, never viewed it as a jewel in their crown, rather an expensive and irrelevant aberration.

Apart from the obvious radicality of its technology, access to the main teaching areas on the first floor were by way of ten staircases. There were almost no corridors to speak of and, as mentioned previously, circulation takes place by way of the entrance lobbies and the communal hall which is at the centre of the plan. '... *The hall is used for everything, it's used for assemblies, it's used for naughties at break time, it's used for feeding, and 700 would go through that canteen, so it's actually quite a hive of activity. In many schools the hall is a sort of administrative corridor*

through which you wouldn't be allowed to walk, now I can't be doing with all that. So the architecture probably does hold itself open to sort of stopping in corridors and chatting which helps the relationship with staff.'[28] Perhaps within these final comments some lessons can be learnt from the sad affair of Hunstanton School. The circulation is an integral part of the assembly hall, which in its better moments becomes a true forum where school staff and children are encouraged to function in an environment of variety and rich social interaction.

Hans Scharoun, Aldo van Eyck and Herman Hertzberger

The major historical developments in school design during the twentieth century would be incomplete without brief mention of Hans Scharoun, Aldo van Eyck and Herman Hertzberger working in Germany and Holland respectively. Where most school facilities are characterized by standardized classrooms, with little differentiation between rooms for younger and older children, Scharoun provided a more tailored humane approach. Whilst influenced by the functionalist ethos, his architecture was anti-modern movement. Van Eyck, with his sophisticated spatial ideas of harmony in motion, and the importance of the 'spaces in between', added another dimension to the theory of schools architecture. Both were immensely influential. Perhaps most important, however, has been the contribution of Herman Hertzberger, which is ongoing (see Case Studies 6 and 7). His work, initially on the Apollo Schools in Amsterdam (1980), illustrated new ways of enhancing the social relationships between the users, through the organization and detail suggested by the built form.

Scharoun was part of the later phase of the modern movement in architecture. Aalto had developed an international reputation before the war; whilst revered in Germany, Scharoun was little known elsewhere. He discouraged writing about his works and wrote little himself. He also remained in Germany throughout the war. As a consequence he was influenced by Hugo Haring's functionalist doctrine which was opposed to the international Modern Movement's interest in geometric abstraction. The clarity of his early work in the 1920s and 1930s was widely accepted by architectural writers as having a certain authentic international flavour. However, Scharoun thought of himself as a designer in a particular Nordic tradition – an approach which he believed contrasted with the Latin tradition, where rules of abstract mathematical harmony had prevailed.

In the post-war period, Scharoun designed three schools, two of which were built. His plans for a primary school in Darmstadt were launched at a conference entitled 'Man and Space', held in 1951. The unrealized

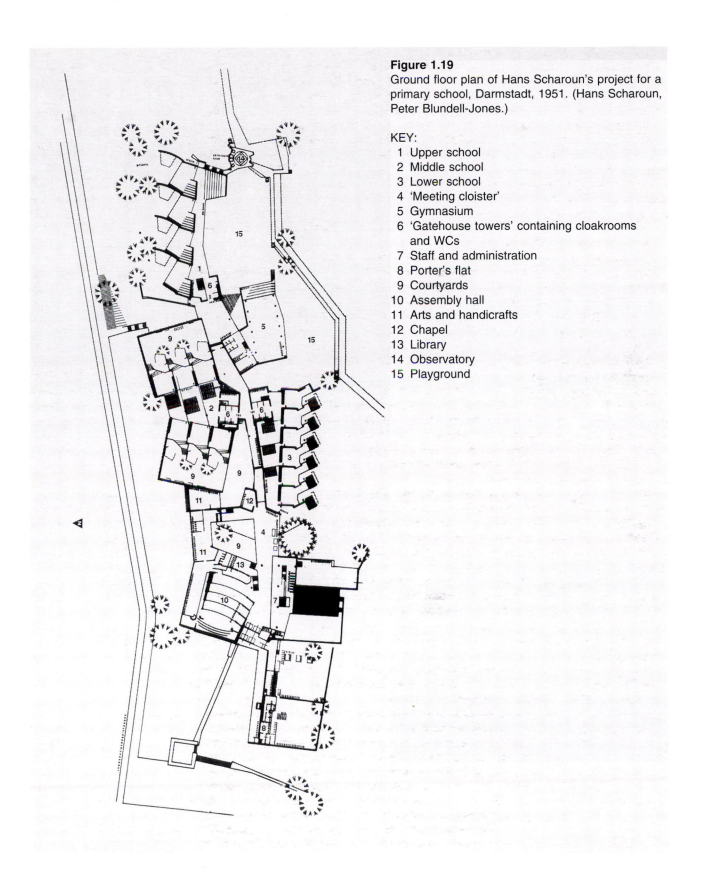

Figure 1.19
Ground floor plan of Hans Scharoun's project for a primary school, Darmstadt, 1951. (Hans Scharoun, Peter Blundell-Jones.)

KEY:
 1 Upper school
 2 Middle school
 3 Lower school
 4 'Meeting cloister'
 5 Gymnasium
 6 'Gatehouse towers' containing cloakrooms and WCs
 7 Staff and administration
 8 Porter's flat
 9 Courtyards
10 Assembly hall
11 Arts and handicrafts
12 Chapel
13 Library
14 Observatory
15 Playground

project was seen as a prototype which displayed the intrinsic social structure of the school community in its planning and organization. Subsequently he was commissioned to design two schools on similar principles at Lünen in 1956 and Marl in 1960. An interesting connection with John Dewey can be made as the designs are not merely about functional requirements, but are also concerned with the school's social role. The wider needs of the pupils were seen as of primary importance. Scharoun believed that the basic principles displayed in the design had a universal relevance which he employed in later public buildings. He saw the school as a microcosm of the city with the classrooms as houses, each with their own communal space articulated as a sort of internal street. Institutional elements of the programme such as the chapel and the assembly hall could be interpreted in terms of urban iconography as the church and the town hall. In this particular instance, the metaphor would be that of the fortified town familiar in that part of Germany, with the plan marked out with walls and tower-gatehouses.

The gatehouses were two-storey cloakrooms which served each wing of accommodation. Classrooms were arranged in three separate units each accommodating three school years with their own common rooms and cloakrooms. They were enclosed small communities within the overall framework of the school. The spatial sequence created a hierarchy which went from private to public. Starting first with the private domain, the pupil inhabits his or her own dedicated space within the classroom, then he or she belongs to the class social group, then the school unit, then the whole school and finally the locality or neighbourhood. The siting of the building and the colours used on the interiors related to the age of the pupils. The activity areas for children aged from 1 year to 3 years face south. Scharoun believed that the youngest children needed plenty of sun and light for physical and spiritual growth. Zones for educational and play activities were provided, comprising external teaching spaces as well as conventional teaching zones.

The second unit comprised classes for 4–6 year olds and was orientated east to west. This middle school wing emphasized a different sort of learning. Scharoun saw it as *'recognizing, understanding and experiencing interest in lessons and independent activities.'*[29] Development of the self within the community was the major issue in the final group for 7–9 year olds. This stage heralded self-identification by children who Scharoun believed were investigating their own personalities and beginning to explore ways of representing their individuality, an indirect reference to Freud's developmental concept of individuation. The classrooms face north and benefit from cool modulated light. The architecture reflects the pedagogical development theories of the time, where each phase of the child's growth is represented by a different type of space.

The area which links the classroom units to the rest of the school is a passage conceived of as a meeting place,

with additional facilities such as the assembly hall, staff rooms, the gymnasium and workrooms. Scharoun described the assembly hall as the 'mediating room'. It was an open area for a social mix of pupils of different ages from the three class wings. Pupils from other schools in the city were also welcomed to this section. Religion and biology rooms were located between unit areas. A domed cosmic room was situated at the eastern end of the school. The dome symbolized the heavens and the floor described a concentric square and circle depicting the earth within its cosmos. It was an important representation of the pupils and their relationship to the wider world, in this rich humanistic setting.

The Geschwister School in Lünen, Westphalia, gave Scharoun the opportunity to use his ideas of the organic in the context of a secondary school. It was a girls' high school for pupils aged ten to 18. The site was overshadowed to the north by the Church of the Sacred Heart, where, logically, Scharoun placed the main entrance. From there, physics, biology and chemistry classrooms were accessible from an elongated assembly hall. Classrooms were designed to be like small flats, homes familiar to many of the students. Included in the classroom cluster was an entrance/cloakroom area, an external teaching space and an annex. The specialized classroom wings utilized at Darmstadt were abandoned here in favour of the same standardized but sophisticated teaching units throughout.

As in the Darmstadt project, the school was divided into lower, middle and upper sections. To the south east, eight lower school classrooms were organized in a serrated formation along a wide internal street. To the south east, eight lower classrooms were planned in a similar linear serrated form. Next to them were the six classrooms of the middle school. The upper school had four classrooms at first floor accessed from the hall. The circular playground was located next to the assembly hall. Scharoun was trying to produce controllable spaces paralleling the child's development, whilst fostering growing independence. The form and layout of the rooms encouraged pupils to identify with their schoolrooms as a whole.

The issues Scharoun was grappling with were complex ones for the period. The architectural representation was compared in the visual arts to the work of the cubists. Different stages of connectedness to the whole, and the establishment of clear polar relationships, were the conceptual basis of the plan. However, they did not have a complementary sectional form, with all the spatial richness that implies, as seen in some of Scharoun's larger public buildings. Like a natural landscape they were spread out and disparate with considerable travel distances between different parts. The schools were a fragmentary assembly of parts. They were organized to respond to the precise needs of the user, and in the case of Darmstadt to the educational needs of each particular age group. In plan terms they were highly sophisticated, laid

Figure 1.20
View of entrance to
secondary school (1976)
at Brondi by Aldo Rossi.
(© Kenneth Macdonald.)

out like geometric landscapes. They succeeded in establishing an alternative approach to the mechanistic layouts of most other schools being built at the time.

In the early 1950s, Aldo van Eyck was commissioned to design a new village community for Nagele, on the outskirts of Amsterdam, which was to incorporate three new schools. Although featureless architecturally, the Nagele schools were composed with an open centre with accommodation rotating around and away from the central square or courtyard. Each school had the 'centrifugal' playground at its heart, not surrounded symmetrically, but eccentrically, with the same block of accommodation bent around two sides of the space, or set eccentrically to the centre point of the courtyard. The classrooms were likewise arranged around small group halls in windmill pattern, encouraging circulation between spaces from a larger to a smaller scale. Halls and playgrounds interlocked and there were axial connections made between larger and smaller components of a similar disposition.

The system was applied to van Eyck's commission of 1955 for a municipal orphanage in Amsterdam. The deeply committed client, Frans van Meurs, had been an orphan himself. He wished to create a small idealized world, where residents could be given a more complete childhood than ordinary children. A utopian thinker, he commissioned van Eyck on the basis of his deep theoreti-

cal approach to design. The brief which the development team created was unusually complex and evocative. It was a clear statement of impassioned prose on the proposed life patterns intended for the new orphans, and was very deterministic. Its image was intended to be anti-institutional and non-controlling; however, it appears to have created almost the opposite effect.

Van Eyck abandoned the static symmetrical form favoured for school institutions, instead adopting a more articulated version of the Nagele approach, with accommodation grouped in L-shaped blocks around open loggias and courts. They mediated between inside and outside, in theory creating a more fluid welcoming effect. Although lauded by the architectural establishment at the time, the orphanage proved less than successful. One young visitor was heard to ask his father: *'Do they lock boys away here?'* The architecture was certainly open and fluid, but it was also rigorously gridded and contained vertical age segregation which proved too inflexible an arrangement for later directors of the institution. Whilst incorporating some beautiful childlike details for integrated seating and sandpits which were in tune with the patterning of the plan, as a whole the project suffered from contractual difficulties. Van Eyck's design ideas were sometimes overruled and diluted by combined client and contractual pressures.

Figure 1.21
General view of the
Orphanage, Amsterdam,
designed by Aldo van
Eyck. (Photo: © Mark
Dudek.)

In the 1970s a new generation of educationalists rejected anything they considered authoritarian. This happened to include the architectural determinism imposed by most of the buildings in which they worked. Education was a process which flowed between individuals rather than institutions. They appeared to interpret the fixed feature configuration of the orphanage as controlling and over-institutional, exactly the opposite to Van Meur's original vision. Perhaps it was; the times had changed from the socialist principles of community groupings organized and fixed in time, god-like, by the client/architect team. The new educationalists saw the equipment and architectural features of the individual living areas as obstacles to their own pedagogic creativity. Perhaps more damaging was their perception of modernist buildings as inflexible and overbearing; an embodiment of the egotistical architect as a social manipulator of the under-privileged masses.

The building was badly maintained and by 1986 was in a dreadful state of repair, having been altered and somewhat vandalized. It was close to total demolition before an international group of conservationists led by Herman Hertzberger stepped in and persuaded the government to support a programme of restoration and to provide a new use. Now it operates as a school of architecture, a fitting epitaph for this highly theoretical work. Perhaps van Eyck and his client's difficulties were encapsulated in Hertzberger's own quotation from the opening section referring to '... *a thing made exclusively for one purpose, suppresses the individual because it tells him exactly how it is to be used ...*', which brings us neatly back to Hertzberger.

Herman Hertzberger was born in 1932. His interest in the school type has realized numerous designs which develop along similar lines. A major culmination of this came in 1980, when the authorities of Amsterdam granted him the commission to design two new primary schools side-by-side on Apollolaan, a boulevard and major axis on the south of the city. Although the programme for each was identical, the pedagogical ethos was radically different, one being a conventional state school and one being a Montessori school based on principles of development through the child's creativity, in contact with his or her peers.

Hertzberger's response to the somewhat degraded urban fabric was to choose a villa typology which referred to the surrounding residential character. The three-storey structures contained eight classrooms organized around a central atrium or communal hall. This was the crucial organizing device; with its open staircases and stepped terraces, the form took on a spatial dynamic which enabled the pupils to develop a constant awareness of their relationship between their own class group and the wider school community. Where most schools were organized horizontally, the Apollo Schools were vertical in disposition. In a much more controlled and spatially sophisticated way, this was a revisitation of the Hunstanton central hall system, which encouraged social interaction, whilst ensuring that the enclosed classes were available to support the needs of the less confident child.

The sophisticated integration of architectural and educational thinking marked these, and subsequent school projects by Hertzberger, as exemplars of a more social

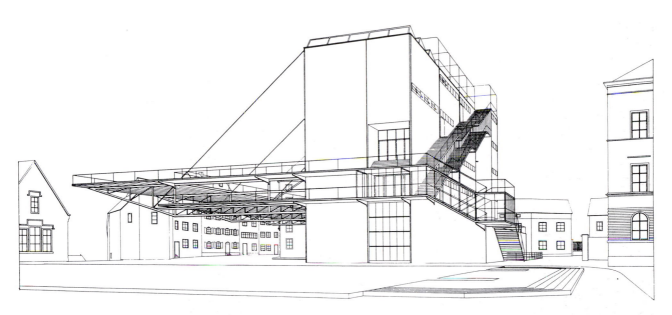

Figure 1.22a
Preliminary study, perspective sketch from the north-west.

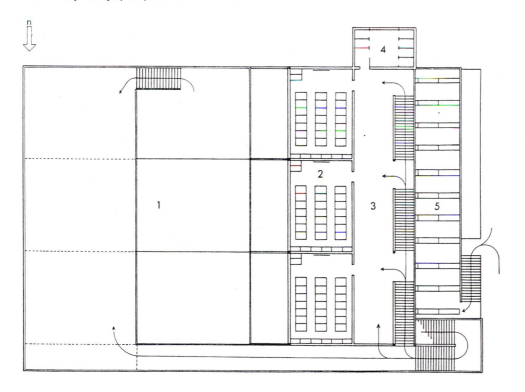

Figure 1.22b
Plan of fourth floor.

KEY:
1 Play area
2 Classroom
3 Hall
4 Toilets
5 Play terrace

This project was designed by constructivists Hannes Meyer and Hans Wittwer in 1926. It is a primary school in the old quarter of Basle. Overshadowed by tall buildings, the school is elevated above street level with a playground on a giant suspended platform above the street. A grand external staircase connects each level of accommodation comprising three classrooms and a play terrace. This theoretical project was an imaginative response to the need for generous circulation areas, light and ventilation within the new urban schools during the 1930s (Schnaidt, Claude, *Hannes Meyer – Buildings, Projects, Writing,* Alex Tiranti, London, 1965).

approach. At a time of threat to the child's freedom to use the wider environment freely, due to stranger danger and traffic stress, this was an advanced strategy which as Kenneth Frampton observed, created: '*... a school as a city-in-miniature, the school as a compensation, one might say, for the loss of a public forum in the community as a whole. It is difficult to imagine a more specifically political gesture than this and it would be hard to find any school built during the last twenty years that is of comparable critical subtlety and depth.*'[30] Twenty years later the schools are still viewed as icons, much copied, and further developed by Hertzberger and others (see Case Studies 6 and 7).

Summary

During this brief canter through some of the most influential people connected with the historical development of schools architecture, these large buildings for mass education have grappled with the conflicting need to create humane environments for learning. Perhaps the culmination of this has been the work of Hans Scharoun at Darmstadt and my description of it as the geometric landscape. However, the focus has been on the built form rather than external spaces. There has been very little mention of the importance of the environment in its totality, or what is sometimes referred to as the 'micro sphere'. During the demolition of the iconic prefabricated school buildings of Alexander and Neutra in Los Angeles, they were dismissed as being: '*constructed in a simple industrial vernacular, had been placed according to a suburban mindset then typical of modernists who treated buildings as machines in the garden.*'[31] The critique ignored the notion of the buildings in their setting and the important relationship they established with the garden, which added a significant dimension to the social development of the pupil body.

Their interpretation as pavilions or little houses, to which each small class community could relate, was a theme which has been adopted by a number of educationalists, particularly in the provision of pre-school facilities. The theme was touched upon by John Summerson in his essay 'Heavenly Mansions' when he described a type of play which is common to every child, where a shelter is formed out of a piece of furniture or a garden bower which takes on the symbolic characteristics of his or her own house. It becomes a necessary haven where the child can withdraw into a fantasy world away from the pressures of the public realm, a requirement which many child specialists believe is of psychological importance to children and school pupils throughout the education system:

> *... At a later stage, the child's conduct of the game is transferred to a new plane of realism; he constructs or uses dolls' houses and insists on a strict analogy between his own practices and those of adult life – the doll's house must be an epitome of an adult's home. But whether the child is playing under the table or handling a doll's house, his imagination is working in the same way. He is placing either himself or the doll (a projection of himself) in a sheltered setting. The pleasure he [sic] derives from it is a pleasure in the relationship between himself (or the doll) and the setting.*[32]

Summerson goes on to assert that even as adults, many people never outgrow the need for this symbolic game, which he believes has much to do with the aesthetics of architecture: '*... camping and sailing are two adult forms of play analogous to the "my house" pretences of a child.*' However, the difference is well explained by this reference to camping and sailing. They are outdoor as opposed to indoor activities which assert the relationship of the sky and the sea at first hand. Whereas the need for the child to appropriate his or her own space still exists, it is no longer contained within the real life house (or school or kindergarten). The adult or older child would not construct the garden shed inside the house, whereas the pre-school child may well interpret the interior space of the nursery school as a microcosm of the world, an indoor garden in miniature, or a kindergarten.

Environmental psychologist Roger A. Hart views the interior and exterior architecture of the ideal school as one in which a child can develop an awareness of his or her surroundings, furnishing them with a lifelong skill which he describes as *environmental competence*. Referring to an earlier study which defined these safe manageable spaces where constructional toys could be laid out, sophisticated skills could be developed through an engagement with a world in miniature, as the 'micro sphere'. He states that: '*... this micro sphere of physical objects allows pre-school children to gain competence and confidence before venturing out into the complex social macro sphere. This makes good sense, but I should note that in my own research I have noticed little or no decrease in children's interest in constructional play until they approach 12 years of age.*'[33] The pre-school and primary school spaces are the context where this very important role-playing should be allowed to develop.

This implies that the role of the interior of the school takes on a more profound psychological significance than simply the machine for learning in. As stated previously, the need to provide a diverse range of internal spaces for the younger school child is perhaps more important than for the older child, who through his or her greater independence will be able to find symbolic shelters within the external environment – the conception of smoking behind the bicycle shed as a territorial assertion of the pupil's growing independence. However, it is my contention that the need for safe manageable social spaces into which the secondary school pupil can withdraw to construct their own 'little shelters' should now be carefully conceived of as part of the schedule of accommodation for any new school.

There is growing evidence which suggests that many children are developing a close relationship with computer games as part of this need to withdraw. Part of the attraction lies in the visual and aural representation of three-dimensional spaces, which can be manipulated and effected by the operator. The little house syndrome is replicated by way of participation most often in the form of violent interactions. The figures or doors and windows of the buildings depicted can be demolished, but rarely are they constructed. The implications of this are firstly that a generation of children is developing a relationship with space, through their computers, which is obsessive and violent. Secondly, their ability to develop environmental awareness is limited, since the spaces of their computer are at best engaging only three of the senses.

With the UK government's emphasis on computer-aided learning, do we risk a generation of spatially impoverished adults? The remedy lies partly in the qualities of both the internal and the external school environment, conceived of in its totality, to provide rich spatial diversity as embodied in a Scharoun or a Lasdun school. The connection between the quality of the architecture and the learning outcome has been explicitly stated throughout this chapter. Whilst difficult to prove, particularly in the context of van Eyck's experience of educational practice during the 1960s and 1970s, it is nevertheless axiomatic and is reinforced by the author's own experience, and my ongoing discussions with numerous adults who benefited from good new school buildings during their formative years.[34]

Notes

1   Hall, E.T., 'The anthropology of space.' An organizing model essay. In Prohansky, Ittelson and Rivlin (eds) *Environmental Psychology* (2nd edn): *People and their Physical Settings,* Holt Rinehart and Winston, New York, 1976. p.158.

2   Hertzberger, H., *Harvard Educational Review: Architecture and Education,* 39, 4, 1969, p.95.

3   Churchill was concerned how the restoration of the House of Commons should be brought about. He feared that a departure from the intimate confrontational public school debating tradition, as the parliamentary debating chambers had been designed, might transform the nature of British politics.

4   Arthur Conan Doyle, *Sherlock Holmes, The Case of the Stolen Naval Treaty.* Selected Stories, Oxford's World Classics, Oxford University Press, 1998. On 30 April 1998, a new government initiative aimed at identifying excellence in schools within the UK and spreading good practice was announced. The 100 centres of excellence 'will be called "Beacon Schools" and will ... act as a guiding light for others to follow, by representing examples of good practice in areas such as: numeracy; literacy; tackling disaffection; or overall performance' (Department for Education and Employment press release).

5   Robson, E.R., *School Architecture* (with an introduction by Malcolm Seaborne) Leicester University Press, The Victorian Library ..., 1972 (first published 1874), p.17.

6   Robson, E.R., *School Architecture* (with an introduction by Malcolm Seaborne), Leicester University Press, The Victorian Library ..., 1972 (first published 1874), p.167.

7   Markus, Thomas A., *Buildings and Power,* Routledge, 1993, p.78, quoting originally from Stow, 1836.

8   Markus, Thomas A., *Buildings and Power,* Routledge, 1993, p.79.

9   Macleod, Robert, *Charles Rennie Mackintosh: Architect and Artist,* E.P. Dutton Inc, 1983, p.12.

10   Dewey, John, *Democracy and Education,* Macmillan, London, 1916 (reprinted 1967), p.142.

11   Dewey, John, *Democracy and Education,* Macmillan, London, 1916 (reprinted 1967), Quoting from Dewey, John, *School and Society,* 1899.

12   Dewey, John, *Art as Experience,* Capricorn Books, New York, 1972, p.265.

13   Dewey, John, *Art as Experience,* Capricorn Books, New York, 1972, p.230.

14   Stewert, W.A.C., *Progressives and Radicals in English Education 1750–1970,* Macmillan, 1972, p.246.

15   Van der Eyleen, W. and Turner, B. *Adventures in Education,* Penguin, Harmondsworth, 1969, p.55.

16   Curry, W.B. and Lane, J., *The School and a Changing Civilisation,* Bodley Head, London, 1934, p.ix.

17   de Carlo, Giancarlo, *Harvard Educational Review: Architecture and Education,* 39, 4, 1969, p.95.

18   Dudek, Mark, *Kindergarten Architecture,* E. & F.N. Spon, London, 1996, p.31.

19   Summerson, John, *Heavenly Mansions ... and other Essays on Architecture,* Norton Library, 1963, p.9.

20   Margaret Macmillan quoted in Dudek, Mark, *Kindergarten Architecture,* E. & F.N. Spon, London, 1996, p.1.

21   Williams, R.P. 'Open air recovery school at Whiteley Wood', *School Hygiene,* 1911, p.132. Quoted in Seabourne, Malcolm, *The English School: Its Architecture and Organisation 1370–1870,* Routledge & Kegan Paul, London, 1971.

22   Seabourne, M. and Lowe, R., *The English School: Its Architecture and Organisation 1870–1970,* (2nd edn), Routledge & Kegan Paul, London, 1977, p.93.

23   Duiker, J., *Jan Molima,* Uitgevery 010, Rotterdam, 1989, p.18.

24 Refer to Mimica, V. and Shannon, K., 'Utopia as tradition'. In Bullivant, L. (ed) *Kidsize, the Material World of the Child* Skira, 1997, p.167.

25 Curtis, W.J.R., *Denys Lasdun; Architecture, City, Landscape ...,* Pall Mall Press, 1974, p.12.

26 Spring, Martin, 'Smithson's School.' *Building*, 28 September 1984, p.10.

27 *RIBA Journal*, January 1997. Masterclass, Dan Cruickshank's history lesson on Hunstanton School, quotation from the headteacher, Kate Shaw, p.51.

28 'Comprehensive Architecture' a diploma dissertation (1998/99) submitted to the School of Architecture, University of Sheffield by Andrew Mortimor. The quotation is taken from an interview with the headteacher Catherine Shaw on 15 October 1998.

29 Bürklee, J. Christoph, *Hans Scharoun,* Artemis, Zurich, 1993, p.105.

30 Frampton, Kenneth, *Modern Architecture: A Critical History* (3rd edn, revised and enlarged), Thames & Hudson, 1992, p.32.

31 'School extensions.' *Architectural Record*, July 1985.

32 Summerson, John, *Heavenly Mansions ... and other Essays on Architecture,* Norton Library, 1963, p.3.

33 Hart, R., 'Summer in the city.' *International Play Journal*, 1, 3 September 1993, E. & F.N. Spon.

34 The author is developing a research methodology which links good new school buildings with educational and social competence as part of his research activities within the School of Architecture, University of Sheffield.

2

The educational curriculum and its implications

Introduction

The first part of this chapter concerns itself with the educational curriculum within the UK, Canada and the USA. What must the teacher do in the modern classroom to be an effective educator? What concerns might the classroom teacher have with his or her environment, relating to the delivery of education, which the school designer should understand? I present an overview of the current educational debate, aimed at architects and designers who perhaps have little conception of the complexities surrounding the role of the classroom teacher. I present tentative proposals for the design of an ideal primary classroom, developed in consultation with an existing school community.

Well over a hundred different schools have been visited during the course of this research. Some of the most memorable observations made to us by teachers and educationalists about their environment and educational methods form the second part of this chapter. Whilst I am critical of certain aspects of the school environments to which I refer, I am also aware that the implications of some of those decisions may not be immediately apparent. I stress that part of the methodology used in this chapter was to challenge teachers to be spatially aware in order to relate their experience directly to the classroom environments within which teaching and learning currently takes place.

I begin with some definitions of school.

Schooling is universal, provided as a right to every child and therefore relatively easy to define and explain. The school is an institution which is intended to nurture, care for and educate children within the framework of structured age-related class groups. Schools will invariably be led by a headteacher, reporting to a board of governors, with one or two streams of mixed ability pupils of approximately thirty children. However there are a number of variations to this format, distinguished by smaller class

Figure 2.1
The Queen's Inclosure, Hampshire, activity in the central 'mall' – a spacious, calm environment. (Photo: © Hampshire County Architects.)

sizes and a particular educational approach, such as nursery, special needs and private schools.

Infant schools, which are often set out as separate buildings from the junior school (yet usually within the same site), provide education for children aged between four and seven. Junior schools cater for the educational needs of children between the ages of seven and eleven. Pupils who have transferred from an infant school to the junior school will move on to a secondary school after four years. Concern is often expressed by educationalists about the negative effects of the sudden transformation from a primary to secondary school setting. Advocates of the 9 to 13 age middle school see it as being quite distinct from both primary and secondary schools, providing the ideal interface between childhood and young adulthood. However, people who have benefited from the stable environment of a single school from the age of 5 to 15 years, as is the case in a number of the Scandinavian education systems, might not view it in quite the same way.

Increasingly, nursery school units or pre-school reception classes are being introduced as extensions to existing infant schools. Interesting variations are evolving which place the UK system into a more European context – for example, the pre-school ethos with its emphasis on exploration through play as opposed to more formal educational methods taking the child up to the age of six or seven. A separate intermediate school would then make a bridge between play and the more formal education of the secondary school. However, the nature of the National Curriculum and its development over the past decade has made flexibility and creativity within the school environment increasingly difficult. This is due to the breadth and scope of the curriculum and the pressures this places upon those expected to deliver it.

I have defined the term 'school' in its most basic sense. But what constitutes a good school and to what extent is the environment deemed to be an important factor in its make-up? Educational specialist Peter Mortimore states that '... *A good school is one which promotes learning; an effective school is one where the pupils achieve more academically than could be predicted from their intake.*'[1] This generalized definition is widely agreed upon throughout the world.

Mortimore's thesis refers to much educational research analysis carried out over the past twenty years into what constitutes an effective school, i.e. a school which promotes learning and above average academic achievement amongst its pupils. The degree to which the environment plays a significant part in this is less clearly defined. For example a recent educational report prepared for OFSTED defines eleven factors for school effectiveness:[2]

1	Professional leadership	Firm and purposeful
		A participative approach
		The leading professional
2	Shared vision and goals	Unity of purpose
		Consistency of practice
		Collegiality and collaboration
3	A learning environment	An orderly atmosphere
		An attractive working environment
4	Concentration on teaching and learning	Maximization of learning time
		Academic emphasis
		Focus on achievement
5	Purposeful teaching	Efficient organization
		Clarity of purpose
		Structured lessons
		Adaptive practice
6	High expectations	High expectations all round
		Communicating expectations
		Providing intellectual challenge
7	Positive reinforcement	Clear and fair discipline
		Feedback
8	Monitoring progress	Monitoring pupil performance
		Evaluating school performance
9	Pupil rights and responsibilities	Raising pupil self-esteem
		Positions of responsibility
		Control of work
10	Home–school partnership	Parental involvement in their children's learning
11	A learning organization	School-based staff development[3]

Although this section of the analysis is brief, the issue of orderliness in the classroom is stated as a key prerequisite for effective learning. Clearly this is linked to the quality of the classroom environment. Factors such as acoustic performance (the restriction of sound amplification) and the ability to display children's work are cited. Beyond that, what might be termed aesthetic factors are not referred to, nor is the overall requirement for specific aspects of the school curriculum such as whole class assemblies. The importance of community spaces is hinted at (above) in 10, home–school partnership. In reviews of numerous publications on educational theory and practice, the quality of the environment is rarely mentioned. Pencils and paper are 'resources'; the surrounding built fabric is presumably not considered to be so.[4] In the scale of value, the architectural quality comes very low on the list of priorities when discussed by educationalists. The 'van Eyck syndrome' (refer to Chapter 1), where educationalists positively reject good purposeful architecture as being restrictive to freedom for the pupils and their teachers, is a prevailing prejudice.

However, there is no doubt that the physical environment in general and in specific ways is deemed to have an effect on the success of the children both academically and socially. Where the school buildings are not well

Figure 2.2
The windows of this primary school are designed to provide some visual connection between the corridor and the room without creating too open an effect which might prove distracting, not just to the pupils, but also to the teacher.

maintained, they tend to encourage vandalism and ultimately a spiral of declining morale amongst the staff and pupils. A recent interview with Geoff Hampton, a school head honoured for his services to teaching, states that the first thing he attended to when he took over the then failing Northicote School in Wolverhampton was the condition of the building: money was found to paint out graffiti, repair broken windows and upgrade lavatories along with other general repairs and improvements. The effect this had was dramatic '... *Within 12 months the smashing of windows, which had been a nightly problem, totally ceased. Something made the kids think before picking up that brick and throwing it. It's about pride. Having a school that looks good is about telling children they're worth something.*'5

Klaus Lehnert, headteacher at the Albert Einstein Gymnasium in Berlin, goes further; having benefited from a recent extension together with a general upgrading of the original post-war buildings, there is an elementary and secondary school on the same suburban site (see Case Study 17): '... *orderliness is essential and this has been re-established by the new classroom block ... generally the architecture is a major factor in the pleasure children express about their daily attendance at school. They actually enjoy coming to school.*' One aspect of the classroom extension is its grid of structural columns cast in concrete and finished in their natural state. The new classrooms are set out to the same grid. The building is the solid framework within which children bring their imaginative, sometimes chaotic, spirits. Yet it is an architecture to be proud of; the order it creates is not oppressive, and it is evident how disciplined and mature the students are as a result. In this example, the strength and clarity of the architecture becomes a metaphor of the orderliness to which Mortimore refers.

Equipment and its context, the school buildings and grounds, is significant because it is the means by which children gain access to different learning experiences. For example, music cannot take place unless instruments and purpose-made spaces are available within which they can be played. In a large US secondary school, different multi-coloured patterns were used in corridors, to help students recognize and relate to their own school 'neighbourhoods'. Bright well-lit circulation areas encourage staff and students to be more open and sociable. However, the most important implication of the above matrices is the extent to which any school is responsible for the order, discipline and organization of a whole community of students, and, less directly, their parents and families. The implied complexity of these competing requirements places a responsibility on the school designer to create an environment which is not only inspiring architecturally, but also meets complex organizational needs.[6]

In specific terms, it is less easy to determine what constitutes an orderly atmosphere and an attractive working environment. Many schools still date from the last century and are based on a model where all classes lead from a central hall. For example, the Morgan's Junior School in Hertford, which was built in 1949, organizes the classrooms around a central core of entrance hall, assembly hall and dining rooms. This was described as a compact 'cluster plan' which was thought suitable to new forms of learning at that time. Buildings from the early 1970s are particularly notable for their open plan classrooms, again a reflection of the more individual approach to teaching encapsulated by the Plowden Report (1967) entitled *Childcare and their Primary Schools* (London, HMSO).

Whatever the form, the classroom remains the essential play and teaching space, and this will be the main focus of this chapter. The constant refrain from school teachers, particularly in infant and junior school settings, relates to the shortage of area; whole class teaching spaces for up to 30 children can only be effective if they are at least 55 m^2 in plan form.[7] However, this figure should be seen as an absolute minimum, and an area of double that would, if used in a purposeful way, be a more appropriate yardstick. Where space is at a premium, it is more important to provide designated areas for special teaching activities, such as quiet zones for reading and computer and storage spaces for materials, than to simply increase the general teaching area. Today the emphasis must be on catering equally for the differential development of individual pupils, rather than simply treating the group as a single homogeneous mass, to be brought along together like sheep.

Angela Anning recently observed that most classrooms in infant schools conform to a particular curriculum-based layout. This makes a basic understanding of the educational curriculum of great value to any would-be school designer. For example, tables are positioned together because children are deemed better at working in groups. Subject-specific 'resources' such as art and craft materials will be stored around a messy area. There will be a carpeted area which young children can use to gather together for registration and story telling and which often doubles as a book corner: '... *There will probably be an interest table reflecting the current theme chosen by the teacher as the focus for topic work, and the classroom displays of children's work, predominantly art-based, will reflect that topic.*'[8]

Access to shared practical areas adjacent to classrooms, external play-spaces, music/drama rooms and multi-purpose halls for whole school assemblies, and dining rooms (and kitchens) will provide essential developmental experiences beyond the confines of the class base. However it is generally agreed that school pupils, particularly the youngest, require the security of a classroom which is well defined. The classroom environment is an important element of any primary school, since it is the zone within which most time is spent. It needs to be a safe haven for insecure or vulnerable members of the group, particularly at the younger age ranges. As children grow through the school, it is likely that they will develop greater personal independence and tend to spend more of their time moving outwards from the secure confines of their class bases using the entire school as the 'learning environment'.

When children arrive at the secondary school, classrooms may be subject-specific, with pupils moving around the entire school throughout the day, to attend language and science laboratories, technology or music rooms, sports, art and recreation facilities, all of which may be functionally specific to the task in question.[9] In the secondary school, even corridor areas may be allocated for the use of children to access information and communications technology, or simply to be adapted for use by children as dedicated leisure areas beyond the controlling eye of adults. The need for student's spaces, particularly for older children, which are in some way out of adult reach, is a theme which many educationalists believe to be important. Geographical studies have drawn attention to young people's ability to subvert the nature of public spaces in a deliberate way. Dr Gill Valentine believes that children are inherently more spatially competent than adult rules and regulations imply. The secondary school can restrict or encourage these skills in the way it constructs its routes and spaces between subject-specific teaching areas. [10]

As previously alluded to, educational theories evolved away from traditional whole-class teaching methods during the 1960s and 1970s. A move towards individual and small group teaching reflected the social shift from collective values to a structure where the rights of the individual were to be at the forefront. The extremes of the so-called 'child-centred' learning method, exemplified by open-plan schools, has generally given way to a more hybrid approach to teaching, which as we will see reflects a range of views as to how children learn: '... *The whole*

Figure 2.3
Older and younger children in their Victorian classroom. (Photo: © Mark Dudek.)

environment has to support active teaching and learning in which teachers and pupils work cooperatively with each other and their peers. Children will be encouraged to explore, share their ideas, solve problems, express themselves and develop their physical and creative abilities through a variety of media. They need freely available resources and access to various forms of technology.'[11]

To view the classroom as the only context within which education can take place, as is being suggested in some quarters, is an extreme view which I will challenge and develop in more detail. It should be stressed that a return to a reactionary system of learning by rote, in whole class groups, is in some respects a natural reaction to the inadequacy of many existing school buildings within which the complex format of the new National Curriculum must be delivered. The quest to make the environment fit seemingly contradictory needs, on the one hand learning through social interaction, and on the other, learning through the adoption of contemplative and disciplinary methods, is one with which the classroom designer and the

class teacher must grapple. From the outset it is reasonable to conclude that the breadth of subject areas covered by the new curriculum requires a sensible balance between control and freedom of movement for the pupils. Both forms are implied by the National Curriculum.

The evolution of a National Curriculum: education as an instrument of political control

... schools are not only institutions for instruction, but at the same time visible symbols of educational conceptions of their time. To plan schools then, it is necessary to become acquainted with questions of education and pedagogy.[12]

The development of the mainstream school curriculum during the twentieth century has either been determined within a moral framework through church schools or within a social framework as exemplified by post-war state-funded schools usually organized in localized education authorities. This distinction can still be seen in most European and North American schools at the present time. The notion of a national curriculum as we know it today, with a strict series of subjects taught in an increasingly prescriptive way, is a relatively recent phenomenon, particularly in the UK. The purpose of this section is to describe briefly the background to the National Curriculum and explain its development during the years of Margaret Thatcher's Conservative governments.

Generally, the structure for the school day, consisting of whole-school religious celebration followed by a series of basic class activities aimed at education for reading, writing, arithmetic and other related subjects, such as science and technology, was universally copied within the state system. The curriculum broadens and expands to as many as ten or twelve distinct subject areas as children mature into secondary school education. This structure has remained intact for most of the twentieth century, a point emphasized by Richard Aldrich when he compared the new National Curriculum introduced in 1988 to the old Board of Education regulations issued to state secondary schools in 1904: '... *There is such a striking similarity between these two lists that it appears that one was simply copied from the other, although the term 'modern foreign language' in the 1987 list excludes Latin which featured prominently in the secondary school curricula of 1904 ... Thus in essence the proposed national curriculum in so far as it is expressed in terms of core and foundation subjects, appears as a reassertion of the basic grammar school curriculum devised at the beginning of the twentieth century by such men as Robert Morant and James Headlam ... This curriculum is now extended to primary and comprehensive secondary schools.*[13]

However, these regulations were not formalized nationally within the UK until the 1944 Education Act, and even then, the only subject to be made compulsory was religious education. Nevertheless, from 1944, infant, junior and secondary schools were required to provide some form of continuous structured education for all children from the age of 5 up to the age of 15, as a statutory right; this became law in Europe and the USA at a similar stage. The intention was to create a national framework for education which would be tailored to the particular child's ability, as tested at the age of 11. Some educationalists would argue that there was a well-established infant school curriculum before 1988, although it was not well articulated.

In Canada new curricula in state schools was influenced during the 1960s by the denunciation of progressive education in the American press. A synthesis arose from the conflicting ideas of the progressives, on the one hand, and the traditionalists on the other. The new curricula established at this time encapsulated a return to a structure of learning based on ideas of specialist teachers in certain disciplines, rather than the ideas of child psychologists. This meant a move away from child-centred to subject-

centred curricula. There was a revival of maths, science and languages in the high schools, which increased pressure on the elementary schools to follow suit. New concepts of mathematics were taught to the primary grades and new science and language courses of an experimental nature became prevalent.

The so-called 'discovery method', where pupils were encouraged to find answers to problems themselves by experiment was introduced. History courses focused on the study of original sources; children were learning the structure of their language by modern linguistic principles rather than through the formal teaching of grammar. Teacher specialization was developed to respond to the new curriculum requirements. The 'open area' elementary school was introduced widely to provide partly secluded teaching spaces arranged around a large open area. Two or more classes could meet for large group instruction, the library was close at hand, and the floor was carpeted to allow for small group teaching within this framework. Elementary schools were constructed on innovatory principles; however, the curriculum was broadly applied and understood throughout the country. Canada's education system was seen to be of an evolving nature, but one which produced high quality well educated children.

Within the UK, the implementation of a nationally determined content to the school curriculum emerged out of a complex educational debate instigated in Black Papers published by Cox and Dyson in 1971.[14] The mobility of children between schools within different parts of the country was flagged as being one of the key issues because of a lack of common guidelines nationally. However, more important and contentious was the perceived skills shortage within the British workforce which was identified as a problem relating to the inconsistent form of education children were receiving. In addition, a lack of clear guidance to teachers and school heads in dealing with changing social mores during the 1960s and 1970s was creating education black spots. Whole communities were blighted by ill-disciplined children, many of whom were out of control during their time at school.

Some educational practices prevalent at that time consisted of experimental ideas concerned more with political ideologies than the content of what children learned; education appeared to be encouraging a particular social spirit relating to freedom of expression of the individual child. Often this seemed to be at the expense of basic skills and practical knowledge. Discipline within many schools appeared to be breaking down. This was exemplified by the infamous events at the William Tyndale School in Islington, where for a brief period of time total anarchy appeared to reign. Widely reported by the popular press as an extreme form of left-wing social manipulation, it helped to give the child-centred ideals a poor reputation. Many teachers continue to view the child-centred approach as one which accurately reflects the culture of society, encapsulating a more social approach to education. Furthermore, 'child-centred' was said to be better for the child since it relied on a firm psychological foundation, as espoused by Dewey, Isaacs, Piaget and many other eminent child psychologists of the twentieth century.

Behavioural problems in UK schools related to a much broader national neurosis, rather than the inadequacy of the education system alone. Nevertheless, schools and, to a certain extent, schoolteachers, tended to take the blame for the ills of society as a whole. Furthermore, the Asian and Australasian systems of education appeared to be producing youngsters better educated and equipped for the needs of industry and commerce, and, ultimately, more disciplined and socially responsible citizens. As a consequence, education became highly politicized during the Conservative years, with successive education ministers undermining the quality of the teachers who delivered it and, through budgetary shortfalls, the buildings and grounds within which it was expected to take place. This culture continues to cause subsidence throughout the teaching profession, and an inheritance of poorly maintained buildings.

Perhaps they were referring back to the late nineteenth century when mass education had first been introduced. Then, it can be argued, a particular form of education was directed at the various social classes: '*... classics for the wealthy, English literature for the middle classes, basic literacy and "clear expression" for the poor. Thomas Crabbe wrote of the way education was becoming a social device to mark out social groups and to control the new industrialized society: "For every class we have a school assigned, rules for all ranks and food for every mind" (cited in Birchenough, 1914, p.5).*'[15] This was a system which educated, yet maintained a clear social hierarchy. During the immediate post-war years, whilst education was still viewed as a means of liberating the working man from slothful ignorance, in some quarters it was also conceived of as a socialist vision of 'knowledge for all'. It would be a system which eradicated social divisions delivered in futuristic school buildings. From the outset of the 1980s, however, the new reactionary Thatcherite view may well have countered this libertarian ethos by seeing the prison as a more appropriate image for the new schools, with teachers as wardens drilling a difficult range of traditional subjects into the unruly inmates.

Much has been written about the failure of the initial National Curriculum implemented from 1988. Sir Keith Joseph, perhaps the most enlightened of the UK Education Secretaries of State, devised a structure which he felt would provide a minimum level of practical curriculum input and which would be understood and therefore implemented consistently in schools throughout the nation. On the one hand, Joseph's desire to broaden the knowledge base eventually resulted in a ridiculously complex nine-subject timetable in primary schools which became even broader at secondary level. On the other hand the move away from practical task-based activities towards forms of learning which would be assessed and, to a certain extent, delivered by way of paper and pencil tests, created profound difficulties for teachers, who became overwhelmed by the weight of bureaucracy. In addition, the concern was (and continues to be so in some quarters) that a more passive form of learning would create a generation of adults who were unable to think for themselves, thus undermining the perceived British virtues of imaginative creativity and freedom of expression.

The conclusion must be that this period came about because too little time was taken to evaluate the effects of change, with much educational policy being made by non-expert politicians to coincide with Conservative Party conferences around election time. Finally in 1992, after a decade of confusion, constant change and over-complexity, Sir Ron Dearing, under the auspices of the School Curriculum and Assessment Authority, was commissioned to carry out a thorough review of the system. His series of recommendations was based on widespread consultation, and the curriculum was slimmed down as a result of the 1994 Dearing Report. The major recommendations were that one day a week should be released to primary schools to use at their own discretion and there would be only three core areas which would be subject to testing. However, testing at the ages of 7, 11 and 14 (SATs) was retained. Anecdotal evidence gleaned from many university academics teaching today's generation of undergraduates would suggest that basic literacy and numeracy skills are in profoundly short supply – partly the effects of an overcrowded and poorly conceived curriculum experienced by this generation of children during their formative years:

> *A great experiment had been tried on the nation's children and had been found wanting. Perhaps, a holistic view of the curriculum and a more rational approach to the introduction of the National Curriculum – involving pilot work and evaluation before wholescale implementation – might have prevented this disaster for a generation of children.*[16]

As if to prove the point that education almost invariably holds the political centre stage, it is constantly re-stated as the most important element of present long-term government policy. Coming full circle, it is presented on the one hand as a moral crusade and on the other as a social revolution as profound as any during the second half of the twentieth century. The government's Education Bill which became law in July 1998 is heralded as the biggest shake-up since Rab Butler's 1944 Education Act. Through education: '*... literacy and numeracy must accelerate at compound rates by the same date (2002). Families must get back together, school children stop swearing and spitting,* *teenagers be deterred from producing 100,000 pregnancies a year.'*[17] And most profoundly of all, everyone must have a stake.

What are the implications of the National Curriculum for the school designer?

The National Curriculum does not refer to the environment specifically, nor indeed does it determine specific methods teachers should use. However, its implications are in practice broad and far-reaching. It is possible to interpret its varying nuances, and identify some of the spatial implications of its content. In trying to paint a brief and generalized picture I have referred extensively to Ashcroft and Palacio's excellent handbook *The Primary Teacher's Guide to the New National Curriculum.*[18] The subjects identified in the curriculum are: English, Mathematics, Science, History, Geography, Art, Music, Physical Education, Design and Technology and Information Technology. These subject areas are termed *foundation* subjects, with English, mathematics and science/technology termed as *core foundation* subjects. Religious Education is a compulsory subject, but since it is not subject to national testing, it is not a foundation subject.

For the purposes of this brief analysis, I intend to explore one of the core subject areas in some detail. However, many of the observations relate equally to other core subject areas. For example, it could be argued that mental arithmetic can best be taught within the context of a small group (of six children) within a dedicated quiet space identified here as the reading room. The element I intend to study in more detail is English, which identifies three specific areas which must be monitored and tested, the so-called attainment targets.[19] They are Speaking and Listening (combined), Reading and Writing. Speaking and Listening at both Key Stages 1 and 2 requires the opportunity for children to have meaningful opportunities to talk within the class setting. The emphasis on speaking and listening skills as a key component of learning within the classroom was clearly expressed by the authors of the English National Curriculum: *'Our inclusion of speaking and listening, thus as a separate profile component in our recommendations is a reflection of our conviction that these skills are of central importance to children's development.'*[20]

Confidence, precision and turn taking can best be achieved by children being given the opportunity to work in small groups involving adult participants, such as parents, learning support assistants and other visitors. Role playing within small groups of three or four children is widely held to be the most effective way to achieve this. Other talking and listening skills can be encouraged through one-to-one conversations between pupils and teachers, where the pupil is asked to justify the way in which he or she has answered a particular question. Drama and media education in larger dedicated spaces have a useful role to play in language development, particularly at a later time. Where the participants can move around freely, relating language to the movement of their bodies, it is widely perceived to have a highly therapeutic benefit.

When Reading commences at Key Stage 1, the differential development of children is a significant concern. The importance of rhythm and rhyme is stressed, in other words listening, hearing and seeing the language used correctly, within whole class groups or preferably in smaller groups, where five or six children can read selected entries from a range of poetry books. Children might be asked if they can identify any words which sound the same. It is important that the acoustics of the space within which this exercise is taking place are reasonably good. One child I heard about had been diagnosed as being dyslexic at the age of 6. He was unable to distinguish between similar sounding words within these group discussions. However, it seems more likely that the source of his problem was simply poor hearing; his difficulties were compounded by the acoustics of the classroom, which had high ceilings and hard reverberating finishes. This created a constant hubbub of background noise. He could hear perfectly well during whole-class teaching sessions, where the teacher was speaking clearly and audibly within a quiet muted atmosphere. During the small group sessions, the amplification of background noise simply made it impossible for him to distinguish between similar sounding words.

The importance of good acoustic performance within the classroom cannot be stressed enough. Contemporary views of the school as a place of learning and contemplation should be tempered by the reality of children at work and play; they are noisy: *'... the silence of the class ripped by the bell, followed by the charge of feet and the yelling and the banging of doors and the thump of bags being thrown and the cumulative effect of screaming and shouting, I yell because you yell and you yell louder because I yell and the whole school yells to make themselves heard above the yelling of the school'*[21]

Given the nature of the performance that a lot of teaching evokes, the designer must respect the needs of the teacher not to be deafened by the noise, or to have to strain his or her voice all day in order to be heard; when designing a theatre, the acoustic performance would be a primary focus of attention. Surfaces and materials should be chosen which do not amplify noise. Environments can be devised which calm the raucous verbosity of many school-age children through their calm minimalist atmosphere. Similarly, the classroom designer should be aware of the notion of the classroom as a stage, with the teacher giving a performance, occasionally of some theatricality, in order to communicate an important idea. Having too many children in a single space can create noise problems, no matter how well the acoustics are designed. In this respect the modern convention of using paired classrooms, to optimize teaching space (as you can do away with corridors), should be questioned.

The demand for hard-wearing and hygienic surfaces in school environments has often militated against the use of more sympathetic materials which ameliorate sound reverberation in the classroom. Controlled tests have been carried out which link error rates to poor noise conditions. The *International Archives of Occupational and Environmental Health* tested and proved increased error rates in mental and abacus arithmetic when students were exposed to 60, 85 and 90 dBA continuous white noise.[22] However, the claims of a manufacturer of acoustic ceiling and wall panels to create a peaceful environment perhaps ignores the aesthetic effects this particular remedy can have on the school.

The need to make classroom spaces fit small group discussions is a requirement which runs across the curriculum. Where special needs reading is offered this should be delivered in a private area where one-to-one concentration can be ensured. A dedicated small reading room which can be closed off, yet is accessible directly off the classroom, is often the best solution – especially as this can fulfil other curriculum functions. A variety of books should always be made available within the classroom. At Key Stage 2, the range and diversity should relate to the interests of all members of the class. Books should be accessible and on show where space allows. The collection should be at child height with facilities for the display of newly acquired texts, either on shelves or in display racks, the theory being that this accessibility encourages enquiry. A dedicated zone where children can browse through new texts undisturbed is a valuable aid to learning; appropriate task lighting can make the relationship between book and child even more intimate.

Encouraging children to explore new areas of their reading experience to extend themselves is often problematic. The natural tendency will be to gravitate towards what is readily understood. Certain picture books will be read and re-read simply because the child has understood the vocabulary and feels comfortable with the rhythm of the text; it is easy. In order to enable new and more difficult texts to be introduced to extend the child's range, they must be explored and presented in diverse and imaginative ways. For example, newspaper reports or interviews can be read out aloud to the whole class. The text can then be shown in an enlarged format, with sections highlighted for dissection. Illustrations in diagrammatic or tabular form, complementary music or recorded interviews can all stimulate interest and aid comprehension. These are modes which can be carried out effectively within whole-class groups.

To summarize, it is clear that strategies for reading development range from whole-class groups focusing on a white board, through to smaller groups reading to each other, to one-on-one sessions either in the classroom or in a separate reading room. Reading niches off the main classroom enable better concentration and audibility. If this is not possible, adapting existing classrooms by the introduction of temporary screens which provide some visual and acoustic separation can be a very effective alternative. As a separate resource, a mini-library within or close to each classroom is highly desirable.

If the task of learning to read suggests a range of spaces to encourage diverse methods, the implications of the National Curriculum in terms of writing are equally demanding. A writing corner can be instigated as the focus for different forms such as notes, records and messages. These can be introduced by way of everyday forms of written communication: postcards, greetings cards, notes to the milkman and shopping receipts. A piece of writing on a particular sporting theme can be introduced by way of newspaper reports from the back page. Children will require writing paper and scrap paper to make greetings cards and even the means to construct their own books, all of which can be used for different writing tasks. These tasks need to be supported by planning and discussion, either one-to-one or in groups. An area of the classroom dedicated to the display of individual writing may be appropriate at certain times of the year.

Role-playing followed by individual writing sessions is also encouraged with groups acting out verbal exchanges from real-life situations such as family visits to garages, banks and shopping centres which often takes place in the 'home corner'. Writing about their own experiences can be carried out as a whole-class activity in the form of an individual writing exercise; however, the initial stimulus should be in the form of group discussion concerning out-of-school activities. Other areas of the classroom such as science or construction corners can stimulate reading activity, especially where subjects relate directly to the activities. Word processing programs can help children to focus on the structure of sentences. Terminals connected to the Internet can, if used in an appropriate way, encourage less motivated children to read and write.

An example of software technology recently developed for this purpose in the USA has been the virtual world known as 'Pueblo'. Phoenix College faculty members Hughes and Walters, together with faculty and students of Phoenix Longview elementary school, have been using so called Multi User Dungeons (MUDs) to teach reading and writing. MUDs are a software technology for creating group narratives on the Internet by writing textual descriptions of settings and characters. Social interaction takes place within the context of these textual narratives. You talk to a character which might be represented as a knight on horseback, as you, a powerful wizard, pursue your quest in search of the holy grail: '... *Elementary school students find college-level mentors in the virtual world who show them how to build their own worlds, and encourage them to read and write expressively and skillfully. Longview students learned social skills, and they learned that college is a possible future for them. Then some of the students, most of whom are from low-income families, can help their parents learn to read and write, using the same technology. The response was so overwhelming that the project had to add higher speed access lines ...'* The programme has had a real impact on at-risk children in the school.[23]

At present, due to a lack of computers within classrooms, groups of three or four working together can be beneficial. Within ten years it can be predicted that all secondary school children will bring their own lap-top to school each morning, which will undoubtedly require more space.[24] However, for the moment their use within the framework of the curriculum at Key Stage 1 is limited. Those computers that are in use should be positioned in a special niche or computer zone, preferably off the main teaching space. It is important that the flickering screen does not become a distant distraction for other children within the classroom. As with most of these distinctive activities, by creating special areas with dropped ceilings and a more enclosed feel, the 'my house' effect can often be triggered which can give children intense feelings of value and comfort, essential aids to concentration.

In their essay first published in 1995 entitled 'How Children Learn', Neville Bennett and Elizabeth Dunne stressed the importance of talking within a cooperative setting; they believe that this approach has profound implications for the way in which the classroom is managed and the nature of the classroom design itself. This is because talk must be carefully directed and controlled in order for it to have optimum educational value. They describe teaching as a cycle which commences with the teacher's preparations:

> *... the cycle begins with the teacher planning and preparing tasks and activities for children which are then presented in some way (e.g. through discussion, an experiment, a television programme, etc.) The children then engage with their work within a classroom management system set up by the teacher (e.g. individuals working on individual tasks; mixed ability groups in an integrated day arrangement; the whole class working in small cooperative groups on the same technology task, etc.) Once this work has been completed, it would be expected that teachers would assess or diagnose it, using that information to feed back to pupils, and to feed forward to inform their next round of planning.'*[25]

The ideal classroom

The teaching process described in the previous section would appear to place almost impossibly diverse functional requirements upon the conventionally constituted single volume classroom. To be added to this is a more recent trend towards the imposition of a stricter curriculum framework to enforce the acquisition of basic skills. The notion of the reflective teacher is one in tune with these dilemmas and contradictions. Although the term was first applied by John Dewey back in 1933, its use has never been more appropriate than in the context of today's classroom.[26]

Essentially it refers to the need for the teacher to monitor, evaluate and revise their own practice continuously; to learn on the job, and to adapt to the ever-evolving needs of a particular social structure. It can be deduced from the above thesis how important this must be. How does one make simplistic decisions about the design of a classroom environment when, at one point in the day, the curriculum implies that the children should be organized on an individual basis and, perhaps ten minutes later, as a whole class? On the one hand children should be given a degree of control over the use of their time, their activities and standards of work, and on the other, the curriculum implies a tightening of control of both time and content. Authority and routine are traditional aspects of educational practice; however, a willingness to take the spirit of childhood seriously and the ability to engage in constant self-appraisal is the necessary gift of the modern class teacher.

What of the reflective architect? This phrase may imply that a similar self-critical approach is adopted, where the designer questions the conventional view of architecture as being fixed to a particular set of functional requirements, and frozen in a particular time. If the teacher must be flexible, then the environment within which he or she operates should also be flexible in use, without compromising essential performance criteria. For example, if removable partitions are specified to enable parts of the classroom to be opened to the corridors or adjacent spaces, then those partitions must effectively prevent noise transmission when the classroom is being used in its conventional mode. Particularly at Key Stage 1, the teaching space must be a fluid one: the distribution of resources affects the way in which children use the space. The reflective architect must, in my view, take on the whole notion of consultation in a serious and committed way.

Sandra Horne, who is studying the ways in which existing classrooms are used, has carried out extensive interviews with teachers regarding the design and re-design process:

> *... the architects ... they seem to come in with preconceived ideas of what they are going to do or they've already got a prescribed plan. By the time it gets down to us seeing an architect ... it's too late because the plans and everything had already been drawn and it's going to go forward anyway. So ... they haven't involved the staff at the beginning.*

Basically what we've got is liaison that is looking at the curriculum and maintaining the curriculum for the school. He's [the architect] not actually looking at the fabric of the building. What he is looking at is if we close that classroom where we can relocate maths to for two weeks while that gets built and where we can move to next. He's not actually looking in terms of "wouldn't it be nice if we had this facility" ... As far as I can tell, the plans were already developed, that's what we are going to get. He is purely there to make certain that as they close this classroom down, another classroom will open up so that we can actually function as a school. Not in terms of the quality of the building we get.[27]

Horne rightly points out that the architect's perceived role is primarily to liaise with the education department. Only after the scheme is designed would the school itself have sight of the proposed plans. The active involvement of more than one or two members of the school community is unusual. No matter how rigorous the designer's vision, it is the teacher who has to deal with the environment in use. In Horne's terms, the architect merely provides the 'finished beginning'. All the complexities implied by the National Curriculum must be catered for, yet the class-room teacher is often given little more than a room deemed to correspond to the statutory area requirements, without consideration of other essential criteria, such as light, colour and texture.

It is generally perceived to be the case that teachers can only change or modify the furniture within their classrooms to make necessary changes to suit different times of the school year. To make more fundamental changes to the actual forms of the space is exceptionally rare. It is Horne's thesis that they cannot influence anything more than the superficial repositioning of furniture. The clue to resolving this problem can be found in the following quotation: '... *One of the reasons we have so little good architecture in Canada is that architects and clients are not committed to refining a project before it is built, models are useful as predictive devices, allowing architects to resolve complex connections and to explain a building to clients.*'[28]

A recent research project carried out by Melanie Evans at the University of Brighton Department of Architecture set out to challenge this view. Through extended consultation it was hoped to explore the possibility of meaningful dialogue between the teachers and the architect during the design process. Initially curriculum needs were analysed and related functionally to a new classroom design at Key Stage 1. Based on a real site in the east end of London, the project used three-dimensional models to aid consultation. Each stage of the development brought a larger and more explicit model of the classroom interiors (the roof and overall roof structure are not introduced until workshop

consultation 3) to which a focus group of approximately four class teachers from the school were challenged to respond at each stage.

From the outset the interiors were interpreted in the form of large-scale three-dimensional models, so that teachers were able to make informed comments not just about functional issues, but also on design and aesthetic criteria. Each stage included the same core group of teachers. The participants were ultimately surprised and satisfied by the end results. This was not simply because the layouts appeared to be elegant and purposeful, but also because they actually understood, and felt they were part of the design process, which indeed they were. Subsequently it was found that the exercise assisted their own spatial knowledge, enabling them to make better use of existing classroom spaces.

The consultation method requires the preparation of questionnaires and a number of scale models of varying sizes; it can be led by architects or student architects. The three-stage methodology is summarized as follows:

Stage 1

a) Present a brief history of the classroom showing its relationship to the educational framework illustrated by key examples some of which are still in use today – this should be to the whole school teaching staff and be carried out as a fifty-minute audio visual presentation. The aim is to stimulate the teachers and identify four participants willing to commit themselves to the subsequent six-month development programme.

b) Prepare questionnaires in order to determine how classrooms should be organized during a typical teaching week: in what kinds of classrooms do teachers currently operate? What kinds of equipment and aids to teaching should be provided? Establish common failings and suggested remedies. The questionnaires should be brief and are intended to encourage the teachers to draw their own ideal classroom layouts.

c) Analyse questionnaires. Contact teachers willing to participate in stage 2. Identify common problems and solutions. Define 'typical' classroom options to be studied during the initial workshop session. Clarify the environmental issues relating to the site. Construct alternative model layouts (developing three or four different options) at a scale of 1:200, incorporating broadly agreed features.

Stage 2

a) Using basic models, carry out workshop **consultation 1** with the school focus group: 'How would you like to design your classroom bearing in mind the National Curriculum implications – you can adjust the size and position of walls, doors, windows and partitions.' The session should take approximately six hours and

Figure 2.4
The consultation process is particularly important in the design of large public buildings such as schools and colleges; it has longer term benefits, encouraging teachers and pupils to become more involved in the formulation of their environment and aware of the design/development process.

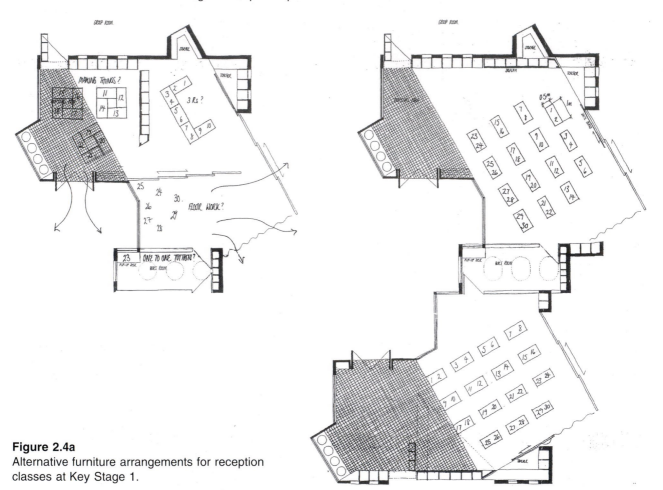

Figure 2.4a
Alternative furniture arrangements for reception classes at Key Stage 1.

include radical amendments to the models prompted by teachers' observations, making and remaking the basic shape and form during the session. Initiate discussions on colours, materials and furniture.

b) Review the initial workshop session then make a single larger model of the preferred layout at a scale of 1:100; carry out workshop **consultation 2**, suggesting furniture and equipment. Introduce colour options: 'You can change colours, textures, floor and wall surfaces and introduce new furniture and fittings by the use of collage techniques.' Images from magazines can be torn out and used to replicate different colour and texture ideas. The focus group are encouraged to be as imaginative as possible; however, they should attempt to articulate why they have reached each decision.

c) Retain a record of the responses. Photograph the models and print as computer simulations. Record and annotate verbal exchanges. Revise and prepare enlarged classroom models at 1:50 or 1:20. Include roof structure and roof forms. Carry out workshop **consultation 3**. Revise the model accordingly to create the definitive classroom layout.

Final review
Evaluate the consultation sessions and design the ideal classroom profile. Formulate a range of components, modifications and general strategies for improvement. Produce a comprehensive technical report. Request formal feedback from workshop participants. Design the classroom and arrange a final presentation to the whole school community

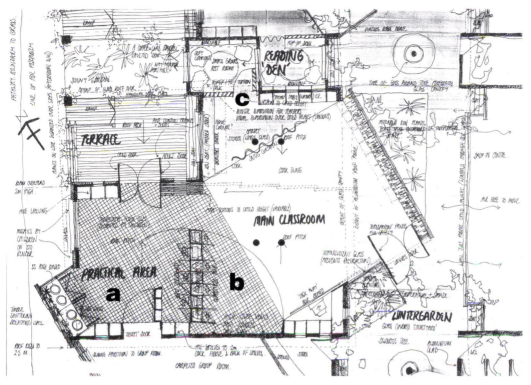

Figure 2.4b
Melanie Evans' ideal classroom, part of a layout for a school site in East London.

Key:
a: practical area
b: computer technology area
c: reading corner

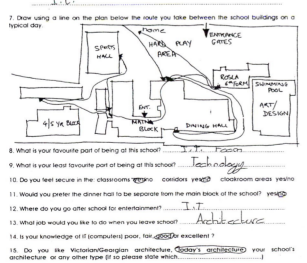

Figure 2.4c
A questionnaire prepared during the development of a new wing of accommodation at De La Salle School, Liverpool. The consultation process was incorporated into IT and technology teaching periods.

Figure 2.4d
The 'School Works' approach to the makeover of existing secondary schools seeks to engage pupils, staff, parents and the wider community. Their School Action Audit involves pupils in mini-surveys of different areas in the school which they identify as being problematic or successful. School Works is currently being promoted by The Architecture Foundation, 30 Bury Street, London SW1Y 6AU. Students measure their school corridor as part of the mini-survey.

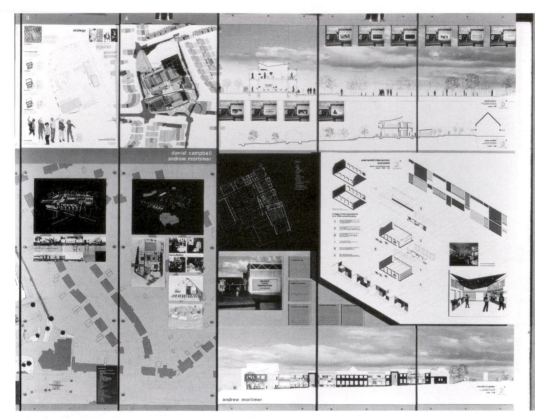

Figure 2.4e
These panels were prepared for a community consultation session at Wisewood School, Sheffield, by Diploma students Andrew Mortimer and Daniel Campbell. Measuring 6 metres by 3 metres, their scale and high quality graphics using collage techniques enabled the presentation of preliminary ideas to a large audience of parents and pupils.

The process as applied by Melanie Evans was completed over a period of six months. The given site conditions suggested that a double orientation would be appropriate, with mainly glazed west-facing walls overlooking the school playing fields. East light is 'borrowed' from the inner activity corridor. Screens and partitions retract and extend to provide a number of different modes in which the classroom can be constituted. These comprise of whole-class groups, half-class groups with one larger and one smaller space, and one-third class groups with the larger of the two spaces divided by way of a pivoting storage wall. In addition, there are two spaces shared with one other adjacent class, providing a quiet reading room with a lowered ceiling and soft fabric interior. There is a group room for drama and music, when the main school hall is deemed to be too large for a particular activity.

The concession is that space standards are on the whole 40 per cent greater than the norm for this type of facility (with the group room accounted for as a part of the classroom space). This was seen as the only way in which this level of spatial diversity was possible. A further dimension is added by the creative use of the edges of the classroom space. Walls and wall thicknesses are exploited in a way which is reminiscent of Sir John Soane's Museum in London's Lincoln's Inns Fields, where the whole experience is defined by a series of layers, which unfold and become manifest by degree. The designer is aware of the way in which she has created a mysterious or playful aspect, so beloved by children. At one point, the library wall reveals a hidden door which lets onto the adjacent space. The two storage cupboards (which also double as computer niches) are deceptively large, hidden in the 'fold' at the corners of the room. So this space seems to be devoid of corners, emphasizing its sense of spatial fluidity.

Each wall or edge has a distinct role to play within the functional life of the room. Thus the practical area (a), (see Figure 2.4b), overlooks the gardens and opens onto a raised play terrace which effectively extends its use during the warm summer months. Children can take painting easels out onto this terrace, which is shaded by the overhanging roof. There is also an outdoor workbench. The interior has hard tiled floor surfaces and is surrounded by useful storage and hanging areas, for drying paintings and for the use of wet materials such as clay. The external walls are described as lightweight 'breathing' elements, which contrast with the thick heavy party walls.

The computer technology area opens up to provide space for seven work stations (b), (see Figure 2.4b). The large pivoting wall unit provides computer terminal points which merely need to be connected to lightweight screens and consoles to provide the necessary workstations. Although this was initially considered as a fixed area during consultation, the focus group felt that they did not wish to make 'a big thing' of the computer within the classroom at this stage. Teachers may choose to set the space up for special periods during each term.

There is a lockable teacher's cupboard, covered by a large blue sliding panel, which enables the teacher to leave the room without carrying his or her possessions away. It also allows him or her to 'leave the desk in a mess' – a request frequently made to us by teachers during the course of this research. The blue panel serves a double function; it is the door to the teacher's office/cupboard, but also acts as the visual focus for whole-class teaching. There is no raised dais within the space; however, this screen becomes the backdrop to the teacher's performance, which will be aided by the use of a portable electronic white board, and various other demonstration modes. The notion of an entire 'teaching wall' was considered to be a valuable focus within the classroom. A number of teachers felt that if too much information was provided as a backdrop, it could distract from whole-class teaching.

The final edge space in this sequence is the reading corner (c), (see Figure 2.4b), which comprises child-height bookshelves fronting the quiet room. The children are encouraged to dwell around this area and perhaps remove a book to the haven of the room. The shelves are deliberately placed to partially obscure views into this area. A degree of transparency is designed in to allow views by the teacher for at least some of the time. Partitions vary in height depending on the age of the children. However, they allow the teacher to see over, whilst affording a sense of privacy and some acoustic separation for the children. The overall aesthetic is one which avoids the display of too much of the children's work. This was agreed upon during the consultation; it was conceded that the environment is cluttered enough anyway. Instead, children's work is displayed in the activity corridor, a sort of long gallery. How far it is realistic to expect children to perambulate, rather than to run full pelt along this corridor, depends upon the discipline of the children using it; however, entrances to the class bases loop back on themselves to deter children from running into and out of classes at full speed. The walls along the back of the classroom can be retracted to provide an occasional open plan area for parents' evenings and open days.

Teachers are uniquely equipped to throw enlightenment on the particular social and physical context of their classroom spaces. Just as the teacher must be flexible, equally the modern environment needs to be flexible, so that it too can evolve, to create an architecture which is reflective in its own right. I have described a particular form of classroom as 'the ideal classroom'; however, it should be borne in mind that this design relates to a particular context, in this case the infant wing of a proposed primary school on an inner-city site in the east end of London. It was determined through close consultation with teachers over a period of six months. The physical devices which are so important to its success, such as folding and sliding partitions and dividing walls, depend on safe, efficient technology. No teacher could afford to devote time to rearranging the form of their space if this is not easily achieved at little more than the touch of a button.

Melanie Evans' 'ideal classroom' is specific to its context and should be viewed as an indicative design only. It sets out to provide accommodation which is flexible, yet at the same time specific to a given interpretation of the UK National Curriculum. In this sense it may be viewed as a little fanciful. However, it challenges the traditional view of the classroom as a squat rectangular form. The rigorous process of consultation set out here may be time-consuming; however, it is intended to address the criticism that architects and interior designers do not listen to the needs of teachers and their pupils. It is a process that specialist school designers may consider carrying out at least once, as a meaningful way to understand the curriculum in relation to teaching spaces.

Classrooms in secondary school settings generally require more specialist facilities. So, for example, the range of teaching spaces at the recently opened Admiral Lord Nelson School in Portsmouth is broad, yet highly tuned to the curriculum; there are rooms for art and design, technology, science, music, languages and other vocational subjects. These spaces simply provide for specific activities which are usually prescribed in educational department guidance notes. However, the extent to which the architect can enhance activities is critical. This can range from simple technical care, such as the need to provide heat extraction, where a large number of computers are in use within the same space, to the addition of a rooftop terrace adjacent to the art rooms. Here pupils can take easels and tables outside during the warm summer months.

Classrooms for teaching subjects such as English, which essentially involve traditional desktop reading and writing activities, were simple rectangular forms, warm on the winter day I visited yet well ventilated, and acoustically effective. The headteacher at Admiral Lord Nelson stressed the simple message about the space. This was not a multi-functional zone as would be required at primary level. Here children only stayed for one or at most two lessons. The space was provided with as much pin-up board as possible, with related wall displays on all four walls. It was a little under the required area but this was a factor of the curved plan of the building. The ceiling had acoustic tiles and was shaped to reflect sound down and into the class with an inverted pitch all the way round. Any child could be heard clearly within this calm environment.

James Dyck in his article 'The Case for the L-shaped Classroom' argues that the conventional classroom shape is far from ideal. He states that after much research, the conclusion must be that the form of the classroom has a considerable effect upon learning outcomes. He points out that in the past, most public facilities were planned to prepare children for a life in the factory. As such, the school room itself was viewed as a kind of factory for the receipt of knowledge. Hence children sat in serried ranks. In recent times, although the overall form of school buildings has changed, with the addition of common areas, gardens, assembly halls, etc., the classroom form itself has remained unchanged. His list of prerequisites for a modern classroom broadly coincides with Melanie Evans' conclusions:

It has to accommodate the formation and functioning of small learning groups while providing a sense of separation, because groups working too closely together will experience distractions and nonproductive interaction.

It has to be flexible enough to allow the continual reorganization of the whole class into various sizes and numbers of small learning groups. This means the space must be as free as possible of permanent obstructions.

It has to be manageable by a single teacher who has command of the entire space. This means the space must be compact and open.

We found that the modern classroom has competing requirements: distance and separation on the one hand; compactness and flexibility on the other. While the squat rectangle scores well on compactness and flexibility, it does poorly on distance and separation. The challenge, therefore is to find a shape that meets both requirements.[29]

To summarize his theory, a short fat L-shaped form was the ideal layout since it provided all the above possibilities at an economical cost. Interestingly, a school designed by Herman Hertzberger in Delft, Holland also features an L shape. However, it cannot be seen in isolation from the communal hall/street immediately outside. Within the space a range of different floor levels have been introduced to aid the concept of distance and separation between pupils within a relatively small space. However, this feature goes further; the floor levels can be extended by way of a kit of wooden elements, forming additional stage areas inside or immediately outside the classroom. For Hertzberger the classroom within this Montessori school is a far more architectural space than Dyck's L-shaped Classroom, with the potential for its use in numerous different modes:

... everything we make must be a catalyst to stimulate the individual to play the roles through which his identity will be enriched ... form makes itself, and that is less of a question of intervention than of listening well to what a person and a thing want to be.[30]

The notion of the ideal classroom, like Palladio's Ideal Villa, is a Platonic vision rather than a standard for imita-

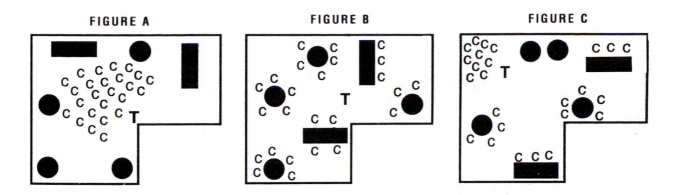

FIGURE A **FIGURE B** **FIGURE C**

Figure 2.5a
Alternative classroom layouts within the Fat L: figure A shows the class meeting as a group with all the children (c) gathered together in the centre; figure B shows children working in small groups at tables and figure C shows about half the children gathered around the children for reading time whilst the rest work in small groups. James A. Dyck, who carried out this research, believes that the L-shaped classroom can be most easily organized to permit a wide variety of pupil groupings, and with bookshelves and storage cabinets can enhance the sense of separation individual pupils need within the classroom. (James A. Dyck, The Architectural Partnership, Lincoln Square, 121 S. 13th St, Suite 702, Lincoln NE 68508.)

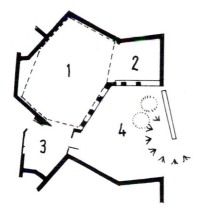

Figure 2.5b
Hans Scharoun, Geschwister School, Lünen. Plan of a classroom unit: 1, classroom; 2, annex; 3, entrance/cloakroom; 4, external teaching space.

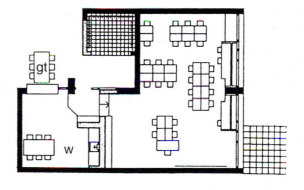

Figure 2.5c
Montessori Primary School, Delft, designed by Herman Hertzberger. A classroom layout which incorporates a sophisticated L-shape form with floor-height variations and an openable 'hatch' to the communal corridor or 'street' which accommodates a group table (gt) and a wet area (w), extending the classroom zone.

tion. To reiterate, it depends on a whole series of variables specific to a particular context. What is clear is the extent to which the traditional classroom form is open to question, and here I refer not just to single volume forms, but also to more recent (post-Plowden) open plan forms. Of far more significance is the process which brought this design to fruition, and its imaginative use of space within the framework of a specific physical context. It deals with

a range of variables which must be considered by every designer in their own right. The only aspect that relates across the board is the form and make-up of the National Curriculum, which applies to schools throughout England and Wales.

The educational debate is changing, even as I write, with visions of a complete transformation in the ways classrooms are used as a result of ICT; one can't help thinking that the next generation of children deserve a degree of stability within their education, which enables both whole-class teaching groups and freer more sociable teaching spaces, together with a diverse array of rooms to accommodate the special needs of all pupils. Designing an inner-city school within a tightly defined site is wholly different from the same project located in rolling fields on the edge of a leafy suburb. If the school designer is willing and able to listen to the teachers he or she is designing for (and by implication their pupils), the social context of the school will remain intact in any new building.

Working within the classroom – the open plan/closed plan debate

In primary school settings, children spend much of their time in the 'home base' and require a cloakroom area (a peg) and, of course, their own seat and table space. Today, children move around much more freely than they did in previous generations, partly an effect of more relaxed teaching methods which were in turn reflecting the spirit of more socially liberated times. In the 1970s, radical educational experiments were carried out. For example, fewer chairs than children would be provided within the class to encourage movement and fluid behaviour.

Post-Plowden, interaction within the whole class setting became the emphasis and a typical teaching period for year one (Key Stage 1) children might consist of a 50-minute lesson beginning with 10 minutes of finger counting as a form of warm-up exercise. This might be followed by 15–20 minutes on the subject of money. This activity could take place on the carpet with the teacher showing pictures of money and asking questions. During the final 15 minutes, the children would be expected to be active, working in small groups at desks, drawing pictures of coins and carrying out exercises in basic arithmetic. Finally the class would return to the mats and review the lesson. This pattern would be repeated in the form of an English or science period.

In primary and pre-school settings, one factor which can enhance or detract from the quality of the classroom environment is the extent to which teachers choose (or are expected) to decorate their spaces with children's drawings and paintings. An experience of different school environments and methods brings with it a range of ideas from the overwrought chaos of classrooms dripping with children's drawings and paintings, to the classrooms of teachers who perhaps give little thought to the quality of the environment and reinforce a dull uninspiring atmosphere. Outdated and inadequate school buildings can create problems for class teachers which hinder educational development no matter how carefully teachers may treat the decoration of their classroom interior.

One school classroom I visited had three doors on each corner of the room. In addition the room had windows punctuating each of three walls, whilst the fourth wall accommodated the washing-up sink. No matter where the white-board was positioned, children always had direct or thirty degree views into adjacent rooms or external playspaces. During whole-class teaching sessions, concentration was difficult because of the visual stimulation occurring in every direction. The headteacher, whilst bemoaning the 'business' of the interior architecture, almost in the same breath reassured us that the room would be decorated by children's work within a month of the commencement of the autumn term. One class teacher was heard to murmur that it would look like Santa Claus' grotto by November. What the headteacher failed to recognize was that the room required little or no decoration; the cluttered nature of its interior architecture meant that the space needed calming generally, with some windows obscured, to limit visual distractions.[31]

Many teachers are beginning to question the need to over-decorate classroom spaces, seeing it as an outward manifestation of activity which impresses the school governors, other teachers and OFSTED inspectors, but rarely benefits the children themselves: '... *Half the time the pin-up spaces are so high the children can't even see them; it's a kind of internal competition aimed at getting teachers to compete with each other. However, it is not competing in academic excellence rather in triple staple gun mounting excellence.'*

Martin Bennett, until recently a class teacher at Warwick Road Junior Infant and Nursery School, Battley, believes that the environment of his school is in conflict with the teaching methods he is expected to adopt. If he tries to run four different activities in his lofty Victorian classroom, the so-called 'integrated day', where subjects such as maths, art and reading are expected to take place in the same space at the same time, effective learning becomes almost impossible. He explains that whereas handwriting is a concentrated activity which should take place in a quiet scenario, art is more boisterous and expressive. It is a discipline that benefits from lots of talking and movement, with children checking on other activities in the group: '*How can you teach reading when there is an art class going on in the same space?'*

He strongly believes that the classroom environment should not be over-stimulated. Small, quiet spaces should be provided as adjuncts to the conventional open classroom area. A much more minimalist approach to teaching spaces should be adopted: '*Today children are over-stimulated, with information overload becoming a real problem for the teacher; everywhere the children look outside the school, they will be bombarded with advertising of the most pernicious type, encouraging them to buy this or that toy or game. Television is a real problem but there are other factors. It means that children have a very short attention span and will find it difficult to concentrate. It is neither their fault nor the direct fault of their parents, rather it is*

Figure 2.6
Displays of children's work are critically important to the classroom environment: this is particularly evident when visiting Italian schools where the artistic endeavours of the pupils are usually presented without over-elaboration within a clear and ordered aesthetic which complements the architecture and helps to make learning a pleasure.

down to the culture within which they are developing. However, the classroom should act as a foil to this and be cool and calming with minimal interventions in the way of wall displays, and visual interruptions.'

The implication of this class teacher's experience would appear to be that the educationalists are largely oblivious to the environment within which it is expected to take place. If the quality of the environment is poor and therefore incapable of supporting a particular form of learning, dependent on basic factors such as quiet spaces where children will not be distracted from their work, my evidence is that no matter how good the teaching, the end result will be compromised. It would appear that in the current climate of computer, televisual and video culture, the need to attend to the quality of the school environment in a clear and uncompromised form has never been more critical.

The Glastonbury Thorn First School in Milton Keynes, Buckinghamshire, is a purpose-designed building which illustrates problems of an educational briefing process which is evolving with uncertainty within the UK at present. The plan is essentially an elongated 'hall' beneath an arched roof with open niche-type classroom spaces appended to the main hall. With its 'funnel'-shaped rooflights, and great arched window openings establishing an order which is comprehensible from outside to inside, it is undoubtedly a very powerful form; clearly it photographs very well (looking splendid within the journals). However, the semi-closed plan teaching spaces are physically incapable of holding a class of 30 children (they are only 35 m² as opposed to the normal plan size of 50–55 m²). Most teaching takes place in the single open-plan 'hall'.

This does not relate well to recent changes to the educational curriculum; there are too many children within a single space, with all the distractions that entails. Although I visited the school one evening when there were no children on site, the impression remains that the classrooms are too small and the shared space is, for much of

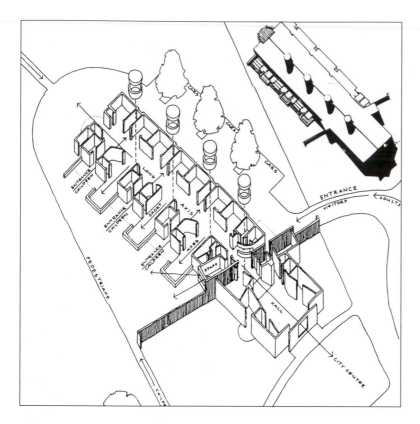

Figure 2.7
Glastonbury Thorn First School.

Figure 2.7a
Exploded axonometric plan.

Figure 2.7b
Floor plan.
Note the level change between 1, hall, and 2, entrance lobby.

KEY:
1 Hall
2 Entrance lobby
3 General teaching
4 Home-base
5 Coats
6 Practical
7 Specialist
8 Store
9 WCs
10 Central store
11 Plant
12 Chair store
13 PE store
14 Caretaker
15 Utility
16 Family
17 Medical Inspection
18 Secretary
19 Headteacher
20 Activity
21 Staff
22 Electricity
23 Cleaners
24 Accessible WC
25 External store

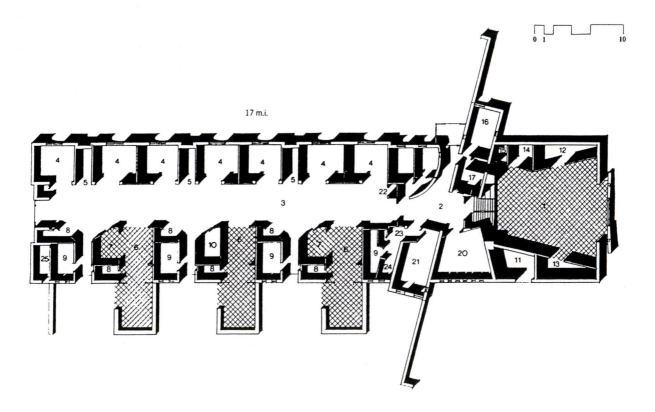

the time, too noisy for effective teaching. As adjuncts to the main teaching space, the classrooms tend to add to the difficulties at the start of each day. The impression remains that here is a building which is in need of drastic surgery soon after it was completed; alternatively, the class sizes could be reduced to around about 18, and the building would work very well. The then deputy chief architect at Buckinghamshire County Architects, John Stewart, accepts that the form is compromised. However he believes that during the period of its conception, the building was wholly in line with educational principles within the Buckinghamshire Education Department:

> *The home bases are deliberately undersized so that they cannot be used as conventional classrooms. In that sense it is quite deterministic. The idea was that the children would have a secure space to arrive at in the morning, make their first contact with the teacher, and from there, venture out into the open area, where most of their time would be spent.*

Stewart observes that this is a first school (for children aged 4 to 7 years), and as such it represents the initial opportunity to build relationships outside the family. He believes the open plan provides a rich learning experience encouraging social interaction. In his view the alternative of closed classrooms with corridors would have been overly harsh, particularly for the very young children who would find the lack of contact with brothers, sisters, friends and the wider community problematic. This is a view which is at odds with the experience of many class teachers whose task it is to bring the rigorous demands of the National Curriculum to children of this age. Open plan arrangements may well provide a richer social experience for the children; however, where the emphasis is on formal educational activity from the earliest years, the Glastonbury Thorn First School struggles to provide an environment which adequately supports these needs.

Stewart believes that the architecture sets the tone for the pedagogic approach, and given time then teaching methods will adapt themselves to meet the combined demands of the environment and the evolving curriculum. The implication is that the environment creates a more challenging scenario within which teachers must deliver the overly structured teaching day, therefore a richer curriculum will evolve organically. There is a certain veracity in this argument; if the educational curriculum evolves constantly, as surely it must, the environment can play a vital stabilizing role in accommodating these changes. Here the openness of the teaching areas encourages a more play-based ethos, hinting at an educational approach more in line with European systems of education, separating pre-school from the more formal educational methods of the primary school.

One must sympathize with teachers in the UK and the USA who are under pressure to achieve quantifiable results which are tested as early as the second year of infant school (Key Stage 1) when children are aged 6 or 7. A comment from a class teacher, which counters Stewart's argument, is that today, schools need to be flexible in order to accommodate changing strategies. However, the highly determined form of this building will ensure that teachers must be ingenious in the use of its spaces. This poses the question of whether teachers are equipped to deal with space in more than a rudimentary way. Certainly there would appear to be little in the way of spatial awareness instruction within university teacher training departments at present to rectify this problem.

The modern classroom – a machine for learning

By contrast, the Queen's Inclosure First School in Cowplain, Hampshire, was designed in a way which accepted a clear educational philosophy, yet one which encompasses a degree of flexibility. Hampshire County Architects who designed the building took their cue from an earlier school project by Michael Hopkins and Partners. The architects formed a partnership with the existing school's headteacher, who wished to take a minimalist approach to the interior architecture. The planning strategy accepted the need for pupils to have their own group spaces in the form of conventional classrooms. The clarity of the plan is reflected in the architecture, which is elegant and stylish yet effects a cool, calming atmosphere. The classroom displays are controlled and qualitative, with selective items of children's work contained within a limited range of display panels. These have been designed as integral elements of the building's fabric.

'Working in Queen's Inclosure is like an enjoyable day spent in your favourite botanical garden – open, light, airy, spacious, warm and bright. Everything flourishes – the common meadow flowers, the exotic bougainvillaea, the rare orchids and the irritating and persistent weeds; all fed and encouraged to grow and flower by the light and warmth which is the essence of this building ...' Despite the reservations of some parents who liken its appearance to an industrial building, many parents and visitors view it as a refreshing and therefore a more relevant style for a late twentieth century school building. The overall success of this more minimal approach, both socially and academically, is testament to this integrated care through the environment. The calm neutrality of the architecture would appear to bring about a calmness in the behaviour of the children who use it.

The area of the class bases is 62 m² (including ancillary storage). The spaces are planned to provide focused views towards a white board which is positioned along the flank walls. The pinboards are specially made to suit the width of the internal partitions. They are fabric coloured

Figure 2.8
Classroom activities spill out into the central 'mall', Queen's Inclosure. (Photo: © Hampshire County Architects.)

'Sundeala' 900 mm wide by 710 mm deep. Each class originally had three pinboards although some classes have now doubled this number. The space is conceived in a way which combines formal whole class teaching sessions with more conventional mixed activity groups. It allows for a hybrid approach accommodating many diverse aspects of the curriculum. There are no doors to the classrooms; it was felt that this would make the building too claustrophobic, and that a more open feel would enhance the general sense of 'space and light' which is the overwhelming message conveyed by its aesthetic. *'Because it is so light and airy, with no heavy-looking brickwork, you get the feeling of being under a shade rather than being inside a building. Just like the feeling you get snuggled up in a caravan on a rainy night. Access to places, and pupils, is immediate and there is a feeling of movement and flowing – it reminds me of the film "Santa Claus", where the little helpers are in a lovely colourful environment, light and comfortable and producing toys – whereas in QI it is work and enthusiasm that is being produced.'*

However, it has been a constant refrain during the course of this research that teachers want to be able to close themselves off at certain times of the school day. This not only for acoustic reasons, but also because a natural sense of ownership and discipline can be imposed by the class teacher on to the class group. Achieving this is difficult when the headteacher or a school governor may be loitering outside. Teaching is a performance, which is not directed towards an adult audience; a self-conscious teacher may not perform to his or her best. In addition, teachers as well as pupils need to be able to concentrate whilst 'delivering the goods'.

Gerry Sheridan, headteacher at the Good Shepherd Junior School, Nottingham, believes that the needs of the primary school curriculum have changed so much in the forty-year period since the school was designed that teachers have to be imaginative in the way the classroom spaces are used. *'We limit the amount of wall art since there is so little sense of space within the classroom at the best of times. When you have thirty odd children inhabiting rooms which are too small anyway. Then [when the school was designed] the curriculum relied more on whole class teaching methods. Perhaps children were more disciplined socially. Today children talk, move around and interact more freely. At one point they will be working individually on the computers, located within the classroom, or engaged in activities which involve a degree of group dynamism. Individual children will be receiving extra help in reading, so quiet niche type spaces are required where this can take place. Another issue is the amount of luggage children bring to school these days; for some reason, the cloakroom areas provided here are totally inadequate. The classrooms should be larger and be provided with much more storage space. More little bays are required so that teachers can find the right environment for the activities their children are involved with.'*

Instead of the indeterminate use of paintings, a limited number of focal points are created which have a particular pedagogic purpose. These foci do not need to be garish or large to achieve the desired effect. A single group collage, engaging with a particular theme which is considered important, reinforces the sense of community which was evident within this school environment. This can be a statue of Christ in the entrance foyer, or a mathematical puzzle explained in a particularly visual way. The emphasis is clearly on the quality of the display, its meaning and significance within the culture of the school. Because

quality is the main factor in choosing what goes on display, it is inevitable that certain children will be held up as exemplars through the public presentation of their art. Sheridan believes that this is a positive factor in showing that some people are better at some things than others. The emphasis is subtly religious, with group belonging engendered through wider community activities generated between the school and the local churches. This spirit, believes Sheridan, is integrated into the everyday life of the school, so that even children with low self-esteem are enveloped in a communal spirit of care.

The first primary school in the UK to be based on Buddhism was the Dharma School in Brighton. Housed in a beautiful house on the edge of the Sussex Downs, it maintains small class sizes (20 or under) and an open attitude to its garden and grounds. Children appeared to be wandering in and out freely when I visited. However, there is no single space where children can gather together as a whole community. The limitations of the house form, whilst highly appropriate to pre-school settings, is compromised as a truly community-based institution. However, the cellular quality of the building, conventional rooms with doors which are closed during class periods, encourages particular qualities within many of the children.

The children are allowed to have periods of quiet time during each day, when they are encouraged to meditate and reflect on spiritual aspects of daily life. Statues of the Buddha are positioned around the building to act as foci for this activity, and the rooms which are closed off from the circulation areas during class and meditation times provide the natural foil to the freeness of other periods of activity. The ritual closing of the rooms is an important way in which disciplines such as concentration and reflection are developed. The environment is a key factor in this ethos and, according to the teachers, the house form is an ideal way of keeping the children calm and sociable. The school is the children's home, and the rooms of the house provide a spatial diversity which is difficult to achieve when designing new purpose-made school buildings.

Each class base offers a different and distinct environmental experience. The children feel secure and focused during class times, with doors closed, and only window views out into the garden causing any real form of distraction. The informality of the system is exemplified by the kitchen which was hosting a small group reading session around a four-metre-long work table, as if at home, filling in the time before a family lunch. The image of the family house creates a homely, relaxed environment, precisely because the teaching spaces appear to be so different to any conventional school room. However, the system depends on the involvement of bright motivated parents to actively support teachers. Also of significance is the ability of teachers to ensure that small groups spread throughout the numerous rooms of the old house are kept under supervision.

Figure 2.9a
Thomas Carlyle School, plan with the classes marked 1–7. The letter q indicates the quiet zone, an open plan arrangement based on dated curriculum applications.

a

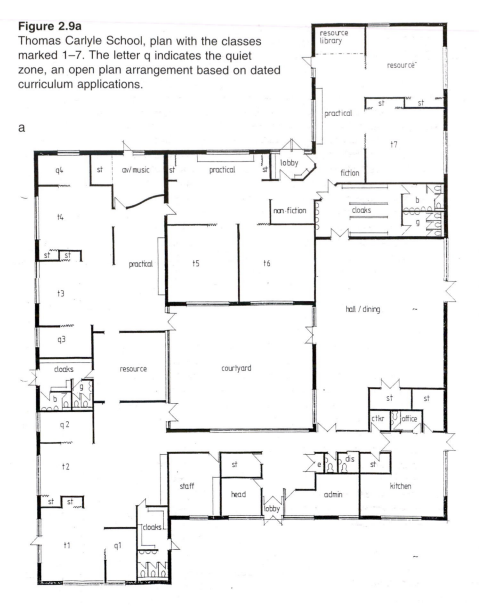

Figure 2.9b, 2.9c
Open plan taken to its extreme: rather than emphasizing the space, the layout is based around four storage units or objects linked to the curriculum, which generate their own particular use patterns within the classroom. The units each have a strong visual presence acting as 'counterpoints' to the dreary fabric of the existing building. 'Identity' is the cloakroom and storage module adjacent to the existing entrance; 'knowledge' contains books and computers; 'creativity' is part wet area, part art storage, and 'landscape' contains equipment for practical outdoor play and science. Each unit unfolds to provide a diverse range of activities. Student project by Susan Stringfellow, Sonia Gohal, Maria Kariolades.

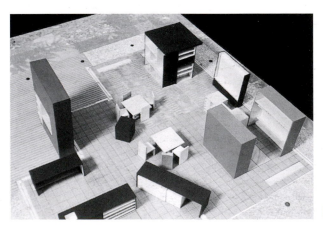

b

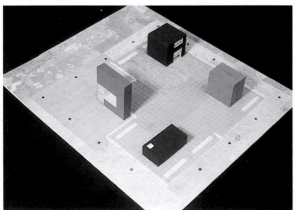

c

By comparison, a more recent Nottingham school, the Thomas Carlyle Infant and Junior School in Nuthall, which was completed in summer 1996, is almost totally open plan. A series of classrooms are ranged around a central courtyard with a multi-purpose hall breaking the sequence. The entrance is 'guarded' by the headteacher's office. Whilst the arrangement creates a pleasant enough environment, the open-plan nature of the building would appear to enforce a particular pattern of teaching. There are no dedicated circulation areas connecting the classrooms. In order to reach spaces on the far side of the site, circulation through the ongoing class activities is necessary. The benefits of this arrangement are clearly related to space saving; the rooms certainly felt much larger than the conventional cellular class spaces. However, the distraction caused by people walking through classes may be too high a penalty in terms of the levels of concentration children are able to maintain.

These concerns reflect the way in which teaching is structured: as described earlier, even in its slimmed down form, the UK National Curriculum is complex and broad. It is almost constantly evolving, therefore the school environment needs to be flexible. Where the numerous enclosed rooms of the Dharma School enable this separateness, in this particular plan the only teaching space which was separate from the rest was the dedicated music room. Not surprisingly a number of the teachers at the Thomas Carlyle School would have preferred more quiet rooms for concentration on special needs. Case Study 1 (The Speech, Language and Hearing Centre, Christopher Place, London) is worth referring to in this respect.

The final project I discuss in this section is the Cleves *Fully Inclusive* Primary School, which is reviewed in more length within the section on Special Needs (Chapter 3). This recently completed building in London's East End caters for 420 primary school pupils. It also includes a 52 full-time educational nursery, of which 32 places are for children with severe learning difficulties including pupils with profound and multiple disabilities. These pupils are included within the mainstream education system, in a modified curriculum structure; it is a deliberately open and fluid form, delivered in an appropriate setting. Every morning children fill out their own timetable and decide in which classes or activities they wish to participate. As long as maths, reading and English is carried out at some time during the course of the day, they are free to do whatever they wish. The theory is that if the pupils are at least partly responsible for the choice of subjects they study, enthusiasm and motivation will follow.

The school is divided into four wings, relating to the Key Stage learning areas. The wings have four rooms organized into curriculum subjects: writing, reading, finding out and maths. These rooms are arranged around a central shared practical area with easy access to the toilets. There are also two small quiet rooms which the staff use for a variety of purposes. Every classroom has access to a secure external play-court. Although there are no doors, it was apparent that the system was working well. However, class sizes were small, and, conversely, staff to child ratios were high. Given these factors, there is no doubting the effectiveness of the system which the headteacher believes to be in direct conflict with the new National Curriculum. Quite sensibly it would appear, since they are carrying out such an effective job anyway, they will simply continue, despite their failure to comply with the statutory requirements of the National Curriculum.

Interestingly, a scheme for a new village school to replace two existing smaller schools, developed by the Architect's & Buildings Branch at the Ministry of Education during the early 1960s, exhibits many of the radical qualities of the Cleves layout. The fifty children on the school roll do not need to be divided into age-related groups of equal size. According to the somewhat speculative theory, village children do not need constant supervision as they are quite capable of getting on with the job on their own: '*One can go into this school for example, and be almost unaware that the teacher is "teaching", simply because she is giving quiet, unobtrusive, individual attention which the teacher in an over-crowded room full of 40 or more children cannot easily give.*'[32]

The accommodation consists of a series of small working areas, one in the form of a covered veranda. All of the spaces have a degree of privacy, but are still part of the whole. Each has a certain character of its own: '*One is a sitting room, designed mainly for the younger children. This is furnished as any sitting room might be, with table and chairs – including a rocking-chair, a window seat, book shelves, curtains and a rug; there might have been an open fireplace, but instead there is an electric radiator to sit around. A small bedroom alcove, which can be curtained off, has a bed, drawers, mirror and shelf. Three more of these small areas are furnished as studies, with tables, chairs, book shelves, a wide sill and some pin-up and chalkboard panels. Two others are workshops, and are therefore near the veranda so that materials and work can be taken easily from one to the other. They have a fixed work top under the window with a washable plastic finish, a long sink with two cold water taps, shelving pin-up and chalkboard panels. Another is a kitchen with sink, working surfaces, wall cupboards and cooker. And lastly there is a library, with tables, chairs, shelving, wide sills, and curtains – and a rug which the teachers moved from their own room.*'[32]

These rooms replicate the home environment in a similar way to the Dharma school. Rooms for individual or small-group work open onto a larger communal space divided by sliding folding doors. The large space is uncluttered and can be used for music and movement and whole-school assemblies. Children generally do not have to clear their work away at the end of each lesson. As with the

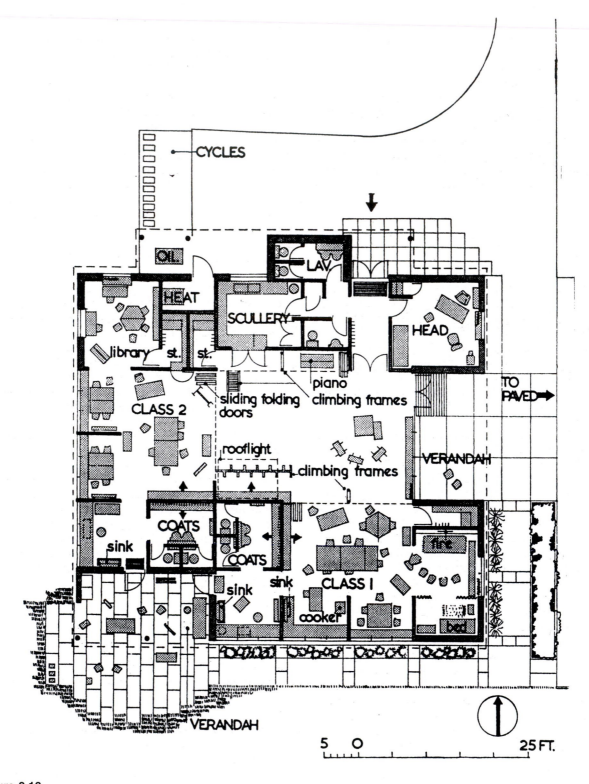

Figure 2.10
Plan of the Finmere Two-Class School, Oxfordshire. An arrangement which only functions if sited within a green-field setting.

ideal classroom, concerns expressed by teachers about the prescriptive nature of this layout suggested that teachers like to create their own environments. Clearly an appropriate balance between the complete finished environment and an empty shell must be struck. The more that is understood of the educational curriculum by the designer, the further it will be possible to strike this balance. Empathy is generated where the architect and educator work together. It is interesting to note how similar this scheme is to the fluid qualities of the Cleves school and, indeed, the specificity of the ideal classroom. The common bond is the extent to which architects and educators have collaborated.

At Cleves School the physical environment is recognized as being of profound importance. The teaching wings and the equipment within send messages to the children about expectations and attitudes. As such, the environment becomes the most powerful tool at the teacher's disposal. However, the staff and children have a shared responsibility to ensure that resources and equipment are maintained. The school has a handbook which is distributed to each family with a child in attendance. It is a checklist which ensures that safe use, care and maintenance of the environment are the essential learning outcomes, almost above and beyond those of the National Curriculum. This valuable checklist is reproduced in the notes at the end of this chapter.[33]

Although architecturally modest, the radical structure of this school's teaching spaces (it is almost misleading to describe them as classrooms) goes far beyond most others I have visited in delivering a learning strategy which is effective both educationally and socially. It is a structure which represents a vision of the future, with more diverse spaces, higher staff to pupil ratios and smaller class sizes. The architecture is far from perfect; for example, the senseless extended eaves restrict light penetration. However, its users feel sympathetic towards the layout and are able to work within the framework of its other shortcomings. Optimizing its environmental qualities is an essential aspect of the educational curriculum. Here one is left wondering how much better their experience might have been had the architecture in its entirety lived up to the aspirations of its teaching methods.

Finally, the use of artificial lighting within the classroom environment is an important factor which, due to its specialized nature, was not part of the design process for an ideal classroom included in this chapter. This factor will become increasingly critical with the incorporation of more computers within the classroom. An example of a school which was recently subject to a close focus study of its lighting was the Mary McLeod Bethune Elementary School in Rochester, New York. A typical 90 m² classroom used continuous rows of pendant mounted fluorescent uplights. These specially made fixtures have two rows of slots on the bottom, which contain perforated white metal panels whose openings provide a small amount of surface brightness. Uplighters are spaced nine feet apart and suspended from the ceiling with aircraft cable. To add visual interest, soffits and soffit faces are painted in bright colours.[34]

The very act of switching on task lighting when the teacher commences a lesson adds a useful sense of theatricality. Students learn to use computers at the rear part of the room, which adopts a different form of lighting again. At Bethune, the discreet use of surface colour reflected up into the space by uplighters provides light which is warm and varied. This complements the task lighting. The system provides scope for variations within the space at a reasonably economic level. Lighting specialist Professor Peter Tregenza of the University of Sheffield School of Architecture believes that electric lighting, daylighting, view and colour are interlinked in design. In almost all buildings, people prefer rooms that appear daylit to those where electric lighting is dominant. The changing pattern of daylight playing on the surfaces of a room provides information about the world outside. Its natural variation tells of the weather and the time of day.

Professor Tregenza believes that the best classroom does not necessarily rely entirely on daylight: there are many factors that limit the area of glazing. Some are environmental – for instance, dazzle from direct sunlight and thermal discomfort from large windows must be minimized. The optimum solution is usually one in which electric lighting is designed specifically to be used in conjunction with daylight during daytime hours. Thus electric lighting must increase room brightness in spaces distant from windows and provide additional illumination where needed for tasks or display; but it must not swamp the natural variation of daylight. Such design leads to the most economic use of energy: several research studies have shown that whether measured in lifetime monetary costs or in primary energy, the lowest costs occur when daylight and electric lighting are designed to be used together during daytime hours.[35]

Summary

Reflective teachers are likely to be concerned about the quality of the learning environment within their school and will aim to maximize the learning potential of the building and space which they have available.[36]

A lack of facilities can severely limit curriculum activities. If the classroom environment does not have quiet spaces for reading, or is badly ventilated, there is very little the class teacher can do to remedy the situation. However, there are ways in which imaginative teachers can optimize a poor classroom environment, even if this requires adapting their own teaching methods to suit the needs of the space. One

Figure 2.11
Neutra's experimental school of 1935, Corona School, Bell, Los Angeles. Due to its radical open-plan form, when it was completed some parents described it variously as a drive-in market, a hangar or a penthouse on Mars. Neutra explained: 'The old time listening school where children were taught in an academic way could get along well with fixed sitting arrangements and with desks screwed to the floor. The teacher faced the pupils and poured instruction into them. Now the teacher has become an active member of the group who works freely around the classroom, constructs, sews, dyes, handles all the material and tools with the children ...' From W. Boesiger's *Richard Neutra Buildings and Projects*, edition Girsberger, Zurich, 1951, p. 150. This image was published in *The New Architecture*, 1st ed., edited by Alfred Roth, edition Girsberger, Zurich, 1940, p. 109. (Photo: © Alfred Roth *New Architecture*.)

teacher I met had arranged for full height doorwindows to replace the existing high-silled windows. She organized the immediate outside space to be a garden. It was, she said, like her own lounge and garden at home, which made it more comfortable for her as an environment in which to teach. However, this type of direct action is unusual within most UK state schools.

The importance of ICT within the classroom has been touched upon. As I write, however, of the 25,000 state maintained schools in England and Wales, the current pupil to computer ratio is 19:1. In secondary schools it is 9:1; however, 75 per cent of the machines in schools are over five years old. This problem is compounded by the fact that around 70 per cent of teachers have received no training in ICT. Computers and communications technology are rightly central to the government's drive to raise standards in the classroom. This makes no sense unless enough pupils have access to the machines and software which will enable them to exploit the National Grid for Learning, and other resources available on the Internet.

Since the UK Education Reform Act was introduced in 1988, there has been a period of continuous demand, pressure and change on schools and their teachers. It has to be concluded that the views of children were largely ignored during this time. Most of the focus centred on the content of the curriculum. The development of children as people was neglected. It is important for teachers to listen to children and for children to listen to each other. As stated in the introduction, special needs require special spaces. Every child, to a greater or lesser extent, has special needs, one of which is to be heard. Increasingly there will be a requirement for social and educational priorities within schools to recognize the rights of the individual child within the classroom, as well as the overall standing of the class group in relation to the institution's standing in the educational attainment league tables.

It is conceivable that the pressures of the National Curriculum will draw attention away from a more holistic view of children's development. On the continent, emphasis continues to be placed upon group and collaborative methods, particularly during the early years. Teachers are given advice as to the use of space within the school, to aid and broaden the field of learning. Within the UK, the emphasis is increasingly on pencil and paper tests. To reiterate, there is little advice at teacher training level as how best to use the facilities and spaces of the classroom. The trainee teacher is told how and what to teach yet little or no attention is paid to the context within which this takes place.

Whilst the excesses of child-centred pedagogy have matured into a richer and perhaps more complex educational form, it is clear that the continued development of the National Curriculum will be made on the understanding that no child's potential is fixed: *'Ensuring equality of opportunity in the classroom will continue to require imaginative solutions, where the best developments of the past years in cooperative teaching and learning strategies, effective communication, and a principled mix of whole class, flexible groupings, pair and individual work, are supported and improved.'*[37] The classroom environment is an essential partner in this task. The classroom teacher should be encouraged to make the best use of their environment and create an ideal classroom in his or her own image.

Notes

1 Penn, Helen, *Comparing Nurseries* Paul Chapman Publishing, London, 1997, p.7.
2 OFSTED: Office for Standards in Education, a government-funded agency which has the power to censure poorly performing schools.
3 Sammons, P., Hillman, J. and Mortimore, P., *Key Characteristics of Effective Schools* OFSTED Publications, London, 1995. A subsequent *Guardian*/Institute of Education debate on whether universities are doing an effective job in training teachers questioned this research. In his paper Chris Woodhead states: 'of course good schools are well led and pupils learn most in well-ordered classrooms. I am simply not convinced that research of this kind

generates additional insights that justify the considerable sums of tax payers' money spent on them ... my problem is that they [research findings] are all obvious' *Guardian Education*, 15 Dec 1998, p.17.
4 Although Andrew Pollard, *Reflective Teaching in the Primary School, A Handbook for the Classroom* (3rd edn) Cassell Education, 1997, refers to 'adequate resources' as essential, he distinguishes four kinds of resource: 'people, buildings, equipment and materials', p.34.
5 'The miracle-worker: he used to be Sir, now he's Sir Sir', *Independent*, 26 January 1998.
6 An appropriate balance needs to be struck between organizational quality and spatial quality, particularly in secondary school situations where children move around not just for assemblies but also for different lessons throughout the day. The Heathland School, which has 1800 pupils, uses a colour coding system for each of its four teaching sections which in turn connect via staircases to the main assembly hall and other parts of the school. A one-way system of movement gives the whole complex the air of a treadmill, with little sense of spatial quality. However, organizationally it is highly efficient.
7 The Area Guidelines for Schools (Building Bulletin 82, DfEE Publications, PO Box 5050, Annesley, Nottingham NG15 0DJ) sets out a methodology for assessing existing buildings against existing and proposed curricula. It gives a range of target gross area standards for pupils by type and size of school, and percentage target teaching/non-teaching area ratios. It also sets out a method for analysing outside areas. The approach can be used to develop a schedule of accommodation for existing or new schools
8 Anning, Angela, *The First Years at School* Open University Press, Milton Keynes, 1998, pp.76–77.
9 For example refer to Case Study 12, Haute Vallée School, Jersey.
10 Refer to Valentine, Gill, '"Oh yes I can." "Oh no you can't": Children and parents' understanding of kids' competence to negotiate public space safely.' *Antipode*, June 1997.
11 *Design for Learning*, Hampshire County Council Education Department, June 1996. ISBN 1 85975 1148, p.5.
12 Otto, Karl, *School Buildings*, 1, 1966, p.9.
13 Aldrich R., 'The national curriculum: an historical perspective.' In D. Lawton and C. Chitty (eds), *The National Curriculum,* Institute of Education, London, 1988.
14 Cox, B.C. and Dyson A.E. (eds) *The Black Papers on Education,* Davis Pointer, London, 1971.
15 Moon, Bob, and Shelton Mayes, Ann, (eds), *Teaching and Learning in Secondary School*, Open University, 1994, p.26.

16 'How children learn.' *Teaching and Learning in the Secondary School*, p.52.

17 *Guardian Education*, 16 December, 1997, pp.4–5.

18 Ashcroft, Kate, and Palacio, David (eds) *The Primary Teacher's Guide to the New National Curriculum,* The Falmer Press, 1995.

19 Three terms are used to describe each subject within the National Curriculum: *programmes of study*, which set out the ways each subject area is to be studied; *attainment targets*, which set out the expected standards of pupil performance; and *level descriptions*. Each attainment target is divided into eight levels. Level 1 is the first that a child should try to achieve after a short time in primary school. Level 8 is the standard you would expect of a 14 year old. A further reference should be made to the Key Stages, which are the age ranges by which the National Curriculum is ordered. Key Stage 1, 5–7 year olds in year groups 1–2; Key Stage 2, 7–11 year olds in year groups 3–6; Key Stage 3, 11–14 year olds in year groups 7–9; and Key Stage 4, 14–16 year olds in year groups 10–11.

20 *English in the National Curriculum Key Stage One*, National Curriculum Council, York, 1989.

21 McCaverty, B., *Grace Notes*, Vintage, London, 1998, p. 56.

22 *International Archives of Occupational and Environmental Health*, 60, No. 2.

23 MUDS – MariMuse: Online Fantasy Worlds Benefit Inner City School. Howard Rheingold – Internet.

24 Bennett, Neville, and Dunne, Elizabeth, 'How children learn – implications for practice.' In Bob Moon and Ann Shelton Mayes (eds) *Teaching and Learning in the Secondary School,* Open University, 1994.

25 Moon, Bob and Shelton Mayes, Ann, (eds) *Teaching and Learning in Secondary School*, Open University, 1994.

26 Dewey J., *How We Think: A Restatement of the Relation of Reflective Thinking to the Educative Process,* Henry Regnery, Chicago, 1933.

27 Horne, Sandra Christine, 'Shared Visions? Architects' and teachers' perceptions on the design of classroom environments' Paper presented to the conference ... as part of a PhD study at Goldsmith's University of London, p.9.

28 'Award of Excellence – Strawberry Vale School.' *The Canadian Architect*, December 1994, p.20.

29 Dyck, James A., 'The case for the L-shaped classroom.' *Principal*, November 1994, p.44.

30 Hertzberger, *Harvard Educational Review*, 1969.

31 In fairness to the headteacher this was a standardized CLASP building constructed in the late 1960s with a plethora of faults relating directly to non-site specific design and outmoded technology. Under these circumstances the staff were coping well.

32 *Village Schools*. Ministry of Education Building Bulletin No 3, June 1961. Text and illustrations taken from Section II. Examples of New Village Schools – A Two-Class School in Oxfordshire: Finmere. pp.8–12. A & B Branch stands for Architects and Buildings Branch.

33 From the *Cleves Primary School Handbook*. 'Key Stage 2b Organization and Management: The Learning Environment – a checklist for teachers and pupils':

Preparation
– is there scope for group, paired and individual work
– have you left enough room for rotators and people
– are activities on different levels
– is every activity given equal status by its position
– was it out yesterday – how has it been developed
– is there a large enough range of equipment
– can every child in the wing be challenged in this area
– are the equipment and resources ready to use
– is the equipment presented creatively
– is there enough room to work at the activities
– is the equipment stored in an accessible way for all children
– are labels and instructions big enough, clear enough and simple enough
– has the area been reserviced for the next session

During session
– is the area kept tidy and reserviced
– does every child get equal time
– are you ensuring that each child is on task
– are you aware of what all the children are doing
– do you have enough extension activities planned and on hand
– are staff fully deployed and sure of their roles
– is there a mixture of children involved, gender, race, need
– is group work cooperative
– are you supportive to the children's initiatives
– are you covered when you leave
– does the child know where to store completed work
– have you and your child evaluated the activity, completed the diary
– do they know where to go next

End of session
– is everyone equally involved in tidying up – do they know the expectations
– is it efficient
– are instructions clear
– where do they go now
– is the equipment complete and put away in its correct place
– is there a way of tasks being continued in the next session

– have they been warned that the session is ending
– have you completed the observation file
– have you pulled out the trolleys and picked up the equipment
– are the children ready to go home

34 Rodgers, Paula A., 'Case Study: An elementary school that saves energy and is visually comfortable.' *Architectural Record*, August 1998, pp.159–163.

35 Tregenza, Peter and Loe, David, *The Design of Lighting*, Spon, London, 1998.

36 Pollard, Andrew, *Reflective Teaching in the Primary School: A Handbook for the Classroom* (3rd edn), Cassel, 1997, p.35.

37 Bourne, Jill, and Moon, Bob, 'A Question of Ability?' *Teaching and Learning in the Secondary School*, p.36.

3

Making the case for architecture in schools

Introduction

Something of a boom in school building can be anticipated within the UK and elsewhere over the coming decade. According to a US Department of Education report, school enrolment will keep growing until the year 2007. At

Figure 3.1
Cottrell and Vermeulen's 'lunchbox wall', Westborough Primary, Westcliffe-on-Sea. (Photo: © Paul Ratigan.)

the same time, schools and their educational needs are changing; information and communications technologies are predicted to transform the classroom. Local control, decentralization, and the introduction of private funding are just three of the factors which may bring about change.

However, is architecture valued by client bodies responsible for the development of education? In discussion with an eminent headteacher, the point was made that the primary function of school is to structure and organize a complex community; to consider the architecture of schools as anything more than this was a waste of scarce resources. The rather polemical thrust of the argument went on to say that the priority should be the repair and upgrading of existing schools, rather than the design and construction of new school buildings. Often school design incorporates technical considerations, without consideration of wider aesthetic issues. As pointed out in the previous chapter, classrooms are often designed with little thought to more complex architectural concerns.

In this chapter I analyse a number of contemporary school buildings which take overtly architectural forms. I believe these combine the highest organizational and imaginative qualities, to create environments which optimize learning. I assess how important this architectural input is to the learning experience, and seek pointers towards future developments in the design of school architecture.

I include sections on special needs, Early Excellence Centres and pre-school classes as well as primary and secondary schools. Developments in the procurement process, such as the modular school, will be considered to provide an all-round picture of educational needs, now and for the future.

To start, I use a quotation from Will Hutton's apocryphal analysis of the post-Thatcherite state education system:

The same three riders of the apocalypse – systematic under-funding, competitive contracting and a burgeoning private sector – are undermining the notion of a universal education system in which everyone has a stake and where individual educational needs can be met by local structures. Class sizes in primary and secondary schools are too large for adequate teaching, and are typically twice the size of those in the private sector. Teachers' salaries have slipped markedly even as the demands on teachers have risen. School buildings, equipment and playing fields are inadequate.[1]

This identifies a UK system which if not already on the verge of collapse is certainly run down and in need of drastic surgery. The major cause of this has been budgetary shortfalls and a lack of interest in the education service generally, during the Conservative years. However, the laissez faire attitudes of some architects and commissioning bodies have also contributed to this state of affairs; by failing to consult with the end users, and adopting untried, poorly performing technologies, previous generations of school designers diminished the importance of educational environments, and the role architects and architecture should play in the process.

Today, the procurement process is moving towards new levels of transparency where everyone should have a stake in determining how public funds are allocated. The contemporary debate only has meaning if the dual criteria of value for money and community involvement are part of that process. It is fairly pointless to assume that any schools can be built without these two functions playing a pivotal role in the architecture which is proposed. It is from this starting point that I begin to examine the contemporary debate. I briefly consider how examples of high quality schools architecture have been funded over the last ten years, before commenting on the nature of that architecture in more detail.

Over the past decade, many UK local authority architects have been privatized and disbanded. Expertise built up over many years has in some cases been lost overnight. As one director of education pointed out, employing architects who have never designed a school before requires immense amounts of briefing time, and no little faith, in order to avoid even the most basic errors. Equally, employing a large commercial 'contractor' with no local knowledge, who for commercial reasons may be unwilling to consult widely, will limit the quality of the end result. In the pre-school sector, the 'learning curve' is even steeper. Local authorities have a somewhat confused view as to how they should cater for this rapidly expanding service; as alluded to above, architecture is often viewed as an indulgence.

However, new building is proceeding. Private finance is being drawn upon to provide an alternative to traditional public sector funding routes. Effective architects draw on their own experience of education and coordinate their ideas together with the end users throughout the design process. Extensive consultation culminates in the form of friendships between architects, school clients and educationalists, which helps to bridge the knowledge gap. Effective communication lies at the heart of this process with design days involving the school community followed up by consultation sessions to make new proposals more tailored towards the needs of the end users. Efficient exchange of knowledge is crucial in modern education, and this applies equally to the design process.

It is evident that the investment of substantial public money (even when it is mixed in with private finance) requires that the school effectively extends its life to the wider community. Certainly this happens in the pre-school sector throughout the continent, with parenting classes, evening and weekend activities using school facilities as the venue. This extends community life. Parents need help and advice on how best to support their children. If they are introduced to other parents through the school, the mutual exchange of skills and ideas becomes a by-product of the school social structure. The problem of single parents stuck within an isolated and consequently demoralizing role of caring for young children at home alone is also addressed. It will be argued that the best way for the whole community to learn is through the school.

David Blunkett, Secretary of State for Education, made a speech at the NAHT Conference in May 1996 and talked about 'The Primary School in the Wider Community', observing that schools do not exist in isolation: *'A family of schools can form a cluster to link with the secondary school into which the children generally move. It can help to make coherence out of a national curriculum which is still not integrating the key stages of the education process. Small schools can benefit most from working together, continuing to contribute to the life of their community. In Dorset, four small rural schools have "federated". They share administrative staff and buy in services from a local secondary school.'*[2]

The role of the primary and secondary schools can be similarly extended, providing facilities for local people who may not even have school-age children. In order to be eligible for National Lottery funding applications from schools are required to offer at least forty hours per week community access to school premises. The building should operate equally effectively as a school between the hours of 9.00am and 4.30pm, and as a community centre in the evenings and at weekends. The premises are managed by the school on behalf of local people. In this way additional facilities such as sports halls and swimming pools can be built within the school site, without the need for autonomous management structures.

An example of a school which was designed in such a way to allow its use during the evenings and at weekends is the Hallfield School in Paddington, London (see Chapter 1). Information and communications technology can also be made available (there is at present a gap in access, particularly for those who most need it – the long-term unemployed). If schools are designed to include cabling technology, access and security to the school site are controlled, and the use of the school can be revolutionized for this and other purposes. It is a common complaint that parents feel they are not close enough to their schools. In this respect the use of home computers can be encouraged which are connected to the school. Parents can communicate with class teachers by e-mail and the Internet. New information and communications technology may in time make our schools contemporary community centres.[3]

In the wake of the Dunblane tragedy, security within schools is now of the utmost importance. To allow strangers to wander through a playground at any time of the day or night is clearly not acceptable. Yet the role of school premises in providing a social focus implies that the school needs to be a flexible and responsive structure, which is 'open' both functionally and symbolically. All of this places the practising architect at the centre of an act of financial and political judgement which will take immense energy and commitment in order to properly address the needs of all involved, at an economic cost.

The cost of new-build extensions carried out at the Westborough School in Westcliff-on-Sea was £232,156 whereas Frankfurt Greisheim-Sud children's day-care centre and after-school club cost approximately £729,000. Comparable costs are £600 per square metre (Westborough) and £1068 per square metre (Greisheim), which is perhaps a comment on the paucity of funding available to UK educational authorities at present. However, even the City of Frankfurt is no longer able to fund such lavish projects. An equitable balance needs to be struck between the real need for large-scale children's centres and the limited funds currently available. As pre-school facilities are not a statutory requirement within the UK, local education authority spending priorities are currently directed towards primary and secondary schools. In Europe, there is a long tradition of funding pre-school which comes directly from regional governments via a range of selective taxes, including taxes on the businesses which benefit most from full-time child care.

Apart from the private financing of nurseries and a small number of so-called public (i.e. privately funded) schools, funding for primary and secondary schools is structured in three distinct ways. There are special schools, usually church schools where a percentage of the total budget must be met by the institution or the diocese itself. At present these are referred to as voluntary aided schools. The second category, and by far the majority, are referred to as County Schools. These are funded through local education authorities (LEAs). The final category, and what some believe to be the most pernicious form of funding, are the so-called grant maintained schools which

were allowed to 'opt-out' of local authority control, being funded directly by central government through the Funding Agency for Schools.

The system of opting-out narrows the local educational resources available for all schools and creates troubling inequalities between schools within regions of most need. Some would say that the 'opt-out' approach was a political device introduced in 1985 by the then Conservative government to weaken the power of local government. Certainly the opted-out schools received substantially more funding than their LEA equivalents during this time. In the case of Westborough, the architect Brian Vermeulen believes that the direct (opt-out) route effectively cut out the middleman, so that the school community itself (the headteacher and her governors) acted as the client, enabling a more meaningful process of consultation to take place: '*Some LEAs have cumbersome bureaucracies which impose higher costs on the development process, and engender a spirit of caution which often has a detrimental effect on architectural quality. At Westborough we can say with confidence that every last penny was squeezed out of a very tight budget, with the architects giving far more time to the project than might otherwise have been the case. As a result of this, the client in consultation with all the teachers got exactly what she wanted with a commitment from all members of the design team. Ultimately this proved to be a rewarding and highly enjoyable experience.*'

Here the process of allowing the school to hold its own budget has certainly worked in its favour. However, as discussed in Chapter 4, it might not always be the case that the school selects such a skilful and responsive consultant to carry out their design and (of equal importance) their building works. Nevertheless, the present Labour government is in the process of restructuring the funding regime in an effort to delegate budgets down towards the schools, and make Westborough a model for future school developments. Precisely how this will happen is unclear. However, the concept of 'fair funding' for schools is central in the present political climate, where the equitable distribution of educational spending is key.

An example of special funding which comes from European community sources is Birmingham City Council's Single Regeneration Budget (SRB). This series of ongoing community-based projects have been developed between the local authority architects, landscape architects and the schools themselves by way of a sophisticated consultation process which has been developed over a number of years by freelance educational environmentalist, Sue Fenoughty. This highly effective programme links school grounds improvements to the educational curriculum, converting previously unused external areas into pocket gardens which are partly maintained by the schoolchildren themselves. The projects are linked to lesson plans and closely monitored to assess the numbers of children directly participating in the cultivation and tending of the areas. This, believes Roger Hale, the team architect responsible for the funding programme, is an essential aspect of the success of the project: '... *by going directly to the school staff, and more importantly, the children, results appear to have a more direct effect on the quality of the learning process.*'

The success of the Westborough and Birmingham initiatives suggests that a more community-based approach has succeeded in radically transforming a number of existing school environments at minimal cost. How far this has deprived other schools in the area of funds is hard to judge. Schools which are on a downwards trajectory of low morale and poorly maintained run-down facilities require special attention, and perhaps discretionary funding to 'stop the rot'. However, an ethos of competitive bidding for relatively limited funds will ensure that value for money, community involvement and flexibility within new school environments is incorporated into the development process. Ultimately, well-funded and well-managed schools will help to provide higher standards of education and lifelong learning for the whole community. In future, the emphasis may be on the school community itself determining the way in which their facilities will develop.

Pre-school classes and nursery schools

The extent of this section on pre-school facilities is limited to identifying broadly agreed prerequisites for any nursery building, and exploring some of the current problems and anomalies which exist in the UK, compared with the healthier and much more established European system of pre-school provision.

Whether it is within an existing school, or in a separate self-contained institution, the requirements of pre-school facilities can be summarized as follows: access to secure and protected outside space; facilities for external play, i.e. covered play spaces; a light, airy and well ventilated internal environment; and, most importantly, a range of rooms which are equipped to meet the requirements of a diverse curriculum. In short, a simplistic open-plan arrangement should almost certainly be avoided. Added to this is the need to provide some kind of architectural autonomy for the pre-school so as to distinguish it from the main areas of the primary school.

Clearly the provision of a varied range of spaces linked to an efficient environment will make that building better suited to the task of providing full day 'educare' for pre-school children. However, budgets are tight and space standards minimal, particularly in the UK and Denmark compared with similar European countries such as Germany and Italy. Having more space *per se* is by no means a guarantee of quality.[4] If the inherent complexities of the pre-school curriculum are addressed in both functional and aesthetic terms and attention is paid to child-orientated issues such as scale and flexibility, then good quality pre-school facilities can undoubtedly be produced within existing school environments, or as part of a new primary school.

A further requirement which distinguishes pre-school from the needs of the later secondary school environment is the need to 'fascinate' young children through an architecture which is in itself playful. Although this point is not wholly agreed upon, playful architecture is viewed by some as a requirement in primary school environments; and it can also be argued that where young children experience an environment which is light-hearted and distracting in its own right, then they will be more willing to participate in the life of the institution. However, the scale of these distractions need not be Disney-esque and an appropriate balance between pastiche and real architecture needs to be struck. It is possible to conceive an architecture for pre-school which is light and engaging, without resort to plastic egg cups or teddy bear doors.

For example Cottrell and Vermeulen's four new reception classes for Westborough Primary School in Westcliff-on-Sea adopts various devices which are both functional and engaging. Equally they have provided a rich and diverse range of spaces within the framework of tight budgets and, by necessity, limited space standards. The single-storey structure houses four teaching areas for the youngest 'reception' pupils. This is not considered to be a pre-school facility as such in that it caters for the needs of one hundred 4 and 5 year olds attending normal infant school sessions (9.00am to 3.30pm). Nevertheless, the new block assumes an appropriate level of autonomy from the main school, sitting on the south side of the existing school's playground.

The structure is simple, consisting of a mono-pitch roof and a relatively deep 10 metre plan which enables a 'spatial layering' to take place. This layering commences with a covered entrance 'deck' on the north side, through the entrance lobby, into the classroom and finally into two light- and air-giving open courtyards sandwiched between the rear party wall and the kitchen/wet areas. The sequence is identified functionally as entrance, washroom/toilet block, quiet area, classroom and shared area. This is both functionally economical and architecturally rich.

The space itself is articulated by using a limited range of rich primary colours; a blue and green in the entrance hall and red, blue, yellow and green to distinguish each classroom area, orange for the kitchens and turquoise in the courtyards. Yet the colour never seems to overwhelm the experience of the spaces themselves. It is used in a sparing, almost painterly, manner. The colours are mixed and adapted to the mood of the space and never used in their primary factory condition. This care is undoubtedly inspired by the use of colour by Le Corbusier; the designers met

Figure 3.2
The cortile at
Westborough Primary
School reception classes.
(Photo: © Brian
Vermeulen.)

whilst working on the restoration of Corb's Unité at Briey, and were strongly influenced by this experience in much of their later work. Similarly the physical structure of the building is robust and wherever possible exposed externally. This becomes part of its fascination. The most extreme example is the use of transparent polycarbonate panels in one of the entrance walls. This allows the children to peer at the layers of the building, rockwool insulation, steel fixings and plywood veneer, as if they have X-ray eyes.

A further device is what has been dubbed the 'lunch box wall'. This is exactly as it sounds, a series of racks on the outside face of the building where the children leave their packed lunches. It is a clever idea, restricting interior clutter, and throughout most of the year, ensuring that the food remains fresh and cool. It also looks wonderful, like an advertising hoarding, at once expressing the individuality of the children and also producing a colourful group collage which changes from day to day. Perhaps the most pleasing feature of this small yet intense scheme is the twin courtyards on the south side of the plan. Although measuring only 2 m × 5 m, they provide a play space which can be appropriated by an optimum number of four or five children. Light bounces back from the rear party wall flooding the interior with a calming pool of blue light. It is a safe and secure alternative to the garden and playground spaces which matches the scale and rhythms of childhood play. It is a little shelter within the greater world of the child care institution.

Architecturally the Westborough scheme illustrates all the characteristics of best design practice outlined in the opening paragraph. It provides a rich range of spatial experiences within the framework of a relatively small building. Although Westborough is for pre-school children, the range of its facilities is limited to 4 and 5 year olds attending school mainly on a part-time basis. The lack of integration between different age ranges diminishes the quality of the pre-school experience and fails to recognize properly the rights of pre-schoolers to their own social structures. The extent to which children can support and learn from each other should not be underestimated, particularly if they are allowed to mix within different age ranges. One must also be concerned about the older so-called 'latchkey' children, who have a period of time between the end of their school day and the return of their parents from work.

For reasons of economy, 'after-school clubs' within the setting of the main school appear to be the solution favoured in Britain. In Germany a more sophisticated approach is taken, providing purpose-made activity rooms within the pre-school structure. This means that school-age children leave the environment of their formal school at the end of the day and return to the Kinderhort, which is part of the pre-school itself. Because the kindergartens are located within or close to residential areas, the children return from school to the pre-school, which is always in closer proximity to home itself. This is deemed to be an important psychological shift which is not achieved by after-school clubs taking place within normal school premises. Levels of social interaction are achieved which encourage an integration of the age ranges to create

Figure 3.3
Kindertagesstatte,
Frankfurt (1989) designed
by Bolles Wilson; the
garden façade. (Photo:
© Mark Dudek.)

Dewey's *embryonic community life*, that reflects the complexities of the larger society.

A good example of the European model is a Frankfurt Kindertagesstatte in Greisheim-Sud.[5] Designed in 1991 by Munster-based architects Bolles Wilson, it combines a large-scale facility with many of Westborough's architectural qualities in its attention to child-orientated details. Located within the suburbs of Frankfurt close to residential areas, the building is provided with only two car parking spaces. However, public transport is excellent and the area itself was identified as requiring a children's centre, so that most children are delivered to the centre on foot from the immediate locality. The centre caters for sixty full-time pre-school children (3 to 6 year olds) and provides afternoon study spaces for forty schoolchildren.

One of the most delightful approaches to the building is by way of a narrow pedestrian footpath. The south-facing garden façade with its strong anthropomorphic qualities gradually reveals itself, like a friendly face, welcoming the children to a building which is in itself a metaphor of growth. Although architect Peter Wilson explains it in a much more serious manner, there is no denying the use of scale and imagery to communicate this sense of frivolity which imbues the whole building. The tapering of both the plan and the elevation, from small, narrow and low around the entrance, to the large double height multi-function hall at the other end of the building, provides a hierarchy which works on two levels. Firstly, the smaller, younger children who are accommodated at the west end of the building feel comfortable in the more intimate scale of the entrance areas; as they grow and move along to activity areas further along the plan, so the building grows with them. The second function of this spatial twist in plan and section is to create a natural sense of movement within the circulation areas of the building; tight and constricted parts tend to slow the children down, wider more expansive spaces encourage movement. Thus safe natural pathways or routes are created that encourage controlled movement through the building and outside into the garden.

Thus the building operates on two levels: firstly as an institution with its own home base areas for coherent age groups, each with their own self-contained activity area with toilet block and quiet area, much in the way Westborough functions. Beyond that it has a secondary structure, the circulation paths through and around it where older children and younger children have the opportunity to meet. As designer Peter Wilson states: '*The relationship between the inside and the outside is very important: the children are free to run in and out from each group room. It's really about group management, ensuring the spaces are comfortable, the loos are located in the right place, and are spacious and architecturally reassuring.*'[6] The building provides safe, secure areas for more insecure vulnerable children, but also enables independent exploration to take place in and around the building for those children with greater confidence. It is a world within a world.

The distinction between the relatively closed activity areas of Westborough and the equally closed activity areas of Greisheim-Sud with the additional structure of the articulated routes and pathways may appear to be subtle. However, it symbolizes the differences between a coherent educational system, where the location and scale of the centre is considered on an integrated city-wide basis, and the inward looking UK system in all its competitive opted-out autonomy. Greisheim-Sud is not an add-on to an existing school. It is a stand-alone institution, located strategically to cater for the needs of a specific geographical area, largely negating the need to 'Volvo' children in from further afield. It is not competing with other schools for children as, it could be argued, is the case with Westborough. Instead it is part of a system catering for children and their parents as a whole community, and as such it complements other local educational facilities. It is designed specifically with young children in mind, and had a budget which enabled the architects to add fascinating distractions to the environment.[7]

Wilson's pragmatic statements about group management disguise the inherent sociability designed into the scheme; the structure of the plan, whilst addressing the rights of the individual child to privacy and security, also recognizes the need for the child to be able to operate comfortably within a wider, more diverse range of group structures. Perhaps the internal routes replicate the city/street and the garden becomes a representation of the countryside. Within this framework the children are allowed to play at being grown-up. Perhaps an obsession with individual rights, particularly in England, has tended to negate the importance of group structures within society. This is an area which can be addressed at the earliest time within the framework of pre-school 'educare':

> *Our image of children no longer considers them as isolated and egocentric, does not only see them engaged in action with objects, does not emphasize only the cognitive aspects, does not belittle feelings or what is not logical, and does not consider with ambiguity the role of the affective domain. Instead our image of the child is rich in potential, strong, powerful, competent, and most of all, connected to adults and other children.*[8]

It can be seen in countless examples of pre-school architecture throughout Europe how careful consideration for the whole community can create an architecture which encourages sociability. This will not only serve the basic needs of the most vulnerable children, but also encourage a sense of group belonging, and ultimately create future citizens equipped socially, to deal with the crowded and competitive world in which they will participate. Even within the framework of existing school buildings, creating a separate pre-school with its own distinct spatial qualities and clearly defined boundaries will provide the healthy foundations for lifelong learning.

Devising new solutions: the prefabricated school

As has already been hinted at, one of the most significant differences between the UK education system and most of the rest of the developed world is the school starting age. Here children have traditionally commenced school at the age of 5. In Europe and the United States for example, the school starting age is 6. This has created a number of more profound differences between the systems which have evolved partly as a result of this anomaly.

Most profound has been the tendency in Europe, as a result of the longer time period prior to first school, to treat pre-school as a distinct and particular form of educational provision, an example being the Frankfurt Kindertaggestatte described above. In addition, women have tended to voice stronger political views over a longer period of time to greater effect. In the United States, the need for pre-school education has been enshrined within a social structure for over twenty years with projects like the Start Right scheme. Women have demanded and received the right to go out to work whilst raising young children, a social and economic function which requires full-time 'educare' for young children.

By contrast the UK approach has been less coherent, the tendency having been to treat the period of time prior to first school as a kind of extended babyhood, to be dealt with by a stay at home mother. As a consequence childcare has evolved either as an ad hoc part-time affair, comprising of two-hour play groups run from church halls, or as full-time state provision sanctioned by Social Services departments usually for vulnerable or at-risk children. Private nurseries sometimes connected to the parent's workplace were until quite recently the only possibility for those working parents who could afford it.

It is hard to say why attitudes to pre-school have recently changed, but changed they have. The demand for nursery education and full day-care with an educational agenda has resulted in all the major political parties promising nursery places for all 3 and 4 year olds within the UK. The new Labour government is considering ways of extending this provision to younger children, placing the onus on local authorities to produce their own strategy documents for more integrated forms of pre- and primary school education within their regions.[9] It is clear that nursery schooling will become an integral part of the educational infrastructure over the coming decade, as it currently is in Europe.

This brings with it previously stated concerns, not least because no substantial new money has been promised to fund this expansion.[10] Where European funding mechanisms have for decades distinguished between pre- and first school, with purpose-designed facilities managed and funded independently, the tendency in the UK is to extend existing infant school provision to incorporate the requirements of pre-school under one single umbrella. This has brought about the notion of a nursery class next to or part of existing infant school classes intended to cater for 4 year olds on a full-time basis. Where the Westborough example achieves a sense of its own autonomy from the main school, many of these new reception classes are accommodated in existing school buildings, or in low quality hutted accommodation.

New initiatives are evolving which are intended to address the dramatic problem of a lack of pre-school care and educational facilities within the UK. Strategies for the replacement of so-called 'temporary classrooms' littered across numerous school sites within the UK and USA are also part of this approach. Whilst good quality school buildings can be provided at economic levels through the traditional procurement and construction route, the argument in favour of prefabricated systems is that they bring better economy and speed of erection with a ready-made educational theory as part of the package. Where the system is supported by in-depth research and extensive development funding, within the framework of the design, arguments in their favour are particularly convincing. It is also reasonable to surmise that build quality is significantly improved by factory assembly. Finally, and tentatively, I suggest that their qualities are more suited to the needs of young children; they pass the 'my house' test (see Chapter 1). I explore two recently completed projects with which I have been involved.

One of the first nursery projects to be conceived of in this way was the Expanding Nursery commissioned by the Nursery School Association in 1937. Designed by architects Erno Goldfinger and Mary Crowley, it provided three alternative layouts to accommodate 40, 80 or 120 children. It was intended to be mass produced by the joinery company Boulton and Paul and was designed in a gridded unit system based on 6 ft modules. Although a prototype was erected, the project never went into production. In the immediate post-war years, the Expanding Nursery was not revived, due partly to the anti-pre-school culture prevalent within the UK, and alternative priorities in other parts of the education system. Critics might refer to the perspective views of its proposed interiors, which appear to be rather neutral and anonymous play spaces, suggesting that the designers had little idea of how the spaces would actually be used by the children and their carers.[11]

Different forms of prefabrication were explored within the UK during the post-war years. These were mainly within the primary school sector. Of particular note was the work of the Consortium of Local Authorities Special Programme (CLASP). This was a system developed for the South Notts coalfield area where undermined land made conventional construction problematic. The system combined a factory-made steel frame with other lightweight materials such as tile cladding to the walls, and flat sheet coverings to the roof areas. Under the leadership of Sir Donald Gibson at Nottinghamshire Education Authority, over fifty schools were constructed between the period between 1957 and 1970, producing a particular architectural form which combined a lightweight airy aesthetic with robust and extendable forms. Unfortunately, many of the buildings have outlived their natural life span, and are proving difficult to adapt to new teaching conditions. Furthermore they are expensive to maintain.

The task and responsibility of the new men will be to build in sufficient quantity and therefore at an industrial rate, schools first, but not just school buildings but schools for real children, and children who later will travel to the moon; universities different from those under construction at present; houses by the million with their ancillary extensions.[12]

During the 1950s, Jean Prouvé designed prefabricated building elements and structures in France. Prouvé stated that by incorporating advanced methods of prefabricated construction, it would be possible to radically transform the school environment to create more appropriate places in which children learn. Spurred on by the need for large-scale production during the immediate post-war years, he established a factory at Maxéville and developed prefabricated systems which radically transformed the spatial quality of what had previously been viewed as low quality buildings.

His thesis was that a school should display the architecture of the epoch rather than some sort of regressive historical form. The new designs were highly engineered constructions using state of the art methods of fabrication. However, it was necessary to observe higher than average standards of design within his new systems, as the education board were uncomfortable with the idea of prefabrication. Despite much resistance, Prouvé won a competition with his experimental approach, which resulted in two building commissions. He also took part in the construction of schools in some communities headed by enlightened mayors. School buildings constructed at Villejuif in 1953 were made with robust cantilevered structural frames which were propped at the edges, infilled with planar steel frame windows to create extremely elegant and robust buildings.

However, despite their advanced design they were condemned as temporary buildings within fifteen years of their completion. The irony is that many huts with negligible architectural and very little environmental qualities were subsequently built in France which then remained in use much longer than the Prouvé system. Currently many UK local education authorities will still refuse to commission prefabricated buildings because of the stigma attached to the temporary concept. Nevertheless, a number of manufacturers are currently working on the development of factory systems for use as schools.

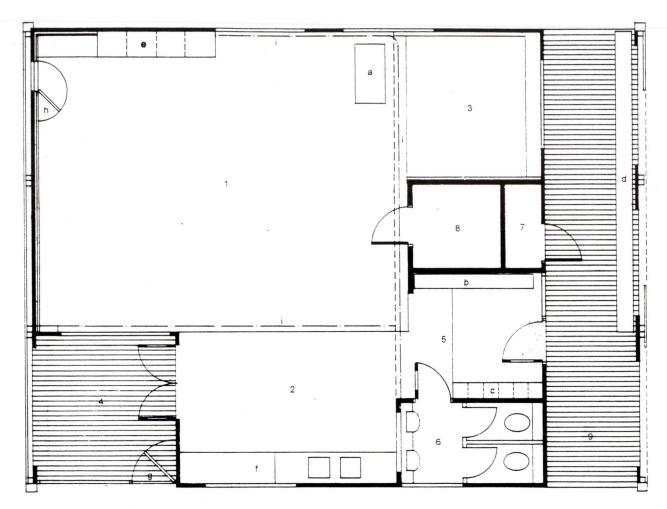

Figure 3.4
Portakabin's 'Academy' modular classroom is laid out to accommodate a diverse range of activities within the framework of a single class group.

KEY:

1	General teaching	7	Boiler	d	External storage
2	Wet area	8	Store	e	Classroom storage
3	Quiet area/book corner	9	Covered walkway	f	Worktop/sink
4	Covered external teaching area	a	Computer station	g	Balustrade and gate
5	Entrance	b	Coats	h	Display board/shutter
6	Toilets	c	Bags	i	Curtain track

The 'Lilliput' Nursery evolved out of a two-year development process and is arguably the first UK system to take the needs of pre-school children seriously, within the framework of a prefabricated system. The design was a joint effort involving the Portakabin technical team headed by development engineer, Chris Hogarth, in collaboration with architects Richard Cottrell and Brian Vermeulen and the author. The conventional Portakabin is an advanced steel framed 'box' system, which is rigid enough to be transported from site with all its finishes in place, including almost everything from plasterwork and light fittings to toilet-roll holders in the bathrooms. Portakabin build prefabricated buildings which have evolved over a number of years; technical problems relating to thermal performance and longevity are not an issue. The system does impose limitations on the design, since

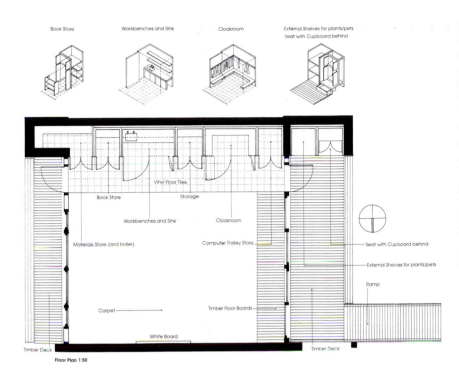

Book Store   Workbenches and Sink   Cloakroom   External Shelves for plants/pets Seat with Cupboard behind

Floor Plan 1:50

Figure 3.5
Plan with storage units. The Community Classroom has been developed as a fully pre-fabricated unit with a range of cladding options which can be altered to suit alternative sites. Designed with a robust steel and timber frame construction, the key architectural device is a storage wall which provides structural stability as well as a neat solution to the perennial problem of classroom clutter.
(© Michael Beeton, Abe Fineberg, Richard Perry, Education Design Group, 4 Westbourne Grove Mews, London W11 2RU.)

the format is dependent on a module of pre-sized rectangular 'boxes' (to enable transportation). These fit together side by side once delivered to the site.

One of the key concerns during its development was the image and appearance of the 'box'; rather than attempting to disguise the Portakabin with a pitched roof or other devices to make it appear like a more conventional nursery building, the design team took the view that the Portakabin 'box' image should, if anything, be enhanced. Children, they felt, would appreciate the caravan-like qualities of the building. The format of the initial prototype comprises four zones: the wet/toilet area, the entrance/play area, the quiet room and a covered play deck accessible directly from the activity area. Storage walls are provided, one within the play/activity area and another externally on the covered play deck. Low windows are fitted which are designed to be safe yet child-friendly. Much of its interior is ergonomically designed specifically with younger children in mind. The first prototype has a yellow external colour with a white slatted rain screen which gives it the striking appearance of fairground architecture. It is bright, gay and thoroughly inviting for children. Yet it actually provides an anticipated forty-year period of maintenance-free life.

The Portakabin prototype was designed as a school reception class for a specific client in Harlow, where 4–5-year-old children were only in attendance during school hours. As such it does not cater for full day-care for younger children. The intention is to extend and increase the range of its facilities to cater for full day-care, if in due course a commission presents itself. However, for the moment, the proposal is a limited yet stylish alternative to a conventional, one-off nursery class. In contrast, the Community Nursery is intended to provide all the benefits of full day-care, part-time education for 3- and 4-year-olds, and after-school facilities within the framework of a single building. The scheme is currently being developed by the Education Design Group (EDG).

Established in 1998, EDG are a collaboration of educationalists and architects working together to produce an integrated childcare package. The initial idea for the building came about through individual members of the group, who recognized the potential of modular hotel bedrooms for adaptation to the needs of nursery education. The hotel bedrooms were constructed in a factory, transported with all their fittings to site, where external brick cladding walls provided a robust external finish. The concept of a nursery made up not of large open plan spaces, as would normally be the case, but of 'cosy' little rooms, like hotel bedrooms, seemed particularly appropriate for the needs of young nursery children.

From this beginning, the concept of a complete package developed incorporating precise costing, advice on staffing levels, ideas about parental involvement, food, sleeping and play. Benefiting from economies of scale, the modular prototype provides a speedy yet high-quality solution to the needs of pre-school care. A radical pre-school care and education strategy, integrated with an economic high-quality building, to fully support the educational philosophy, could in theory be implemented within a period of

Figures 3.6a and 3.6b
The Community Classroom, design development models. Figure 3.6a – section; Figure 3.6b – external view showing a paired arrangement of two classrooms side by side illustrating the storage walls and activity deck in the foreground.

twenty-two weeks from the receipt of an order; all the client requires is the site and the funding. The typical ready-made package provides accommodation for ten babies (0–12 months), twenty-five 1–2 year olds, twenty-five 2–3 year olds and one hundred 3–5 year olds, and space for after-school children. However, it can be adapted for smaller group sizes.

An open approach to parental access is encouraged, which takes the notion of community involvement seriously. The building takes a more continental view of the rights of children, locating a semi-open access kitchen as its communal focus, the symbolic heart of the project where children have access; indeed, it is intended that the children would use the kitchen as a play/education space. Central to its philosophy is the notion that fresh food would be prepared in full view of the children. Perhaps most importantly, all parts of the building will (at certain times of the day) be open to all of the children. It is a socially advanced model where children support and learn from each other and (amongst other benefits) have the right to select the spaces they wish to inhabit.

As with the Portakabin project, the modular principle imposes limitations in terms of the architectural aesthetic. Whereas Portakabin present a design which is clearly and proudly prefabricated, the architecture of the Community Nursery is a little more circumspect. A range of cladding options and alternative roof profiles are offered which allow for a certain amount of customization to each site context. The cladding could either be a shiny metallic rain screen panel, or a heavy masonry parapet wall. The roof is a high performance flat element, which is integral. However, in theory a client can select a roof profile to their own taste, which could be pitched and tiled. Other add-on options include canopies, fences, walls, pergolas and play terraces to suit the needs of the site. It is, states project architect Mike Stiff, a building which will mould itself to the site.

Both of these schemes deal with the problem of appropriateness in different ways; where Goldfinger's Expanding Nursery fails is in its ability to fulfil the needs of young children in providing the context for a variety of learning experiences, both inside and outside. These two projects offer purpose-designed environments for pre-school children with space for movement, small intimate areas for rest and quiet with warm, comfortable child-scale bathrooms. The limitations of the Portakabin Nursery are reflected in its lack of provision for full day-care, and its failure to provide a personal space for adults. However through its quirky design it is 'owned' by the children and organized to be as accessible to the children as possible, promoting their development as autonomous individuals.

Children's centres for care and education

I have already briefly described a German model for pre-school which incorporates designated activity areas for after-school pupils. In the UK the need to provide facilities for children whose parents are still working at the end of school is being increasingly recognized. After-school clubs are often located in existing schools or in shared community buildings. Usually these premises offer a limited range of activities and are of an inappropriate scale and environmental character. Furthermore, children of different age ranges and various developmental stages naturally require distinct kinds of facilities; for example, young children will be happiest playing on the floor whilst older children will be more interested in table-top activities or challenging physical tasks. The possibility for children to appropriate their own space in their own way, the 'my house' pretence, is discounted in environments which are not purpose-made.

A project initiated by the University of Sheffield Schools Research Unit explored the possibility of adapting

Figure 3.7
The Forest Kindergarten, a modular unit designed for location in rural settings in Denmark. As part of an advanced educational curriculum, children make the journey from the main day-care centre to these single units to spend days exploring nature.

and amending existing environments for the temporary use of children as after-school facilities. Activities were identified which were appropriate to different age ranges. A number of these were then interpreted and incorporated into a schedule of temporary installations and storage pods which were capable of being packed and unpacked with ease by the children themselves. Consideration was given to the provision of temporary devices which enclosed or transformed the spatial quality. Fold-away shelters, sight and acoustic screens and climbing frames were devised which could be 'inhabited' by children without physically altering the fabric of the existing building. They enabled children to create 'rooms within rooms', yet also enabled their use as climbing structures, construction exercises, and, in good weather, for use outdoors.

One of the few purpose-designed after-school clubs visited in the UK during the course of this research was a facility for eighty children located in the grounds of Dunblane Primary, Stirling. Architecturally the facility is modest, and on this level does not warrant further comment. However the care leader in charge, who had a close hand in developing the plan, has created a series of niche spaces which can accommodate groups of two to four children playing relatively undisturbed. There is also a private study space for older children with a fully stocked library. The building replaces older temporary stock, and the effect of the new building has been to markedly improve the behaviour of the children who spend time there. It enables undisturbed play to happen with games which can be left out and extended for weeks on end if desired. Its message is in its development; if those who work with the children are involved in the development process, the end result is more likely to be in harmony with the rhythms and needs of all who are involved.

As I write, the government is inviting local authorities and other interested parties to submit proposals for a pilot programme for what they are calling 'Early Excellence

Centres'. Precisely how these centres are to be constituted is very much at a formative stage. What is clear is that a number of functions and concerns, previously unlikely bed-fellows perhaps, must now come together. It is intended that the centres would act as the focus for all other family provision in a particular area or region, providing guidance in best practice across a range of childcare and community functions. In this respect, the government attaches importance to cooperation and partnership rather than competition, and will encourage flexible and innovative approaches.

It can be envisaged that the centres will comprise the usual spaces to service the needs of full-time pre-school children such as kitchens, dining areas and rest spaces. In my view particular emphasis should be placed on food preparation and meal times and their integration into the life of the building. The outside space and its potential as a learning resource should be seriously considered. It might be conceived of as a natural extension of the activity areas themselves. The ecology of the building should be in evidence. It should be designed not just as a comfortable environment, but also as a building which is responsive to climatic conditions, with an overtly responsible attitude to the use of scarce resources in its construction.

Additional functions such as training and assessment should also be accommodated. The need to make provision for the use of the building out of hours, perhaps for local community use, should be developed within the framework of the brief. A sensible extension of the building's use after hours, with additional 'sentry' functions tacked-on, such as after-school clubs and evening classes, can help to protect the building against vandalism. Strategies for providing a broader usage of the nursery site should be explored to encourage more integration of community activities into the childcare environment.

All of this promises to be a heady mixture, requiring levels of control not just by people and curricula, but also in terms of the thresholds and territories defined by the architecture itself. The aspirations of the design team must discuss the project on these levels from the outset. Otherwise the brief will develop as little more than a schedule of accommodation, devoid of any architectural and educational intentions. The design team should bring both educational and architectural aspirations to bear in a constructive way. This will ensure that best practice emerges not just in terms of childcare/education, but also in high quality environments with clearly defined goals and outcomes. Certainly one of the messages to be learnt from the Frankfurt Kindertagesstatte programme, is that architectural solutions should be matched to an educational programme from the earliest stage.

As a centre of early excellence, this building must be a resource base for others, and the local authority of which it is part should provide documentation about its activities for dissemination amongst a wider audience. It should anticipate receiving lots of visitors and their members of staff participating in courses and training elsewhere. The centre should also contribute to authority-wide curricula developments. Accommodating visitors and researchers, providing information and supporting others is demanding, and the obligation to do so needs to be fully understood and budgeted for as well as being planned for in the new building. This will inevitably take a lot of time and energy, but it will also be exhilarating for staff. Without the wider promotional and supportive role of the local authority, the centre will be working in a vacuum.

In order to integrate pre-school children, including perhaps even children up to the age of 6, into a single pre-school institution requires serious funding and a re-ordering of priorities. In many European countries, levels of provision have reached 90 per cent full-time places for children aged 3 to 6 and 15 per cent full-time places for children aged 0 to 3, and the lack of comparable provision detracts from the UK's economic competitiveness. An obsession with health and safety concerns which currently dominates social services regulated provision in the UK, infecting the ethos of many nursery school facilities, must be overcome. This limiting philosophy deadens the life of the pre-school child. A more optimistic concept of well-being, with full-time provision incorporating children's need for regular exercise, a healthy diet and rest, can only be accommodated in buildings which are purpose designed. This holistic view should be central to the ethos of the Early Excellence Centres.

Special needs schools

In a plea to designers to make the school environment fit diverse educational requirements, I wrote earlier that every child has special needs of one kind or another. However, it is clear that some children have more pronounced degrees of need which require special attention. The more extreme ends of the needs spectrum can be defined as those children who find it significantly harder to learn than most children of the same age or those who have a disability which makes it difficult for them to use conventional educational facilities. For example, a child may have learning difficulties caused by a problem with sight, hearing or speech, a physical disability, a medical or health problem and emotional or behavioural problems.

On a recent visit to a special needs school I noticed a child and what appeared to be his teacher walking together within the boundary fence, and approached the pair to ask directions. Before they caught sight of me, the two began to struggle with each other. I watched as the child made off across the playground with his special needs teacher in hot pursuit. Eventually the teacher caught the child and forced him to return to the school. They were

Figure 3.8
The Kompan
Kindergarten, designed
by Helle Grangaard, a
model of early years
excellence: the play-deck.

both struggling violently as they returned. I then went into the school and found the pair sitting happily together. When I asked, the teacher explained that this occurred every day at around about this time. The child had extreme behavioural difficulties, and the ritual was always similar. The child would run away, the teacher would catch him, and then everything settled down. The teacher was clearly offering care and no little love in maintaining this demanding ritual, day after day. She was determined to ensure that the child fitted into a school scenario which fully integrated special needs children into the life of a normal school.

Witnessing this performance underlined to us how extreme behaviour can be within special needs schools of this type. A key challenge is how to integrate more extremely disturbed individuals into the life of the school. The Cleves Primary School in Eltham, London, describes itself as a fully inclusive school, combining special needs children within a radical curriculum structure (see also Chapter 2, p.61 'The Modern Classroom'). The purpose-designed school includes an early years section, and five wings each relating to the curriculum key stages accommodating children up to the age of 11 years. Each wing forms its own private external courtyard. The teaching wings are set out in five main areas: reading, writing, maths, finding out (science, humanities and religious education) and a practical area at the centre of the plan.

Small-group activities are apparent throughout the building as there are no doors except in the pre-school areas. Within each wing there is a quiet room and an office. Communal facilities comprise a sensory room, a fully equipped assembly hall, a gym and a dining area, all of which are used in strict rotation.

The form of the building supports the curriculum very precisely. Indeed, it would be difficult to imagine any other layout supporting this very particular philosophy of education. Unfortunately, the architectural aspirations do not complement its radical layout. Designed by a local architect, the building is of a rationalized traditional form with low quality standardized components. The pitched roof extends beyond the line of the external walls providing covered areas around the edges of the building. However, these prevent the penetration of daylight even on the sunniest of days. This most important aspect of the school environment is diminished. It would be interesting to take this enlightened educational philosophy and match it to an equally responsive architecture. This is a reflection of the current mismatch between educational and architectural aspirations in many new commissions.

Rather than being segregated in distinct institutions which may accentuate their differences, special needs children can be more integrated – indeed, there are evident social benefits. However, without support, in the

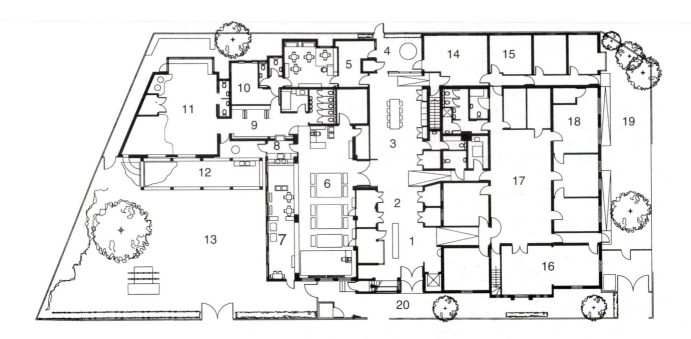

1 - Reception
2 - Toy library
3 - Community space
4 - Courtyard
5 - Meeting room
6 - Nursery main activity area
7 - Art, construction activities
8 - Open access kitchen
9 - Cloakroom/WC
10 - Store
11 - Day care 'house'
12 - Covered play area with
     sand pit & water feature
13 - Outside classroom
14 - Autistic Room
15 - Interview rooms
16 - Social Workers
17 - Croft centre atrium
18 - Assesment Room
19 - Sensory Garden
20 - New combined entrance

Figure 3.9
The Windham Nursery School/Croft Centre, Richmond upon Thames – Early Excellence Centre bid designed by Education Design Group. The scheme integrates two separate institutions: a day nursery and a special needs centre for children with learning difficulties. A new entrance court is created between the two existing buildings which provides a forum where staff, parents and children can share ideas and facilities. (© Education Design Group, 4 Westbourne Grove Mews, London W11 2RU.) Here the aim is to enhance the social lives of all who use the building; this is identified as a key educational objective, an idea which is often ignored in secondary school settings.

shape of both special needs teachers and complementary environments, their progress through the education system will be slow, laboured and potentially disruptive. Frequently there can be a disparity between their physical growth and mental development. Severely mentally handicapped children are usually dealing with a number of associated disabilities. Therefore the environment is a factor which should take into account their need for ease of movement around the building. This places an onus on the provision of group bases which are readily identifiable, so that learning can take place without distractions. A sense of the environment in its totality, incorporating sensory aspects such as sight, touch and aroma should be even more keenly considered. For example, sensory gardens can have considerable therapeutic benefits for mentally handicapped children.

Figure 3.10
Window seat at the Speech and
Learning Centre, Christopher Place,
London. (Photo: © Alan Delaney.)

One of the distinctive gardens I visited in Birmingham was the so-called 'sensory garden' at Highfield Nursery, Saltley. Containing a range of plants and shrubs which provided different colours and aromas all year round, it acted as a constantly changing stimulus to the youngsters. Plant species which are velvety or prickly to the touch, or have a particular aroma such as mint or juniper, are thought to be particularly beneficial for children who have special needs. The Speech and Learning Centre in Christopher Place, London, is confined within a restricted urban site in central London; similarly it optimizes the external spaces, creating two gardens which broaden the experience of planting and vegetation for its city children. There is a robust ivy garden on the ground floor where children use their tricycles. The lush aromatic planting boxes which surround their roof terrace garden contain a variety of plants and shrubs which create a calm, soothing environment right in the centre of London.

The garden is only one important aspect of this environment for the senses, which aids the development of children with varying degrees of speech impairment caused by their hearing difficulties. The centre has places for thirty-two babies and children under the age of 5, who attend on a part-time basis. Described as an assessment and therapeutic centre, it stresses the partnership between parents and the work of the school. It is a building which balances health and safety aspects in a form which encourages social development amongst the parents as well as the children. The building is a self-confessed homage to the Esherick House designed by Louis Kahn in the late 1950s. Architects Troughton and McAslam have taken the house form to create a warm, intimate yet playful building using natural materials which have distinctive textures and colours; thus fair-faced concrete sits next to warm natural timber and smooth white render. Harsh primary colours and synthetic materials such as plastics are avoided.

Kahn's notion of the served and servant spaces is seen in the ground floor plan, where rooms for one-to-one (or two) therapy are articulated by curved walls clad in timber. The shape is then repeated at a larger scale in the group therapy rooms, accentuating the enclosing womb-like form. These spaces provide a solid core to the building, symbolizing the children's need for support and encouragement of the highest quality. Sectionally the three-storey building is divided in two, with a light glazed frontage containing four classrooms and two therapy rooms on the first floor, and offices and assessment rooms on the ground floor. The rear part of the 'slice' contains the toilets, staffrooms and a bright glazed family meeting room with a semi-circular wall, echoing the curves of the therapy rooms. The care and attention to child scale is nowhere more evident than in the large windows on ground and first floors: from the outside there appears to be a window box slung beneath each. Inside, each contains two deep boxes of beech laminated MDF. Thus classrooms are provided with a window seat upon which a child and teacher can sit, and beside it an orange coloured box to store books.

The windows themselves are full height vertical slits opening at the side, safe for children yet allowing good ventilation around the whole room. Most importantly, they enable staff and parents to exchange greetings as they pass through the entrance courtyard. Full height storage cupboards complete the picture of a room which is purposeful and ordered with just a touch of intrigue; what, one might ask, is behind all these panels and doors? A fine balance is struck between a serious heavyweight architecture and one which relates to the senses and playful enquiry of young children; one which avoids the use of overtly playful references which children (and adults) often find patronizing.

At the heart of the Stephen Hawkins Primary School in the London Borough of Tower Hamlets are the building's communal spaces: the open-plan hall and dining room and the more closed library and cookery rooms. There is a hydrotherapy pool, now a prerequisite for any special needs school. Architects Haverstock Associates designed the scheme in such a way that it is readily understandable to the children and staff. A doubly pitched butterfly roof runs over the whole building supported by dramatic steel 'Y' beams. Where the main roof meets the lower mono-pitch, glass clerestory windows allow light to cascade into the heart of the building. The domestic scales often seen in this type of building are avoided; instead, a semi-industrial form is appropriated which is tough and fits the context, a site which is adjacent to one of the main London traffic arteries, in a generally run-down part of the city.

The school caters for children commencing at the age of 2 years, who are accommodated in the enclosed nursery. Beyond its confines, the form of the building opens up to provide accommodation for children up to the age of 11. There is a play frame within the activity area which enables children with mobility problems to pull themselves up to a standing position and move around the space relatively unencumbered. This ethos of mobility is an overriding concept for the design of buildings, which encourages the exploration of their whole environment. However, an awareness of the dangers this entails for some children is dealt with by the installation of a double handle on every door; the theory is that when children have understood and mastered the system, then they will be responsible enough to use the whole school as their zone of learning, and move around more independently.

Primary/elementary schools

Infant schools and junior schools are usually located within the same building, or at least within the framework of a single campus setting. The purpose of this section is to identify distinctive characteristics of the some of the best recent primary school buildings. I also consider strategies adopted in designs for a new primary school in Baden, Switzerland, which integrates itself physically into the urban fabric to become a genuine building for the community.

The difference between the physical and psychological make-up of the school child at the beginning of the primary school process (aged 4 or 5) and at the end (aged 11) is huge. The tendency to treat first-year infants as novices to the whole experience of social relations is one the school designer should bear in mind. Whilst gender separation was abandoned during the 1920s, infants may well benefit from having their own entrance, even their own school, which is separate and distinct from the junior school. On the other hand, access to shared resources, such as music rooms and sports/assembly halls, is necessary where infant schools are not designed with their own assembly and sports facilities. Therefore most new initiatives comprise primary and junior schools forming one coherent entity, the typical format being a seven-class single-form entry for 245 pupils aged 5 to 11, with associated play, sport and work areas. Administrative support spaces such as offices and staff rooms should be closely connected if not fully integrated.

As with nurseries and nursery schools, the definition of territories between different classes and, to some extent, infant and junior schools themselves is essential if the needs of the smallest and most vulnerable are to be properly nurtured. Often, a historical development has come into play, where one section of the primary school received funding some years before the other. This can create completely separate schools designed by different architects a number of years apart. Both buildings share the same grounds, yet are physically and architecturally distinct. Although the dichotomy between two alien architectural forms can be perplexing to young children, the effect is often one which successfully reinforces the difference between the young and the not so young. They both benefit from shared facilities, but must make a short journey across a school landscape to do so.

A recent example of this development process was the King Alfred School in Hampstead, London. Founded in 1898 as a progressive school, the original lower school buildings were designed in 1934 in an advanced modernist style with large steel and glass fold-away shutters to allow the pupils to spill out into the landscape. By 1995 these buildings were crumbling, whereas the older more traditional brick buildings constructed during the nineteenth century remained serviceable. Rainwater was falling

Figure 3.11a
King Alfred School,
Hampstead, London,
interior of classroom; Van
Heyningen and Haward
Architects. (Photo:
© Dennis Gilbert.)

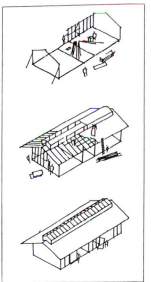

Building the winner in simple stages.

BACK TO SCHOOL FOR COMPETITION WINNER

Van Heyningen and Haward has won a limited competition for the design of school buildings in Golders Green, north London.

Three practices — the others were Chris Wilkinson Architects and Weston Williamson — had been invited by the King Alfred School to prepare sketch schemes for the replacement of the existing buildings which form the lower school.

The winning scheme was based on a strategy which would replace the existing classrooms, two at a time, in the holidays and as funding allows. The school will maintain its present layout, a series of low buildings grouped round a field, which was originally planned by Charles Voysey, a former pupil.

Most of the buildings which are to be replaced were designed by the Modernist E.C. Kaufmann in 1934-5. They are now in poor condition.

The client felt that Van Heyningen and Haward's scheme had the best

chance of being buildable in the brief holiday periods and without snags. The architect describes its design for pairs of classrooms as 'a gentle pitched roof cabin with a wide "eyebrow" for undercover teaching on the field side'. (Outdoor teaching is a tradition of this progressive school.)

Joanna Van Heyningen and Birkin Haward are themselves parents of former pupils of King Alfred's.

The buildings will be timber framed with timber cladding, and floating slab foundations will cope with settlement problems. The brief specified that North London Polytechnic's Low Energy Architecture Research Unit should be used as a consultant.

The proposal by Chris Wilkinson Architects was based on largely prefabricated units of lightweight steel structure, clad with timber. A timber board walk, beneath a fabric canopy, would link the classroom units and double as an external teaching area.

Figure 3.11b
King Alfred School, the
construction process in
simple stages.

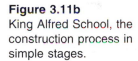

Figure 3.11c
King Alfred School, plan
of a typical classroom
unit.

through the leaking flat roofs of the 'modernist' blocks, and rendered walls were flaking. The architects Van Heyningen and Haward were commissioned with a brief to create a replacement which was sympathetic to the ethos of the original, yet at the same time established a new architectural language, one appropriate to the 1990s. The most fundamental concern related to the eight-week construction programme required by the client in order to fit in with the school's summer vacation.

The architects adopted the form of a series of timber 'pavilion' buildings, paired together providing two classrooms, with shared cloakroom and toilet blocks sandwiched between each. They included a deep, partly covered open colonnade, extending the use of the classrooms into the landscape. This reflects the openness of the original buildings, yet in a more practical way. The new classrooms and library are accommodated beneath a single pitched roof. The eaves hang over to form the colonnades, and create what the architects describe as an ordering structure, under which the messy activities of the school can develop.[13] This principle extends into details of the classroom spaces themselves. The walls are broken up into a grid by strips of wood covering the butt joints of the panels behind. Teachers use this structure to frame the pupils' drawings. The overall effect is a calm, neutral architecture which is in harmony with the more solid Queen Anne styles of the older buildings. Indeed, the system of modular pin-up boards may be carried into other parts of the school, to further enhance this notion of difference within sameness. The pavilions ensure that each pair of classes retain their own levels of autonomy, yet feel at one with the rest of the school campus.

By contrast, the Woodlea Primary School was developed as a single architectural concept, which nevertheless provides the territorial distinctions referred to above, without recourse to separate detached buildings. The development is very much site orientated, which is a picturesque sloping woodland running down from Iron Age earthworks in Whitehill, Hampshire. The aim was to set the building into this magical landscape, without losing the spirit of the place. This is no mean feat given the number of trees which needed to be removed in order to accommodate both the new building and a playing field. The plan of the building closely follows the contours of the land, developing as a variegated crescent shape. Whilst the three infant classes are architecturally part of the whole, they are slightly off-set from the main entrance forming an autonomous wing, protected and sheltered from the activities of the main school.

This separateness is further emphasized by each infant class having its own semi-private entrance immediately off the outside play area. In addition, views from the infant classrooms are orientated diagonally towards the wood and away from the junior school wing. A subtle balance is achieved between the needs of the youngest children to feel secure and protected from the 'big people', yet at the same time maintaining their sense of belonging to the whole school community. From within the building, views of the woodland are composed specifically to enhance the inside/outside relationships. Likewise, the woodland surrounding the site breaks up the scale and form of the whole, providing tantalizing glimpses of the building framed by the trees. The end result is like a forest shelter, in total harmony with its setting. This effect is further enhanced by the use of rustic materials, natural slates for the roofs, stone dressings for exposed parapets and timber cladding for the walls.

The architects of the King Alfred School announce their agenda as one which creates a clarity of structure with the architecture becoming a part of *'the whole learning process'*. A similar statement by Nev Churcher, of Hampshire County Architects, who designed Woodlea, defines the concept as one which enables the children to 'read' the structure, so that the building becomes *an education in itself*. For Churcher, it is important they do not feel overwhelmed by technical concerns. Whereas some of the more overtly modernist designs referred to elsewhere, such as the Queen's Inclosure (also designed by Hampshire County Architects), are more overt in the articulation of their structure, both King Alfred and Woodlea effect a harmonious relationship with their setting. They are, in addition, constructionally legible. The structure at Woodlea is not so much 'exposed', more 'revealed' in a gentle almost playful manner. Its materiality fits perfectly with the picturesque setting, to create a harmony between architecture and space.

Consultants are constantly being prompted to make economies in the design of school environments. Indeed, it is unusual to find entirely new school developments, particularly in existing urban settings. Robin Bishop, Chief Architect at the Department for Education and Employment, A & B Branch, anticipates that by far the greatest demand of architects working in the primary and secondary school area over the coming decade will be to adapt and refurbish the existing school stock. Often minimal interventions can have a marked effect by enhancing the overall quality of a school building. By carpeting classrooms, greening external areas and making other relatively minimal changes, great improvements to the overall spirit of the establishment can be brought about. The effect of a well-designed entrance can, as if by magic, not only provide more space but enhance the whole ambience of a previously dowdy building. I include at least one example of a school environment improved by such interventions (see Case Study 4).

Strategies to bring about new projects within the UK and elsewhere will increasingly rely on partnerships with private developers, or in the case of some secondary and specialist schools, with commercial organizations. I refer to an example of this in the section on funding, where a

Figure 3.11a
Conceptual plan
of Woodlea
Primary School,
Hampshire.

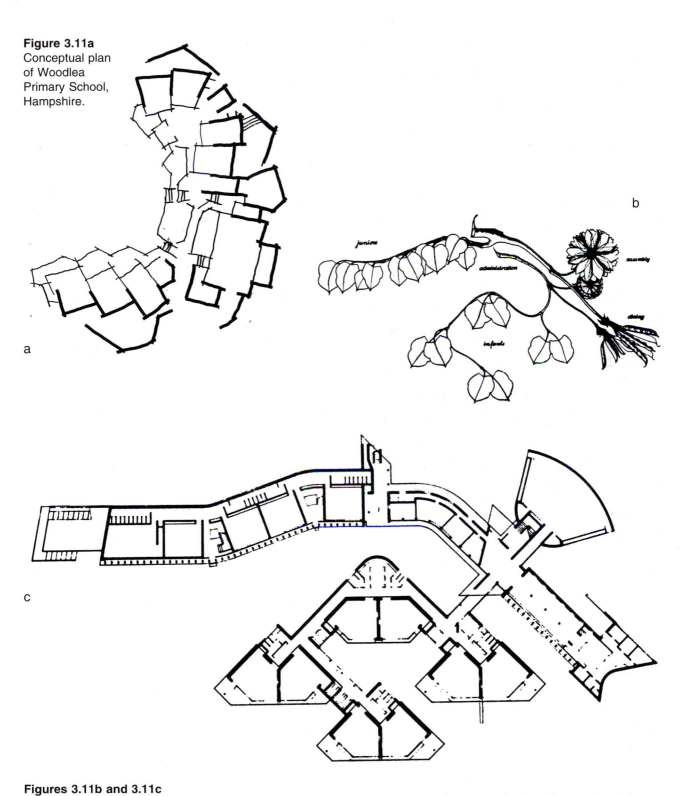

Figures 3.11b and 3.11c
Drawing of plant (Figure 3.11b) as metaphor for the layout of an urban school, Lasdun's Hallfield School, Paddington (Figure 3.11c). From *Denys Lasdun, Architecture, City, Landscape*, William J.R. Curtis, Phaidon Press, London, 1994, p.42.

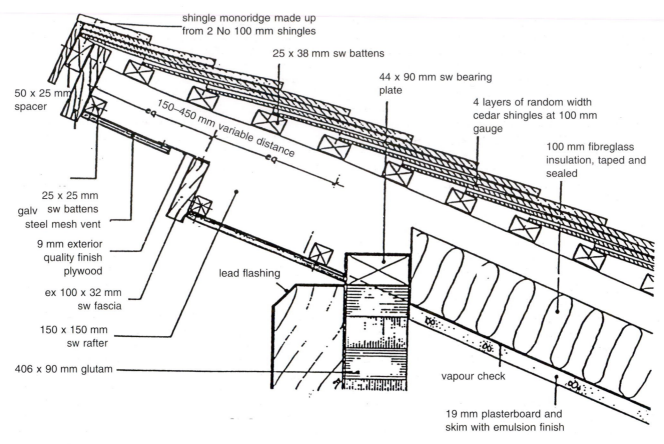

shingle monoridge made up
from 2 No 100 mm shingles

25 x 38 mm sw battens

44 x 90 mm sw bearing
plate

4 layers of random width
cedar shingles at 100 mm
gauge

100 mm fibreglass
insulation, taped and
sealed

50 x 25 mm
spacer

150–450 mm variable distance

25 x 25 mm
galv sw battens
steel mesh vent

9 mm exterior
quality finish
plywood

ex 100 x 32 mm
sw fascia

150 x 150 mm
sw rafter

406 x 90 mm glutam

lead flashing

vapour check

19 mm plasterboard and
skim with emulsion finish

Figure 3.12
Woodlea Primary School, detail section through pitched roof eaves.

developer paid for the construction of a new school and, in return, was granted permission to develop a residential site. Frequently such partnerships create an architecture which is second rate and hardly comparable to the standards achieved by experienced local authority architect's departments. However, new school developments are increasingly funded in this way, an example being the Heritage Park School, sited on the edge of Peterborough, Cambridgeshire. The new school lies at the heart of a large residential development, and has been designed and built to a high standard, by the developer's architects, based on designs by Cambridge County Architects.

Encompassing a two-form entry, the building has a pitched roof and a traditional brick construction. Yet it is tasteful and almost universally admired by staff and pupils alike. For example, the assembly hall has high-quality finishes, with hardwood floors and skirtings, and an acoustic ceiling with an expressed roof structure which provides an attractive combined assembly, dining and sports hall. Additional resource areas, such as a dedicated music room and a generously proportioned drama space, add to the

educational experience. Material qualities have not been compromised by the inherent economies of the system; for example, a gently curving brick wall runs into the entrance area. The detail is subtle yet, to an inquiring mind, sends out the right message, that someone has taken the effort to make the entrance welcoming.

Similarly, rather than adopting the 'developer' approach, and installing the ubiquitous powder-coated aluminium window systems, instead a warm and texturally rich composite timber window/door system was chosen. Architect Mark Benns describes this as being in line with the local authority policy on the use of environmentally sound materials, and confirms that the product *'adds a touch of quality to the building, without sacrificing essential economies.'* All of this raises the so-called developer solution to a level which is above normal expectations.

The only area where economies are questionable in the Heritage Park School is in the combination of two classrooms into what is effectively a single space. The two-form entry is dealt with by the pairing of teaching rooms; consequently there are no corridors. Circulation takes place outside the building by way of external courtyards. This provides more teaching space. However, the effect of having two groups of thirty or more children in one room is questionable. It is an enforced economy which ensures that teaching techniques remain fluid and incident-laden. The large space makes concentration for both teachers and their pupils difficult, being analogous to open-plan arrangements which are highly desirable for some class-room activities, but extremely problematic for others. It will be interesting to see how long it will be before separating walls are introduced. However, the layout makes this amendment feasible.

Like most of the school projects reviewed during the course of this research, the Heritage Park School sits within its own site, largely surrounded by ungainly wire fences. In the wake of Dunblane and other tragic attacks by outsiders both in the UK, the USA and Australia, security has become a crucial issue. Peter Buchanan, in his review of the Hochi-Dattwil complex, a combined primary and special needs school, makes the point that twentieth-century schools are generally designed as the most un-urban of building types. This was the case even before recent security concerns surfaced. However, the school, designed by local Baden architects Burkard Meyer Steiger, is arranged around a public piazza which makes a meaningful urban gesture, helping to integrate the school into the wider (sub)urban fabric: '... *Porticoes on Dattwilerstrasse flank an entrance to a pedestrian route that leads into the piazza and beyond into the suburb. This new entry sequence, and the urbane porticoes that animate and overlook it, confers a certain identity to the settlement to which it leads.*'[14]

The identity is one which recognizes that public buildings have both a front and a back. The parts are divided into three and surround the piazza, taking up the axis of the existing urban blocks which hem the site in on three sides, a memory perhaps of the form and structures of the traditional city. The hall and gymnasium comprise a single self-contained group which can be used outside school hours, almost as a provincial theatre. The primary and handicapped school form the other three sides of this new civic space. Each part has its own distinct entrance; the primary school with its prominent portico leading into a double height entrance loggia is dominated by a formal scissored staircase, beneath which the children must pass in order to enter and rise up through the building. The staff room and principal's offices are strategically placed just off the entrance space to maintain discreet control over the building. The very fact that it has three storeys adds to the sense of efficient urbanity; after all, why shouldn't children be trusted to use stairs and lifts safely, since these hazards are commonplace at home?

Peter Buchanan observes that compared to most new school buildings in Britain, similar European projects are far more lavish in their use of common and circulation spaces. Here they are viewed as important meeting points within the building, adding to the social life of the institution. The corridors open up into balconies overlooking the theatrical spectacle of pupils moving in large, often boisterous groups up and down the staircases. They use the various parts of the building as any city might be used: freely yet under constant discreet supervision. This happens as a factor of the planning – all windows and balconies look out onto the piazza space, which becomes an extension of the field of learning, and a forum for public life: a sort of auditorium in its own right. From the relative privacy of the classrooms and small group rooms, to the publicness of the piazza, a spatial hierarchy is established which enables its pupils to experience different levels of social interaction; in itself a valuable social experience.

The overall effect of this thoughtful strategy is urban. The school is accessible only by foot, as there is no dedicated parking. Parents are encouraged to walk with their children to and from school, enjoying the natural pace of the city and its institutions. More significantly, this organization de-institutionalizes the institution; its seamless integration into the city makes it a place. That place is not one which its citizens necessarily become excluded from after 3.30pm, or indeed when they move onto their secondary school after the age of 11. It becomes an integral part of the city itself, both formally and functionally. The proof of its success can be seen in the way its former pupils return, reusing and reinventing its patterns to suit their own needs. Sadly it is a strategy that would be hard to justify in today's security conscious climate. It is urban but far too open to the threat of stranger danger.

Secondary schools

Many aspects of school design discussed in the context of previous sections apply equally to the secondary school. For example, colour, texture, acoustics, and the principle of defining safe secure territories within the overall structure of the institution, are all concepts which should apply equally to pre-, primary and secondary school settings. The responsibility of the designer to create environments which address these requirements in a balanced and holistic way does not diminish as children grow older. My contention that aesthetic quality is fundamental in establishing an appreciation of their environment, and raising self-esteem, is one which applies throughout the life of the school pupil. Within this final section I analyse four alternative approaches to large-scale high quality secondary schools.

Students are infinitely more mature and independent at the age of 11 or 12 than when they first enter the education system at the age of 3 or 4. Younger children are more

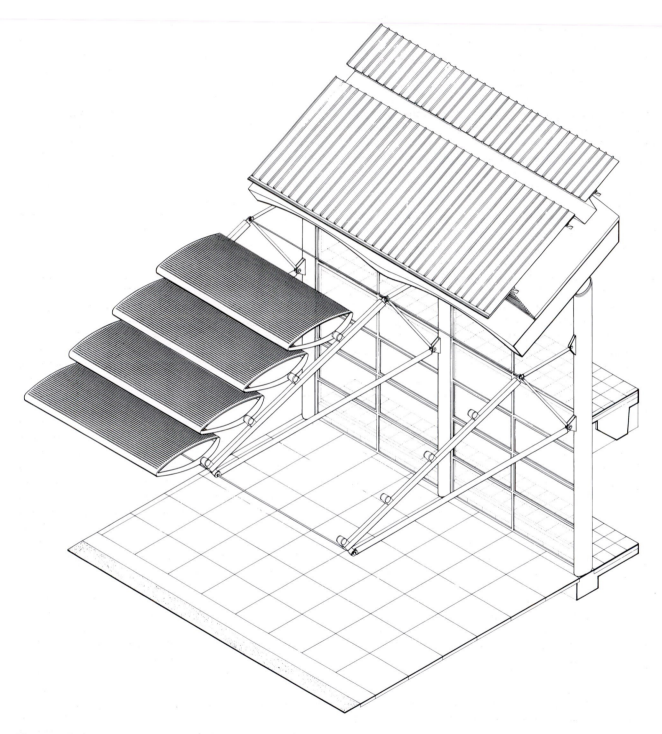

Figure 3.13
Detail of the Lycée Polyvalent designed by Sir Norman Foster and Partners. The structure is intended to be adaptable with, here, sunscreens clipped to the main frame. (© Foster and Partners.)

focused into their immediate surroundings whereas older children will generally be more outward looking, interested in the wider social and spatial environment. Secondary schools are almost always larger both in terms of the physical size of things, and the numbers accommodated. On average they cater for 780 to 1200 students. However institutions dealing with larger numbers are not uncommon. Schools architect Richard Jobson believes that the organization of different subject areas is crucial. The specialized nature of secondary education generally means that children move around the school campus more frequently. Curriculum areas can be organized to minimize travel distances. Jobson states that art and craft departments should be close to the hall to enable the movement of props and scenery; science and technology faculties should be clustered together for similar logistic reasons. Circulation areas should be interesting and spatially varied to reduce conflict during changeover periods.

The new Lycée Polyvalent in Fréjus, France was designed by Sir Norman Foster and Partners and completed in 1994 following a successful competition entry. Constructed in just eleven months within the constraints of a tight budget, the school is used by nearly 1000 students and staff. It is perhaps appropriate that the building is for the training of technical and vocational skills as there is little concern for spatial diversity provided by variations in texture and the use of surface colour. There are no alternative routes around the building except a long straight internal street. This is an exercise in pure unrelenting techno-space, with little or no decorative embellishments; an example of early 'Foster', with everything seemingly subservient to the rigours of the system.

When described in terms of its environmental performance, however, this approach would appear to make very good sense. Fréjus can be very hot in summer, the climatic pattern frequently being stormy: torrential rain can be followed quickly by hot, very sunny intervals. The building section has a central double height 'street' with classrooms on either side. The street is topped by a canopy running the entire length of the building which acts as a solar chimney, heating up in the sun and drawing hot air out through openable vents, by way of the stack effect. The classrooms which are orientated towards the sunny east–west facing side, are protected by a sophisticated system of brise soleil canopies to provide a shaded area in front of the classrooms. They also act as rain canopies. Despite the lightweight nature of its architecture, Foster has used a concrete frame, in order to lend some thermal mass to the structure. This is articulated on the façade by edge vaults clad with metal panelling. This concrete vaulting system is an aid to the environmental control generally, storing heat in winter, and acting as a cooling mass during the summer months.

A similar section runs the entire 243 metres of its length. The spatial quality is very similar to the ITN building, designed by the same practice, which is an office and recording building in London. Why the two aesthetics should be so similar is not clear; however, many of the details, such as the glazed balustrading, are identical. The atmosphere is clinical and a little bland, like an up-market car showroom. One of the teachers made the point that it was a beautifully calm environment within which to work, but mechanistic and humourless. Her observations on the quality of light which reflects from these bland surfaces is telling: '... *the surfaces are so reflective yet colourless, half the time people walk around looking like they are suffering from some sort of anaemic disorder.*' In a sense this is its problem. As a member of staff, you have to walk from one end of the building to the other end where the staff room is located. This is a long walk with little spatial variation to make such a journey interesting.

The Admiral Lord Nelson School, designed by Hampshire County Architects, is similar in scale and form, with an enclosed atrium/street arrangement which the architects describe in shopping centre speak as a 'mall'. This runs the entire length of the plan. The space is generally lively, with a range of activities taking place around and within, to make it much more than a circulation area. However, perhaps more importantly, where the Fréjus project has a street/atrium which is straight, here the Hampshire County Architects Department have introduced a gentle curve to the form, which adjusts its scale to a more human level.

The nature of its site was one of the key determining factors in the so-called banana-shaped plan. The ground is low-lying, just above sea level, facing a sea estuary a few hundred metres to the east. The level of the site was raised a nominal height above sea level and to avoid having to import a large volume of fill, raised foundations were installed from a platform which subsequently became the formation level for pile caps and ground beams. Drainage was also laid within this level before pre-cast floor slabs were installed, finished with a topping slab which was power floated to receive the final finishes. This proved to be an economical form of construction.

The superstructure is divided centrally by a glazed mall on a north–south axis, and three-storey classroom blocks to the east interconnected internally by balconies and staircases. Externally, each floor has a sun terrace which allows rapid evacuation to the three escape staircases. The mall is covered by a curving lightweight roof supported on structural steelwork. The glazing is designed to provide adequate natural daylight, whilst avoiding excessive heat gain. On the west side of the mall, large spaces for music/drama, gym and sports are located together with dividing partitions to aid flexibility. There is a two-storey administration block with kitchens and the assembly hall to the west. Initially a courtyard solution had been suggested; however, the 'banana shape' solved the constraints of the servicing and soil conditions, maximizing green areas for playing fields, with minimum land wasted around the rear service side of the building.

The strategy for the design of the engineering services also played a significant part in determining the form. The designers wanted to provide a high level of environmental control using passive means wherever possible. This included a structural mass and distinctive cantilevered concrete soffits on the south-facing façades, to facilitate natural shading. The orientation of the mall and the perimeter classrooms was specifically selected to maximize daylight and provide the best teaching conditions with good natural daylight to all parts of the school. The heating plant and low energy light sources also form part of the energy strategy.

Environmental conditions within the teaching block are tempered by natural cross-ventilation through openings in the glazed east wall of each classroom, which is exhausted out into the mall. This is in turn ventilated by the stack effect created through high-level openings in the great glazed roof. The openings are orientated to maximize the benefits of local breezes coming off the sea. The use of the central mall as a semi-external zone onto which the perimeter classrooms are ventilated creates high levels of through ventilation. However, one teacher commented that sometimes this ventilation becomes so fierce that papers fly around the room.

Despite environmental dexterity, here it was the architectural qualities which impressed. The building was designed to be low energy, low maintenance and eco-friendly. Light floods through the central atrium bringing life to the mosaic floor which can be seen three storeys below the access decks. The floor design was inspired by a map of the local Langstone Harbour mud flats. The space has been further enhanced by the introduction of stunning wall-mounted collage models and a dramatic thirty-foot relief of a human figure produced in the art department. It is a space full of life and energy. This is particularly evident at lesson change-over times. From a vantage point high above, children can be seen flooding across its length. They are waving and shouting at us and at each other, yet good acoustics and sufficient volume within the volume never create a disorderly atmosphere. This is no mechanistic school of the future. It is rugged, part ship, part ark, actively inspiring its staff to provide high quality education within a diverse range of spaces. As headteacher Dianne Smith commented, it was the 'wow' factor we wanted to elicit when first entering the atrium. This is the heart of the school with all the classrooms like little houses along a street, constructing a perfect foil to the great internal street.

Another Hampshire school which features an unheated glazed arcade is the Crestwood Secondary at Eastleigh. The roof spans between two eccentrically curved buildings which house the school accommodation. However, it is open at both ends. According to the caretaker, the arcade is a useful addition providing areas for concerts and other social and community events that take place during the summer. Apart from the problem of low temperatures during the winter months a significant problem is birds, which become trapped inside the arcade. The mess they cause has put a stop to its use as a venue for lunchtime eating. Despite this, the undoubted strength of the scheme is the links it encourages with the local community. Circulation through the arcade follows on directly from adjacent shops. There are community rooms off the space, which are open and available during the weekends.

Based upon these three examples, it is apparent that the concerns of the secondary school designer are directed predominantly towards the environmental issues which will be explored more fully in Chapter 4. The size and consequent costs of a new secondary school building means that any area of cost savings which can be gained by a positive environmental strategy should be considered. It will pay back over subsequent years. However it is also the refreshing concern for the future well-being of our planet that this should be the case. A project which works on this basis and on other more community-centred principles is Brampton 2000. It is an appropriate point at which to complete this section.

The project comprises a long-term strategy not only to transform a failing educational community, but to do this by way of evolutionary improvements to the existing buildings and surrounding environments. The architects Initiatives in Design won the commission on the basis of a combined business plan and a so-called vision statement. This addressed the problems of the existing school buildings, proposing their subsequent development over a period of some thirty years. The strategy also activated a series of funding 'pots' which would enable the whole area to benefit from a general upgrading of the landscape and associated buildings. This was the essential concept in the success of their pitch.

The location is in the heart of the London Borough of Newham, in a neglected area of land around which seven disparate community facilities were located including a hospital, a leisure centre and the large secondary school. Isolated from each other by old refuse tips, they were also cut off from their surrounding residential areas by major trunk roads and a sewage outfall pipe. 'Brampton 2000 – Creating Access' was the first and instrumental factor in the overall improvements to the school which would enable its integration into the community. Not only was the central wasteland transformed, but the worn-out school buildings would be transformed into an exemplar of a community-centred school for the twenty-first century.

The project achieves major improvements to the quality of the education by facilitating easier movement around the disparate parts of the campus. At its heart there is a new pedestrian street providing a ready link to the fifty-five new classrooms planned for the north-east section of the site. Within the secondary school curriculum, specific

Figure 3.14a

Figure 3.14b

Brampton 2000, before
(Figure 3.14a) and after
(Figure 3.14b).

lessons are functionally specific to particular rooms. However, lesson times cannot be too long, so the overriding need was to reduce travel distances and make circulation around the complex labyrinthine campus more fluid. As project architect Alan Brown explains, by relocating key functions such as the library and restaurants to the middle of the plan: '*... the centre of gravity of the site is shifted and a clear hierarchy is created which enables children and staff to understand the building, not just as a system, but as a three dimensional landscape within which they can feel comfortable.*'

Glazed screens are introduced to corridors so that transparency between the classrooms and common parts is increased, suggesting a more open-plan office-type environment that appears to work quite well at this educational level. Place trust in the students, suggests Brown, and they will be happy to work independently, with teachers acting as intermittent guides. This is a theme reinforced by architect John Waldron of Architecture PLB who designed and built a number of landmark school buildings in Jersey. He contends that in the future, the number of secondary school teachers, who are the major cost in any school budget, will be reduced. Information and communications technology will be exploited, with lessons held in lecture theatres hosting fifty to sixty children at any one time. The communication of ideas and facts will be in the style of higher education. The teacher's role will be limited to occasional group seminars and the organization of the system.

Waldron predicts that the school of the future will become more office orientated, adopting multi-media technology and distance learning. This will transform the way children learn and the nature of their educational environments. Aiden Boustred, who has carried out a dissertation on the subject of computing in school, takes a more circumspect view.[15] Whilst he accepts that more learning will take place via the computer, he believes that the 'virtual classroom' will have to be much more than the talking head of the teacher appearing on the child's screen. This negates the importance of interaction with their peers, learning from their achievements and mistakes. He predicts advances in technologies such as voice recognition, head and eye tracking and video display technology will make it likely that the current 'desktop on a TV' interface will be replaced by something more intuitive and varied.

The integration of technology is the challenge that must be taken up by the next generation of school designers and educators. Perhaps more importantly, the school will become a twenty-four-hour resource available for the whole community. This will transform schools into buildings which are actively sought by the young. As a consequence, education will be viewed as user-friendly and accessible. Only by becoming truly community oriented, as is the vision for Brampton 2000, will funding flow in to rehabilitate the current run-down secondary school stock within the UK.

Summary

This chapter began with Will Hutton's introductory quotation which emphasized the importance of funding education properly. It never ceases to surprise, how lavish the average high street bank can be, compared with the generally dilapidated and second-rate quality of so many school environments within the UK at present. The science of selling a product or a commercial service has reached a level of sophistication within a society largely driven by economic pragmatism. It is recognized that the environment within which this activity takes place has a crucial role to play. Hence the provision of high quality finishes, sophisticated lighting and fluid ergonomics. It will help to sell the product.

The value of architecture for its own sake is rarely linked to positive educational outcomes. It is more readily identified with financial profligacy. The values that bring this about are clearly entrenched within the social framework, and may take generations to transform. Schools, particularly within the UK, appear to be profoundly introspective institutions, and whilst education is rarely fun, it is clear that until the school becomes more user-friendly and gains value in the minds of the majority, poor funding and poor quality will go hand in hand. The alarming comment of one headteacher I spoke to, that we are 'custodians' of the children in our care, is a troubling perception. It can be anticipated that the more educated the populace become, the more open and democratic the modern school will be, to transcend these reactionary views.

Designers can begin to redress the balance by developing a service which optimizes the value of the school site for the whole community. Simplistic philosophies are inappropriate. The science of education is one where the developing aesthetics of childhood must be complemented by an altogether more intriguing range of spatial qualities. As stated in Chapter 1, the Soane Museum is one of the most child-orientated spaces in terms of its educational value. It achieves this by combining a clearly articulated architectural layout with intriguing child-height distractions. It incorporates humanity into ideals of simplicity. The kind of challenge evoked by spaces of this nature lifts the experience of education out of fickle fashion into something altogether more interesting and enduring. These are the values to which schools architecture should aspire.

In Chapter 2 I referred to a number of classroom environments at primary level which were over-decorated; fixed distractions such as windows and doors placed within the field of vision could draw the child's focus of attention away in a negative manner. Having spent much time observing secondary school pupils, I believe that classroom distractions should be minimized. Social interaction between secondary school students is all very well in principle – unfortunately I have observed the negative learning environment in the form of classrooms which are too open. Such are the difficulties caused by even mildly disruptive students that any form of concentration is difficult for those who wish to learn. My view, admittedly as an informed school architect (rather than an educationalist), is that classrooms should in some cases actively prevent social interaction. The notion of the classroom as a machine for learning is not a negative one; it is a concept which views the time spent in school as precious. We should ensure that all children optimize educational opportunities.

The effects of social interaction in other parts of the school environment have not been well studied. However, outside the classroom it would appear that features which encourage good social interaction between differentially aged children can be very positive '... *highly stimulating, perhaps even stressfully so, environments seem to promote greater cognitive development especially if the organism is allowed to freely explore.*'[16] Beyond the classroom, the best schools become a sort of aquarium within which children float, stimulated within a warm friendly atmosphere. Inhibiting this sense of freedom for reasons such as health and safety, fears of bullying and difficulties of control, are the greatest limitations to the well-balanced school environment. School students, like any community of people, learn as much from each other outside the classroom as they do from their lessons. This notion of community was central to the original thinking of the early educators, such as John Dewey.

In this chapter I have illustrated how good architecture can significantly enhance the experience of education. In practical terms this does not simply mean the provision of minimal comfort conditions. It requires architects to go further. To use playful distraction in pre- and primary school settings and at secondary school level to encourage meaningful social interaction between students and their teachers by providing pleasant social areas. By considering the wider urban environment architects can help to integrate schools into the community and develop mutually supportive structures. Well-designed buildings stimulate the users to be more spatially aware, by making the design process interactive and inclusive of the community which it will serve. The work of many of the designers featured within the case studies show that today, perhaps more than ever, schools need architects.

Notes

1   Hutton, Will, *The State to Come,* Vintage, London, 1997, p.16.
2   Young, Hugo, 'Tony Blair: Turning Leadership into an Art Form', *Guardian*, 1 October 1997.
3   Esther Dyson is chairman of EDventure Holdings, New York and author of *Release 2.0: A Design For Living in The Digital Age.* Her comments published in the *Guardian*, 7.1.98, encourage the Internet to be used in this way. A focus group of parents express concern that they have limited contact with their children's teachers: 'All four of the parents [who were consulted], hardly rich people, have computers at home. All of them would like better communications with their children's teachers, but no one had ever thought of sending e-mail to a teacher.' Where do teachers get the time to respond?
4   Bidtrube, Vibeke, *Children and Square Theatres,* Paedagogisk Bogklub, Copenhagen, 1993.
5   Kindertaggestatte literally translates as 'Children's Day-Care Centre'.
6   Peter Wilson quoted from Dudek, Mark, *Kindergarten Architecture,* E. & F.N. Spon, London, p.79.
7   Areas per child in the Frankfurt project equate to approximately 6.8 m² per child and Westborough 2.3 m² per child. The 1989 Children's Act section 10 sets minimum space requirements for 'set floor areas' per child as follows: under 2 year olds, 3.7 m²; 2–3, 3.2 m²; 3–5, 2.3 m².
8   Malagasy, 'For an education based on relationships.' *Young Children*, NAEYC, November 1993, pp.10–12. Referred to in Penn, *Comparing Nurseries,* Paul Chapman Publishing, London, 1992.
9   The government's Early Years Development Plans are now complete, as are the first of 25 planned Early (years) Excellence Centres. However the architectural qualities of these facilities are far from excellent. Refer to 'Co-ordinate', the Journal of the National Early Years Network, article by Dudek 'Going-up' p.8, Issue 75, January 2000.
10 One of the Government's new initiatives is the 'Sure Start' programme. Funded to the tune of £540 million, it will focus on pre-school children and their families and initially covers 125,000 socially disadvantaged children. The government plans to open 250 centres over three years commencing in January 2000. Existing buildings such as clinics, schools or community centres will be used and extended.
11 Dudek, Mark, *Kindergarten Architecture,* E. & F.N. Spon, pp.36–37.
12 Prouvé, Jean, 'Prefabrication.' In Benedict Huber and Jean-Claude Steinegger (eds), *Structures and Elements,* Pallmall Press, London, 1971.
13 Welsh, John, 'School of thought', *RIBA Journal*, July 1993, pp.28–29.
14 'Pedagogic piazza', *Architectural Review*, Schools Special 1991, pp.58–59.
15 Boustred, Aiden, 'Computing in schools.' University of Sheffield School of Architecture Diploma Dissertation, July 1999.

16 Saegert, Susan, 'Stress inducing and reducing qualities of environments.' In Prohanski, Ittelson and Rivlin (eds) *Environmental Psychology – People and their Physical Settings,* Holt Rinehart and Winston, New York, 1976, p.219. However, if there is not enough space and circulation around the school site this brings older children into conflict with younger school students, and the effect can be extremely detrimental.

4

The community in school and the school in the community

Introduction

In the make-up of these complex organisms, design decisions can rarely be made in isolation. The architect is often faced with difficult choices ordering competing priorities within the limitations of tight budgets. The inclusion of one feature may by necessity exclude another. Aesthetic values, whilst important to designers, are sometimes difficult to justify when schools are faced by other schools in the competition for funding. Teachers are mainly guided by their own theories on education, which on the whole take little account of architecture and space. The views of architects are often deemed irrelevant within the framework of a more general educational debate.

In this chapter I consider various aspects of the school environment and its operational structures which generally lie outside the concern of the classroom teacher. On the most basic level, they do not carry explicit academic weight, as they do not relate to the National Curriculum. Nevertheless, I will argue that these 'add-ons' are of great educational and therapeutic value to children and their teachers – indeed for the community as a whole. For example, ecologically sound design can create buildings which communicate important social values. The addition of a well-located swimming pool or a sports hall can open the institution to the public and thus enhance its value to the wider community.

External areas, environmental comfort generally and the role of a specific space, the assembly hall, will be considered in this section. Not only can these areas contribute significantly to the well-being of the school community, they can also transform the architecture into a pedagogical 'instrument' in its own right.

We also include a section on the changing funding and procurement processes within the UK at present. This will enable school clients to understand the procurement processes which lead to new and improved school sites.

Figure 4.1
Atrium at Admiral Lord Nelson School, Portsmouth, a large entrance/circulation area which is often used for community events. (© Greg Moss.)

Figure 4.2
Whilst aesthetically pleasing, the reality of many schools designed during the 1950s is problematic, with overglazed facades and low levels of isulation their natural life span has come to an end.

We begin with a brief analysis of the energy-saving context within which school designers must currently operate:

> *Schools in the UK spend approximately £400 million a year on heating and cause the production of 6 million tons of carbon dioxide.*[1]

As previously stated in Chapter 1, the open-air school movement was a response to unhealthy living conditions within the cities of the nineteenth and early twentieth centuries. However, the cleansing effects of fresh air and sunlight within the school environment were often taken to extremes. For example, the use of badly fitting full height folding and sliding windows could create near-Arctic conditions during the winter months. Conversely, orientation which was mainly southerly, to take full benefit of sun penetration, created glaring or overheated environments, even on mildly sunny days.

During the 1940s and 1950s the notion of progressive education seemed to fit neatly with the utopian spirit of modern movement architecture with its emphasis on prefabrication and flexibility. Large areas of glazing often went hand in hand with inadequate levels of heating and ventilation to create extremes of temperature and environmental discomfort. For example, a minimum 2 per cent so-called daylight factor was introduced as a statutory requirement for all new school buildings with a memorandum recommending 5 per cent where possible. This tended to exacerbate the problem of overheating. Linked to the use of untested, lightweight factory technology newly introduced by the construction industry, problems within schools built at the time soon emerged.[2] Even as I write, many school communities up and down the country are still making do with these out-dated forms.

Today, the quest to build environmentally sound new schools and to find ways of upgrading existing educational buildings to provide a satisfactory level of comfort is one of the most important aspects of the school designer's remit. One of the major concerns lies in the need to improve existing buildings. How do architects rectify difficult conditions, without resort to total demolition of what are robust and serviceable structures? Often piecemeal strategies are adopted for upgrading those parts of the building fabric which can be readily replaced during the school vacations, for example: new high performance flat roof membranes; double-glazed windows; window and door panels made with environmentally sound high performance reconstituted timber sections; and the replacement of old uneconomical heating systems. These can all go some way towards remedying the comfort problem.

However, more radical approaches, where the overall strategy for environmental comfort is viewed in a holistic way, will almost always be more effective in the long term. For example, a nursery school in Richmond, west London which was originally built in the 1930s as a community health centre, had large single-glazed metal window frames which were in a serviceable condition, yet tended to be draughty and cold during the winter months. Due to high fuel costs the problem was becoming critical. A replacement system of plastic coated aluminium windows appeared to be the most economical solution. A bid was made for money to construct a new 'lean-to' conservatory on the cold north façade to provide more play space for an expanding school role. This effectively acted as a 'wrap' which insulated the large windows in the winter, allowing the space to remain cool and ventilated during the warm summer months. As well as providing additional space, the well proportioned interior of the original building was thus preserved, whilst the environment was brought up to modern standards. A longer-term review of the institution's needs enabled the school to make a virtue out of a vice.

Another recent example of a school with poor comfort conditions due to its age that was reconfigured rather than rebuilt is the Crookham Junior School, Hampshire. Designed by Edward Cullinan Architects in 1995, it required the unusual refurbishment of a system-built school, originally constructed in 1963. The structure suffered from poor insulation, fabric deterioration and failing roof membranes. Rather than adopting the usual piecemeal approach, a strategy was devised which dealt with the building as a whole. Initial research established the reason for the failing fabric and the building was made watertight. Following further research into all aspects of its performance, other elements were replaced, upgraded and redesigned on a priority basis. For example, in order to retain night heat, large south-facing roof lights with ply baffles were installed. Not only did they boost daylight levels at the rear of the deep plan classrooms, they also increased the flow of ventilation through the spaces without sacrificing heat efficiency. Their introduction became a key strategic decision which improved the psychological comfort of the whole building.

Here a critical evaluation of the classroom environment brought the designers to their roof light solution. One important factor was identified as the need for more natural light in the classrooms; reduced window areas

combined with dark, non-reflective surfaces produce a reliance on electric lighting, which is almost universally fluorescent. This is often wearing, particularly for teachers, who may find they spend their entire working day within the confines of their classroom. The roof lights designed by Cullinan's are more primitive than proprietary makes, but in this particular situation are deemed to be of educational benefit to the pupils as well as facilitating appropriate levels of light and ventilation. With their rope and ratchet opening mechanisms they are child-friendly in a Heath Robinson manner, allowing the children to see (and hear) the workings of the parts.

Thus a subtle but important new aspect is added to the environment, which empowers the children to understand and relate to their building. They begin to impose active rather than passive environmental control systems, an exemplification of education in action. The roof lights are one of a range of integrated improvements to the building which have been made, allowing up to 50 per cent savings in energy, and a complete transformation of its spatial quality.

Energy lessons from school

When the States of Jersey were considering strategies for a range of new schools to be built on the island, they commissioned architects Plincke, Leaman and Browning (Architecture PLB) with a brief which emphasized environmental criteria. Since Jersey imports all of its fossil fuels, this was a sensible approach to take. However, the environmental aspects included much more than financial considerations. The enlightened client sought to encourage a holistic approach which would incorporate aesthetic pleasure within the environment as an essential part of the educational experience: '... *a sense of light, space and visual stimulation should be immediate from without and within. The environment should not be repetitive but provide changing experiences in colour and form.*'[3]

The architects further developed themes from their earlier work, notably their Tanbridge House School in Horsham, West Sussex. There, the school forms were fragmented and articulated as a set of separate linked buildings, with each part serving a different curriculum area, creating what Director John Waldron calls a 'village' of linked buildings. In a similar manner to their new Jersey College Preparatory School for Girls, the elements of the overall composition are laid out in a south-west facing arc, cut into the ground of the sloping exposed Mont Millais hillside at the eastern inland edge of St Helier. This maximizes both solar and wind orientation and the geometry of the occasional views across the bay. The final result appears to be much smaller and child-oriented than it actually is, with a reduced physical impact upon the surrounding environment.

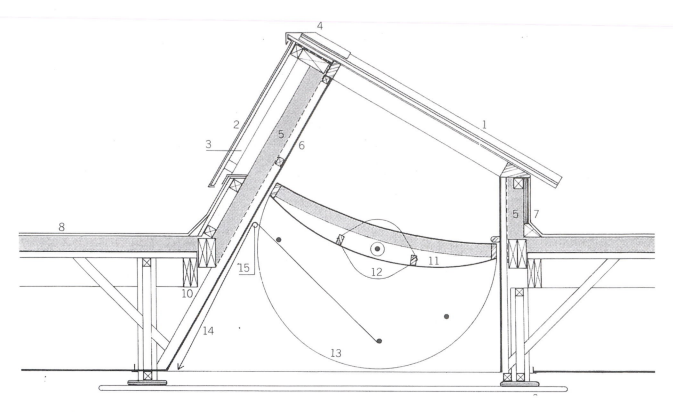

Figure 4.3
Rooflight detail at the refurbished Crookham Junior School, Hampshire.

KEY:

1   6 mm wired glass in proprietary glazing bars with lead flashing
2   Built-up weatherproof membrane on felt painted with solar reflective paint on 19 mm wbp plywood sheeting over breather paper
3   Ventilation space
4   19 mm wbp plywood fixed to treated softwood frame
5   100 mm glass fibre insulation quilt with polythene vapour check
6   12.7 mm plasterboard on 38 × 44 mm battens painted gloss
7   Built-up weatherproof membrane dressed to 19 mm wbp plywood kerb on softwood framing
8   Chippings on high performance felt over minimum 70 mm cork insulation to falls on new wbp plywood
9   19 × 200 mm mdf supported by timber batten hung from joist painted gloss
10 Twinned 150 × 50 mm softwood joists
11 Revolving shutter 8 mm plywood facing on plywood former and 150 mm glass fibre insulation quilt
12 30 mm diameter stainless steel spindle and casing in 14 gauge stainless steel plate
13 19 mm birch plywood
14 Waxed nylon rope
15 Stainless steel pulley

The latest to be completed as part of the sequence of new schools on Jersey designed by the same practice is a large secondary school for 750 students. The sophisticated approach developed here is worthy of analysis. The Haute Vallee School at Mont l'Abbe near St Helier, whilst building upon PLB's previous experience, included a whole range of expert consultants during the design development period. The initial fear was that incorporating expert advice to this extent was tantamount to design by committee. Three different consultancies were employed to advise on energy and thermal optimization alone. A daylighting consultant was used, and separate ventilation, acoustics and even aeronautical research on wind were incorporated. At times the input became an organizational nightmare for project architect Richard Jobson. However, the design of passive low-energy architecture requires a subtle balance.

That balance is evident in the sophisticated system of user-friendly controls which adjust the internal environment to take maximum advantage of the changeable temperate coastal climate. Shading devices have been carefully designed in order to control solar heat without restricting the penetration of too much daylight. Here the challenge for designers was how best to enable the build-

Plate 1
The main courtyard façade, The Speech and Learning Centre, Christopher Place, London. (Troughton and McAslam. Photo: © Peter Cook.)

Plate 2
Exterior view of Seabird Island School showing the rich and powerful form which appears to be in a harmonious relationship to its physical setting. (Patkau Associates. Photo: © James Dow.)

Plate 3
Exterior view from the woods of Strawberry Vale School.
(Patkau Associates. Photo: © James Dow.)

Plate 4
Typical classroom interior, Strawberry Vale School.
The adjacent classroom block and the rocky outcrop are
framed by this dramatic corner window, which forms a
cosy reading corner. (Patkau Associates. Photo: ©
James Dow.)

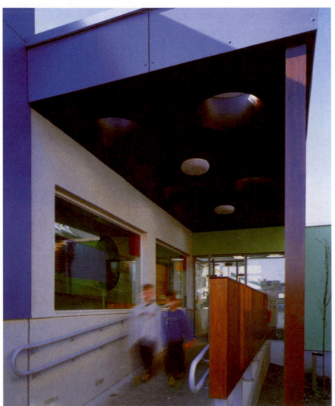

Plate 5
Access ramp and canopy to the new nursery unit, Westborough Primary School,
Westcliff-on-Sea. The architects deal with entrance as a critical symbolic and
functional threshold between existing and new parts in all their school buildings.
(Cottrell & Vermeulen Architecture. Photo: © Paul Ratigan Photo/Graphics Ltd.)

Plate 6
Resources area with coordinated furniture, Woodlea Primary School, Bordon, Hampshire. The level of transparency through the interior varies between closed classrooms and more communal group and circulation areas. (Nev Churcher, Hampshire County Architects. Photo: © Tony Weller/The Builder Group Library.)

Plate 7
Despite the post-modernist form and neutral materials, a human scale is retained at the Anne Frank School, Papendrecht, The Netherlands. (Photo: © Architectuurstudio Herman Hertzberger.)

Plates 8 and 9
The external form is created by a complex geometric relationship between the plan and the vertical circulation, The Bombardon School, Almere, The Netherlands. Details of the fenestration relate quite precisely to the human child-sized scale of its users, in a modern industrial aesthetic. (Photo: © Architectuurstudio Herman Hertzberger.)

Plate 10
Resource and library area with vivid zebra skin decorations, Pokesdown Primary School, Bournemouth. (Milton Forman. Photo: © Charlotte Wood.)

Plate 11
Interior of a classroom in use, Ranelagh Multi-Denominational School, Dublin. (O'Donnell and Tuomey. Photo: © Dennis Gilbert VIEW 14 The Dover Centre, 109 Bartholomew Rd, London NW5 2JB. 020 7284 2928.)

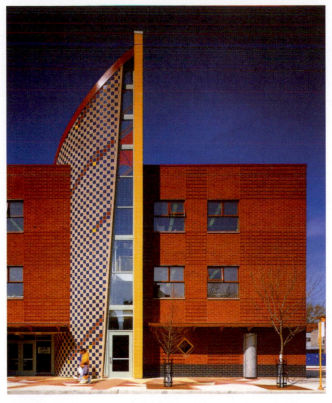

Plate 12
Vibrant decorative tiles wrap round the external
curved staircase wall embedded in the city block,
Little Village Academy, Chicago, Illinois. (Ross, Barney
and Jankowski Architects. Photo: Steve Hall © Hedrich
Blessing.)

Plate 13
The staircase contains a big red sundial which has
been adopted as the key motif for the new school,
Little Village Academy, Chicago, Illinois. (Ross, Barney
and Jankowski Architects. Photo: Steve Hall © Hedrich
Blessing.)

Plate 14
Glazed entrance hall with main staircase,
dramatically structured to reflect the
uneasy geometry of the building's plan,
Saint Benno Catholic Secondary School,
Dresden. (© Behnisch & Behnisch.)

Plate 15
Sports hall interior with exposed industrial-style metal roof and laminated timber roof beams gently curving up towards the ventilated north-west elevation to create natural air movement throughout the year, Haute Vallée School, Jersey. (© Architecture PLB, Winchester.)

Plate 16
View from lowest level 3 showing the main playground with the castle in the background, Elementary School, Morella, Spain. (© Carme Pinõs.)

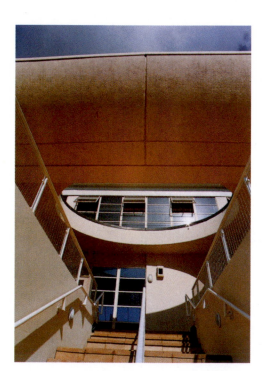

Plate 17
The architecture at Admiral Lord Nelson Secondary School, Hampshire, has a strong horizontal emphasis with the accentuated cantilever supporting projecting terraces; it appears like a grandstand overlooking the landscaped areas to the south, it's immense scale stating unequivocally the importance of the educational environment. (Hampshire County Architects. Photo: © Paul Carter.)

Plate 18
Internal corridor gently curving, full of afternoon sun, Heinz Galinski School, Berlin. (Zvi Hecker. Photo: © Michael Kruger.)

Plate 19
The two-storey colonnade provides classrooms and science rooms linked by the covered route, North Fort Myers High School. The media centre roofs touch the colonnade without disturbing its symmetry. (Perkins & Will. Photo: Nick Merrick © Hedrich Blessing.)

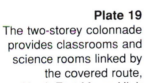

Plate 20
The entrance foyer is at the end of the new block, Albert Einstein Oberschule, Berlin. Note the structural grid marked by the row of columns delineating the site boundary, and the 1950s buildings behind. (Stefan Scholz. Photo: © R.Görner.)

Plate 21

The interior atrium, Barnim Gymnasium, Berlin, a circulation and social space sandwiched between the outer wall of classrooms constructed in brick and the inner world of the white-rendered science and art rooms. The heavy exposed concrete ceiling structure is lightened by the introduction roof light, some as circular domes, and some as edge strips articulating the horizontal and vertical planes. (Stefan Scholz. Photo: © Ulrich Schwarz.)

Plate 22

The architecture is surprisingly domestic in scale considering the size of the building, Waldorf School, Chorweiler, Cologne. (Photo: © Peter Hübner.)

Plate 23

The image is of a tree house straddling the ground and the branches, an appropriate metaphor for education, Odenwaldschule, Frankfurt. (Photo: © Peter Hübner.)

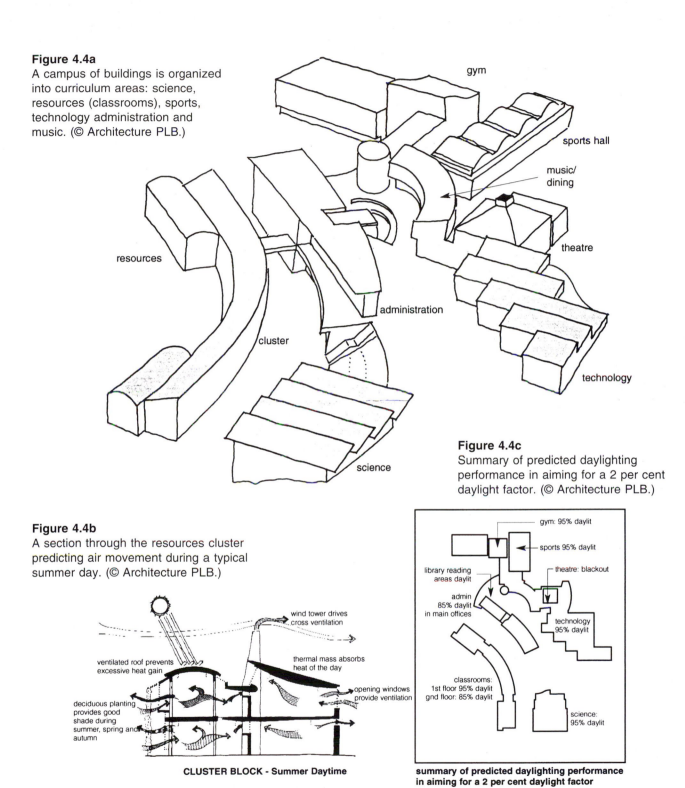

Figure 4.4a
A campus of buildings is organized into curriculum areas: science, resources (classrooms), sports, technology administration and music. (© Architecture PLB.)

gym

sports hall

music/ dining

theatre

administration

technology

resources

cluster

science

Figure 4.4c
Summary of predicted daylighting performance in aiming for a 2 per cent daylight factor. (© Architecture PLB.)

Figure 4.4b
A section through the resources cluster predicting air movement during a typical summer day. (© Architecture PLB.)

wind tower drives cross ventilation

thermal mass absorbs heat of the day

ventilated roof prevents excessive heat gain

opening windows provide ventilation

deciduous planting provides good shade during summer, spring and autumn

CLUSTER BLOCK - Summer Daytime

gym: 95% daylit

sports 95% daylit

library reading areas daylit

theatre: blackout

admin 85% daylit in main offices

technology 95% daylit

classrooms: 1st floor 95% daylit gnd floor: 85% daylit

science: 95% daylit

summary of predicted daylighting performance in aiming for a 2 per cent daylight factor

Figure 4.4
Haute Vallee School, Jersey, designed by Architecture PLB. Diagrammatic representation of the organization based on a combined curriculum and environmental strategy.

Figure 4.5
Jersey High School for Girls, the access ramp.

ing's users to understand and, through minimal modifications such as the opening and closing of windows and the adjustment of blinds, determine their own environmental comfort.

This relates directly to the previous theme touched upon in the reference to the Cullinan school, with its adjustable roof lights. The controls must be obvious to the users, who should be educated in the correct control of their environment. Barrie Evans' observation accurately evokes the potential for energy inefficiencies with such a system: '... *blinds down, lights on and heating on, windows open.*'[4] It is an approach which imposes responsibilities

106

upon the users. With guidance, these features will be reflected in daily practice. It is the concept of an environment which cannot be taken for granted and has to be communally cherished.

The source of much of this section is drawn directly from Evans' excellent article 'Energy Lessons from School'. In dealing with a complex issue, it is clear and succinct in setting out seven crucial issues in creating environmental control and responsibility for it amongst the users:

1 *Landscape and wind – some cutting of buildings into the slope but also preserving views. Creating courtyard spaces between buildings. Use of deciduous trees for shelter belts close to buildings; strong winter winds would lead to turbulence immediately behind evergreens. Wind blows through leafless trees but loses significant force in the process.*

2 *Heating and insulation – U-values of 0.3 W/m²K for walls, 0.25 for roofs and typically 50 mm insulation in floors. Careful attention to fabric sealing to control heat loss through air leakage. Double-glazing, some low emissivity. Passive solar gain supplemented by heat from occupants and perimeter room heating. (Fuels supply about a third of the heat requirement.) Internal blinds in frames provide solar gain control by day and insulation at night – by trapping air and limiting radiant heat losses the effective window U-value is brought down from 1.9 to 1.5 W/m²K.*

3 *Thermal mass – mostly thermally heavyweight, though infrequently used spaces, such as gym, sports hall and dining room, are lightweight.*

4 *Ventilation and cooling – high-level and low-level windows provide cross-ventilation seasonally and diurnally. Wind towers assist ventilation in some buildings. The two sections of the classroom block, for winter and summer, illustrate how these towers are integrated into the thermal design. The swimming pool is mechanically ventilated. Peak summer temperature of 23.5°C should be exceeded for only 5 per cent of the time. Temperature stability is aided by the thermal mass; this mass can also be pre-cooled overnight by natural ventilation. This use of mass reduces peak temperatures by about 2°C. Main shading is to the south-west, but some is also likely to be needed in the early morning to the east.*

5 *Daylight and artificial light – evenness is important in daylighting. Contrast can give an impression of darkness and lights are more likely to be switched on. For most spaces daylighting is from at least two sides, so shading one side leaves significant daylighting. The internal blinds also provide glare control. Almost all the school can achieve a 2 per cent daylight factor, in practice likely to be achieved variously for 71–83 per cent of the year; lighting controls are simple, low-cost (dimming is too expensive). Lighting is to be pulsed off every lesson.*

6 *Building management – a building management system will provide control settings in response to building use patterns and weather, and will monitor system performance and energy use. Individual rooms have temperature controls. Occupants play a big role too. The headmaster has agreed that each classroom will have an energy monitor responsible at least at night, for setting the dampers on the wind towers (some automation is still a possibility), adjusting windows and closing thermal blinds. Excess ventilation heat loss is where the building can most easily run out of control. Excess artificial lighting is also a risk. If the simple controls and user awareness are enough, low energy light fittings are hardly cost justified. But they are to be included because if lighting use does rise, they soon become cost-effective. More generally, the idea is that the building performance and the output of monitoring will become part of the educational process, helping to promote general energy awareness among building users.*

7 *Heating – fuel choice. Gas has significantly lower CO_2 emissions and installation cost. But on Jersey oil is significantly cheaper to buy and will pay off the extra installation cost in about a year. Oil has been chosen.[5]*

The concept of a campus of buildings which stand partly linked and partly isolated breaks down the institutional nature of the school. However, it means that children often get wet when going from lesson to lesson. Yet the spaces between are so well considered that the aesthetic itself becomes the overriding quality, with these practical drawbacks assuming a secondary role behind the strength of the architectural ideas. Nevertheless, they are central to the overall concept of the school and achieve an integrated and balanced role within the framework of the architecture itself.

An approach to environmental control simply based on reducing energy bills at the expense of comfort is unacceptable. Children and their teachers will be the first to complain about stuffiness and a lack of ventilation. Here the prevailing atmospheric conditions are stable enough to allow a degree of changeability, rather than a constant predetermined atmosphere, without the risk of creating temperature extremes. As well as being part of a total environmental strategy occupants should be able to add heat or increase ventilation instantly and locally if required. Thus ventilation effectiveness and thermal mass will be balanced together. This balance is achieved in a seemingly effortless manner despite the cumbersome development process. It is a quality to which every modern building should aspire.

A recent report by the National Audit Office concluded that energy and water supplies form a significant part of school expenditure.[6] Based upon an energy review of sixty-five schools, they found that the main factor enabling schools to reduce energy consumption was the effectiveness of their energy management practices. Bearing in mind that the overall condition of the school fabric must meet certain quality thresholds (there is very little a teacher can do if the roofs leak, for example), then energy systems can be harnessed by the teachers themselves. This knowledge and responsibility, linked to an efficient overall management structure of the school environment, will have a positive effect upon the health and mood of those using the building, as well as on its maintenance budget.

More aggressive approaches are currently being considered by school funding communities both within the UK and further afield. For example, grey water systems of great complexity are being explored by some designers. Here the rainwater from the roof is collected and, as a first stage, simply filtered into storage settlement tanks. The water can then be used for low quality requirements such as flushing toilets and irrigation. It is possible to go further than this with total grey water systems, employing natural filtration through reed beds to remove phosphates and nitrates and subsequently sending the water through complex micron and UV filters. This process can sterilize water to a drinking quality, but is, at present, expensive and largely untried technology.

Similarly, the widespread use of photovoltaic cells is hindered by their unit cost. It is estimated that current prices would need to reduce by a factor of five before they became viable for the average school construction budget. However, one advantage they have is as cladding components, with their technology being well developed. They can be spaced out in a grid of clear glazing, providing both translucent shading and electricity generation. Their integration into the fabric of the building can have magical effects upon schoolchildren, who can relate to their technological edge much in the way they might view any high-tech gadget. In rural locations where the cost of connecting to mains electricity may be high, they are certainly worth considering. The down side is that, as with advanced grey water systems, photovoltaic cells are complex and underdeveloped in terms of their practical serviceability; they naturally lack client confidence. The poor level of performance during overcast conditions may in any event require subsidiary mains back-up.

In his review of the Stuttgart-Stammheim School, Peter Blundell Jones points out that radical green consciousness in the way we construct our public buildings is not neces-sarily to do with high-tech devices. The primary school was designed and largely built in collaboration with the local community.[7] He believes that truly green architecture is more likely to come about through a collaborative fully inclusive approach to design and build initiated and developed at local level. He asserts that building has become the most hidebound, least spontaneous, activity on earth. Its bureaucracy therefore limits experimentation, particularly where existing budgetary regimes may be upset – for example where a higher than average capital outlay at construction stage is required.

However, according to Blundell Jones, an approach which combines practical self-build methods with the avoidance of materials which have high levels of energy input at the manufacturing stage is only half the story. Green architecture will become acceptable and therefore mainstream when existing orthodoxies of centralized bureaucracy are challenged. Building or extending a school would then become an act of political will, involving people at local level. If the world declares that the end result is ugly, it does not matter: '... *Trivial aesthetic judgements are pushed to one side, for the look of the thing is bound up with its identity and biography, and therefore accepted.*'[8] However, the designer should take his or her own view as to how far it is realistic to go along this route, and consider the full cost of adopting aggressively green strategies.

We advocate a more evolutionary approach to the design of the new generation of green schools. As proved by the experiences of Architecture PLB in Jersey, consulting widely with so-called experts does not always resolve the problems of a complex architectural puzzle. For example, the acoustics of the music rooms at the Haute Vallee School are disastrous, primarily because of a number of unpredictable factors. The combined effects of the shape and proportions of the space and its hard resonating surfaces have created unacceptable levels of reverberation, despite the use of an acoustics consultant. However, that aside, the rest of the school integrates its energy-efficient strategy into a campus of great architectural quality in a sensible and low-key way.

External space – learning through landscapes

The imaginative use of school grounds and their potential for curriculum activities is, for obvious reasons, rarely mentioned by overworked classroom teachers. However, one issue which came to the fore following the tragic events at Dunblane during 1997 is that of security. And this factor became particularly relevant when casting a critical eye upon the external areas of a number of schools I have visited. For example, the Thomas Carlyle School, Nuthall, sits well back from the public sides of the site, enabling easy access from the street. It is difficult ever to imagine a perimeter security fence high enough to prevent the ingress of unwelcome guests after school hours. In any event, this would transform the welcoming image of the school. The building sits in the centre of its site, a tempting prospect for any burglar or vandal. On the other hand, it is overlooked by surrounding houses.

A slightly older building, the Good Shepherd Primary in Nottingham, uses the form of the building itself to shield the external play areas from the street. There are two entrances, one central to the school building which is 'guarded' either side by the headteacher's office and the school secretary. The major point of access for children arriving and departing is the main school gate at the western end of the site. Although this entrance tends to make accessibility too free, it benefits by having the full-time caretaker's house immediately adjacent, a symbolic if not a real control to the access of strangers onto the site. An even more secure arrangement can be realized when the whole school hugs the site edges and the building itself becomes a security in its own right.

In a recent discussion document written by early years expert Helen Penn, a distinction is drawn between nursery schools run by education departments and the more overly protective social services nurseries: '... *In the education based nurseries, staff were constantly inventive about the activities – more than a hundred activities were available to the children at any time – and children were allowed to move freely in the nursery and outside. The buildings were constructed so that they could. In the childcare [social services] nurseries, by contrast, there were only six or seven activities, which had been on the menu many times before, and the buildings and spaces themselves restricted how children could move. Children in the social services nurseries were generally under exercised.'[9]

Here Penn is not simply referring to the physical under-exercise of the children, but also to a lack of intellectual stimulation. The implication is that the curriculum should be rich and the children encouraged to develop autonomy within the safe secure framework of the school. The more outside spaces were integrated as an extension of the field of learning, the better the children fared both emotionally and developmentally. The extent to which these possibilities can be extended beyond the pre-school to the primary or secondary school in any meaningful way is open to question. As stated elsewhere, the concept of open learning with its libertarian associations is currently being questioned.[10] There is no doubt, however, of the potential for outside space to be used more positively as an aid to teaching activities in primary and secondary schools, as well as pre-schools. This concept was certainly explored in the past.

For example, at Edward O'Neil's experimental school at Prestolea in Bolton is the so-called Fantasy Garden O'Neil created to fulfil the school's motto 'Learn by Doing'. The idea began during O'Neil's recuperation from a serious illness. To mark this event, he drew on the therapeutic benefits of the garden at his own home. He believed it to be central to his recovery. A similar school garden could engender similar qualities of contemplation and thoughtfulness within the children. He set about creating a garden which would thus become a positive aid to child development rather than being a hard austere area for physical exercise and a limited number of games.

The focus was a pool of water filled by a fountain that was allowed to flow down into another lower pool, forming a stream. This was spanned by two wooden structures. Additional rustic features were added: a windmill, stiles, gates, ladders and steps. The whole playground area was broken up into interesting smaller enclosures, which were planted and suffused with the sound of flowing water. Most importantly, there were things for the children to do in the garden, creating areas which O'Neil saw as outdoor classrooms:

One comes upon a garden lounge. Children sit at it drinking their milk and by it is a brazier. In colder weather it is alight and the drinkers can warm themselves. There are flights of a few steps at either end. If you sit on the topmost, you have a new prospect. Indeed, you can see into the sandpit. This is a low, walled enclosure, with a rather wild garden round it aglow with flag irises, dusty-miller, logan-berries, crab-apples, pears, and roses; you might easily miss it and the four small people who are busy building castles in the deep sand. And you will only come upon the wishing-well by a chance turn. Its parapet is about thigh-high, and it is this parapet that really holds the water. Overhead is a roof and under this is the bucket-winding gear. The parapet was built by girls; just bricks, dipped in creamy cement, but properly bonded and brushed over internally with a cement skin and touched up here and there with the aid of a pastry knife. Boys made the wooden structure overhead, and the axle of the winding gear, an old railing, was bent to form a handle at one end by heating it in a small bonfire. The bucket is rather fun. In the bottom are rings of holes, and a disc of rubber fitted, which acts as a valve, so that when the bucket is lowered into the water this latter, entering through the holes in the bottom and pushing past the rubber disc, fills the vessel. When it is wound up it will empty slowly through an outer ring of holes not covered by the valve, forming a shower-bath, which aerates the water in the well. This is a good thing because those are real fish which you can see swimming in the well and they like it. Children love to play with water, especially when it sprays and splashes, and there is grand exercise to be had winding the bucket up, holding it while it discharges, and lowering it to refill. The water in the well is not really deep, just eighteen

Figure 4.6
Helling Street Park, London by Lyn Kinnear Associates. The blue wall divides the space into two zones; this side is full of seating and soft grassy areas for reading and quiet contemplation, the other full of climbing equipment for rumbustious physical play. Unfortunately, since this photograph was taken, the wall and other parts of the park have been covered in graffiti and generally vandalized by older teenage children, perhaps emphasizing the need for children's play areas to be supervised and attached to institutions such as community schools with evening and weekend activity programmes.

inches or so, and when a child leans with his elbows on top of the parapet, the surface is just at hand. There is a wide step at one side for smaller people to get on to.[11]

Edward O'Neil died in 1958, and his fantasy garden fell into disrepair. It was concreted over in the 1960s. So what, the reader may ask, does this have to do with the contemporary debate? It is that the dearth of real gardens for the use of school children is a real concern. So many school grounds are neglected and under-utilized as spaces for imaginative free play. The garden at Prestolea became an essential extension of the teaching space of the school itself. Whilst the school buildings remained the context for more formal teaching activities, the outside spaces become

the freer context for children to learn through play. In this way the primary and the secondary school can continue to extend some of the important roles of the pre-school in providing the milieu for imaginative uninhibited free play, by way of its outside spaces.

Landscape architects Lyn Kinnear Associates have recently completed the Helling Street Park in London's Docklands which takes an imaginative approach to the needs of outside space for children. Although not part of an educational institution, it is worth describing for its unusually picturesque child-friendly qualities. For safety reasons the client wanted a fence around this urban park. The designers saw the fence as a symbol of division and exclusion, which was inappropriate to children. Instead they tried to make the boundaries playful, using a range of

Figure 4.7
A caring landscape with a garden bench positioned within the school yard which breaks the space up to create quieter areas. (© George Spicer.)

scales and textures; so at one stage the boundary is a vibrant blue wall, an undulating galvanized steel fence and then a sinuous ivy-clad wall. The wall becomes transparent in winter as the leaves drop, emphasizing the changing seasons.

Within the playground, boundaries are suggested by what the designer describes as 'carpets of colour' which have contrasting tactile qualities: there is a grass 'carpet', a multi-coloured undulating rubber surface and a hard bitmac surface with line markings. The territories are defined and articulated to look like different postcard scenes, one surrounded with pine trees and flowering plants and one with a vivid blue background, like a Mediterranean beach

edge. Another has more straightforward undulating areas enclosing flat zones of robust play equipment. A third area is defined by a raw steel box frame surrounded by climbing plants which is intended to remind one of a New York apartment roof garden. Here the dynamic of the built form is contrasted with soft organic objects. It is a clever reference to the dialectics of childhood.

Although not part of a school playground as such, the play space is adjacent to a school involved in consultations at design stage. It engages dimensions of intrigue amongst those who use it in its adoption of different images and ideas focusing on children's play. Its use of poetic metaphor to structure diverse play experiences provides spaces for contemplation as well as conventional areas for raucous physical activity in a similar form to O'Neil's Fantasy Garden. Its careful manipulation of form and image enables and encourages a diverse use of all areas of the playground. As such it is a true learning environment which appeals to adults as well as children; a focus for the wider residential community.

The Winchester-based organization Learning Through Landscapes (LTL) was established in 1985 as a research project to explore the real possibilities of the use of outside classrooms in primary school education. In 1990 LTL became a charity and as the National Curriculum was being introduced, demonstrated to numerous schools that it was possible for significant elements of most academic subjects to be taught outside. Its research has demonstrated the enormous impact school grounds have on the behaviour and developing attitudes of school pupils. Children 'read' the landscape of school and see powerful, often negative, messages 'written' in its tarmac spaces. LTL would claim that children do not stop learning when they leave the classroom, although certain kinds of outdoor spaces such as hard open tarmac areas will encourage a less thoughtful use of the space. If treated in an appropriate way, any outside space can be designed to encourage activities, such as painting, sculpture, drama and story telling, music and dance:

> *By focusing their interaction with the school grounds, pupils develop visual and emotional literacy and begin to identify with the place in which they spend so much of their lives. It has often been remarked that one valuable spin-off from such a developing relationship is a sharp decline in vandalism. Indeed, when pupils come to see the school grounds as their space, existing in their imaginations and containing their own experience, they will be drawn into valuing and nurturing that space. They will also experience that relationship with their immediate environment which has been termed 'a sense of place'.*[12]

In practical terms this might mean constructing a pond which will enable children to monitor the way the habitat attracts different creatures and plants during the year. Its

Figure 4.8
Children planting vegetables in their school garden. (© Learning Through Landscapes.)

use within the curriculum would incorporate the analysis of data using IT, maths and science. It would introduce children who may see very little green space within their own domestic environments to the full cycle of growth. The organization can advise on the siting of the pond, its surrounds, depth, access and many other practical factors which would make it usable for groups of children within the context of the school curriculum. Interventions in more urban situations might include wall and floor murals perhaps carried out by a local artist, small enclosed fruit and vegetable gardens, and the planting and nurturing of individual trees and shrubs within the playground. Funding and implementation strategies would also complement these curriculum ideas.

LTL do not go into schools; all their advice is disseminated by way of publications, videos and conferences. Ultimately the implementation of any initiative is dependent on individuals within the school itself. The most successful projects involve teams of highly motivated people including parents, governors and teachers. A friendly local landscape architect willing to donate free advice can be a formidable asset. However, LTL can act as an effective catalyst in what is an onerous but worthwhile undertaking, the implementation of the outside classroom.

Tending the landscape

Dealing effectively with outside space can take as much planning, organization and finance as the construction of a new school building. Sue Fenoughty, an environmental education consultant, has worked with landscape architects at Birmingham City Council on over a hundred school projects. In 1991 she identified a concern for children's health due mainly to inactive lifestyles and set up a partnership with the city landscape architects to work with schools to improve the design of their school grounds. She visited many school sites, recognizing their sterile character and aimed to create areas where pupils could grow food plants using organic methods to introduce biodiversity: *'It is hoped that by growing their own food pupils can be encouraged to eat more fresh fruit and vegetables.'*

Figure 4.9a
Larmenier School, Hammersmith. This urban school benefits from the imaginative use of tree logs and boulders to create a challenging climbing area for the primary school pupils within what was formerly a hard tarmac playground area. (Photo: © Mark Dudek.)

Figure 4.9b
St Benedict's Infant and Nursery School in Small Health, Birmingham has utilized the left-over spaces around the site as planting areas for the cultivation of vegetables, herbs and flowers. Maintenance and upkeep requires a commitment from pupils, staff and parents. (Photo: © Mark Dudek.)

Sue Fenoughty visits each project on average twenty times during the design and development process. Her aim is to link the design of the school's outdoor spaces with the school timetable itself, so that the educational benefits are explicit. This she believes makes it easier to raise funds. She will advise on how to draw up a long-term development plan which involves the pupils, within the framework of the educational curriculum. She can also connect the school to other local, national and European sources of funding and 'translate' the wishes of the school to the professional team working within the LEA architects and landscape architects departments. Pupils and teachers work together by way of curriculum activities to redesign their grounds, using the following steps:

Step 1   Identify the need to improve the grounds.
Step 2   Make a map of the school grounds, indicat-

ing the flora and fauna, micro climate, pathways, all physical features. Conduct a playground survey for each class ('who plays what and where'). A 3D model could be made of the school site.
Step 3   Analyse the map and identify opportunities for improvements.
Step 4   Design the improvements and draw up the whole site design plan.
Step 5   Start to implement the plan, beginning with the first priority.
Step 6   Plan maintenance/care of the site, divided between the classes.
Step 7   Ensure continued use of the grounds[13]

We might add to this list the following two points. Firstly, since these projects will usually rely on private/parent

113

funding, or require significant speculative design and administrative input in order to formulate funding bids, as part of step 2 contact the local university design or landscape design department. If the proposition is interesting and there is real need for imaginative interventions, they will welcome the involvement in what may later become a real project. Secondly, at step 4, encourage as much publicity as possible, both locally and nationally, as a way of levering sponsorship from commercial companies. The more national the publicity, the wider the sponsorship net can be spread.

There is much evident quality in the work of the Birmingham schools I visited, so the development processes refined by Sue Fenoughty can only be welcomed. For example, St Benedict's Infant and Nursery School in Small Heath is housed within an old Victorian building which is believed to be the largest in Europe. The school building sits in an unrelentingly austere landscape of tarmac surrounded by high security fences. The leftover external spaces between the buildings and the boundary fencing have been transformed into more positive play and activity spaces. The plan form of this somewhat austere Victorian edifice is set slightly within the boundaries of the site with a series of indentations, forming naturally sheltered areas. On the southern side of the site, close boarded fencing, pergolas and rustic stone walls have been ingeniously added to provide more enclosed courtyards. The tarmac and concrete have then been removed, and various types of garden are developed within each of the new courtyards: an aromatic herb bed with exotic Asian varieties such as okra and mooli is located near the entrance 'court'. Aromas waft into the adjacent assembly hall, assisted by prevailing winds. A vegetable garden has been planted, with different small plots allocated to groups of children, allotment style. During the visit, I was offered some very tasty soup, the ingredients having been cultivated and cooked on the premises.

The children's curriculum is geared towards an integrated approach to these environments with lessons which revolve around planting seasons and the wildlife encouraged by these natural additions to the school grounds. Thus children's knowledge of plants and animals is extended by a 'minibeast hunt' as part of the written curriculum: *'use a magnifying glass to identify snail, worm, spider and beetle to understand that there are a range of creatures to be found in and on the soil.'*

Many children can be found returning of their own accord to tend and plant their gardens outside of school lesson times. In this way, an introduction to gardening can become a lifetime interest for many of these children. A large proportion of the children are from Asian families, whose parents have never previously appreciated gardening to be a form of relaxation. Initial capital costs and some maintenance support comes from regeneration funds won through local authority bidding to the European Social Regeneration Budget (SRB), but the projects do take some maintenance. It is anticipated that parents and former pupils will offer their own time to tend the gardens in years to come. However, the sympathetic support of the headteacher is also deemed to be of fundamental significance in developing and maintaining these initiatives.

Sue Fenoughty believes that every school site should have at least nine identifiable habitats to provide a rich and diverse natural environment which can flourish in the most urban of sites. She lists them as follows:

- a pond;
- a wet area;
- short grass;
- long grass or meadow land, which encourages butterflies and other scarce species;
- a hedgerow, which can help to dissipate particulates from polluting traffic; this feature can be a source of encouragement for wildlife, particularly birds and small mammals;
- an old dry wall;
- a roofed garden for wet days;
- vegetables and fruit for cultivation;
- a woodland or coppice.

In the ways in which new school projects are planned, the landscape is often seen as a bolt-on extra to be lost or found at the end of the process depending on the state of the budget. By the time planting is due, the budget has frequently been exhausted by building costs. Thus a vital aspect of the school environment is lost, not just as an educational resource, but also as a pleasant place to be for children. Hard open areas for some children, usually boys, to kick balls around is required, but if that is all there is, the needs of the rest of the school community are obscured.

Tending the landscape of school reduces vandalism and engenders a sense of respect for their environment. The UK government-funded Elton Report of 1989 specifically linked bad behaviour in schools to the quality of the outdoor environment. *'We are an indoor society at present,'* believes Fenoughty, and this is having a disastrous effect on the physical and mental health of some of our youngest children. She emphasizes the positive effects of cultivating the grounds, encouraging the child to assume responsibility for his or her plot. Present a finished or 'complete' environment and the tendency for the minority of disturbed or insecure children is to deface or vandalize the fabric. Where the architect might view a tree merely as a pleasant aesthetic shape, she states, we appreciate it as a learning resource which teaches children about the ecology of their world.

Children wish to use their school facilities at all times, rather than being excluded at weekends and during the

Figure 4.10
The School Hall at Jersey High School for Girls, designed by Architecture PLB. (Photo: © Mark Dudek.)

evenings. It is frequently the case that teachers have no time to engage with the outside landscape; in pre-school settings, keeping children cooped-up indoors throughout the winter. If the curriculum is matched to the outside spaces, the beneficial effects are beyond question. It is vital for architects and designers to understand and appreciate the ways in which school grounds can become a true learning resource. If teachers and carers do not have time to harness the benefits of outside areas, interested parents and other community-minded individuals should be encouraged to participate more actively.

On a more general level, children need fewer aids to imagination designed in elegantly abstract forms such as climbing frames in the form of trains and castles. Rather, adults must adopt less prescriptive approaches to the external environment – a few old logs left in a dug-out corner of the school yard, compost heaps or an old bath-tub filled with waterlogged earth to encourage decomposition can very quickly become natural environments which

allow the imaginations of the children to create landscapes in their own images. Gunter Belzig, a designer of children's environments for over twenty years, believes that it does not matter if the results are ugly or kitsch. It is the possibility for constant change and adaptation by the children themselves that is important.[14] In this way a sense of ownership and respect for their environment will develop naturally.

Finally, some brief observations about the effects of gender differences within conventionally constituted school grounds. Much research has been carried out into this area and the scope of this publication does not allow greater coverage. It can be broadly summarized into the dominant/subordinate relationship between girls and boys acted out in the school playground. Avoiding the politically correct clichés inherent to much of this research, predictable patterns of use described in the following quotation are worth considering when designing external spaces for mixed school communities:

The boys' games of Superman, cowboys and Indians, and football can keep the whole playground in a state of tension and excitement as they 'charge' and whoop their way through the ranks of other children. This does not mean that girls cower at the edge. The boys dominated the available space in most forms of play in the playground ... If by chance the girls wandered into what was seen as the space of the boys, they were viewed as intruders who do not know 'their place' and who try to take that which is not theirs.[15]

Assembly halls – the school as community and the community as school

Due to a shortage of dedicated rooms at the Good Shepherd Primary in Nottingham, a number of the schoolrooms are used on a rotational basis. Music or remedial reading takes place in a spare classroom. The hall caters for a two-class singing group as well as assemblies, sports and community activities; this is a profoundly multi-functional space. The hall is in constant use throughout the week, and although this entails a certain amount of movement, with classes crocodiling across playgrounds at various times of the day, it was felt that the movement enhanced rather than detracted from the educational and social experience.

In addition to its role within the school curriculum, the hall and adjacent dining areas form a generous (in terms of measurements) communal space where the whole school, its parents and friends can come together at various times of the year to celebrate religious festivals, and discuss community concerns. On an everyday level, the spaces form the setting for numerous different activities, some engaging the whole school, others simply enabling a single class to experience generous amounts of interior space while bodily expression is taking place.

As touched upon in the previous section, this aspect is particularly important for girls, who may find outdoor play spaces dominated by boisterous football games. Often girls appear to be pushed towards the outer edges of the playground areas by the physical exuberance of these activities. With its light beech sprung floor and airy atmosphere, the hall of the Good Shepherd provides the perfect environment for activities such as line dancing which requires lots of space (and is fashionable at present), gymnastics and aerobics. All of these are activities which cannot readily take place outdoors. The hall is the focus of the school, generating a natural sense of community, beyond the limitations of the class bases.

Previously I have been critical about the Glastonbury First School on the level of its open-plan teaching areas. However, with regard to the hall, both architecturally and functionally it works very well. According to John Stewert, it is *'located between the school and the community'*. The

Figure 4.11
Schools need not necessarily be designed on a single level; here a two-storey building optimizes the tight urban site so that a small garden can be provided. The Greisheim-Sud Kindertagestätte Frankfurt designed by Bolles Wilson and Partner uses a distinctive timber staircase with on the top landing, a bold abstract image, a colour-form language. The red and white logo is elegant, complementing the architecture, but it also alerts the children to the potential hazards of this important feature.

plan develops from the axial relationship between the streets and the public 'green' adjacent to the school site. The original intention had been to provide doors at the back of the hall which could be opened onto this space. However, for reasons of security, this idea was abandoned. The hall can still be used at weekends when the rest of the school is closed off. During the week it provides flexible spaces for assembly, sport and music activities.

With its faceted non-orthogonal plan form, it has excellent acoustic properties. The 'poche' provides useful storage space and an added 'twist' to the ways in which the space can be used. It has a theatrical quality, an effect which is enhanced by the stepped threshold. The hall accommodates site level changes which mean that it is 1 metre below the level of the teaching areas. Although the level change is identified as a hazard to children by some teachers, from my point of view this provided a welcome spatial distinction between the two parts of the school. The scale changes and physical separation of the hall from the rest of the school appeals to the imaginative perceptions of the group, and underlines the importance of the whole school community coming together in collective celebration.

It is widely accepted that the transfer from primary to secondary school is a traumatic one for many children. Enthusiasm is naturally high, but age differentials can present a daunting spectacle to many young children new to their secondary schools. Lydia Picton, who is the deputy head at a large multicultural comprehensive school in West London, believes that, in essence, the experience of large group assemblies is no different to what the children have experienced in their primary schools. Indeed, she believes this is one aspect of school life, unrelated to formal teaching activities, which is nevertheless essential in fulfilling the school's ethos: *'Spiritual awareness is most evident in the organization and delivery of assemblies in which the themes of reflection, meditation and prayer are reinforced by devotional messages and a deep appreciation of the power of musical expression.'*[16]

Schools are required to teach religious education. However, it is not one of the foundation subjects within the National Curriculum, and arrangements are agreed upon at school and LEA level. An important forum for the teaching of religious education is the school assembly. Lydia Picton is clear about the formality of the assembly as an almost ritual event where all the children are asked to stand, before the staff process onto the stage. This she believes is an inheritance from the earlier grammar school tradition of the Heathland School, where deference and respect were engendered as a form of clear hierarchy. It may not sound very modern, but it is, according to Picton, nevertheless effective. All the children stand up in perfect silence as the staff enter and circulate around the hexagonal form of the assembly hall. These come from behind the children, before gathering on the raised stage. It is deliberately theatrical, yet serious, focusing the children into academic life at the beginning of each day.

The assembly itself will almost always begin with music, either performed live by school students or members of staff, or pre-recorded classical music. The theatricality of the event is often enhanced by the multi-media facilities within this purpose-designed space. There are large-format videos and a state of the art quadraphonic sound system to enhance the acoustic experience of the 'event'.

A video of a politician or a religious leader can fill the space before a member of staff talks about the message which lies behind the superficial image. Although the theme of Heathland School assemblies is often religious, it is never overtly denominational.

For the children, assemblies represent a continuing socio-cultural experience throughout their life in the school. Where the major area of concern is described as spiritual, moral, social and cultural, the assembly is the point where the staff are presented to the children in a formal setting. It can provide a sense of stability, an important bedrock for the children, as they grow and develop towards adulthood. In this sense Lydia Picton likens the school hall to a sort of medieval town square, where contact can be made between the townsfolk and their leaders. Set at the heart of the building, all four staircases leading to the class blocks suggest a different analogy; that of the fortified castle. It is the physical and symbolic centre of this huge community. Unfortunately there is not enough space for the whole school to congregate at one time. However, twice a week there are main school assemblies for 500 children in each. Year groups rotate over the term.

Having enough space within which the whole school community can meet is particularly important in secondary school settings. Peter Clark, who assumed responsibility of the troubled Ridings Secondary School in Halifax, believes that the school assembly was an essential element in the school's rehabilitation. It is the context where a head can communicate directly with the entire student body, and the point where he or she can most easily lead the staff by example. Clark sees assembly as an important way of explaining the social ethos which establishes behavioural benchmarks for the pupils to follow; it is through the assembly that the students get to know the head: *'Building up the self-esteem of both staff and pupils was essential at the Ridings School and assembly allowed us to come together in large numbers, although it was never possible to bring the whole school together – due to a lack of space.'*

Clark avoids assemblies with hymns and prayers as he feels it is not his style. He often bases his assemblies on television adverts or programmes as most children can relate to these. He tells 'moral tales' which he believes to be relevant and important, but rarely with an overtly religious message:

I think it's important to encourage youngsters to be inspired by others. Humour is important too, even though some of us think we are wittier than we actually are. Humour helps to gain a perspective and that enables us to see ourselves as we really are.[17]

School assembly is keenly observed by OFSTED inspectors as an exemplification of the particular spirit of the institution. It is significant that inspectors rarely comment on the lack of physical space for these ritual events to take place. However, the importance of addressing the needs of the school as a single community is exemplified by the experiences of Lydia Picton and Peter Clark. The school hall can be a multi-functional space, a role it more usually fulfils at primary school level. In secondary school, that role is more circumscribed, and the designer should take into account the specific activities which lie at the heart of the school day. These can only be carried out within an assembly hall of a particular size and specification.

The designer should also bear in mind the community role these spaces can support, such as hosting evening events, to truly extend the life of the institution. In the Peter Hübner designed primary school at Stuttgart-Stammheim, the plan takes on a large circular form, with the hall at its centre. Not only does this represent the symbolic heart of the school, but on a practical level it enables children to enter and leave their classrooms through or adjacent to the space. Meetings, gymnastics and singing become a central part of the life of the school, as everyone is aware of their proximity. On wet days it serves as a place where children spend their break-times. It is made available for the use of the local community in the evenings; a wholly appropriate gesture since the community participated so actively in its procurement and construction. This space becomes a community hall which is integral to the school, built by the community and designed in a user-friendly and welcoming form.

Funding and procurement – an introduction

Increasingly the economics of the marketplace are dictating new approaches to the procurement of school buildings. In the USA, organizations such as the Edison Project and Educational Alternatives apply private sector management practices to schools. In the UK, Education Action Zones and Private Finance Initiatives seek to adopt similar free-market strategies. Some critics of the present system have suggested that schools should adopt corporate approaches to property, renting column-free space which can be flexibly organized, and used for as long as required. In the UK, commercial pre-school operators such as Kids Unlimited and Jigsaw, catering to a corporate market, adopt these privately funded initiatives. They build childcare centres on the basis that if the market for childcare changes, the building can resort to office use, without compromising architectural quality.

Educational reform is firmly on the agenda, and this is being expressed by profound changes to the legislative framework. This is taking place at present within the UK and elsewhere. Reform reflects the concept of delegating responsibilities down to the school communities themselves, yet with a very firm eye on the marketplace model. The 'micro-society' concept of education sets out to create a simulated market place where secondary school students behave as they would in a larger, albeit highly

controlled, civic society. New schools would have streets and shops, banks and a choice of restaurants adjacent to more traditional teaching spaces. According to Thomas Fisher, this concept is no more than a controlled version of John Dewey's educational vision of the school, as a microcosm of society: *'But it raises a question about the role we want schools to play in our society. Should schools "educate for the status quo," as Dewey asked, or should they "take an active part in directing social change, and share in the construction of a new social order?"'*[18]

The answer must lie somewhere in between. To destroy the solid basis of a communal education for all, which reflects a traditional concept of institutions defined by dedicated buildings, would undermine its very role in providing the physical heart of the community. The notion of carrying out education in cheap industrial buildings, with big open-plan spaces and negligible architectural quality, would be an anathema. Yet radical thinking of this nature is being applied, and may be incorporated in future school designs. The quest for efficiency will apply to any new proposals, now and in the future. Architects for their part should understand and be able to explain the evolving funding regimes which will enable this balance between public and private finance to succeed.

In this section I will explain the various channels by which funds can be drawn within the UK, and complete the picture with a basic guide to the way in which the revised development process can operate to the benefit of the end-users: teachers and children. It should be stressed that this area is highly complex and what follows should be viewed only as a summary. It is neither comprehensive nor is it completely up-to-date since legislation is being formulated even as I write. However, the principles outlined can be viewed as pending. *Architects would also be advised to refer to the extensive guidance publications provided by local and central government.*[19]

The UK state education system – explaining the funding terminology

Since the 1988 Education Reform Act, all schools have 'locally managed' budgets. Income is distributed annually from each LEA or direct from central government, on the basis of a formula. This formula allocates a certain amount for each pupil on roll, plus a certain other amount in respect of social disadvantage, special educational needs or school size. Expenditure is the responsibility of the headteacher and governors. However, school managers often have relatively small sums to spend at their discretion, once fixed costs are taken out of the overall budgets.[20]

Here the distinction should be made between school running costs and financing major improvements to existing schools or the construction of completely new schools.

Running costs are met on an annual basis and distributed as part of the public spending round. They are generally described as **recurrent funds** and are specifically earmarked to meet fixed costs such as teachers' salaries and general maintenance. For example, the repair of a broken window or the construction of a new classroom partition would be considered to be running costs.

In theory, the school has discretion to use its budget entirely as it wishes, but it has obligations in certain areas such as salaries and premises' running costs. These are essentially fixed costs and, in practice, most schools have little notional funding for maintenance or improvement purposes after fixed costs have been covered. Additional sums which may become available will usually be allocated to items such as additional equipment for teachers, rather than the implementation of basic improvements to the fabric of the school environment. Since April 1999, recurrent funding has been delegated 100% to schools as a statutory requirement. Local Authorities must have an approved 'Fair Funding' plan. This is a formula by which the available individual schools budget is shared between all schools in the area.

Conversely, **capital funding** for new or refurbished schools is determined on a once yearly cycle by government and allocated through the Annual Capital Guidelines (ACG). However, there are rigid bidding rules for ACG which relate to the need for additional places within an area, or the requirement to rationalize and reorganize as a result of population movements. During the 1980s, for example, Hampshire experienced a boom in new school building largely as a result of population growth within the region, which brought with it ACG borrowing approval. Since April 2000, so-called Formula Capital is a new annual budget available for school governors to spend. It is allocated on the basis of information contained within the school's Estate Plan; this is a fundamental part of the School Development Plan, which is intended to make the best use of the school's resources, and to constantly review and update the way in which the school manages itself. Formula Capital can be used for repairs to the fabric of a school, and for minor improvement projects, such as security and classroom improvements, however it is not intended for furniture and equipment such as computers. The crucial spin on this is that the annual allocation of funds can, by agreement with the DfEE, be rolled forward, so that rather than repairing a patch of leaky roof, the repair can be carried out more completely.

Also from April 2000, Seed Challenge Capital is available. It is not a formula allocation to each school, rather schools must bid for between a third and a half of the costs for a project to the LEA. Past funding must be available from other sources outside usual capital or recurrent funding.

Initiative funding is targeted allocations for specific problems and areas of neglect. These come under the guise of the New Deal for Schools (NDS) or the 'Class Size Reduction Initiative'. Generally this is in the form of Specified Capital Outlay for premises which are in a state of serious disrepair or for improved facilities which are required to meet curriculum needs.[21] NDS is an additional capital grant of £1.086 billion being distributed over the first five-year term of the Labour government, primarily to eliminate the extensive backlog of repairs to existing school buildings. Without significant direct increases in taxation, it is unlikely to provide sufficient funds for the required reconstruction of thousands of existing schools, which is likely to be provided by privately sourced finance initiatives.

School staff sometimes find it difficult to differentiate between running costs and major one-off capital grants.

In primary schools staff salaries usually amount to around 80 per cent of the entire annual recurrent budgets. Essential building maintenance costs can come to another 10 per cent. So, for example, in 1995/96, a medium sized primary school in Bristol, with 145 children on roll with a total budget of £226,100, only preserved £13,000 for expenditure directly on educational equipment, books and materials. This represents genuine hardship for many schools within the UK, a direct effect of sustained budgetary shortfalls where high quality maintenance has been sacrificed on the political altar of low taxation. This is a state of affairs with which class teachers struggle almost everywhere.

Invariably their concerns are translated not just to shortages of equipment such as classroom computers and books, but to wider issues relating to the fabric of the building and the quality of the architecture itself. For example, a teacher I talked to who runs a class in an elderly north London primary school, commenced our interview with a series of general complaints about condensation on the large single-glazed windows, poor heating and the drab colours in the corridors. On cold days, the children had to wrap up whilst inside the classroom. As a consequence, they were less willing to go outside during break times. However, all of this was just about manageable, as it only became a real problem on the twenty or so coldest days of the year.

For the remainder of the time, the double height classrooms and large north facing windows, plus the benefits accrued from its high thermal mass (an attribute of its traditional brick construction), made the classroom environment comfortable, particularly on hot summer days. This, she said, was in marked contrast to her previous experience in a lightweight 'modern' school building. However, it was the niggling factors which most frustrated her. For example the lack of rubber dampers on the chair legs which made a terrible noise and constituted a considerable distraction to both her and the children. This problem could be simply rectified by their replacement or, better still, the installation of a carpet on top of the existing wooden floors. The noise and distraction caused by this basic shortcoming seemed to be totally unnecessary and yet out of her control.[22]

In a sense, these comments reflect the lack of control many teachers feel within the UK. Not only must they cope with large class sizes but also the demands of the National Curriculum (explored in Chapter 2), with its emphasis on testing and evaluation. The Local Management of Schools (LMS), a principle which the government is keen to extend, would appear to have little meaning for most class teachers at present. They are too overworked to involve themselves in capital bids, and there is usually little money left over from the recurrent funding budget in order to carry out seemingly minor remedial works such as the replacement of rubber dampers on chairs.

The mechanism by which funds are made available through the ACG for what might be termed emergency provision is called a statutory Basic Need proposal; because the population moves around the country in patterns which cannot always be anticipated, this mechanism is intended to provide additional places within a particular area either by increasing capacity in existing schools or building an entirely new school. This form of funding reinforces the traditional concept that children should travel minimally between home and school. It also underlines present government policy which sees schools as resources local to and ideally available to a particular community outside of school hours.

Conversely, if a number of local schools experience falling rolls, the LEA may choose to close two schools, combining them together in one new building if the cost benefits of such a decision can be proven. ACG funds are available for capital works associated with this rationalization process. However, closing any school is always politically fraught at local level. Communities feel particularly vulnerable when their local school is threatened, underlining the deep attachment felt by many people to their early school years and the associated memories of the buildings which provided the context for this formative time.

Capital funding has to be bid for by the Local Education Authority (LEA) on behalf of the schools. The agency dealing with all educational bids is the Department for Education and Employment (DfEE). These funds are usually allocated to larger projects, mainly because the bidding itself is such a time-consuming process. A new entrance area and toilets may be worth bidding for, but the money to pay for thirty new chair dampers simply has to come out of the hard-pressed annual budget allocation for running the school.

Despite this, the political will to improve education within the UK is genuine. Recognizing the inadequacy of existing educational environments, the government has pledged that 10,000 UK schools will have received money for general improvements to the fabric of their buildings within their first term through NDS. In September 1998 a further addition of £1.5 billion was added to the original figure of £1.086 billion; however, at the time of writing, it

is unclear how this will be distributed. Imaginative new initiatives such as special Internet pricing packages will be offered with costs expected to be as little as £1 per pupil. £19 million worth of books will boost the government's literacy drive, described by Prime Minister Tony Blair as: *'the biggest assault on poor literacy and numeracy standards this country has ever seen.'*[23]

Most of this initial 'seedcore' funding, which was an addition to existing recurrent budgets, was drawn from a windfall tax on the privatized utility companies. However, all resources have to be paid for year after year, and on a national basis, education is a significant expense. For instance, the total cost of education in 1991/92 was £29 billion, or 14 per cent of all government spending. Primary education in England and Wales alone costs almost £5 billion. At local level, education is by far the largest item in council budgets; about 70 per cent in some cases, of which the most significant item is teachers' salaries. Many LEAs cannot increase education budgets because of 'capping' on local Council Tax levels. Funding available for schools is fixed, unless other services are closed. The act of political will required to substantially increase funding both for running schools and building or improving them is immense.

Redefining the terminology – who is the client?

Recently, not only has the terminology relating to state schools changed, so too has a number of crucial aspects of the legislative framework. The driving force behind these changes is the desire by government to extend delegation to all schools and to remove the inequalities which developed between the majority of LEA schools and those schools which opted out of LEA control, adopting instead 'grant maintained' status, effectively receiving their funding directly from central government.[24] Ultimately it is hoped that these changes will enable schools to use their discretion and either choose to buy-in services from their local education authority or provide those services themselves by fully managing their budgets in a way that only grant maintained schools could do previously. This will make the concept of the *local management of schools* more real.

Although the LEA framework will be available to support those schools which choose not to be autonomous, it may be anticipated that very many schools will opt to run part or all of their budgets. All recurrent and some significant capital funding is now in the hands of the schools themselves. As I write, there is no clear decision about the precise future of capital funding and how it should be determined.

However, it may be anticipated that schools will be given increasing autonomy to decide how and where funding is spent. They will be responsible for bidding to central government for limited funding for capital projects.

The four main categories of school are now called Community Schools (LEA), Foundation (formerly Grant Maintained), Special Agreement (Voluntary Aided) and Specialist (formerly in the guise of City Technology Colleges).

The crucial distinction between Community Schools and Foundation Schools is one of ownership and therefore responsibility. The LEAs own and act as landlords of the Community Schools and are at present the real clients. Foundation Schools are those which have previously 'opted out' of LEA control, choosing instead to control their own budgets. As previously stated, the reality of LMS allows little control for Community Schools since most of the recurrent budget is taken up by salaries paid directly from LEA sources. At present the LEAs have no statutory obligation to allow the schools under their control to administer their own larger scale capital spending by, for example, allowing the schools to employ an architect of their own choice, if they so wish.

In the case of Foundation Schools it is the governors who effectively own the school, therefore formal responsibility as client rests in their hands and those of the headteacher. The school would even control the budget which pays salaries, although these funds are held by the LEA and are paid directly to the teachers. The troubling inequalities this system created are outlined in the introduction to Chapter 3, and is the main reason why the present government wants all state schools to retain the levels of control which suits them, without removing the safety net of a full LEA service for those schools which choose to concentrate on teaching. It can be anticipated that in the years to come, the distinction between community and foundation schools will become hazy. Indeed, some pundits believe the changes are all to do with the abolition of GM schools.

Without the support of the LEA architects' department, fully opted out Foundation Schools (GM) must at present manage all building projects themselves. Sometimes this can work well, as was the case with Westborough Primary School (see Chapter 3, 'Pre-school classes and nursery schools') due to a responsive and energetic architect. Other Foundation Schools have been less fortunate in their choice of consultants. The alternative, which is a return to full LEA control, allows them little say in the management of their budgets. Often hard-pressed schools speak with disdain of some local authorities, which misdirect funds intended for repairs to their school towards other less deserving causes, often for what would appear to be political reasons.

Despite these concerns, many of the schools who chose to become grant maintained when the scheme was first introduced in 1987 are now returning to full LEA control. The work and responsibility entailed in making complicated bids and managing even minor capital projects proved too great. For Foundation Schools, bids were made to the

Funding Agency for Schools (FAS), until this agency was phased out by March 1999. Its responsibilities were usurped by the DfEE, who are expected to exercise discretion in funding capital improvements to only a few of the numerous deserving schools. Only the statutory Basic Need proposals are fully financed through the ACG. The introduction of Challenge and European Community funding usually allocated to deprived urban areas, and recent changes in legislation allowing Foundation Schools to borrow on the capital markets, are potentially providing more diverse funding sources.

The so-called Special Agreement (VA) schools are those which belong to a larger charitable trust, such as a church community. They will provide part of their annual recurrent funding from their own resources with 85 per cent coming directly from central government. In return for their 15 per cent contribution, they will receive a degree of autonomy in matters such as spiritual guidance, but must still fulfil statutory education requirements enshrined within the National Curriculum. Increasingly these schools require potential students to pass onerous entrance examinations. According to Gerry Sheridan, headteacher at the Good Shepherd Primary School, selectiveness is not usually based upon academic ability, but on the notion of a 'shared vision'. However, the high-flying secondary schools which have special agreement status in London, such as the Oratory School, are tending to 'Hoover-up' the most academically able students. This creates an imbalanced academic picture when viewed in terms of the annual examination league tables.

With Special Agreement schools there will usually be a diocesan board of education which may employ a building surveyor to direct day-to-day maintenance. He or she will be able to guide individual schools towards funding applications for larger capital projects, although the bids are actually submitted by the LEA. In this case, the client should be seen as something of a synthesis between the diocesan board and the headteacher. Where professionals become cynical of teachers' attitudes, the client relationship can become less democratic. To a certain extent, the closer the headteacher is to understanding his or her building, the more likely the school community will be to bid successfully for capital funding.

The final category I am concerned with here is the newly designated Specialist Schools (as opposed to Special Schools, which are Community or Foundation schools dedicated to children with special needs). Although they are generally referred to as technology colleges, in fact they are essentially secondary schools specializing in one of the following disciplines: technology, science, languages, performing arts, visual arts or sports. In order to achieve Specialist Status, they must formulate detailed bids to the DfEE.

Existing secondary schools wishing to make bids to become Specialist Schools must formulate the proposal

Figure 4.12a
This Art, Music and Drama suite was designed as an extension to the existing Clarendon School in Hampton, Middlesex, a Special School for children with learning and behavioural difficulties. The extension was conceived as a stand-alone building with its own entrance, which could be accessed and used by the local community after school hours; indeed, this was a requirement of the funding. The modular construction provides fast, flexible accommodation. Architects: Education Design Group, 4 Westbourne Grove Mews, London W11 2RU.

Figure 4.12b
The Lilliput Nursery manufactured by Portakabin initially installed at this school in Harlow. A fully modularized construction period. Architects: Cottrell and Vermeulen, 1a Iliffe Street, London SE17 3QA.

themselves; however, they need the tacit support of their LEA. The bid would be in the form of a three-year development plan. They must make links with local businesses and raise £100,000 in sponsorship money (which must be cash, as opposed to equipment or other payments in kind). If approved, this will then be match funded by the DfEE. Government has specially earmarked funding in order to expand this area. The central aim is to make education more responsive to the needs of local industry and commerce, and generate excellence to which other schools within the area would theoretically aspire. It is anticipated that fifty such new schools will be funded every year.

It is important that changes currently in hand are understood by both the client and the design team. They are intended to iron-out inequalities enshrined within the current system. In addition, the principle of devolving budgetary spending and direct control to the schools, by implication taking power away from distant beauraucrats, is a central tenet. Although a long way from realization, it is a principle which lies at the heart of the present government's policy.

Bidding to fund capital projects

Resourcing levels for running schools vary somewhat between local education authorities. They are always dependent on different levels of government support and the degree of priority given to education at any one time. The funding formula differs from one LEA to another, depending on the amount at which government allows each local authority to pitch its Council Tax. Generally, the poorer the region (or the most politically sensitive to tax rises), the less likely is government to allow increases in the local taxation levels in order to provide adequate levels of funding for schools. One school governor within a deprived Labour ward commented that because their school was not located in a marginal constituency, the need to fund education was not seen as a political priority.

Due to the fact that contributions to total school incomes can be made by parental fund-raising, further disparities emerge. The level of resourcing in particular classrooms and schools is dependent on a number of factors which can be summarized as: school-based decisions; the degree to which teachers, governors and parents can act cohesively to press for increased funding; numbers of pupils on roll; the priority given to education by national and local governments; and variations in LEA funding. More wealthy areas inevitably spend more on their education system, when all these factors are taken into account.

A good deal of political as well as professional judgement is involved at all points of the procurement cycle, with energetic individuals such as headteachers, governors and parents making some difference at local level. Added to this is the importance of having a cohesive switched-on LEA. It is surprising how modest, well-conceived bids for funding which have the support of both the school and the LEA can succeed, whereas grander more elaborate bids may be overlooked year after year. The process can then be repeated to create a virtuous cycle of continuing improvements to the school environment, one bid building upon the success of another.

Decisions about the allocation of scarce funding for capital projects are often taken at a distance from the schools themselves. Those under LEA control, which are by far the majority within the UK, can lobby their education authority, which then represents chosen schools in funding applications to central government. Information for all of these bids will increasingly be provided by school level promoters and their consultants, who will usually comprise an alliance between the headteacher and the school governors. However, at present, bidding information appears to emanate mainly from the LEA.

Sometimes architects drawn in at an early stage, and who are willing to do some initial legwork on a speculative basis, can be useful catalysts to the development process as a whole. Since the bids are made on a competitive basis for limited budgets, value for money will be the main criterion for the success of any bid. However, the more 'weight' behind the bid from groups and institutions within the community, the more likely to be its success. To reiterate, one successful bid can often lead to another from a different source, as the 'tricks' become known and understood.

For example, substantial funding to improve the Brampton Manor Secondary School came about through the formation of the Brampton Manor Champions Group, aptly named as they were championing the cause of the school by way of a wider raft of linked community projects. The group comprised representatives of the school, parent governors, council departments, the Hospital Trust (located on a site adjacent to the school), the local technical college and the East London Partnership, a government agency established to fund projects in designated deprived areas. The breadth of interest gave the promoting school genuine leverage in accessing funds not just from the DfEE but also from commercial and European sources.

Whether they are LEA controlled or not, all school projects must be submitted to the DfEE for scrutiny at various stages. Even projects which are funded entirely without grant aid, such as from fee-paying public schools assisted by alumni benefactors or state schools where projects are wholly paid for through the activities of wealthy parent/teacher associations, must be scrutinized in the usual way. The LEA certifies compliance with the School Premises Regulations (1996) for all schools in its area. This is a health and safety issue and the DfEE Constructional Standards allow exemption from the Building Regulations of LEA-controlled schools.[25] Grant Maintained schools must apply for Building Regulations permission in the usual way.

The clearest cases which can be made for new schools at LEA level are the statutory Basic Need proposals made through the ACG. For example, at Gamston in Nottingham, a thousand new houses were being developed as part of a new estate. The formula relating 22 primary school children per 100 new dwellings is applied before a new school can be built. The LEA must also prove that there are insufficient places within a two-mile radius of the new development. The process takes approximately three years from the submission of the bid to the DfEE in early autumn to completion and handover. If borrowing permission is available the following April (corresponding to the financial year), a start on site in the late autumn can be assumed.

Rather than building a new school, it is often possible to meet a Basic Need case by extending existing schools, assuming they comply with the two-mile criterion. 120 is the minimum number of pupils for a new primary school to be viable. This will comprise initially four teaching spaces with core services. Eventually there would be thirty pupils per class with a reception (also of thirty), three infant classes and six junior classes. The school should be no greater than 330 pupils in size, located on a three-acre site with a junior size football pitch and separate playground areas relating to pre-school, infants and juniors. The need for staff parking will depend on the availability of local transport facilities. The bid for such a project is clear-cut in the case of Gamston due to its isolated location. However, most bids will be far less certain as regards priority need and value for money.

Increasingly, the success of any LEA in bidding for school funds will depend upon its Asset Management Plan. This is a coherent strategy statement for school premises which relates a whole series of factors in order to plan and prioritize school building works across the LEA area. Sheffield City Chief Architect, Andy Beard, describes the three criteria which help to determine priorities when analysing school buildings; they are condition, sufficiency (gross area and the quantity of different types of teaching spaces) and suitability (quality of the learning environment). In addition, educational priority criteria will be identified which may have a bearing upon schools which are failing educationally.

The key factors which enable an AMP to be formalized are: the condition of the external fabric; structural information based on surveys; and the condition of the electrical and mechanical services previously carried out by qualified testers. In addition, security, capacity issues and educational priority all form part of the matrix. A category entitled 'the quality of the learning environment' includes an additional range of factors such as the provision of IT, numbers of temporary buildings on the site, and interior quality. These all contribute towards an all-round picture of the condition of each site within the authority.

However, the nature of priority is determined on the quality of the information known about each school. To quote from Sheffield's preliminary AMP, '... *this is the first attempt to bring all this information together in one document. The quality and age of the information is variable, and some of it therefore has to be treated with caution.*' It is worth noting that most European state education systems have operated on this coherent level for many years, coordinating information on the condition of their buildings, to anticipate and respond to needs and problems before they occur.

As the system gathers momentum, it can be anticipated that the LEAs will have a more complete picture of all schools in their area, presented in a way which identifies key educational criteria, so that future planning can be matched to funding. The Asset Management Plan will become the cornerstone of the whole funding process. Every LEA will be required to draw up a plan based along similar lines. At present Sheffield is one of three pilot LEAs participating in the development of a national model.

Involving private sector finance

The Private Finance Initiative (PFI) was introduced to create a framework for private sector investment in public sector infrastructure projects. It is gradually being applied to educational buildings and services. The principle is that private sector management expertise is brought to bear on the public sector. This is intended to transfer the risk of borrowing money away from the tax-payer and on to commercial organizations which are, in theory, best at dealing with capital funding of this nature.

In addition to borrowing money, the private sector will normally take on design construction and operating risks on the basis of a long contract (in excess of twenty-five years) in return for an ongoing unitary charge. It can cover a wide range of capital and revenue activities including new buildings, refurbishment, IT provision or complete new heating installations, including fuel and maintenance costs. This appears very attractive to central government. The public sector will retain a regulatory and legislative role as well as those consequences associated with changes in the school roll over the operating time of the contract. Government subsidy is via the SSA (Standard Spending Assessment) and effectively reduces the size of the unitary charge.

Where optimum risk transfer can be achieved, both the public and the private sector are in theory able to concentrate on those activities they do best. As can be seen in the case of some of the privatized railways in the UK, this can also mean that the service deteriorates although direct costs to the taxpayer remain fixed, thus achieving one side of the equation. In the case of school projects, the operation is usually more controlled and less susceptible to cavalier management techniques. Nevertheless, considerable resistance to this new approach can be discerned. Many believe it has long-term cost implications far in excess of conventional approaches to funding. Some of the main types of PFI schemes are:

- Design Build Finance Operate (DBFO) projects; a private contractor, sometimes linked to a new commercial development, constructs and operates a school building for an agreed period of time. The numbers of new school pupils can be clearly assessed (using the equation of twenty-two primary school children per hundred new dwellings), therefore the need is tangible. The contractor receives a performance-related operating fee to cover borrowing, running costs and profit. Capital outlay is funded privately; therefore funding and operating responsibility is taken away from the LEA, although in theory they should regulate the quality of the service provided.

  This should not be confused with a straightforward deal between the local authority and a private developer. In exchange for land and permission to develop, a contractor will build the school and hand it over to the LEA who will then operate it in the usual way. This is called a Section 52 Agreement.[26] However, both types of financing potentially hold similar pitfalls in that the contractor will usually employ their own architects and not necessarily implement detailed guidance from the LEA on design matters. In a commercial world, the temptation to water-down quality and architectural authenticity may be a drawback for those who adopt this approach to funding.

- Dual use schemes are those where a private sector contractor constructs a facility such as a sports hall, tennis centre or a swimming pool, to which the school has access for an agreed period of time each day. The contractor is free to generate income for the rest of the time including weekends and holidays. The revenue from school and commercial use would enable the contractor to maintain the facilities whilst ensuring a market return on his investment. This approach is particularly attractive to the private sector where a school is located on a valuable site, where development would otherwise be restricted.

- Facilities management schemes are those where a specialist private contractor takes responsibility for providing a service such as heating or grounds mainte-nance. Here the contractor will not only provide the fixed asset, such as a tractor or a heating boiler, but will also agree to provide heating for the buildings to a stated temperature range over a set contract period. These agreements can be handed on to PFI.

When making bids for substantial public capital, the promoter will normally be required to show that they have explored the PFI route. However, operational modes of this type in which LEAs feel confident are largely untested. Consequently, very few schools have opted to go down this route. By its very nature, commercial stringency is imposed which can compromise architectural quality. One practice I spoke to refused to countenance such work since it involved cut-throat fee bidding, and unreasonable specification constraints. Other architectural practices will take a less circumspect view.

Until the link between high quality environments and learning outcomes is made, the potential for mediocre school design will be a potential problem when commis-sioning authorities are vying for the cheapest new option. However, it is worth mentioning the DfEE Architect's and Buildings Branch, who not only provide guidance to potential bidders but also have a role in vetting LEA capital schemes, including PFI bids. Theirs is a crucial role within this process, ensuring that standards of design are maintained as procurement processes are privatized and opened up to increasingly competitive tendering processes.

A note to clients: 1. PRE-CONTRACT – you have the money – what next?

Often the appointment of an architect will go hand in hand with earlier development work, a trusting professional relationship having already evolved between the client and the architect. However, if this is not the case, schools will expect guidance from the LEA on the selection of their consultants. This can be in a form where specialist archi-tects pitch for the commission in limited competition with two or three others. The school will then expect their agent (a private architect or the LEA equivalent) to employ a

contractor on their behalf. Any temptation to save money by the client appointing a contractor directly will at best be a false economy, at worse a potential disaster. Even the smallest of projects will require a detailed knowledge of safety regulations, British Standards and legislation result-ing from European Community Directives. For example, the Disability Discrimination Act (1997) requires that all public buildings over a single storey must have a lift and is therefore part of the regulations which govern any new building.[27]

The Construction (Design and Management) Regulations (CDM), which came into force in 1995, require that clients appoint a planning supervisor and a principal contractor, except where the works are deemed to be minor. The planning supervisor has specific responsibilities in connection with site safety. Initially the project-planning supervisor prepares what is formally called a health and safety plan. This is then transferred to the principal contractor who will subsequently develop the plan further. Clients have a responsibility to ensure that both documents are competently drawn up and implemented. The health and safety executive have published guidance on CDM Regulations, and local education authorities will sometimes have a dedicated health and safety inspector.

All school building projects, except those in the private sector, are exempt from the Building Regulations unless they are budgeted at less than £200,000, in which case the promoter can choose to go through building regulations. Otherwise they are expected to comply with the DfEE's constructional standards. All schools, or in the case of Special Agreement Schools, the LEA must certify compli-ance and will look to the lead consultant for assurances that this is the case. Foundation Schools will be required to gain approval from the DfEE. However, the DfEE is currently consulting on ending the exemption of school buildings from national Building Regulations approval.

An aspect, which should be clarified at an early stage, is how furniture and fittings will be financed, and whether or not this needs to be included in any bid. Funds can be wasted by selecting furniture from a domestic catalogue which may be incapable of standing up to the rigours of school use beyond the first three years. Guidance is avail-able in the form of DfEE building bulletins.

The range of consultants required will depend upon the size of the project. Small projects will be carried out by a single architect in conjunction with his or her nominated structural engineer. For larger projects, over approxi-mately £150,000, there will need to be a full team of consultants including specialist mechanical and electrical engineers, possibly a landscape architect, and almost certainly a quantity surveyor who will be responsible for the initial accurate and finite costings, and will have a continuing role in cost-controlling the project on-site. Upon appointment, the architect should be given respon-sibility as the team leader to nominate and approve specialist consultants. A Clerk of Works is sometimes employed on larger projects. Usually located on the site, their responsibility is to ensure that the building is constructed in accordance with the specification. They are employed by the client and will report to the lead consultant.

Peter Foale, who is Assistant Director of Education at Nottinghamshire Education Authority (speaking to me in 1996), believes that their design philosophy has changed over the past few years as a result of competition from independent practices. Their architects' department is less dogmatic than previously. They believe in extensive consultation with the school community during the development of a project. Initially a 'wish list' of facilities they want to see at the school will be drawn up. Subsequently, discussions with the headteacher and the school governors will bring about a preliminary consensus as to how the brief should evolve. The curriculum advisor at the education authority may be consulted. Then the headteacher and one or two governors will visit different model schools prior to the preparation of sketch schemes. These are presented to the school community, which would include interested parents, for evaluation and discussion.

Foale resists the appointment of consultants who have no previous school building experience. As a local authority with their own architect's department, they would always maintain the value of using their own in-house team. However, the extent to which this particular local authority are prepared to consult, in order to 'get it right', illustrates the competitive climate within which job procurement is now taking place. Local authorities no longer get the school building work as a matter of course, as used to be the case. They are sharpening the quality of their service to counter the possibility of appointments by the schools themselves, as is currently the case in the voluntary aided sector. As discussed earlier, although not without its pitfalls, this will further emphasize the quality of service provided.

The implementation of such a regime might mean that scarce funding will be distributed evenly amongst all schools in a region rather than being targeted by way of carefully drawn-up asset management plans. Large schools with greatest need will simply not receive adequate funding. This suggests that mechanisms will be implemented to ensure sensible distribution, a role that will most likely fall on to the LEA in any event. A further criticism echoes Peter Foale's fear that schools may simply appoint the wrong consultant, perhaps choosing a local parent who happens to be an architect, with little experience of school work.

Schools vested with the power to choose their own consultant should at least visit one previous project designed by the practice (the LEA architects' department or any private consultant should certainly be willing to show off their work), in order to assess competence and get a 'feel' for the type of architecture on offer. They should also speak to previous clients. It is important that the person who has responsibility for the day-to-day running of the job is interviewed, not just partners who may have little involvement once the project has been assigned. From the outset there should be clear lines of communication established between the client and the consultants. The ability to place trust in, and develop a working relationship with, the person running the job is important. This can be partially assessed through preliminary meetings; it is in my view a good sign if the prospective architects have previous experience of consulting with parents and classroom teachers as well as the headteacher and its board of governors.

An architect will be expected to prepare information in order to get prices from at least three contractors competing for the same commission. This element of the service is a statutory DfEE requirement and normally ensures an independent unbiased assessment of a range of contractors, as well as a competitive price for the job. European Procurement rules stipulate an even tighter competitive framework. If the client (understandably) wishes to apply the same criteria when selecting a lead consultant, then a number of different architects can be invited to compete on the basis of fee levels and the scope of their previous experience. The quality of the service should in theory be uniform since it is governed by the RIBA code of professional conduct. However, as with any service the final deciding factor can be down to personalities involved. Increasingly, fee competition is becoming commonplace. Sometimes this can include a long list of practices; however, a shorter, more focused, set of potential consultants will avoid excessive bureaucracy. Guidance from the Royal Institute of British Architects (RIBA) is available on selection of consultants appropriate for the project.

The size of the consultant's fee will vary, depending upon the extent and complexity of the job in question. For a capital project, as against a maintenance project, consultant's fees should not exceed 15 per cent of the construction costs, including expenses but excluding VAT or any planning charges or building insurance costs. For an independent consultant carrying out work, these will be retrieved from the local authority except in the case of a capital grant, where the DfEE pay directly; they are likely to reject any consultant whose fee level exceeds 15 per cent of construction cost. This is based upon an analysis of a range of new building projects, and it includes the planning supervisor's fee required under CDM regulations. However, fees for simple projects and straightforward repairs are expected to be significantly lower. The RIBA recommended fee scale is an appropriate guide. However, where particularly large projects are concerned, keen competitive fee bidding can be implemented.

However, I reiterate that the level of service each consultant is capable of providing, particularly in design terms, should be carefully weighed up. It should be remembered that lowest fees might not always represent the best value for money. The quality and scope of the service should always be carefully assessed and previous experience (not necessarily in the design and construction of school buildings) should be considered. It is far better to have a well-designed building completed efficiently and on time than to save a few thousand pounds on fees. This is where the responsibilities of the school acting as client are most crucial. The client should never deal directly with the contractor. Time and effort should be invested in the selection process of both the consultant and the contractor at the beginning of the project, in order to enjoy an efficiently run building contract.

A note to clients: 2. BRIEFING – the programme and a development plan

The traditional method of procurement based on competitive tendering is a statutory requirement of the DfEE. In the unlikely event that an alternative approach is to be considered, such as the adoption of design and build methods, early consultation with the agency is essential. The Code of Procedure for Selective Tendering (as issued by the Joint Contracts Tribunal) sets out the recommended number of tenderers required for different projects. The usual number is between three and six. In the case of PFI bids, architect/developer teams will pitch for full-price services, which would include everything from statutory fees for planning and building regulations to the cost of maintaining the grounds.

The LEA or the local diocese will usually have a recommended list of contractors, some of which may have carried out work previously. If additional contractors are to be added to the list, perhaps recommended by the lead consultant, they will be required to show that they meet all the criteria in terms of operational capability (usually relating to size), insurance warranties and track record. It is important that sufficient time is allowed not just for the tendering process, but also for detailed design. Project programmes are often determined to fit in with the school vacations, although it is certainly possible to run school building contracts during term times. One of the most important tasks for the contractor is to return a feasible programme which suits the needs of the existing school community. Even where a new school is being constructed, hand-over will generally coincide with the new academic year.

All projects are submitted to the DfEE, who have professional teams to advise them and scrutinize proposals for prospective funding. When the proposal has received the initial go-ahead, much more detailed information must be supplied for tendering purposes. Standard forms are available for these applications which must be supported by drawings, specifications, photographs and tender reports.

Submissions for scrutiny must be complete and clearly presented. The risk of delays as a result of a failure to provide good information can cause problems in fulfilling government spending targets within a prescribed time frame. There is no scope for fast-streaming applications except in the case of emergency projects. Although the onus is on the client to implement all matters pertaining to statutory requirements, in reality it is the architect or lead consultant who will arrange these matters. This is not just planning approvals, but also legislation relating to building quality standards in general. Submissions must comply with the statutory procedures which cover health and safety and the welfare of pupils. These rules apply to all school premises and include external areas. Constructional Standards cover environmental design, fire safety and parts of the Building Regulations and Approved Documents. However, I stress that, at the present time, the methodology is subject to streamlining and considerable modification.

The need to provide new or substantially upgraded accommodation is often an obvious and long-standing one. Schools will be informed of potential funding perhaps as a result of changes to government spending priorities and will act accordingly. As previously mentioned, all schools have a statutory requirement to maintain the Estates Plan, as part of the School Development Plan. The more detailed this is, the better. A long-term development plan can aid the process and support the educational objectives. It is much more plausible to submit a bid which is framed in these terms than to act in a knee-jerk way, responding to events as they happen.

Accommodation problems may not always require new buildings. The remodelling of existing facilities can often represent a better solution than launching into expensive new build projects which may in any case have little scope for funding. Advice from architects who can analyse curriculum needs and match them to the existing building stock are valuable supports when developing a meaningful long-term plan. In the case of LEA schools, to a certain extent this will be carried out as part of the AMP.

It is of fundamental importance to match the curriculum and social needs of the wider community to the accommodation which is already available. Too much accommodation may be as much of an encumbrance as having too little. School facility costs, that is the cost of maintenance, energy, cleaning and insurances, are in the range of £30–40 per square metre per year. Therefore, substantial savings can be made by reducing areas surplus to requirement. The reorganization of subject departments, small-scale extensions and modifications to an entrance or circulation areas can be as valuable as the two opposite extremes, either doing nothing to the school, or constructing a totally new building. It is useful to have options drawn up which provide alternative spending strategies, for discussion with the governors and the wider school community.

Figure 4.13
Common areas outside the classroom should be carefully considered as they are essential spaces for social interaction. The corridor link within the resources block at Haute Vallée School.

Throughout the text I have stressed the importance of good briefing when designing new school premises. In the history section (Chapter 1) I point out the way in which space must be flexible enough to accommodate changing aspirations within society at large, underlining the reality of the school as one which responds to social needs. In the section on the ideal classroom (Chapter 2) I stress the importance of matching the needs of classroom teachers to the spaces within which the diverse activities of the National Curriculum must take place. Other areas of the school are no less crucial in fulfilling the functional and spiritual needs of those who are using them. The school environment is for people and not for machines. It is therefore axiomatic that the designer should consult with the end users and match their perceptions with the preconceptions of the funding agencies as to what constitutes an ideal learning environment.

Clients inexperienced in this role may be surprised at the overall length of time it takes to brief adequately. It is

recommended that one person has overall responsibility for carrying out this research work. The results must be balanced so that the personal enthusiasms of the specialist teachers are neither ignored nor wholeheartedly adopted at the expense of other users' needs. Community groups should be consulted as well as governors, departmental heads, premises managers and finally, although I state this tentatively, the children themselves. Within this complex and multi-layered structure, the priorities must be determined by the architect and presented to the client as a definitive set of fully costed options. The end result is inevitably one of compromise; however, the priority must be towards improved social and educational outcomes.

Often the process of consultation enables teachers and pupils to understand and follow the design/development sequence, so that they are more sympathetic to the changes taking place. It is important to recognize that most lay people cannot simply be asked what it is they want, as

Figure 4.14
Melanie Evans' *Strategy for Consultation* included 1:50 scale working models showing furniture and fittings to which school pupils and their teachers could relate. See Chapter 2, 'The ideal classroom'.

if they can articulate sophisticated spatial needs. Rather, they should be given meaningful options, most usefully of a visual three-dimensional nature. For example, Richard Jobson, the design architect for the Hautee Vallée School on Jersey, used extensive models to illustrate the developing ideas. These were initially at a scale of 1:200. Subsequently, larger scales were adopted. These incorporated simulations of colour and texture. Time-consuming it may be, but good briefing is a two-way process which will pay immense longer-term dividends. These can be seen in comparing the client's initial expectations and the way the building works in use, which in the case of the Haute Vallée School is a close match.

A note to clients: 3. DEVELOPING THE DESIGN –
maintaining an input

It may be apparent from all of this that the stages of design development are not strictly linear. Rather, they are three-

dimensional, depending on a constantly evolving process of refinement, with new inputs being made at every stage. However, these development periods are finite and the final design process will often be compressed into a relatively short space of time. It is crucial to ensure that written records are maintained which should be circulated to all parties. It may be useful to consider the following three phases of development as being indicative:

• *Phase 1*
The development of a concept; although this will usually have been determined at the pre-bid stage, it may require a good deal of refinement and re-clarification after confirmation of the successful bid. It may also include sketch drawings, illustrative precedents and ideas about the aesthetic concerns of those involved. Consultation will be a very important aspect of this phase; however, it will veer towards the general rather than the particular. A detailed briefing

document pertaining to the educational curriculum will be required from the LEA.

- *Phase 2*

  At the heart of the second stage is the development of sketch ideas into more detailed planning studies to establish the range, size and spatial relationships of the parts to the whole. It will include the checking of area standards and costs and will incorporate the most meaningful phase of the consultation process. Where possible an entire range of briefing sessions including design workshop days with three-dimensional briefing packages will be matched to the needs of the funding programme.

- *Phase 3*

  The final pre-tender phase will be the detailed design where most if not all the elements of the building are finalized. The specification of doors, windows, walls, heating and other aspects relating to structural and environmental design will be specified. Consultation is still important, especially checking that fundamental decisions which were made at earlier stages are still being implemented. It is important that the flow of communication is fluid, especially relating to the size of spaces, colours and materials. Although a great deal will be left to trust, a process of client inclusion rather than exclusion must be maintained.

At the point when the documents are sent out for pricing, all decisions should in theory have been made. Since the budget is to all intents and purposes fixed, changes and modifications after this stage are not advisable. However, it is likely that circumstances will crop up which force some changes onto the construction team. There are contractual mechanisms built in which can facilitate certain changes and modifications during the course of construction. When preparing documentation for tendering purposes, the client will also be called upon to provide information relating to issues such as site boundaries, access and construction deadlines which suit the existing or new school community.

A note to clients: 4. ON SITE – completing the process

Communication is still seen as being important during each stage of on-site activity. The client should receive minutes of all meetings held. However, instructions should always go through the lead consultant, never directly from the client to the contractor, as they may have unforeseen cost or programmatic implications. Clients do change their minds, particularly when viewing the new spaces coming out of the ground for the first time. Drawings and models can never convey the physical reality of built form. Construction can have a highly emotive effect upon prospective users. When the full reality of complex and distant decisions are becoming apparent on site, control by

the lead consultant is crucial. The effective consultant will make it their responsibility to ensure the client is 'nursed' through if necessary.

It is important for the client to understand that each stage of the work is carefully pre-planned. Materials must be ordered well in advance if delays are to be avoided. Changes at this late stage may have implications for aspects of the work such as structural design and safety which may not be obvious to a lay person. Although there is a contingency sum included within the contract to cover unforeseen occurrences, this is not an excuse to alter the design or specification. Contractors will always be looking for increases in the contract sum. Variations to the works are often seen as their way of making a reasonable profit, particularly in circumstances where competitive pricing is tight. Some latitude in the budget may be prudent. However, savings can often be anticipated when adopting a design and build form of contract.

The tender documents are made up of three parts: the drawings, which show the precise size and form of the new building; the specification, which describes the detailed nature of each part of the works; and the bills of quantity, which set out each element of the work as a sequence of priced items. Provisional sums are included to cover those parts of the works which cannot be known at tendering stage. Work which is designed and installed at a later date to cover uncertain items (which may be dependent upon additional moneys coming through) are called 'prime cost sums'. Applications for additional funding to cover genuinely unforeseen costs can be made to the DfEE, but only as a last resort.

When the building is ready for handover, the client, architect and main contractor's representative will make a final inspection of the building noting any incomplete or defective parts. The keys will be handed over and the building can be used to a greater or lesser extent. If the project is not habitable in time, the contractor will have to pay the client. This is an insurance policy covered in the contract which is called the period of liquidated and ascertained damages. The figure usually relates to the reasonable cost of providing alternative accommodation and is a daily or weekly charge levied until such time the building is ready for use. It is a punitive tax applied in the event of the contractor's inefficiency, and is a vital element of the contract.

When the building is in use, there will inevitably be a period where minor problems come to light. This is called the defects liability period and is usually of six months' duration following project handover. A retention sum will be released upon successful completion of these defects. Sometimes this period can be extended in order to allow for a heating system to 'bed in'. Any defects during this time should be noted and, following a formal inspection at the end of the defects liability period, are expected to be resolved. An extension to the defects liability period will naturally delay release of the contractor's final payments.

When the building is finally handed over, record drawings, maintenance manuals for all equipment and the health and safety plan should be held by the school Also provided should be a user manual which goes into much more detail covering the ways in which a building should be operated, maintenance requirements over a twenty-five year period and a log book to note additional works carried out over subsequent years. It is true that, to a certain extent, recent CDM regulations have addressed these omissions. However, it is often left to the client to ensure that post-occupancy maintenance is recorded and evaluated.

The client should hold a list of all who worked on and supplied materials for the project. This documentation should be retained and kept safely, to be handed on to subsequent generations of headteachers and school keepers. Larger secondary schools will have premises managers who should be fully conversant with the building both in terms of its technical performance and the educational values enshrined in its environmental ethos. School buildings are living organisms, which given appropriate care can last for many years, changing subtly to accommodate new generations of pupils and their teachers.

Summary

We have set out a system which is currently in use where the architect is a stand-alone consultant. As procurement strategies evolve it is likely that architects will become more integrated into the construction team of surveyors, engineers and landscape architects all employed by the main contractor (referred to previously as the design and build, contractural arrangement). In this situation, the point of contact for the client will be the builder's representative rather than the architect. The architect will be expected to nurture contacts with reliable builders, and ensure that the architect's unique talents are brought to the process, interpreting the client's spatial needs through meaningful consultation. In this way, teams will stay together and develop their own specialism, to become expert in the design of a particular building such as a school.

Schools' architecture is constantly evolving, a process which is barely recognized by the cumbersome funding regimes, which bring about change and modernization on a clunking 20–35-year cycle. Changes usually occur when funding is allocated on the basis of highly centralized political expediency. This is crisis management of the worst kind. Perhaps Peter Blundell Jones is right: until decentralization and distant bureaucracy is overcome, this will always be the case. The concept of LMS (Local Management of Schools) is a policy directed towards this end; however, it is in its infancy. Nevertheless, an architect committed to the well-being of a particular school can go a long way towards rectifying these anomalies. We are all custodians of our environments, whether they are private or public territories.

Education in this matter begins at school. Schools' architecture should reflect this duty in every aspect.

Private fee-paying schools within the UK invest around £5000 per pupil per year with staff ratios below 10:1. In the state sector the figure is currently in the region of £2250 per pupil with staff ratios double or triple that. It is striking that in countries such as Germany, France and Italy there is a strong grammar school system which is broad and open. In those countries, poor educational practice is attacked as an inhibitor of social mobility. As a consequence, it can be argued that more public-spirited virtues prevail. If this spirit is to spread within the UK culture, rather than simply tinkering with administrative frameworks, the government must increase investment in the state education system considerably in order to equalize the funding of the private schools.

Many believe that because the academic élite are educated apart, there is no emotional commitment to the welfare state for those who occupy the top positions in society within the UK. They would point to European systems where the strength of a twin-track secondary school system, comprising technical and grammar schools, relies on good funding for both. The end result is two systems which have equal strengths, directing students towards academic or vocational careers as appropriate. However, no matter what the system is, the notion of devolving power and control away from politicians and down towards the communities themselves is a concept which is at the forefront of current political debate. Central to this idea is the need for consultation.

(The speculative nature of this section is inevitable, as the impending changes to the system are determined. Delegation to schools from the LEAs is a political commitment. The arguments for and against, and the degree to which schools will hold real control over their budgets, encapsulate the central educational issues at the heart of our society. The outcome is keenly awaited.)

Notes

1 *Passive Solar Schools – A Design Guide* Building Bulletin 79, A & B Branch, HMSO, London, 1994, p.8, historical background.

2 *Passive Solar Schools – A Design Guide*, Building Bulletin 79, A & B Branch, HMSO, London, 1994, p.12.

3 Evans, Barrie, 'Energy lessons from school.' *Architect's Journal*, 20 April 1995, p.42.

4 Evans, Barrie, 'Energy lessons from school.' *Architect's Journal*, 20 April 1995, p.43.

5 Evans, Barrie, 'Energy lessons from school.' *Architect's Journal*, 20 April 1995, pp.43–44.

6 *Good Stewardship: National Audit Office Examinations of Value for Money at Grant Maintained Schools*

1995–96. Report by the Comptroller and Auditor General, HMSO (HC 697).

7   Blundell-Jones, Peter, 'Green School of Thought – review of a primary school at Stuttgart-Stammheim.' *Architectural Review*, September 1997, p.53.

8   Blundell-Jones, Peter, 'Green School of Thought – review of a primary school at Stuttgart-Stammheim.' *Architectural Review*, September 1997, p.53.

9   Penn, Helen, *Centres of Excellence*, Social Sciences Research Unit, Institute of Education, 18 Woburn Square, London WC1H 0NS.

10 The tendency to return to more traditional teaching methods is explored exhaustively in Philips, Melanie, *They Should All Have Prizes,* Little Brown and Company, London, p.61.

11 Holmes, Gerard, *The Idiot Teacher,* Faber and Faber, London, 1952, pp.26–27.

12 Martin, D., Lucas, W., Titman, W. and Hayward, G (eds) *The Outdoor Classroom* (1990) and *Special Places, Special People* (1994), Learning Through Landscapes, 3rd Floor, Southside Offices, The Law Courts, Winchester, Hants, SO23 9DL.

13 Schools wishing to link to a Birmingham school involved in improving school grounds can contact Sue Fenoughty, 44 Maney Hill Road, Sutton Coldfield, Birmingham B72 1JR.

14 Belzig, Gunter, 'Child-like, childish, child-friendly: is there such a thing as children's aesthetics?' In L. Bullivant (ed) *Kid Size, The Material World of Childhood,* Thames & Hudson, 1997.

15 Clarricoates, Katherine, 'Child culture at school – a clash between gendered worlds.' A chapter in A. Pollard (ed), *Children and their Primary Schools,* Falmer Press, 1987, p.201.

16 King, J.A. (T11354) *The Heathland Inspection Report* Under OfSTED contract number 0/S5/001931, 9 and 13 October 1995.

17 'Hard Choices', *Guardian Education*, 12 August 1995, p.10.

18 Fischer, Thomas, 'No cure-alls for K-12.' *Architectural Record*, October 1997, pp.105–107.

19 Within the UK, the Department for Education and Employment and the Royal Institute of British Architects may be contracted for further information. DfEE: Caxton House, 6–12 Tothill Street, London SW1H 9NA. RIBA: Client's Advisory Service, 66 Portland Place, London W1N 4AD.

20 Pollard, Andrew, *Reflective Teaching in the Primary School* (3rd edn), Cassell, London, 1997, p.36.

21 New Deal for Schools (NDS) is an additional capital grant of £1.086 billion being distributed in five rounds over the life of the 1997 government, primarily for eliminating the backlog of repairs to school buildings.

22 Sheffield City Architect Andy Beard comments: 'The carpet would probably come out of the schools budget (unless part of a larger LEA capital scheme). Boiler replacement is capital. Annual regular maintenance is probably the school responsibility although under the new regime this is not clear.'

23 Hutton, Will, *The State to Come* Vintage, London, 1997.

24 The concept of 'opting out' was an invention of the last Conservative Government, allowing schools to bid for funds directly to central government via the now defunct Funding Agency for Schools. Many commentated on the derisive nature of this, since opted-out schools avoided local control, which was a key Conservative political-objective. Opted-out schools who were prepared to run their own budgets, were far better resourced, depriving other schools of funding.

25 Andy Beard comments that they (Sheffield Design-Build Services) apply for Building Regulations approval for all their projects.

26 Andy Beard comments: 'A planning gain agreement such as this is rather unusual ... planning obligations are more common where residential developers hand over cash.'

27 Andy Beard observes that, for LEA schools, the appointment will be by the council. Schools do not at present enter into independent agreements either with a consultant or a contractor.

Part B

Case studies

Significant points of reference within this case study section include the use of a particular form of technology, the organization of the room programme, and approaches to the process of consulting with the end-users during design development. In some cases area analysis is approximate, but generally gross usable internal area is accurately measured and includes: light well spaces, corridors and courtyards, if they form part of the teaching space itself; ancillary storage areas; and kitchen, dining and assembly areas. The UK flooring conventions are applied to all projects featured, indicating ground, first floor, second floor, etc.

An architect's statement is included where I feel it is appropriate and any particularly significant features illustrating a strong educational/architectural convergence are also mentioned.

What marks these projects out is the imaginative edge they bring, with designers using ingenuity to create buildings of immense educational and social benefit. The featured projects are intended to illustrate a range of approaches to the design of contemporary school environments. What is striking is the frequent rise of urban iconography by the designers when describing their schools. Hence the references to internal streets, villa forms, towers and gatehouses.

1 The Speech and Learning Centre, Christopher Place, London

Troughton and McAslam

Type of project:
Assessment and therapeutic teaching facility for children under the age of five with hearing impairment or speech and language delay.

Client:
The Speech Language and Hearing Centre Ltd (registered charity).

Site area:
185 m². The site is located within a small mews in Euston, Central London. The building is set within a context of variegated back-of-terrace buildings. The site is therefore tightly confined and the building opens onto a south orientated mews.

Number of teaching spaces:
Twenty-four, divided between individual and small group therapy rooms. Essential are the adults' spaces within the building with outreach programmes into the community. There is a high adult to child teaching ratio of 1:3 with typically two professionals to six children per group therapy room. Ancillary staff facilities represent a substantial part of the accommodation.

Type of construction:
Reinforced in-situ concrete frame including fair-faced columns, beams and soffits and power-floated slabs. Structural blockwork perimeter walls and infill fair-faced blockwork walls. Steel-framed double glazed cladding units.

Special features:
Acoustically separated teaching therapy rooms. High specification performance-related fixtures and finishes incorporating: acoustically insulated double-glazing; lead-lined doors with magnetic seals; acoustic absorption panels to walls and ceilings; dedicated air supply and extract system.

A series of projecting bay windows with integrated fitted bench and shelf units 'float' within the fully glazed elevation. These provide opportunities for long views offered by the external space of the mews.

Schedule of areas:

Ground floor	155 m²
First floor	155 m²
Second floor	70 m² (with external roof terrace play space)
Total	380 m²

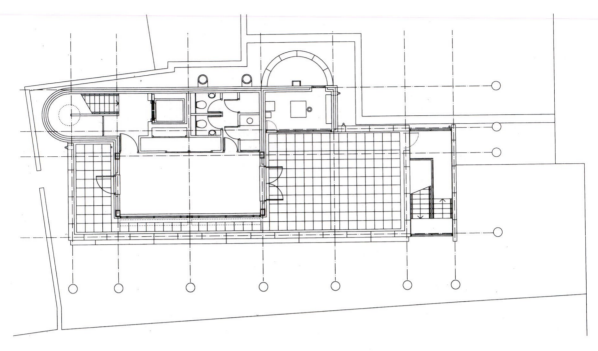

Figure CS1.1
Ground floor plan.

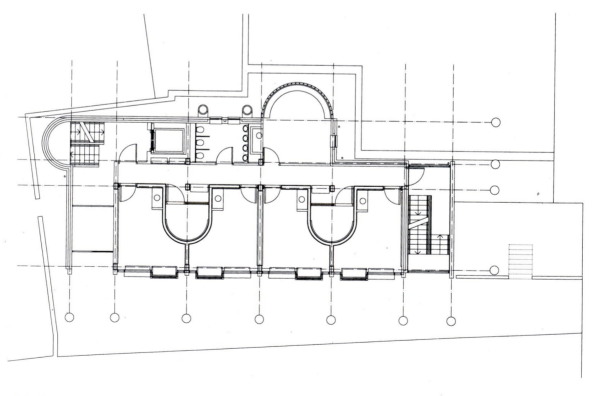

Figure CS1.2
First floor plan.

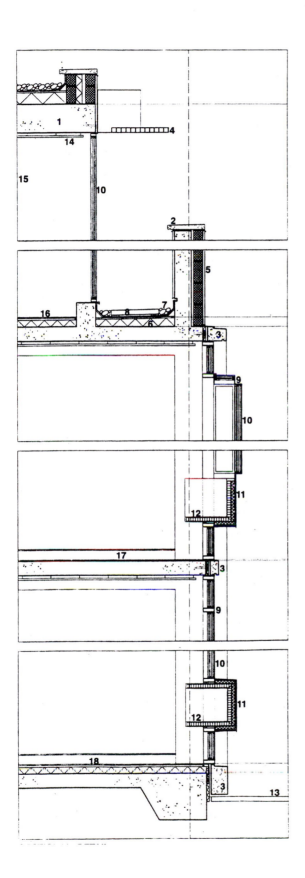

Figure CS1.3
Detailed section.

KEY:
1 In-situ concrete
2 Pre-cast concrete coping
3 Pre-cast concrete cladding
4 Powder coated steel louvre
5 Painted render on blockwork
6 Mineral surfaced felt membrane on roofing board and rigid insulation
7 Washed beach cobbles
8 Concrete pavers on rubber pedestals
9 Micaceous iron oxide coated steel glazing frames
10 Acoustic toughened laminated double-glazed unit
11 Zinc sheet cladding on waterproof plywood
12 Beech lipped and veneered joinery unit
13 Reclaimed yorkstone paving
14 Microporous acoustic boarding on metal studwork
15 Skimmed plasterboard on metal studwork
16 Rubber sheeting on waterproof chipboard
17 Rubber sheeting on power floated concrete
18 Carpet on waterproof chipboard
19 Rendered blockwork

Group therapy room	13 m²
Individual therapy room	5 m²
Multipurpose room	24 m²
Family room	20 m²

Summary

Christopher Place is a charity-run assessment and therapeutic centre for children under 5 who have hearing impairment or speech and language delay. The site is within a confined mews back lot surrounded by taller buildings. The new building is organized in a three-storey block running along the mews street. The main two-storey block to the front of the site overlooking the street entrance consists of the staff and teaching rooms at ground and first floor respectively. All rooms in the new purpose-designed building are orientated towards the south to engage with the narrow mews space and to optimize sun penetration. Projecting window bays maximize the dialogue between inside and out and provide the best aspect within this confined site.

The colour and material palette creates a cool tonal and textural range to the building's envelope, which is offset by

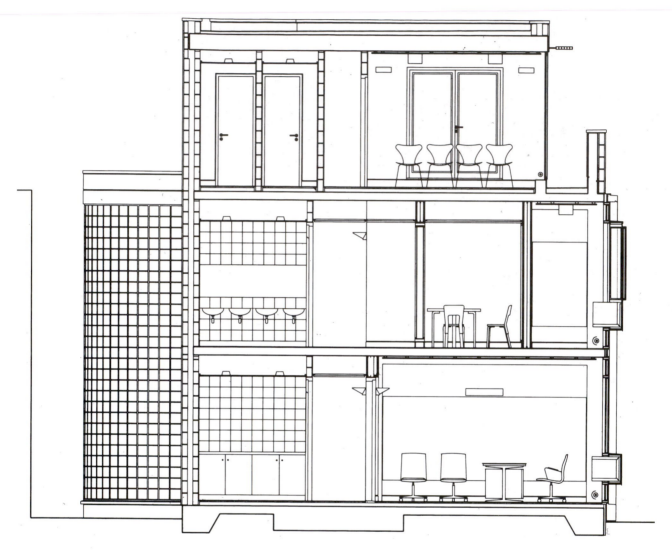

Figure CS1.4
Cross section through courtyard and therapy room showing projecting bay window seats.

the use of rich natural materials inside, utilizing some coloured lacquer finishes. Particular attention was focused on the form and colours of the mews elevation. Glazing frames are silver grey-coated aluminium to balance tonally with internal exposed concrete and rubber flooring, and external zinc cladding. The buff colour of the external pre-cast concrete frame matches with the local context of stock brick, and is echoed internally by elements of fitted furniture.

The mews retains its traditional character and has been upgraded with the original granite cobbles re-laid and a new Yorkstone 'orientation' strip introduced running from the street through to the building entrance. Strategic planting provides a degree of visual softening, and night-time illumination animates the space further. On an urban scale, the massing of the new building as a series of blocks consistent in material and finish creates a tension between the variegated back-of-terrace buildings which surround the site. It does not mimic its surroundings yet is in harmony with its context in a very subtle way.

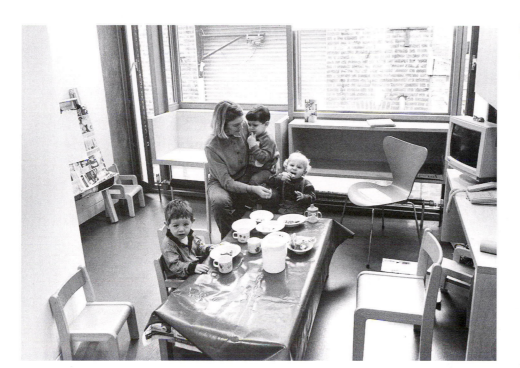

Figure CS1.5
Therapy room on the first floor with fully integrated furniture and fittings.

Figure CS1.6
Family room with glass block wall to maximize natural lighting from the rear of the site.

2   Seabird Island School, Agassiz, British Columbia

Patkau Associates

Type of project:
State elementary and secondary school for children from kindergarten to grade ten (aged 16) providing 400 full-time school places.

Client:
Seabird Island Band Department of Public Works.

Site area:
The site is not enclosed as such; the 23,000 ft² building is simply an integral part of the surrounding public spaces and the Seabird Island as a whole. The island is 120 kilometres east of Vancouver situated on the Fraser River delta and surrounded by mountains. The school is sited along an open northern edge of an existing village square. There is, however, a dedicated outdoor play area of approximately 1000 m² and a secure covered space for the kindergarten.

'The space of the island – a flat delta of agricultural land surrounded by mountains – seemed very much like a great room. We felt that the building which was to inhabit this room should have an animated personality, something that could be perceived on a naive level as a "being" of some kind. We didn't intend that the building represent anything specific.'

Architect's statement

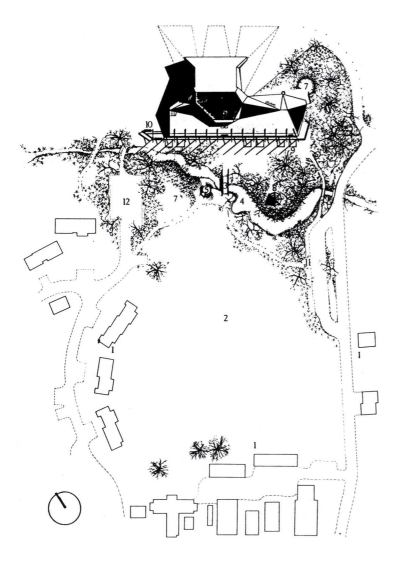

Figure CS2.1
Site plan.

KEY:
1. Community buildings
2. Village common space
3. Bridge
4. Dry creek bed
5. Fire pit
6. Seabird Island School
7. Outdoor play areas
8. Traditional pit house
9. Teaching gardens
10. Salmon drying racks
11. Bus and passenger drop-off
12. Parking

Figure CS2.2a
Cross section through entrance gym.

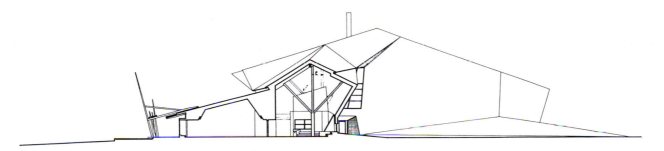

Figure CS2.2b
Cross section through elementary wing.

Number of teaching spaces:
Ten elementary and secondary classrooms with a kindergarten.

Type of construction:
The traditional structure of the natives of the Pacific Northwest is heavy timber post and beam. This approach has been interpreted using parallel columns and beams with steel connections sitting on a reinforced concrete beam and pile foundation system. Walls and roofs are clad in cedar shingles. Beneath the broad eaves of the south and east elevations walls are clad in translucent white-stained plywood panels, reflecting light into the building from the surrounding snow-clad mountains.

Special features:
Much of the structure was erected by members of the community band who are not experienced in large-scale construction methods. A detailed framing model was made, at a scale of 1:20, to make the process more understandable to the amateur construction team.

Schedule of areas:

Ground floor	2190 m²
Area of gym	464 m²
Area of classroom	74 m²

Summary

On an urban level, the school was sited to complete the northern edge of an emerging village square. Classrooms were orientated along the resulting public face of the building. The entrance is marked by a large porch element. The gym was located behind, providing shelter from the winter winds, with the kindergarten on the east for morning light. The library and staff facilities took up the resulting interstitial zone.

Architect's statement

The design is described in simple down-to-earth terms; for example its orientation, the use of materials and a number of urban moves such as the closing of the fourth side of the village square. Yet its spatial complexity creates an environment of great appeal to pupils and adults alike. It shares its outside spaces with the village, encouraging people to enter the building and use its facilities outside school hours. Extreme winter winds which are funnelled between the mountains down the river valley are modified by the large protective roof forms.

Classrooms and the main entrance porch are strung along the protected south side, with the gymnasium and community hall at the rear. There is a kindergarten tucked under the large roofs in the north-west corner, with its own

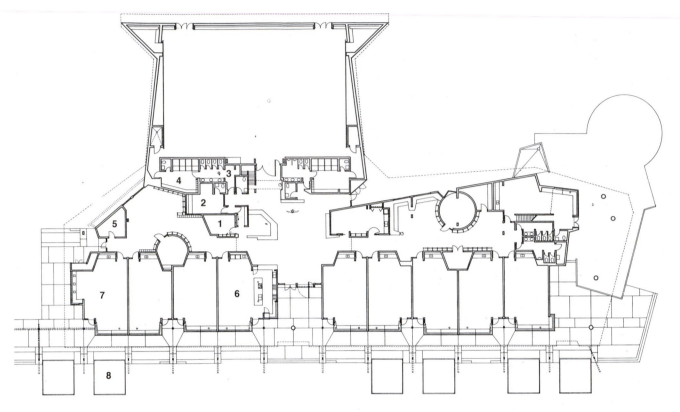

Figure CS2.3
Ground floor plan.

KEY:
1 Principal
2 Health/counselling
3 Washrooms
4 Showers/changing rooms
5 Workroom
6 Home economics room
7 Science room
8 Teaching gardens

Figure CS2.4
Exterior view. (Patkau Associates. Photo: © James Dow.)
Both interior and exterior views show the rich and powerful form which appears to be in a harmonious relationship to its physical setting. Special windows dramatize the structure within the resources area whilst the east elevation appears to mimic the shapes of the mountain range beyond.

Figure CS2.5
Interior view. (Patkau Associates. Photo: © James Dow.)

covered play space. Variety is brought to the traditional linear school form by the introduction of curved and splayed walls. The large shingle-covered roofs pitch upwards in places to provide dramatic and contrasting closed and open forms.

3 Strawberry Vale School, Victoria, British Columbia

Patkau Associates

Type of project:
State Elementary School, triple form entry for 448 students aged 5–11 years.

Client:
Greater Victoria School District.

Site area:
1.8 hectares. The school serves a semi-rural community on the edge of Victoria. To the north there was an existing school beside an oak woodland which forms the edge of a small park.

Number of teaching spaces:
Sixteen classrooms arranged in groups of four with associated areas located in or off common areas, including a library, computer room and additional corridor areas.

Type of construction:
Due to its wooded location, timber was selected as the primary building material. Walls and roofs are framed and sheathed in wood (cedar externally with birch ply for internal carpentry); however, the major structural elements are steel with reinforced in-situ concrete foundations and floors. The shallow roof slopes are clad in aluminium-coated steel. In places white-painted gypsum board are added to complement natural timber finishes. Wet areas are of polished concrete; carpet is utilized in classrooms and in the library.

Special features:
The hydrology of the site has been exploited to form part of the educational curriculum. This begins on the south side of the school where rainwater from wall and roof surfaces is collected in concrete trenches located below roof overhangs. This water is piped towards the lower north side of the school where it is discharged into an open watercourse. This leaks out into the lower site area and creates a shallow marsh. Children plant monitor cat-tail grasses and bulrushes and enjoy nesting birds and waders.

Schedule of areas:

Ground floor	3172 m²
Mezzanine	121 m²
Typical classroom	73 m²
Gymnasium	423 m²
Multi-purpose room	80 m²

Summary

The building is orientated towards the south, symbolically turning its back on the city. All classrooms look out towards the woods and distant hills. By placing windows, clerestorys and roof lights to optimize views and daylight, the building gives form to the rural site and the environmental forces, to create a dramatic new vernacular architecture. In order to dramatize the form and limit the perceived length of its corridors, the building is fragmented into five primary blocks with ancillary accommodation in between.

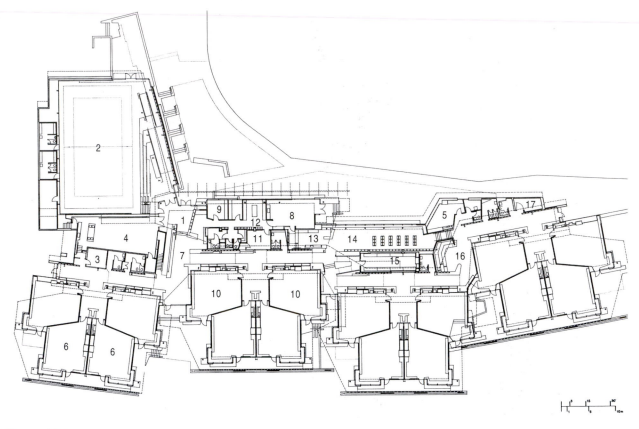

Figure CS3.1
Ground floor plan.

KEY:

1 Entrance	7 Reception	13 Technical centre
2 Gymnasium	8 Principal	14 Library
3 Storage	9 Vice-principal	15 Computer
4 Multipurpose	10 Workroom	16 Story telling
5 Special education	11 Health	17 Recycling
6 Classroom	12 Staff	

The classrooms are grouped in blocks of four, each arranged as a small rustic house, with a gymnasium making up the fifth element. Whilst interesting in themselves (and something of a development from their earlier Seabird Island School), here it is the ancillary areas in between the classroom 'pods' which became the predominant social and educational zones. The meandering corridor route enables smaller areas to be articulated which are beyond the classroom confines. These 'in-between' spaces create an overlap between the classrooms and other facilities establishing a comfortable intermediate scale to which children relate. These places may be used by individuals or small groups from adjacent classrooms. Movable carts for art, science and cooking have been designed for these common areas which can be unplugged and wheeled outside to create the focus for external teaching groups. The form of the architecture can be seen to effectively extend the educational and social curriculum.

The metaphor for this building is expressively environmental, almost anti-urban – perhaps a rejection of city values which at times becomes too overt. However, the double height spine wall of circulation and ancillary spaces (library, computer room and technical centre) places an emphasis on this side of the school's programme, over and above the conventional closed classrooms. Its dialogue with the surrounding landscape and this rich social programme make it a refreshing and radical approach to the architecture of schools.

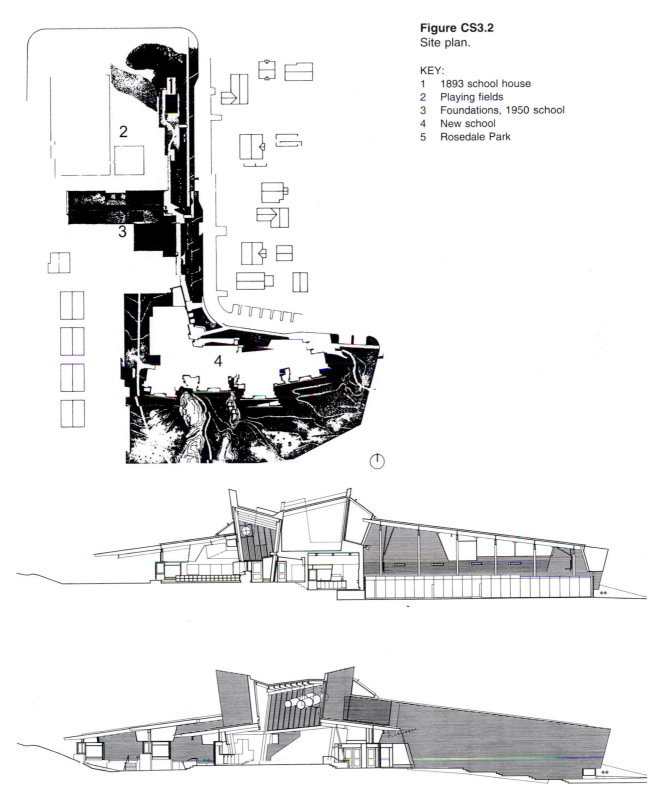

Figure CS3.2
Site plan.

KEY:
1   1893 school house
2   Playing fields
3   Foundations, 1950 school
4   New school
5   Rosedale Park

Figure CS3.3a
Long section.

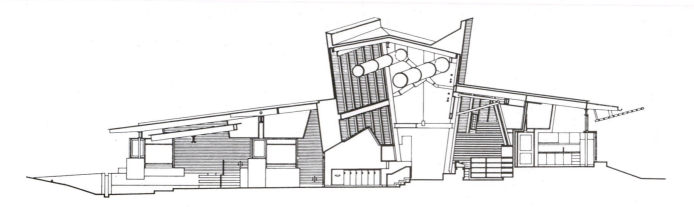

Figure CS3.3b
Cross section.

Figure CS3.4
The oversized sun shade and the cedar clad walls
slope eccentrically outwards on the northern city side of
the building. (Patkau Associates. Photo: © James Dow.)

Figure CS3.5
Spaces in between classrooms and service areas not
only form the corridor link between each block of
accommodation, but also become inhabited by small-
group activities: this science corner is lit dramatically by
the afternoon sun. (Patkau Associates. Photo: © James
Dow.)

4 Westborough Primary School, Westcliff-on-Sea, Essex

Cottrell and Vermeulen

Type of project:
686-place primary school with new 49 place half-day nursery school (4–11 age group).

Client:
The governors of the Westborough Primary School with headteacher Jenny Davies operating as grant maintained status.

Site area:
0.9 hectares. The existing Edwardian school was constructed in 1930 and runs along the street frontage with

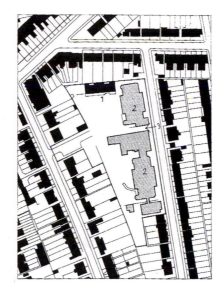

Figure CS4.1
Site plan.

1 New infant and reception class
2 Existing primary school
3 New entrance lobby

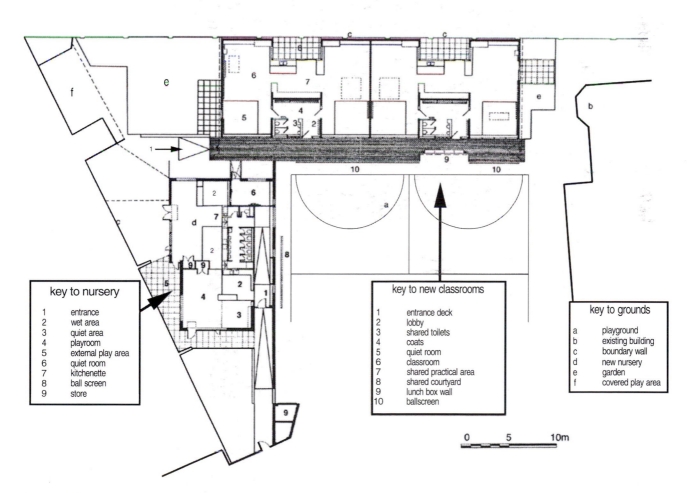

key to nursery	
1	entrance
2	wet area
3	quiet area
4	playroom
5	external play area
6	quiet room
7	kitchenette
8	ball screen
9	store

key to new classrooms	
1	entrance deck
2	lobby
3	shared toilets
4	coats
5	quiet room
6	classroom
7	shared practical area
8	shared courtyard
9	lunch box wall
10	ballscreen

key to grounds	
a	playground
b	existing building
c	boundary wall
d	new nursery
e	garden
f	covered play area

0   5   10m

Figure CS4.2
Ground floor plan: nursery and four new classrooms.

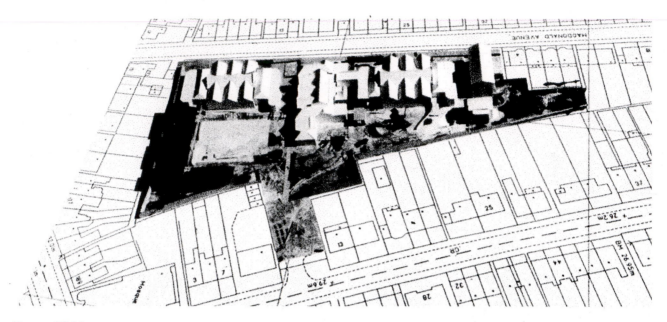

Figure CS4.3
Site development models are used as a key method of consulting with the school community during the development of proposals.

playgrounds hemmed-in around the back of the site which is surrounded by residential back gardens.

Number of teaching spaces:
Twenty-two classroom bases plus two new nursery classrooms.

Type of construction:
The original buildings are of brick and slate construction; the new classrooms are of timber-frame construction with rendered blockwork and mono pitched zinc roof finish.

Special features:
The majority of work carried out in the educational sector is to existing school sites. This project takes a long-term view on improvements to this very difficult site, to provide a vision which, through close consultation, the whole school community can share.

Schedule of areas:

Teaching area	1600 m² (24 classrooms)
Other teaching areas	225 m² (library and special needs)
Total	2464 m²
Typical classrooms	34–81 m² (as in main school building)
New nursery rooms	65 m² (paired)
Nursery total area	150 m²

Summary

Westborough is an attempt to develop a sustainable school community through a structured environmental plan. Schools often suffer from meagre piecemeal funding, disjointed planning and changing government policy. This can inhibit positive action by the school to effect change, and can result in perpetuating neglected and alienating environments which affects the staff, children, parents and the wider community.

Architect's statement

When Cottrell and Vermeulen first commenced work with the school in 1986, they set out a strategy which not only dealt with the building fabric, but also attempted to bring some aesthetic qualities to the school and its hard urban site. The buildings were suffering from a serious lack of maintenance funding, and the architects formulated a ten-year development plan of improvements, in close consultation with the school community.

The first phase of works involved maintenance and repair. However, it also represented an opportunity to improve the architecture. This began with new fire escapes incorporating attractive decks and ramps which appeared like dramatic playground structures. A refurbished entrance foyer provided a new exhibition area and improved the public face of the school. A new stair link introduced the first part of a lateral link across the site to

Figure CS4.4
The playground enclosed by new buildings designed and built at different times. The playground edge is marked by a calming blue wall; decorated mesh screens protect the buildings behind whilst enabling the penetration of light and view. (Cottrell & Vermeulen Architecture. Photo: © Paul Ratigan Photo/Graphics Ltd.)

Figure CS4.5
The covered canopy has a warm iroko floor and transparent polypropylene cladding panels so the children can see the timber wall structure with rock-wool insulation. Simple, cheap materials used imaginatively provide the context and catalyst for education. (Cottrell & Vermeulen Architecture. Photo: © Paul Ratigan Photo/Graphics Ltd.)

Figure CS4.6
Reception classrooms with mini courtyard or cortile. Soft paired colours match the furniture and storage units to the fabric of the building: very little applied decoration is used to ensure the classroom environment remains a calm and neutral backdrop to the activities of thirty children. (Cottrell & Vermeulen Architecture. Photo: © Paul Ratigan Photo/Graphics Ltd.)

connect the three existing buildings and the new nursery/reception classes to make circulation between the blocks easy and legible.

The second phase of works involved the demolition of a 1950s block and the construction of four nursery, or 'reception', classrooms. At the front of the new classroom block there is a ball-screen which provides an enclosing façade protecting the entrance portico. The lunchbox wall provides storage for the children's belongings which is protected from sun and rain. It clearly signals the entrance to the building.

The classroom block is a simple building constructed from inexpensive materials. There is an attempt to create a variety of spaces, modulating light and colour to animate the whole building in a playful spatial sequence. Simple architectural devices further enhance this sequence: the lunch-box wall, a transparent wall made of polycarbonate panels; and two small light-giving courtyards, captured space which adds a significant dimension to the classroom environment.

5   Woodlea Primary School, Bordon, Hampshire

Hampshire County Architects

Type of project:
Seven-class single-form entry for 245 pupils aged 5–11 years.

Client:
Hampshire Local Education Authority.

Site area:
2.85 hectares of mixed woodland (primarily pine and birch), on a steep slope running down from Iron Age earthworks. The woodland lies on the edge of a new housing development. The woodland is held in trust and is managed by a dedicated warden.

Figure CS5.1
Ground floor plan.

KEY:

1	Infant class	12	Music/drama	23 Headteacher
2	Junior class	13	Children's lavatories	24 Staffroom
3	Home base	14	Changing	25 Staff work
4	Shared area	15	Decks	26 Disabled WC/shower
5	Tutorial	16	Kitchen	27 Staff lavatories
6	Library/resources	17	Caretaker	28 Waiting
7	Infant library	18	Plant	29 Main entrance
8	Cooking	19	PE store	30 The bowl
9	Craft	20	Central store	31 Outside work/play
10	Store	21	Administration	
11	School Hall	22	Deputy Headteacher	

Number of teaching spaces:
Seven classrooms with associated resources area, assembly hall and music/drama room.

Type of construction:
The rear part of the building, orientated towards the Hill Fort, is of multi-yellow stock brickwork with tiled solid concrete floors and painted plastered ceilings. The front classroom wings are of timber frame construction, with timber external cladding and natural timber ceilings. External play decks are of hardwood with rilled plank decking. Pitched roofs are covered in cedar shingles with the flat linking roofs in natural slate granules.

Special features:
The essence of this scheme is its harmonious relationship to its natural setting. This is partly a factor of the quality of natural light admitted from a variety of windows

149

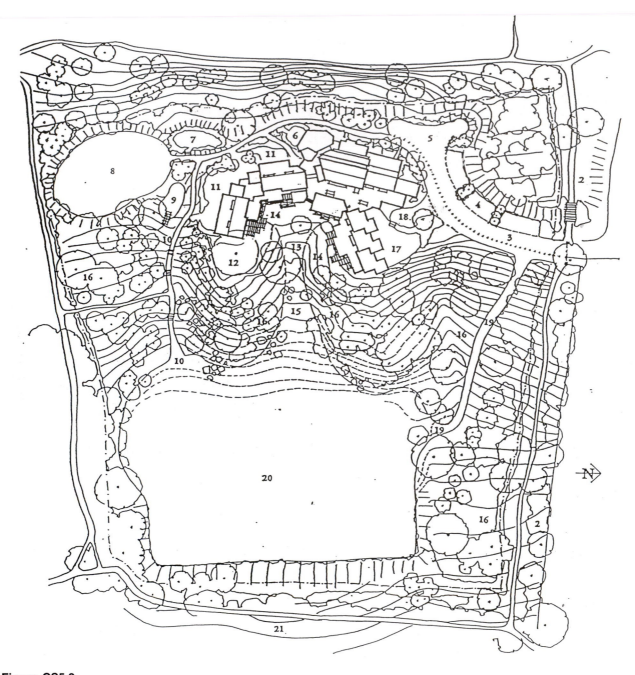

Figure CS5.2
Site plan.

KEY:

1 Iron Age fort
2 Greenway path
3 Drive and footpath
4 Parking
5 Service
6 Drama garden
7 School garden
8 Main playcourt
9 Pond and dipping deck
10 Playing field path
11 Junior work and play
12 Key tree
13 The bowl
14 Decks
15 The funnel
16 Woods
17 Infant work and play
18 Main entrance
19 Playing field track
20 Playing field
21 Ancient woodland

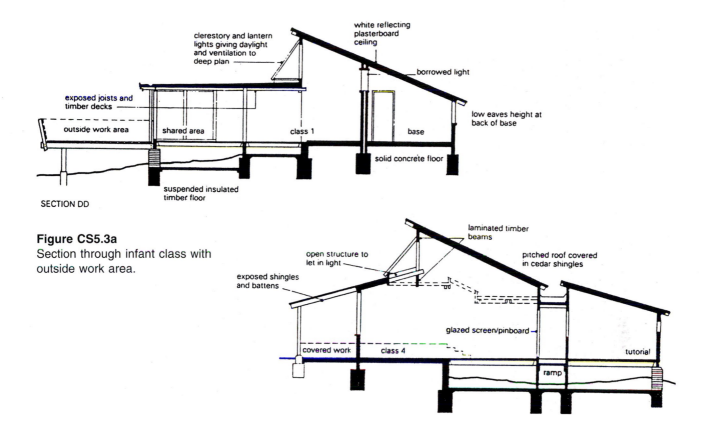

Figure CS5.3a
Section through infant class with outside work area.

Figure CS5.3b
Section through junior class, tutorial area and covered work space.

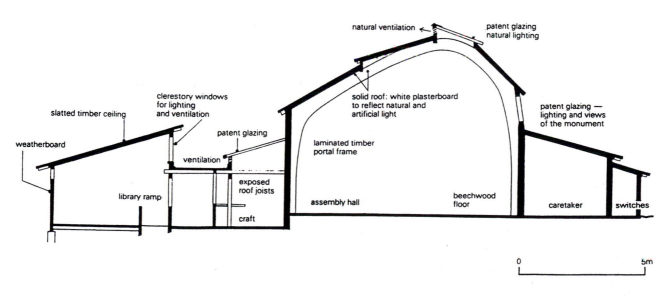

Figure CS5.3c
Section through main hall and resources area.

Figure CS5.4
View into courtyard from the junior school end of the building; external timber decks extend the activity areas out into the landscape. (Photo: © Tony Weller/The Builder Group Library.)

throughout the building. Almost all the remedial and additional planting uses species that occur on the site or in the immediate vicinity. Adjacent to the building is a large wildlife pond with a dipping deck and a hedged school garden.

Schedule of areas:

Typical classroom	42m²
Assembly hall	109m²
Resources area	42m²
Music/drama room	50m²
Total	1157m²

Summary

The nature of the place and project engendered a great spirit in, and degree of cooperation between, almost everyone involved. The building contract was unusually trouble-free and enjoyable, with many people giving their own time to help produce the pond, seats, and to help clear the site.

Nev Churcher, architect

Woodlea is a predominantly timber and masonry structure put together simply, with a stock of straightforward details which nevertheless encapsulate essential site-specific characteristics. For example, the timber sections which support the pitched classroom roofs were worked out on site with the contractors. They are detailed as stepped tapering rafters becoming thinner as they project away from the roof edge. A small detail, perhaps, but one which illustrates the care and attention paid to the realization of this building.

The school is set to the west of the site, adjacent to the earthworks. This has ensured that site level changes have been kept to a minimum. The entrance and resource area are on the middle level while gentle ramped circulation leads naturally up to the hall and music area and down into the infant and junior teaching suites. Thus areas are clearly defined but linked visually. The hard wet noisy areas are on the outside of the curved form and open onto paved play areas, whilst soft, dry quieter zones focus towards the interior. These give onto timber decks used for study and play. Both sides provide maximum teaching flexibility and optimize the inside/outside relationship, both visually and functionally.

High standards of natural lighting have been achieved by means of glazed roof lights which modulate and control the lighting in a variety of ways. Plain-pitched ceilings reflect daylight down and combine with artificial light from uplighters, to give even, glare-free lighting. Care has been taken to achieve a good acoustic environment in

Figure CS5.5
Junior school technology lesson in progress: natural light is introduced in a variety of ways creating an ever-changing atmosphere during the long teaching day. (Photo: © Tony Weller/ The Builder Group Library.)

what is generally an open plan building. This is achieved by a judicious use of screens and baffles and appropriate surface materials. The form of the music/drama room was devised to give acceptable reverberation times. Its shape echoes the organic mood of the rest of the building.

The form and plan of Woodlea have their origin in the landscape. A substantial number of trees were felled in order to construct the building; however, this does not appear to have detracted from the natural beauty of the site. The plan developed from a complex process of marking-out the contours of the land around a natural earth bowl, and sketching, intuitively, the required forms of classrooms and ancillary spaces, until the right shape appeared. No plan or photograph can do full justice to the poetic quality of this building in its natural setting.

6   Anne Frank School, Papendrecht, The Netherlands

Architectuurstudio Herman Hertzberger

Type of project:
A local authority primary school designed as part of a larger housing scheme, for children aged 4–12 years.

Client:
Papendrecht City Council.

Site area:
2700 m². The site occupies a flat corner plot on the edge of a new modernist housing development within a largely residential neighbourhood.

Number of teaching spaces:
Eight, 28 pupils in each with a playroom for the youngest children.

Type of construction:
A steel frame with rendered blockwork walls and a combination of flat asphalt and pitched-curved zinc-clad roofs.

Special features:
The school is designed in what might be described as a typical Hertzberger form. It is organized vertically as opposed to the normal school configuration of predominantly horizontal planning; as such it is economical spatially and adopts a clustered house-type configuration. It has a central hall space which has become the focus of the community with an auditorium arrangement of steps which encourages the pupils to linger and mix across the age ranges. Even if not remaining in the hall, circulation

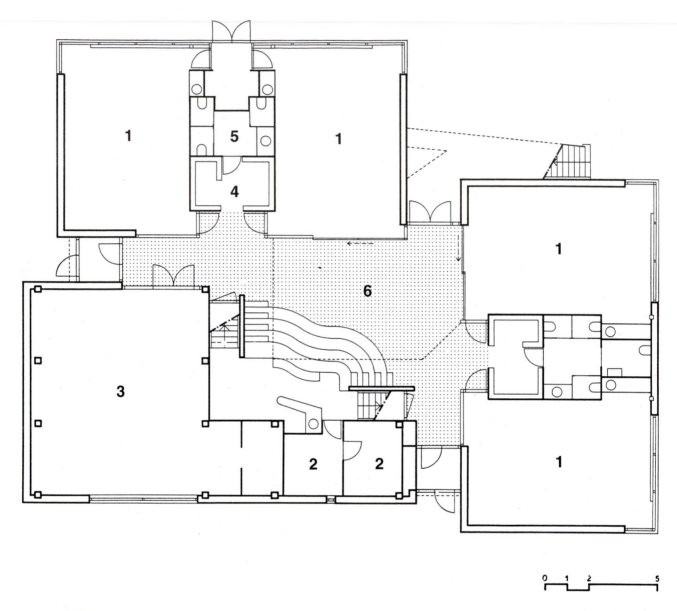

Figure CS6.1
Ground floor plan (refer to key on page 156).

stairs and galleries criss-cross this large volume enabling a relationship to the whole school, not just the class bases, for even the youngest children.

Schedule of areas:

Teaching areas	480 m² (including lavatory store and quiet room)
Area of hall	96 m²
Total area	1200 m²

Typical classroom	50 m²
Nursery playspace	70 m²
Central hall	88 m² (triple height volume which includes vertical circulation)

Summary

This school could be described as a natural development of the architect's philosophy initiated in the 1980 Apollo

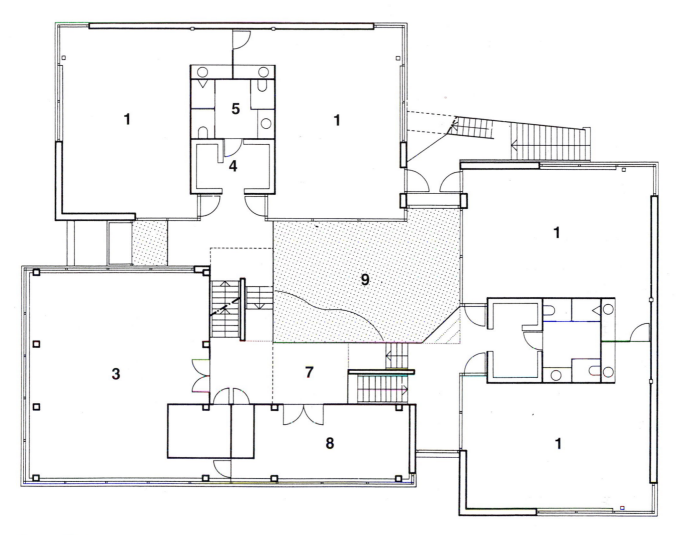

Figure CS6.2
First floor plan (refer to key on page 156).

Schools (see Chapter 1). Designed in 1993 and completed in 1996, the building displays its lineage as a progression from the original prototype; a villa-type cluster of vertically organized floors. Each of the two main levels comprises two sets of paired classrooms with a bathroom and quiet room sandwiched in between. There is a playroom at ground floor and a staffroom above.

On the second floor, a homework room is provided for those children who need to remain after school hours. In addition, the entire school is open for most of the day and in the evening, for parent use. There is a surprising lack of overt security with access provided from three directions of the site. This is a factor of its open, contained internal volume, with many eyes controlling the space against the possibility of intrusion by strangers.

What makes this particularly effective is the flexibility enabled by openable screen walls linking classroom spaces at ground floor to the hall. The ground floor opens up to become a transparent volume melting into the surrounding gardens. This is a surprising transformation from the cellular nature of the normal closed classroom arrangement.

The architecture evokes the language of its surrounding housing blocks with their Corbusian aesthetic of white rendered walls and horizontal 'ribbon' windows. Yet here the form is different enough both in terms of scale and shape to announce its status as a public building. Each element of the programme is expressed, with two great curved roofs looping over the top of the internal hall. Its sophisticated form language is derivative of Gerrit Rietveld.

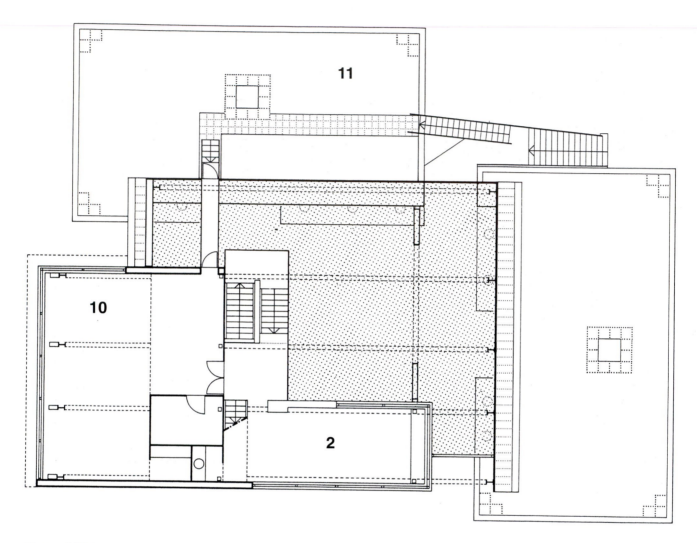

Figure CS6.3
Second floor plan.

KEY: to Figures CS6.1–6.3
1 Classroom
2 Office area
3 Activity area
4 Cloakroom
5 Pupils' shared WC
6 Communal entrance/assembly area
7 Balcony
8 Library
9 Void
10 Staffroom
11 Roof top fire escape

The orientation of each classroom is carefully choreographed to optimize sun penetration with a largely glazed wall to the north-facing playroom, and shaded corner window openings to the south and west. It is a beautifully clear and rational school building, the result of many years of thought and development along similar lines. It synthesizes small-scale domestic forms with larger scale institutional volumes to create a hybrid school of great sophistication

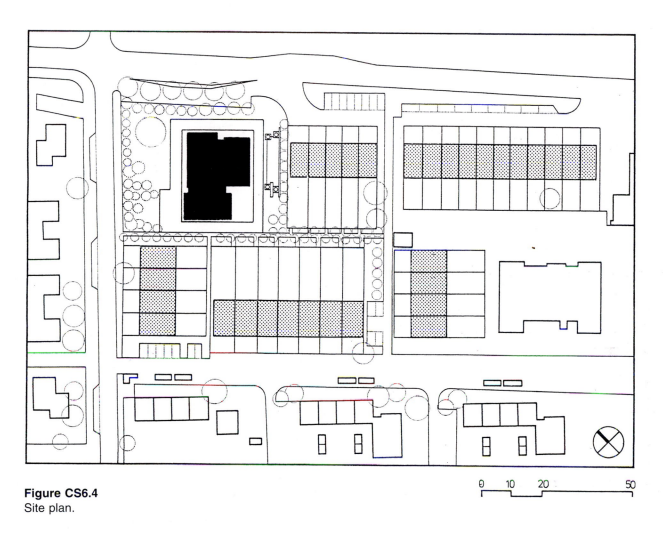

Figure CS6.4
Site plan.

0   10   20   50

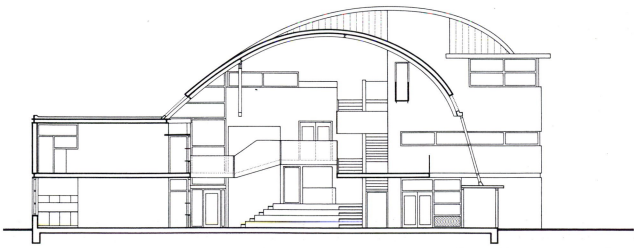

Figure CS6.5
Section.

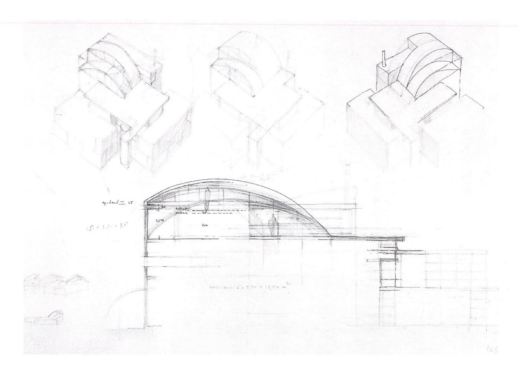

Figure CS6.6
Sketch sections and axonometrics: the designer grappling with the integration of two forms, the classroom blocks and the arched roof shape. (Photo: © Architectuurstudio Herman Hertzberger.)

Figure CS6.7a
Interior view. (Photo: © Architectuurstudio Herman Hertzberger.)

Figure CS6.7b
Exterior view. (Photo: © Architectuurstudio Herman Hertzberger.)
These views show the marriage between the form and its use: the staircase and balconies beneath the great industrial roof form a safe enclosed public space; from the playground the image can be interpreted on two levels, one of clear uncompromising technology, a space-ship, on the other a home from home, intimate and friendly.

Figure CS6.8
The Schroeder House in Utrecht, Holland, by Gerrit Rietveld (1928), inspiration for much of Hertzberger's school architecture.

7 The Bombardon School, Almere, The Netherlands

Architectuurstudio Herman Hertzberger

Type of project:
A special needs school for children with educational and learning difficulties.

Client:
Almere City Council.

Site area:
1500 m². The site is within an existing park surrounded by public playing fields.

Number of teaching spaces:
The school has fourteen dedicated teaching spaces with ancillary therapy rooms for music and movement.

Type of construction:
Steel frame construction with brick steel and timber cladding. Interior finishes are rubber floors, ply fascia panels with ash steps and open treads.

Special features:
Although more linear in form than most other Hertzberger schools, which are based on a more horizontal villa type, the organization is compact. This focuses on the central hall which is described as 'a school square'. There are no corridors – circulation and communal social activity flow through and around this purposeful volume.

Schedule of areas:

Ground floor	1200 m²
First floor	1010 m²
Second floor	700 m²
Total	2910 m²
Typical classrooms	102 m² (bathroom and quiet room not included)
Gym/enclosed hall	265 m²

Summary

The building sits prominently within a park, an elongated sleek object, enclosing its inner secrets like a wrapped gift. Once inside, classrooms, therapy rooms and a gym surround a covered courtyard creating a secure communal space which supports pupil development on a number of different levels. Their requirements for both privacy from the outside world and public life by way of peer group interaction are subtly balanced by this architectural dialectic.

The language of the form is similarly dialectical. The building is explicitly asymmetrical, perhaps referring to van Eyck's Orphanage. Classrooms can be interpreted as static boxes which interlock with horizontal planes of the circulation decks, strapped tentatively onto the sides and top of the walls. This conjunction of light and heavy are

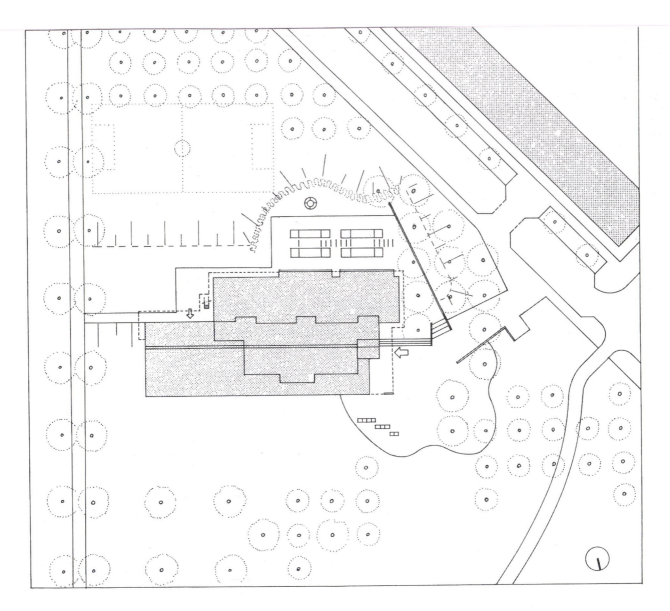

Figure CS7.1
Site plan.

the key ideas. At the end of the classroom link at second floor, the director's meeting area overlooks the park landscape. It controls the surrounding vistas, asserting the importance of the individuals who use the building. Self-esteem flows, perhaps as a result of this languid and complex form.

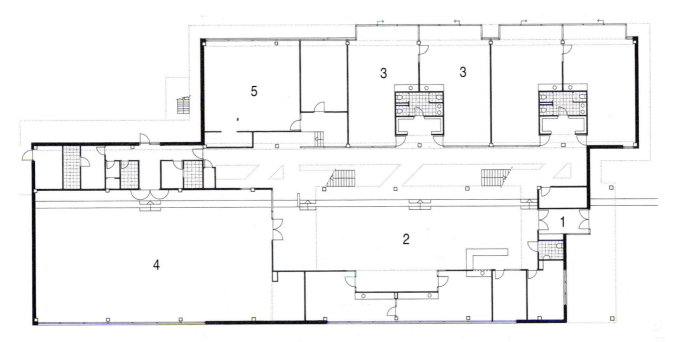

Figure CS7.2
Ground floor plan.

1 Entrance
2 Communal space
3 Classroom

4 Gym
5 Playroom

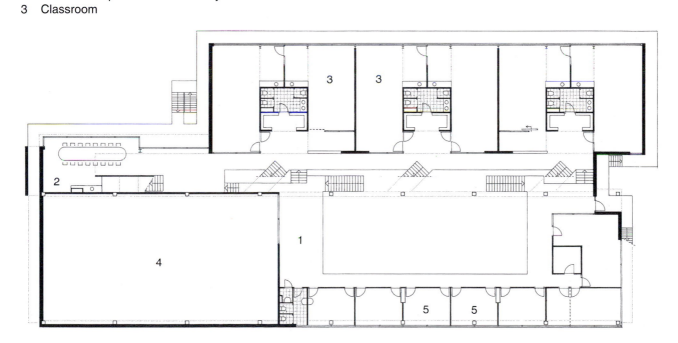

Figure CS7.3
First floor plan.

1 Gallery over entrance
2 Meeting area
3 Classroom

4 Gym (upper part)
5 Office

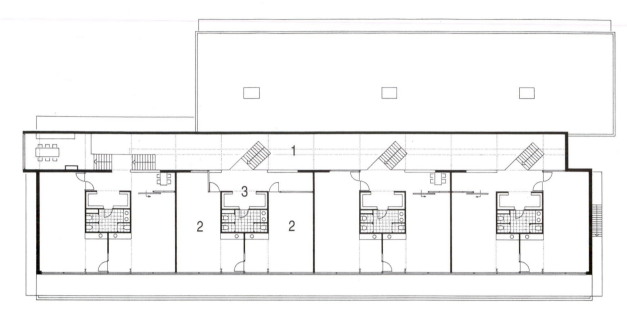

Figure CS7.4
Second floor plan.
1   Gallery access
2   Linked classrooms
3   WC/cloakroom area

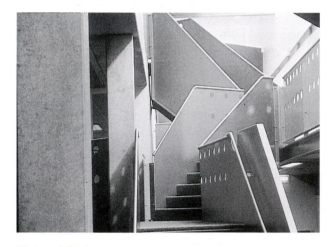

Figure CS7.5
The staircase is a safe 'obstacle' part of the internal landscape as it cascades down to the internal courtyard.

Figure CS7.6
The internal courtyard, a cool neutral backdrop prior to the introduction of furniture and people. Note the theatrical steps on the left side.

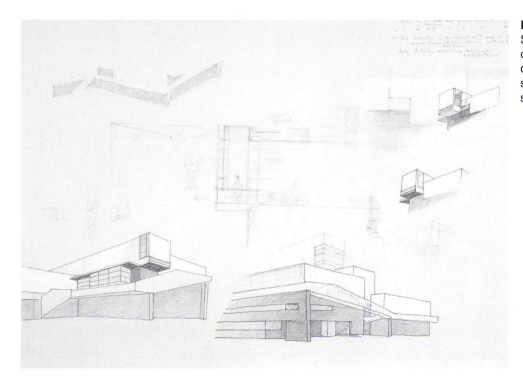

Figure CS7.7
Studies in the development of its three-dimensional form, a subtle interplay between solid and void.

8 Pokesdown Primary School, Bournemouth

Format Milton

Type of project:
420 child primary school: reception entry class, 2 class-room spaces per year (4–11 age group).

Client:
Originally Dorset County Council, subsequently Bournemouth Borough Council.

Site area:
0.6 hectares. The site is within a dense residential district of Bournemouth. The new school had to be constructed within the restricted playing area of the existing Victorian school which was subsequently demolished.

Number of teaching spaces:
Reception class and twelve classrooms of thirty pupils.

Type of construction:
Reinforced concrete raft at ground floor with concrete floor beams at first floor. Structural blockwork walls.

Timber and steel roof structure with aluminium roof membranes.

Special features:
Light scoops, large 'sun light' collectors, reflect light into the back of the classroom. Through the use of computer-operated clerestory windows, a fully controllable flow of natural cross-ventilation is established. The system has been very successful and dramatically cuts predicted lighting costs.

Schedule of areas:

Ground floor	1267 m²
First floor	851 m²
Total	2118 m²
Typical classroom	59 m²
Reception classroom	134 m²
Hall	160 m²
Library	90 m²
Studio	61 m²

Summary

The design ethos stresses the school as a unity, as a single space rather than a number of separate classrooms off a corridor or courtyard. The focus of the school is what the

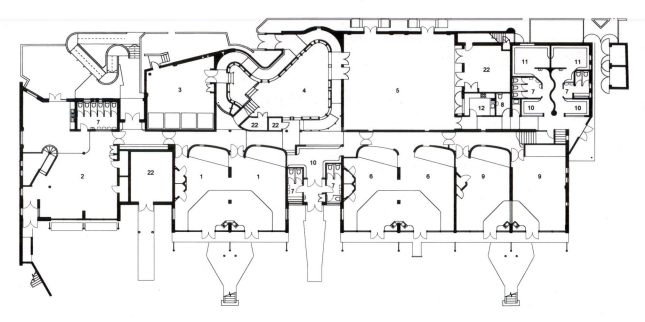

Figure CS8.1a
Ground floor plan.

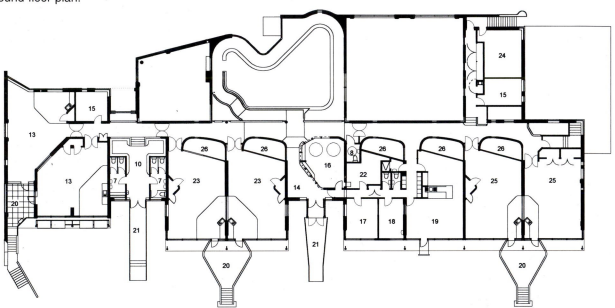

Figure CS8.1b
First floor plan.

KEY:
1 Classroom year 1
2 Reception class
3 Studio
4 Library/resources
5 Hall
6 Classroom year 2
7 WC
8 Disabled WC

9 Classroom year 5
10 Cloaks
11 Changing
12 Kitchen
13 Classroom year 3
14 Office reception
15 Quiet room
16 Office
17 Headteacher

18 Deputy head
19 Staffroom
20 Playdecks
21 Entrance bridge
22 Store
23 Classroom year 4
24 Boiler room
25 Classroom year 6
26 Light scoop void

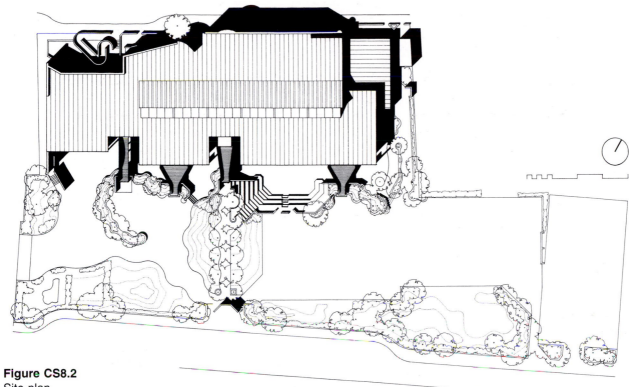

Figure CS8.2
Site plan.

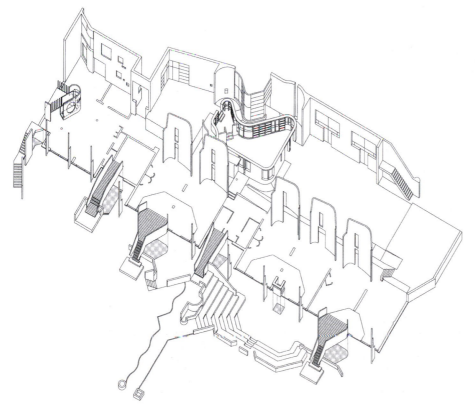

Figure CS8.3
Axonometric of interior where the building takes on a fluid form: the central spaces become a stage for childish fantasy, the classrooms become backstage preparation for the theatre.

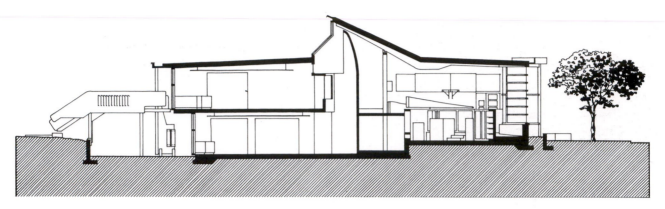

Figure CS8.4
Section through resources area showing a typical staircase ramp down into the playground at the rear of the site.

Figure CS8.5
Site plan and location plan.

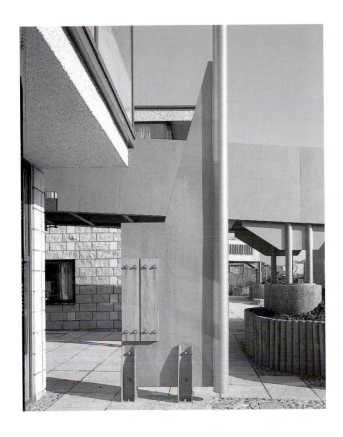

Figure CS8.6
Abstract use of contrasting textures and materials on the external playground façade draw attention to the building's technology, an education in itself. (Photo: © Charlotte Wood, architects Format Milton.)

designers poetically describe as 'the pool of knowledge', a central library/resources area. Vertical movement via a ramp around this space connects the hall/drama space off the ramp at intermediate landings.

Throughout the school there are a series of glass screens which separate and connect the spaces providing exciting vistas. A rich and unusual range of textures and colours makes this an unusual example of contemporary school design which is greatly enjoyed by staff and pupils.

Figure CS8.7
The north-west street façade is fragmented yet urban, relating well to the surrounding landscape of suburban houses and gardens complete with numerous zebra crossings. (Photo: © Charlotte Wood, architects Format Milton.)

9 Ranelagh Multi-Denominational School, Ranelagh, Dublin

O'Donnell and Tuomey

Type of project:
A single-entry primary school (4–12 age group): approximately 250 pupils, 36 per class (maximum).

Client:
Ranelagh Multi-Denominational School Association with the Board of Management.

Site area:
1430 m². The former school comprised a number of haphazard shed-like buildings with corrugated iron roofs on an island site. These buildings were demolished and replaced with the new building. This enabled the creation of landscaped playgrounds between the school and the adjacent residential terrace. Behind the new school are the wooded gardens to the East and West which have been upgraded by the insertion of semi-mature trees.

Number of teaching spaces:
Eight classrooms and a remedial room.

Type of construction:
In-situ reinforced concrete strip and pad foundations. In-situ RC columns typically with structural blockwork infill. To the rear, pitched canopy roofs of terne-coated stainless steel on plywood deck are used supported on iroko flitched rafters. Internal walls are of painted blockwork.

Special features:
Classrooms are clearly visible from the street by way of large openings which frame the activities of the children at work. Thus the school develops a close relationship between interior and exterior, helping to synthesize its life with that of the surrounding neighbourhood.

In-situ RC flat slab floor and roof construction provides attractive fair-faced concrete ceilings which are ideal for maintaining thermal mass in teaching areas.

Schedule of areas:

Ground floor	610 m²
First floor	532 m²
Total	1142 m²
Typical classroom	69 m²
General purpose hall	92 m² with associated balcony space 36 m²
Library	27 m²

Summary

We have used colour as a kind of coding device throughout the inside of the building. The floors are lino, classrooms are yellow, painted wet areas black, corridors terracotta red, and teachers' rooms blue. The unplastered blockwork walls are painted. In corridors they are white. Within the classrooms the 'external' walls are white to allow maximum area for display of posters and children's work. The walls to corridors, bathrooms and adjoining classrooms are painted in strong earth colours, red, blue and green. Taken from Italian frescoes, they are vibrant and strong, yet complementary to each other and to the

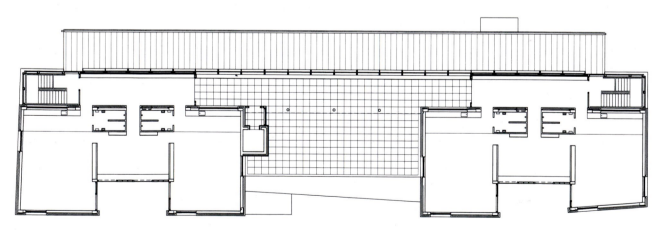

Figure CS9.1
Ground floor plan.

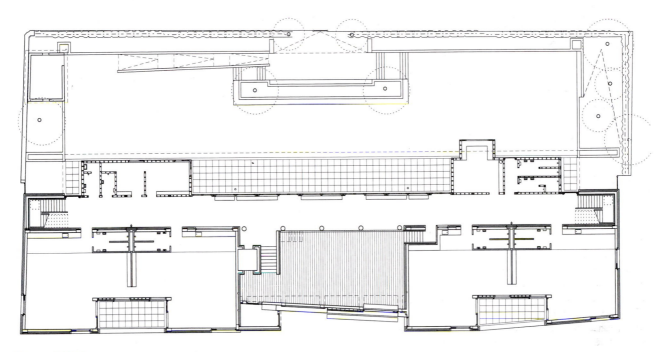

Figure CS9.2
First floor plan.

naturally coloured untreated materials used elsewhere. The colours help to zone the classrooms into wet areas, reading/quiet areas, teaching areas.

Architect's statement

The organization is simple, with a pair of two-storey class-room blocks, a spine of circulation and service spaces making the connection. There are staircases at each end of the spine and a lift in the centre. This zone is intended as more than a circulation space and is generously proportioned with ample seating, pinboards, coathooks and drinking fountains. The balcony link at first floor overlooks the hall to provide glimpses of communal activities.

There is a protected south-east facing yard surrounded by a wrought-iron railing, a remnant from the original school, whose gate still forms the entrance at back of the site. In contrast to the street façade, here the building feels open and transparent. There is a covered loggia space overlooking the play yard with a generous 12 metre long timber bench. Even when it is wet and rainy, many children venture out to the protection of this purposeful inside/outside play space.

The playground is landscaped and provides shelter from the south sun and privacy from the houses to the rear, with canopy roofs and louvres. Plants have been chosen to provide educational opportunities for the students to demonstrate reproduction, the seasons and other aspects of the ecosphere. Plant selection has been carefully considered to encourage varieties of plant and insect life throughout the seasons.

The size, function and finish of each classroom were precisely dictated by the Department of Education; however, the designers have always made more of the predetermined schedule of accommodation. For example, corridors are broad, well lit spaces, with benches, lines of coathooks and pinboards for display and decoration. Finishes are contrasting cold and warm materials, fair-faced concrete columns of the structural frame set against rust-coloured marmoleum floors.

When first seen from the road the school appears as an exploration of local vernacular, with appropriate use of scale and materials yet with a tightly packed elemental form which is totally contemporary in feel. Externally it is almost austere; however, the subtle juxtaposition of colours and materials lend an elegant simplicity to the building which acts as a calm backdrop to the often chaotic life of the users. Here is a new school which is totally in keeping with its surroundings but combines an appropriate balance between openness and defensiveness in a economical package.

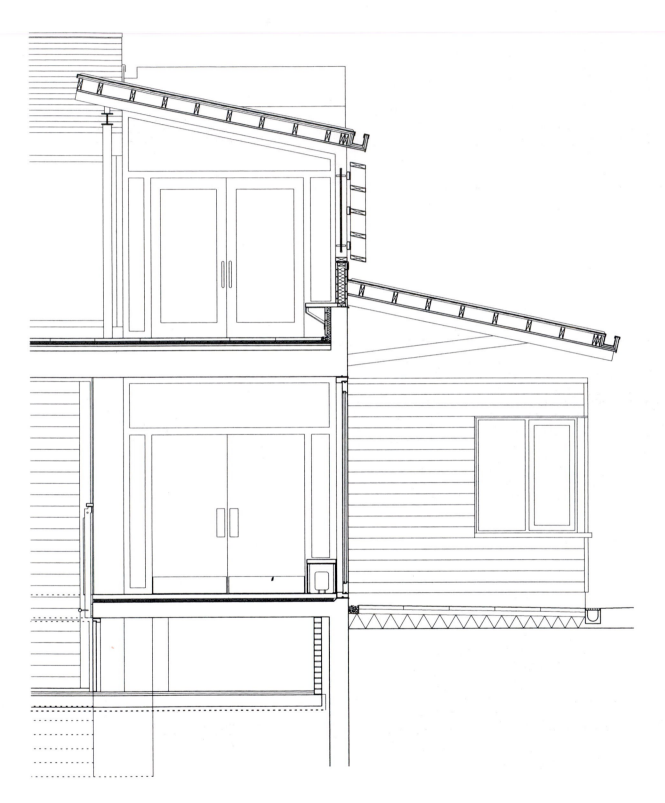

Figure CS9.3
Detailed section through balcony and covered walkway.

Figure CS9.4a
Section through classroom blocks.

Figure CS9.4b
Section through multi-purpose hall.

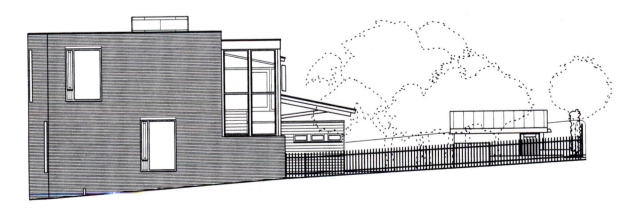

Figure CS9.5
End elevation illustrates the closed street façade opening up to the rear playground.

Figure CS9.6a
Rear playground façade with first floor horizontal louvres which give the building a squat sleek image. (Photo: © Dennis Gilbert, VIEW 14 The Dover Centre, 109 Bartholomew Rd, London NW5 2JB. 0171 284 2928.)

Figure CS9.6b
The street façade is more traditional: windows in brick walls with the form relating well to the Victorian villas opposite. (Photo: © Dennis Gilbert, VIEW 14 The Dover Centre, 109 Bartholomew Rd, London NW5 2JB. 0171 284 2928.)

Figure CS9.7
The ground floor communal spaces utilizing a rich range of natural materials with just a hint of colour; spaces appear to flow seamlessly between inside and outside. (Photo: © Dennis Gilbert, VIEW 14 The Dover Centre, 109 Bartholomew Rd, London NW5 2JB. 0171 284 2928.)

10   Little Village Academy, Chicago, Illinois

Ross, Barney and Jankowski

Type of project:
Elementary school for 688 children from kindergarten to grade 8.

Client:
Public Building Commission of Chicago for the Chicago Public Schools.

Site area:
A constrained urban site measuring 36 m × 120 m of which 720 m² comprises parking spaces. Nevertheless, the compact plan manages to incorporate a varied range of accommodation.

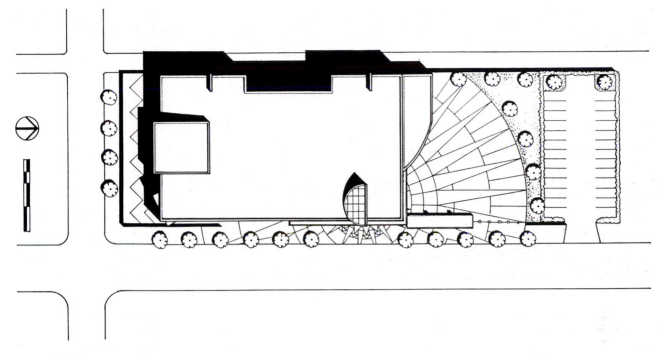

Figure CS10.1
Site plan.

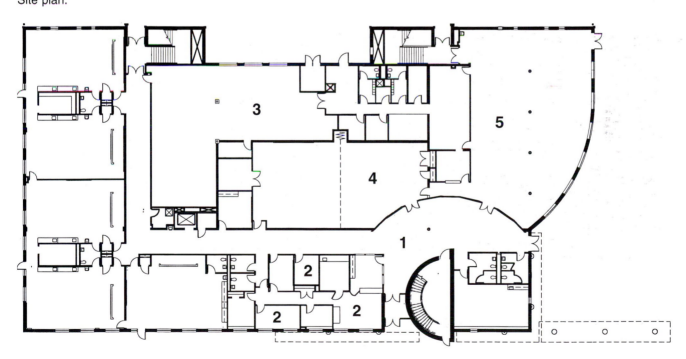

Figure CS10.2
Ground floor plan (USA first floor).

KEY:
1 Lobby
2 Offices
3 Kindergarten
4 Multi-purpose
5 Cafeteria

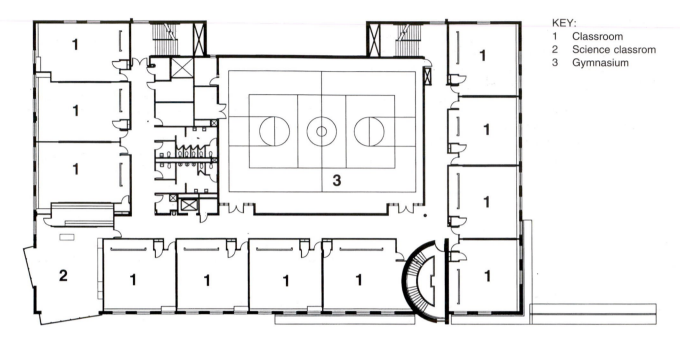

KEY:
1 Classroom
2 Science classrom
3 Gymnasium

Figure CS10.3
First floor plan (USA second floor).

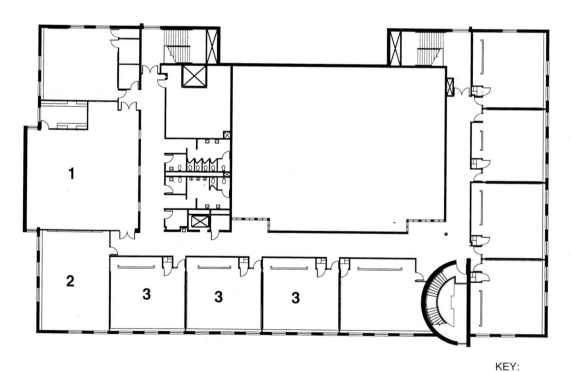

Figure CS10.4
Second floor plan (USA third floor).

KEY:
1 Library
2 Computer laboratory
3 Classroom

Number of teaching spaces:
Twenty traditional classrooms, with specialist science and computer rooms. There is an electronic interactive library. On the ground floor there are three kindergarten activity areas, a community room and a cafeteria.

Type of construction:
Steel frame with masonry infill, pre-cast concrete floors and roofs, aluminium framed window-curtain walling with some aluminium clad wood windows. Features include glazed coloured decorative brick and mosaic tile finishes and various rooflight configurations.

Special features:
The school makes reference to the local Hispanic community with the use of coloured mosaic tile decorations and the incorporation of a sun motif in the form of a semi-circular vertical light scoop within which the main staircase rises. The feature is expressed as a skylit vertical sun dial calibrated to the angle of the sun. The time is shown on the glazed rear wall three storeys above the street. The motif is echoed on the external street courtyard with the axis mundi graphically set out in coloured floor tiles; the sundial refers to the role of the sun in Aztec culture, and is a local landmark. The grand staircase acts as a social meeting point and lynch-pin of this vertically stratified building.

Schedule of areas:

Ground floor	2,303 m²
First floor	2,153 m²
Second floor	2,174 m²
Total area	6,637 m²
Typical classroom	84 m²
Typical kindergarten room	96 m²
Gymnasium	479 m²
Cafeteria	298 m²

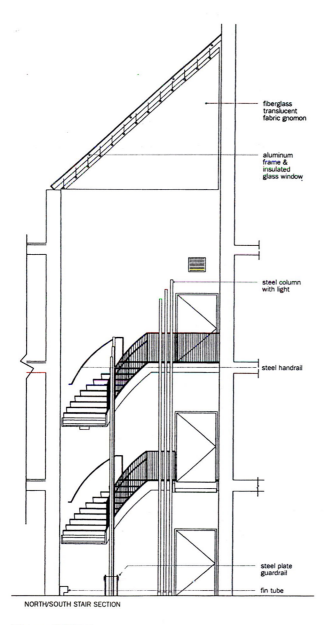

fiberglass
translucent
fabric gnomon

aluminum
frame &
insulated
glass window

steel column
with light

steel handrail

steel plate
guardrail

fin tube

NORTH/SOUTH STAIR SECTION

Figure CS10.5
Section through feature staircase.

Summary

The design is a rectangular three-storey perimeter block with a recessed loggia to the west, playgrounds for the kindergarten on the south and a play 'plaza' for the main school pupils to the north. It provides a simple civic presence yet with the addition of a number of crucial architectural flourishes, such as a dramatic tapering staircase tower and a third floor library block clad in shimmering translucent glass, suspended above the street. These architectural moments add interest which can be savoured either from the inside or from the outside. Strong colours are used in geometric patterns as a reminder of the Mexican heritage of a large proportion of its pupil intake.

The advantages of the planning strategy are firstly that the school is hard up against the street giving very high densities. Its edges act as secure buttresses against an often hostile outside world. Paradoxically they also lend an immediacy to the street edge, which is welcoming to outsiders, yet in a controlled way. The treatment of entrances and thresholds encourages parents and other interested community members to come into the building and use the community room, and at certain times outside of school hours, the cafeteria and gymnasium. Perhaps more importantly, it is an extremely economical layout both in environmental terms and in building costs per

Figure CS10.6
Science classroom with translucent walls providing even natural light set out in the form of a graph-paper grid. (Steve Hall © Hedrich Blessing.)

Figure CS10.7a
A solid redbrick block enlivened by projecting bays, a sundial staircase and the rooftop library volume all help to articulate the internal hierarchy to the outside world. (Steve Hall © Hedrich Blessing.)

Figure CS10.7b
The library interior benefits from generous all-round clerestory lighting and light, neutral colours. (Steve Hall © Hedrich Blessing.)

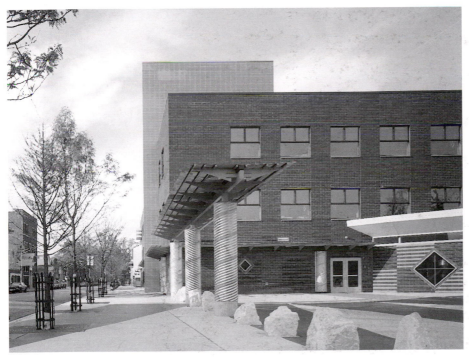

Figure CS10.8
A projecting canopy helps to define the street-level courtyard which is further delineated by rough ashlar blocks with the back of the staircase coloured a vibrant yellow. (Steve Hall © Hedrich Blessing.)

Figure CS10.9
All materials are cheap and durable yet each is carefully considered within the composition of the interior architecture: the cafeteria features diagonal pendant windows and circular structural columns clad in shiny spiralling zinc. Restrained decorative strips within the floor lino make a strong contrast to the gridded ceiling. (Steve Hall © Hedrich Blessing.)

square metre. The minimal external envelope makes good environmental sense in this region which experiences considerable extremes of temperature.

One of the drawbacks, however, is the large areas of internal circulation which only have restricted areas of natural daylight seeping in from the rear of the gymnasium. The architects have used a number of devices to lessen the effect; these range from varying ceiling heights and accentuated lighting fixtures which mark out circulation intersections, to the use of sophisticated colours and textural transformations which aid the legibility of the internal planning. Everywhere the evidence of thoughtful pragmatic design decisions create a building of immense value both to the client and its community of users.

We feel the Academy ... brings the community together in many ways. The design is unique and delightful to look at. The colour scheme is bright and warm, very similar to traditional colours used in Latin America. As the director of the Little Boys & Girls Club, I pass the Academy every day. The parents gravitate around the building at certain hours of the day. I have noticed how relaxed and at ease the parents seem to be. There is a court in the school grounds where the parents wait and this place is a perfect place for neighbours and family to meet and talk.

Robert Cepeda

11   Saint Benno Catholic Secondary School, Dresden

Behnisch and Behnisch

Completed:
1996

Type of project:
720 place church-run mixed secondary school for students aged 11–18 years.

Client:
The Bishop's Diocese of Dresden.

Site area:
26,000 m². This urban site is close to the city centre at the intersection of two busy roads. The site is a long thin strip of land fitting into the urban city plan. Classrooms turn their backs on the busy traffic streets opening up to the residential western orientation. An acoustic wall and generous new tree planting provide a certain amount of protection from the noise of traffic.

Number of teaching spaces:
25 classrooms arranged in faculty blocks of four with special music and drama rooms and a rooftop art studio.

Type of construction:
Reinforced concrete frame, large-scale structural steel and glass infill components. Internal solid walls between classroom areas are of rendered blockwork, with stepped landscaped terraces on the west side.

Special features:
The building is articulated as a series of solidly constructed building blocks, with the parts in between infilled with lighter glazed elements which act as relaxation areas for the staff and its pupils. Over the entrance, the floor plates are cut out to create a large three-storey enclosed atrium or winter garden which is full of life and architectural incidents, the social focus of the building.

Schedule of areas:

Basement	2200 m²
Ground floor	2500 m²
Raised ground floor	2800 m²
First floor	2100 m²
Second floor	1171 m²
Total	10771 m²

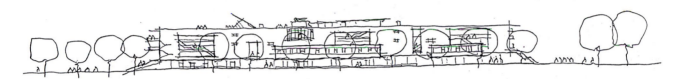

Figure CS11.1
Street elevation – sketch drawing.

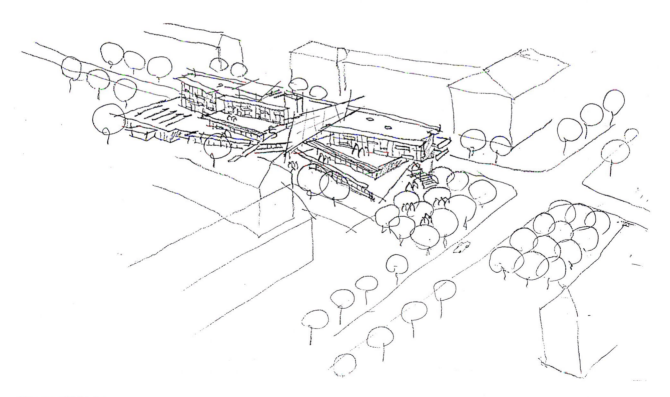

Figure CS11.2a
Conceptual drawings illustrating the fragmented nature of the architecture, a deliberate antidote to the rather austere housing blocks which surround the site, infusing the school with energy and drama.

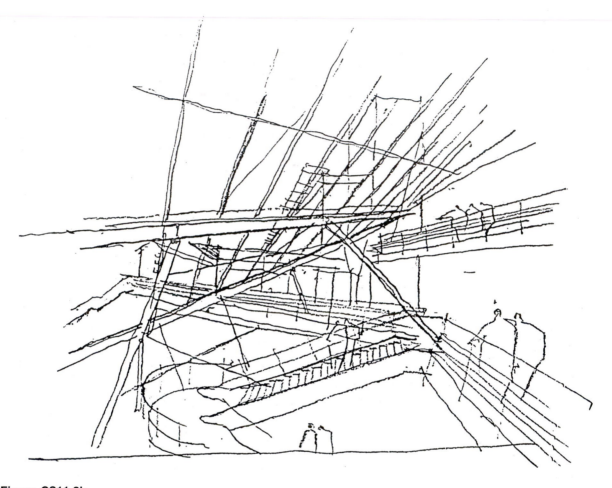

Figure CS11.2b
The entrance atrium or public hall has a similar quality with staircases and roof structure reflecting the non-orthogonal geometry.

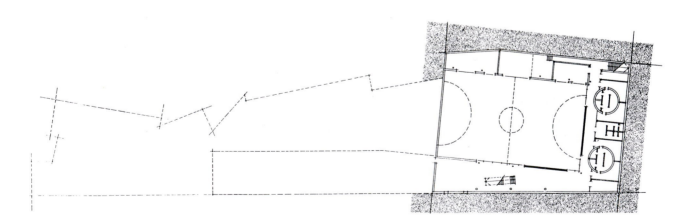

Figure CS11.3
Basement plan and section through sports hall and changing rooms.

Typical classroom   54 m²
Toilet block – female   20 m²
Toilet block – male   25 m² serving 12 classrooms
                           second floor
Two paired music rooms with a single recording studio:
105 m² each
Hall   168 m² (with openable wall/doors to provide a
           single volume of 500 m² when fully retracted)

Summary

The architects describe this as a building where the rooms are positioned logically 'where they ought to be'.

However, the overall effect is much greater than this modest statement suggests. The entrance is on the south side, set back from the busy road. It comprises a grand flight of stairs which elevate you immediately to the raised ground floor, a sort of 'piano nobile' where the main communal spaces are located. From here you can either go down, via a range of open staircases, to the ground or basement levels, containing a sports hall, music and drama rooms and the library; or up to conventional suites of classrooms and the rooftop art studio with viewing gallery providing vistas across the city.

Entering through and into the building, a passageway carries the visitor all the way along its 150 metre length.

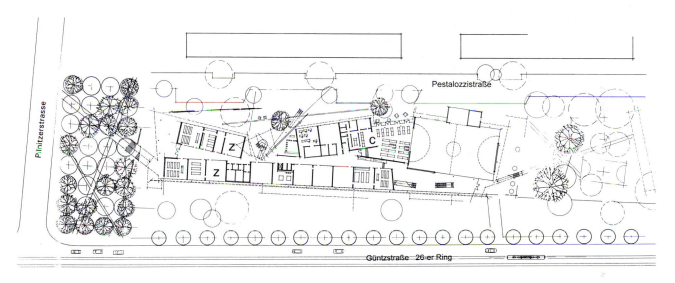

Figure CS11.4
Ground floor service level with cafeteria (c) and classrooms (z).

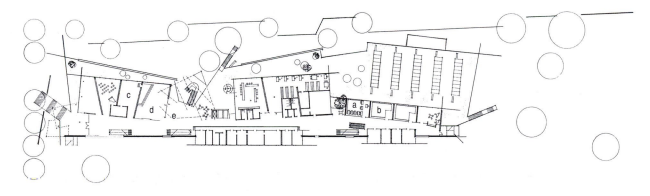

Figure CS11.5
Raised ground floor plan with office (a), meeting room (b), music room (c), and school hall/public meeting area (d) beneath glazed roof and main entrance (e).

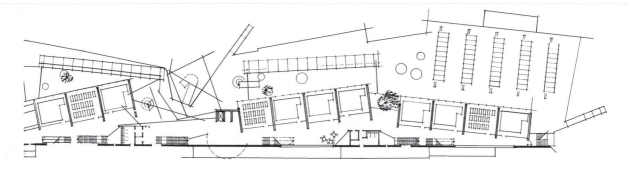

Figure CS11.6
First floor plan with three blocks of four classrooms.

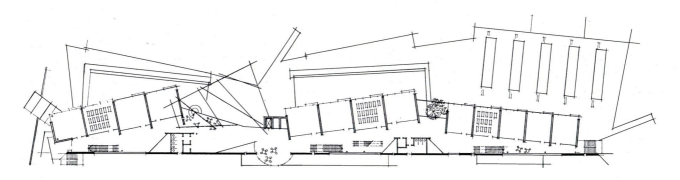

Figure CS11.7
Second floor plan, classrooms and art studio.

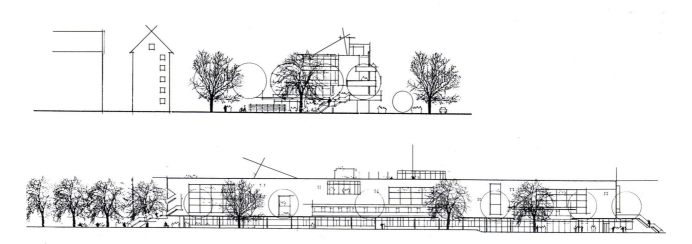

Figure CS11.8
South and east elevation.

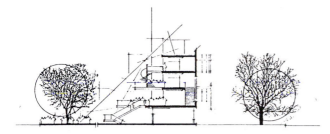

Figure CS11.9
Section through glazed entrance hall.

Figure CS11.10
Exterior view of glazed roof balancing precariously on pin joints from the main frame (compare with plate 14).

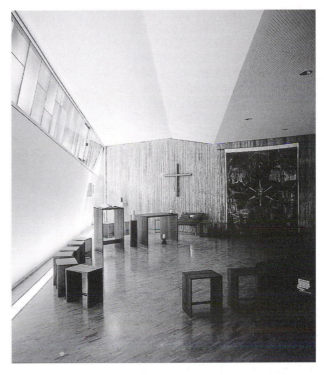

Figure CS11.11
The interior of the chapel with dramatic blue clerestory glazing filling the space with calming blue light.

One is enclosed in an atmosphere of varying modulated light, a route which naturally leads you up towards the glazed roof. Roughly at the centre of the plan is an enclosed winter garden, with angled fenestration, staircases and galleries pitched and skewed to create a dynamic space full of warmth and light. This has become an important social focus for the building, either for children to 'hang-out' in during the day, or an evening forum for concerts and other performances, connecting the school into the patterns of the local community.

In order to reduce the impression of length, the architects have introduced angles into the planning of the solid classroom blocks. The anti-orthogonal organization deliberately subverts the ordered linearity of the housing blocks on the opposite side of Pestalozzi Street, creating a more humane almost organic architectural form which fits its context in scale terms, yet shouts out how special it is in architectural terms. Here is an architecture of schools which is uninhibited about how special it can feel to be in education. Every vista within this internalized circulation world provides a context for social interaction, whereas classrooms are largely conventional enclosed spaces for formal learning.

The building unfolds like an exotic plant, enclosed in thick ochre-rendered walls towards the east, opening up to the west with explosions of dynamic form, individual components merging together into a coherent architectural composition. At ground, first and second floor level, decks and staircases project out like fingers exploring the cultured formal landscape around the edges of the site, an interface between public and private life. The architectural response to its context enhances the life and institutions of this damaged urban landscape.

Figure CS11.12a
Elevation from the east presenting a more formal closed face to the main street in the form of white rendered walls punctuated by window bays and staircase openings.

Figure CS11.12b
The main entrance elevation from the south which begins to open up, hinting at the spatial gymnastics to come inside.

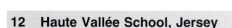

12   Haute Vallée School, Jersey

Architecture PLB

Type of project:
750 place mixed secondary school for pupils aged 11–18 comprising two forms per year.

Client:
The States of Jersey.

Site area:
14,000 m² approximately.

Number of teaching spaces:
Twenty-four classrooms, a science faculty, music and drama, library and IT centre arranged in functional clusters.

Type of construction:
Mixed construction of steel frame with concrete infill, and concrete frame with block and stone cladding.

Special features:
The piazza or town square lies at the heart of the campus where a circular granite clad stair tower sits as a reminder of Jersey's leftover defensive fortifications. It announces the entrance to the glazed dining block which acts as a 'front of house' to the main school hall. Indeed, it is designed as a 350-seat theatre complete with a thrusts stage. It can be operated with or without dining facilities providing a flexible venue for conferences, evening community meetings or local theatrical groups. Technology, visual arts areas and sports facilities are also seen as complementary and grow out of this interpretation of the school hall as theatre, the most public part of the complex.

Schedule of areas:

Total:	9293 m²
Typical classroom	52 m²
Hall/theatre	630 m²
Sports centre	1764 m²
Drama workshop	140 m²

Summary

The States of Jersey assigned the commission following a limited competition. Since Jersey imports all of its fossil fuels, the enlightened brief emphasized the importance of energy efficiency. However, they had strong ideas about

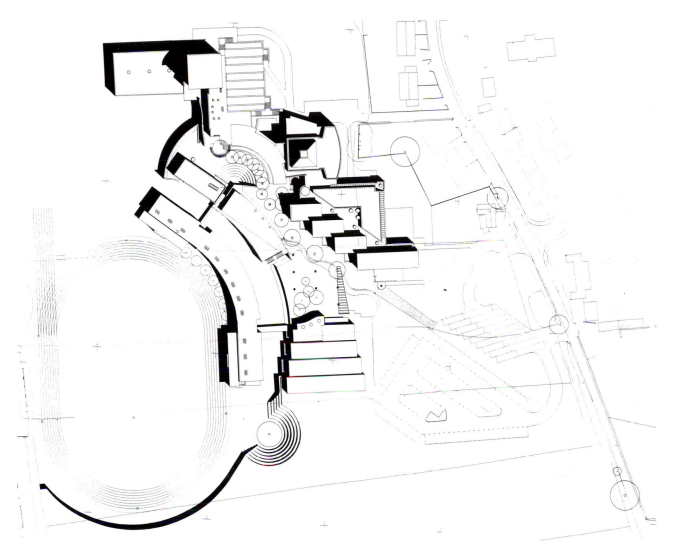

Figure CS12.1
Site plan.

the architecture, stressing the importance of changing experiences in colour, form and texture within the new environment. In short, they wanted a building which would be anti-institutional and welcoming, yet at the same time one with a certain air of technical sophistication.

Design architect Richard Jobson describes his interest in the fragmentation of geometry, expressed here as an axial north–south grid which is broken by a single diagonal line forming a powerful entrance route. The whole campus is organized around this diagram with pedestrian and visual links intertwined through and between the various level changes.

On the south side of the piazza, a vibrant blue concrete wall with an inverted canopy roof slots between the administration and library buildings forming the entrance down into the headteacher's office and other staff and administration areas. Buildings surround and create external areas in a way which is reminiscent of Stirling's Staatsgalerie or the snatched glimpses of the Campo from Via Banchi Di Sotto in Sienna. These spaces act as natural meeting points for adults and children, creating a spatial hierarchy which is rich, articulate and of a particular urban quality.

An analysis of the environmental controls within this building is included as part of Chapter 4.

Figure CS12.2a
Lower floor plan. (See Chapter 4 for sectional and environmental analysis.)

KEY:

1 Sports hall	5 Hall/theatre	9 Technology
2 Gym	6 Library below	10 Science
3 Dining	7 Administration	11 Swimming pool
4 Central piazza	8 Cluster block – classrooms	12 Fifth form

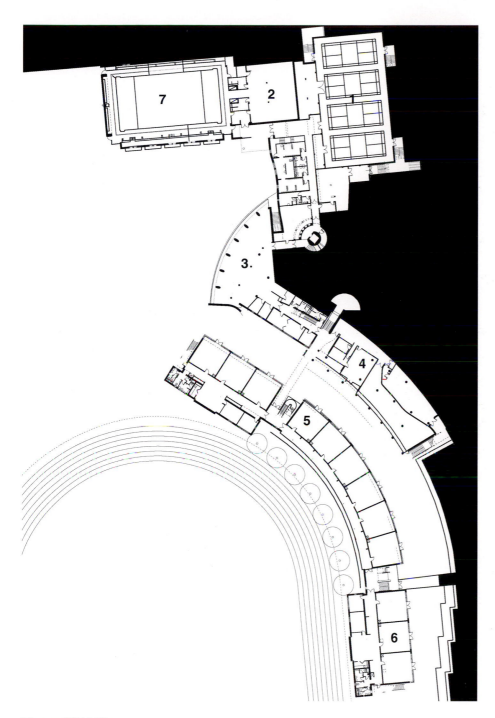

Figure CS12.2b
Upper floor plan. (See Chapter 4 for sectional and environmental analysis.)

KEY:
1 Sports hall
2 Gym
3 Library below
4 Administration

5 Cluster block – classrooms
6 Fifth form
7 Swimming pool

Figure CS12.3
Site model with proposed planting to form the enclosure to the running track. (Photo: © Architecture PLB.)

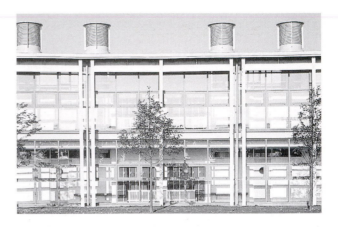

Figure CS12.5
Elevation to resources block with twin ventilation chimneys articulating the classrooms beyond. (Photo: © Architecture PLB.)

Figure CS12.6
The science block with propped mono-pitch roofs projecting over the glazing to provide shading from the afternoon sun. (Photo: © Mark Dudek.)

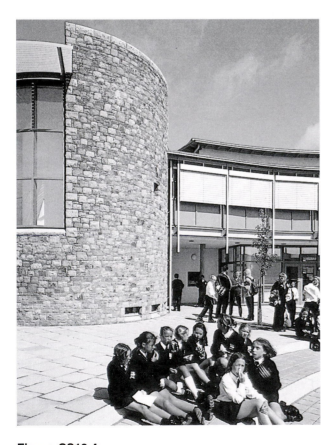

Figure CS12.4
Entrance tower to dining and theatre block wrapped in rough stone – a reference to the vernacular martello towers along the Jersey coastline. (Photo: © Architecture PLB.)

Figure CS12.7
The dramatic canopy behind the piazza marks the route down to the administration block and library. (Photo: © Mark Dudek.)

13   Elementary School, Morella, Spain

Carme Pinõs

Type of project:
An elementary school for 320 students, many of whom come from outlying districts; there is an overnight dormitory facility for 50.

Client:
The General Government of Valencia.

Site area:
0.9 hectares lying immediately outside the walls of this ancient fortified hill town. The building nestles into the sloping contours of the hillside stepping down from east to west.

Number of teaching spaces:
Eleven classrooms, a library and multi-purpose hall accessible from the street for the use of the local community outside school hours.

Type of construction:
In-situ concrete walls with a steel structural frame Triangular roof plains are finished in Cor Ten steel with locally quarried slate wall cladding.

Special features:
The stepped site section is exploited to create a series of external terraces, one for each classroom, which extend curriculum activities. Its historical context is referred to in the scales and tectonic rhythms of the form with the use of exposed concrete and dramatic slate cladding, reflecting the tough dramatic fortifications beyond. The fragmented

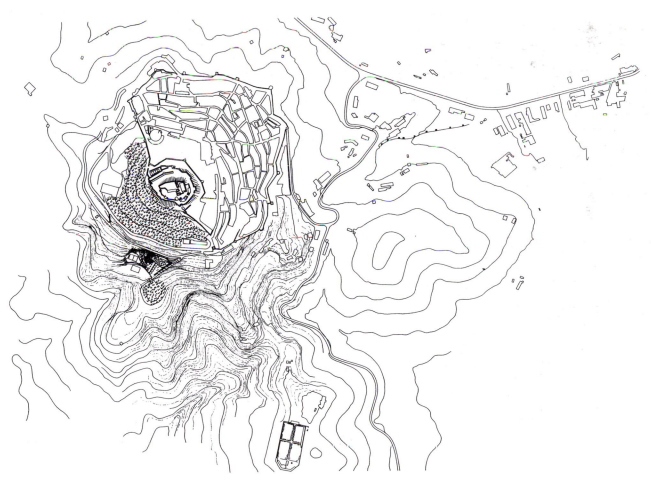

Figure CS13.1
Site plan.

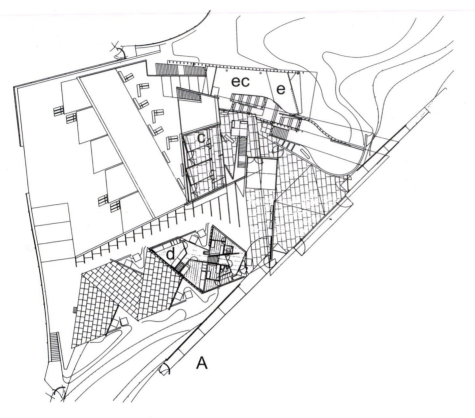

Figure CS13.2
Plan from entrance level 0 (third floor plan) with dormitories (d) and small classrooms (c), refectory (r), entrance courtyard (ec), and entrance from street (e).

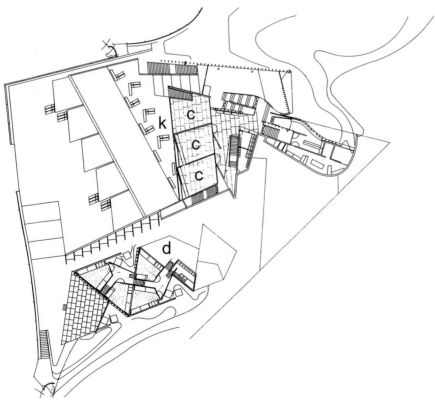

Figure CS13.3
Plan from level 1 (second floor) with classroom (c), cafeteria (k) and dormitory (d).

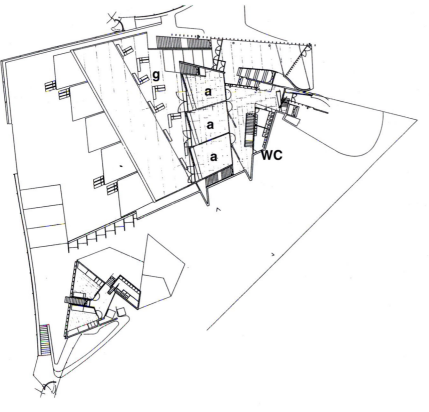

Figure CS13.4
Plan from level 2 (first floor) with classroom block (a), library (g) and WC.

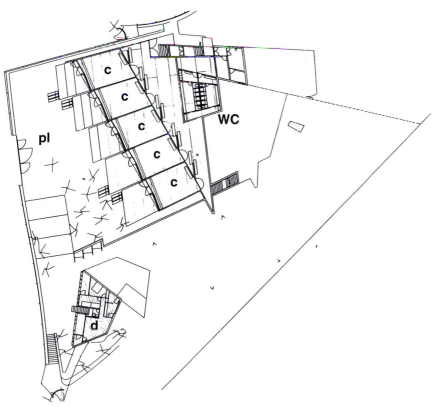

Figure CS13.5
Plan from level 3 (ground level plan) with second classroom block with five classrooms (c), WCs, playground (pl) and dormitory (d).

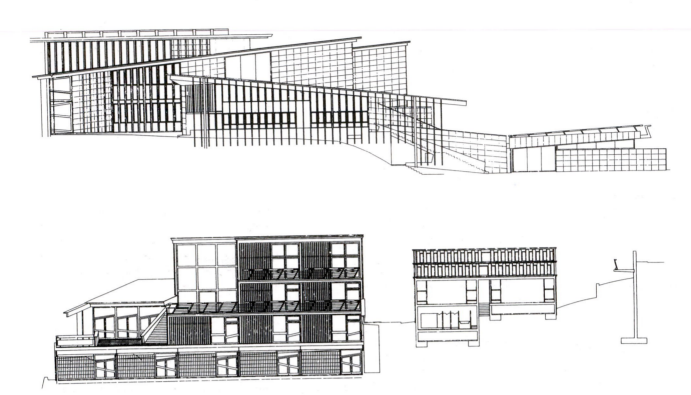

Figure CS13.6
Section A (see CS13.2) and above elevation from the street (alzado).

Figure CS13.7
Colliding geometries create an appropriate aesthetic for this romantic location. Fenestration and cladding elements are designed to create natural shading with recessed windows and doors, projecting roof canopies and heavy reflective cladding materials.

Figure CS13.8
The classroom is a cool, shaded interior which is nevertheless structurally refined, articulating the complexities of the planning.

Figure CS13.9
Interior from the upper level of the refectory looking out towards the entrance courtyard.

form is not only in harmony with its natural setting, but it also breaks down the institutional scale of this large building. Circulation areas are interesting and eventful as they meander down the slope.

Schedule of areas:
Levels 0–3	1820 m²
Typical classroom	78 m²
Dormitory	420 m²

Summary

The building is integral to the site and steps down in a series of wings, each complementing and adding to the dexterity of the whole. The entrance point is at the upper highest part of the site; the ground plain running off the street appears to touch the roof of the new building and the visitor passes down a flight of stairs into the first of a series of courtyards or foyers. The entrance threshold appears secure yet inviting. The first wing of accommodation houses offices, administration and the headteacher's office guarding circulation routes beyond before the route drops down into the first of three primary levels. These contain classrooms and are orientated towards the west, each with its own roof deck/terrace, a natural benefit of the complex stepped section and siting. On reaching the lowest level there is a large enclosed playground with dramatic zigzag concrete benches and play equipment which were designed by the architect. In the southern corner of this play/workspace is the lowest level of dormitory accommodation. This dormitory wing provides accommodation for fifty pupils from outlying rural areas. It is arranged as a mini version of the school itself, with complementary zigzag layout, stepping back up the hillside.

The building's complexity makes it difficult to understand in simple plan form; it is an exploding sequence of external and internal spaces which energize and socialize at the same time by inviting the public to penetrate, yet ensuring that the classroom blocks and the dormitory remain safe, secure territories. '*Pinōs' building is, in effect, an enormous foyer, a public meeting place which is in turn expansive and enclosed*' ('Lyrical Geometry,' *Architectural Review*, 4/6/97).

14 Admiral Lord Nelson Secondary School, Portsmouth, Hampshire

Hampshire County Architects

Type of project:
900 pupil secondary school for 11–18-year-old students with general teaching spaces and a mixed curricula range of science and technology rooms.

Client:
Hampshire County Council.

Site area:
9.6 hectare site bounded to the west by Dundas Lane and beyond that by industrial units. There is a golf course and green open space to the north and east. The site is known to be very low-lying, at or below mean sea level. A degree of flood protection is necessary with areas of the existing site raised.

Number of teaching spaces:
Forty-seven teaching spaces with ancillary accommodation, including a sports centre open to the public at weekends.

Figure CS14.1
Ground floor plan.

KEY:
1 Sports hall
  1A Upper volume
2 Plant room
3 Kitchen
4 Hall
  4A Upper volume
5 Gym – 5A Upper volume
6 Dining
7 Space for possible community use
8 Administration
9 Head
10 Main entrance
11 Courtyards
12 Library
13 Information Technology
14 Business Studies
15 General teaching
16 Staff
17 Music
  17A Upper volume
18 Drama
18A Upper volume
19 Technology
20 Pupils' entrances
21 Toilets
22 Science
23 Science preparation
24 Art
25 Languages
26 Changing
27 Lift
28 Meeting room

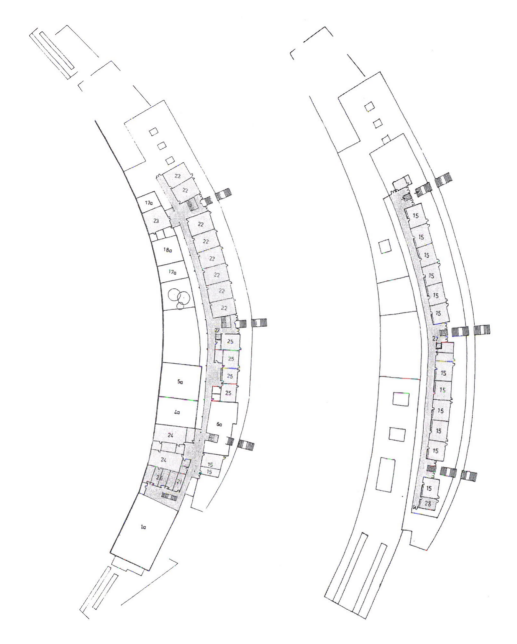

Figure CS14.2a
First floor plan.

Figure CS14.2b
Second floor plan.

KEY:

1 Sports hall
  1A Upper volume
2 Plant room
3 Kitchen
4 Hall
  4A Upper volume
5 Gym
  5A Upper volume
6 Dining
7 Space for possible community use
8 Administration

9 Head
10 Main entrance
11 Courtyards
12 Library
13 Information Technology
14 Business Studies
15 General teaching
16 Staff
17 Music
  17A Upper volume
18 Drama

  18A Upper volume
19 Technology
20 Pupils' entrances
21 Toilets
22 Science
23 Science preparation
24 Art
25 Languages
26 Changing
27 Lift
28 Meeting room

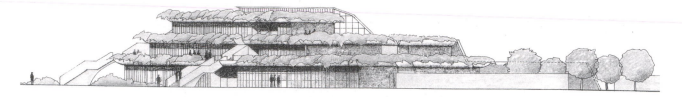

Figure CS14.3
North elevation.

Figure CS14.4
Site plan.

KEY:
1 New roundabout
2 Cycle/pedestrian crossing
3 Cycle/footway
4 Coach parking off Dundas Lane (6 spaces)
4A Future spaces
5 Car parking on site (60 spaces)
5A Future spaces
6 School service bay
7 Tennis courts/overflow parking
8 Access for fire vehicle/ overflow parking
9 All-weather pitch with lighting (equivalent to two winter large pitches)
10 Bicycle storage (215 spaces)
11 Winter grass pitches: 2 medium, 2 small, summer running track and cricket square
12 Shallow wetlands and 'seasonal' ponds. Irregular ground to create winter floor grassland. Ponds to have controlled outfall to prevent flooding beyond site. Ponds to have an expansive area of water catchment adjoining them
13 Rough grass and incidental low planting to banks with appropriate fencing, where required
14 Boundary tree and shrub planting
15 Boundary shrub/scrub planting

Type of construction:
The construction is solid with piled foundations and suspended floor slabs supported by a concrete frame.

Special features:
The building has a stepped section. Each teaching space has access to an external balcony/terrace. This is achieved by providing a series of green roofs giving a decked feel to the development on its south side.

Schedule of areas:

Ground floor	4820 m²
First floor	3800 m²
Total	8620 m²

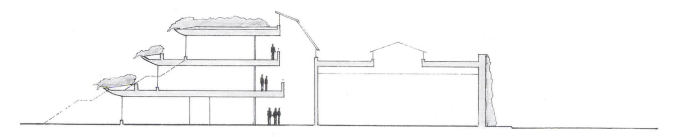

Figure CS14.5
Typical section.

Figure CS14.6
View from the first floor gallery looking across the glazed atrium. Materials and surfaces are light and reflective to create a winter garden full of social activity. Student lockers can be seen along the wall and the top of a five metre high installation prepared by the art department. (Photo: © Paul Carter.)

Typical teaching room   70 m²
Library   420 m²
Music room   360 m²
Sports hall   1000 m²

Summary

The street façade forms an acoustic barrier between the noise of the road and the quieter teaching areas. The class-rooms and the social areas overlook the playing fields to the east and south. The form of the building acts as a visual and acoustic screen between the busy main road and the adjacent industrial development. Between the large volume spaces and the classrooms is a curving glazed 'street' 100 m in length and 12.5 m in height which acts as the main internal circulation space.

The school is three storeys high and to the east presents an open stepped elevation consisting of a series of

Figure CS14.7
The open terrace looking out to towards the coastal marshlands provides planting areas for the children immediately next to the classrooms. (Photo: © Paul Carter.)

landscaped terraces opening off the classroom spaces. These terraces provide sitting areas and with external stairs form a strong link between the school and the playing fields. They are for social use by children during fine weather and, in the case of an emergency, present easy and rapid evacuation routes from all levels.

For the large volume spaces on the west side, the roof comprises insulated profiled metal decking. To the east of Dundas Lane, the roof planting effects an integration of the building into its landscape. On the terraces there is a selection of low planting covering the balustrades. All planting on the terraces have a watering facility for ease of maintenance.

Its integration into the landscape reduces the building's impact and is an appropriate solution for this semi-industrial context. This large building has a minimal impact on its context, which continues to provide enhanced areas for Brent geese and waders which traditionally use the site for winter feeding.

Figure CS14.8
The access stairways give an appropriate nautical feel to this unusual building, piercing the terraces at right angles. (Photo: © Paul Carter.)

15   Heinz Galinski School, Berlin

Zvi Hecker

Type of project:
Special Jewish Primary School for approximately 800 pupils with a communal assembly hall for 500 which doubles as a synagogue.

Client:
Jewish Community in Berlin for the Senate of Berlin.

Site area:
16,000 m². The site is on the edge of the Grunewald Forest with many mature trees.

Number of teaching spaces:
Forty classrooms with ancillary craft/art rooms, gymnasium and art gallery.

Type of construction:
Load-bearing in-situ concrete frame, brick walls with rendered finishes, corrugated metal cladding to parts of the circulation areas.

Special features:
Symbolic fragmented plan with strong community usage.

Schedule of areas:

Ground floor	1630 m²
First floor	1630 m²
Second floor	1636 m²
Total	4898 m²
Typical classroom	70 m²
Reception classroom	85 m²
Hall	480 m²

Summary

The sunflower is a metaphor and a symbol of organic growth. The light of the sun makes its form, it is the source of its life. Education, knowledge, is the light which illuminates children's minds. The nature of ourselves depends on the quality of education we have received. Organic development of our mind demands an organic environment, an organic architecture, the spirit of nature embodied in stone. Education is an organic way of conveying knowledge, from one human being to the other. We plant

Figure CS15.1
Roof plan with shadows.

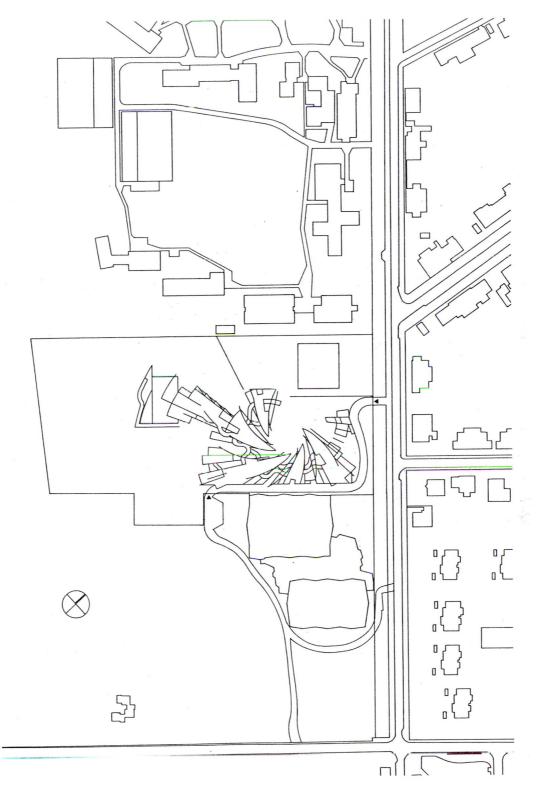

Figure CS15.2
Site plan.

the seeds of knowledge not the knowledge itself. I can't imagine an organic education in a mechanical soulless environment. School is not a production plant. We produce nothing. On the contrary, the results of education are invisible and mostly impossible to evaluate, until much after, sometimes too late.

Architect's statement

In the architect's own words, this is a building which is like a 'big family house'. There are numerous places in which the pupils can hide, and create their own sense of mystery. This is no place for the casual visitor with its labyrinthine passageways and spaces between spaces. The architect's approach is a highly personal attempt to re-create the complexities of the city with its walkways, passageways and cul-de-sacs. The school therefore becomes the city.

The Heinz Galinski School is the first Jewish primary school to be built in Germany after the Second World War. As a result, its construction was not only a functional necessity but also an act of great symbolic significance. Located in Charlottenburg at the northern edge of the Grunewald Forest, the school programme called for a mixture of both large and small spaces. There is a multi-purpose hall for 500, which can be used as a synagogue, a dining hall and two kitchens for meat and milk, in accordance with Jewish tradition. The smaller spaces consist mainly of cellular classrooms.

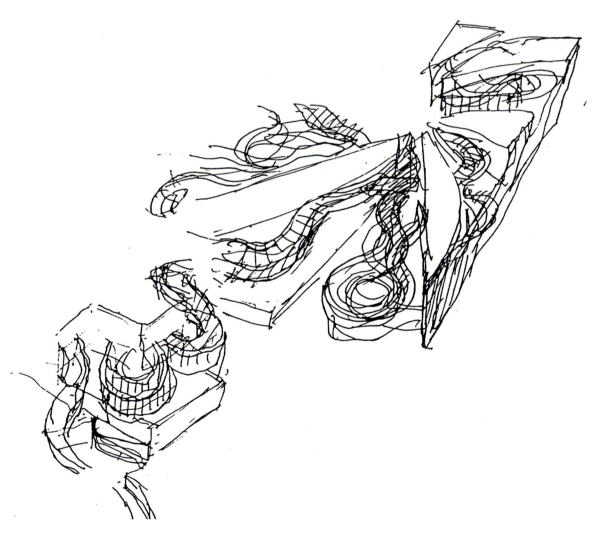

Figure CS15.3
This conceptual drawing appears like an abstract piece of sculpture drawn in two dimensions.

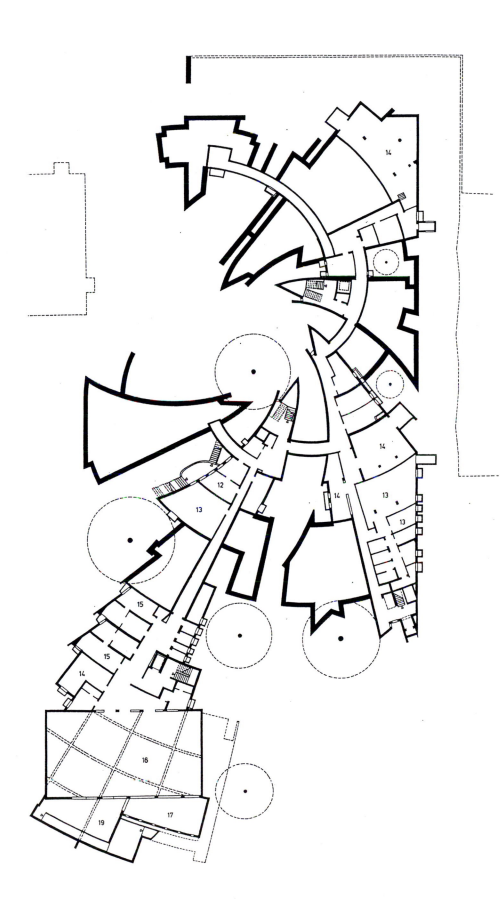

Figure CS15.4
Basement plan.

KEY:
1 Main entrance
2 Secondary entrance
3 Classroom
4 Free time classroom
5 Corridor
6 Art workshop and
  laboratory room
7 Library
8 Conference room
9 Administration
10 Headmaster
11 Staff room
12 Doctor's room
13 Store room
14 Mechanical room
15 Change and shower
  room
16 Gymnasium
17 Equipment room
18 Stands
19 Courtyard
20 Terrace
21 Play court
22 Entrance hall
23 Maintenance room
24 Auditorium and assembly
  hall
25 Gallery
26 Kitchen
27 Dining hall

Figure CS15.5
Ground floor plan.

KEY:

 1 Main entrance
 2 Secondary entrance
 3 Classroom
 4 Free time classroom
 5 Corridor
 6 Art workshop and laboratory
   room
 7 Library
 8 Conference room
 9 Administration
10 Headmaster
11 Staff room
12 Doctor's room
13 Store room
14 Mechanical room
15 Change and shower room
16 Gymnasium
17 Equipment room
18 Stands
19 Courtyard
20 Terrace
21 Play court
22 Entrance hall
23 Maintenance room
24 Auditorium and assembly hall
25 Gallery
26 Kitchen
27 Dining hall

Ground floor plan

Figure CS15.6
First floor plan.

KEY:
 1 Main entrance
 2 Secondary entrance
 3 Classroom
 4 Free time classroom
 5 Corridor
 6 Art workshop and
   laboratory room
 7 Library
 8 Conference room
 9 Administration
10 Headmaster
11 Staff room
12 Doctor's room
13 Store room
14 Mechanical room
15 Change and shower room
16 Gymnasium
17 Equipment room
18 Stands
19 Courtyard
20 Terrace
21 Play court
22 Entrance hall
23 Maintenance room
24 Auditorium and assembly
   hall
25 Gallery
26 Kitchen
27 Dining hall

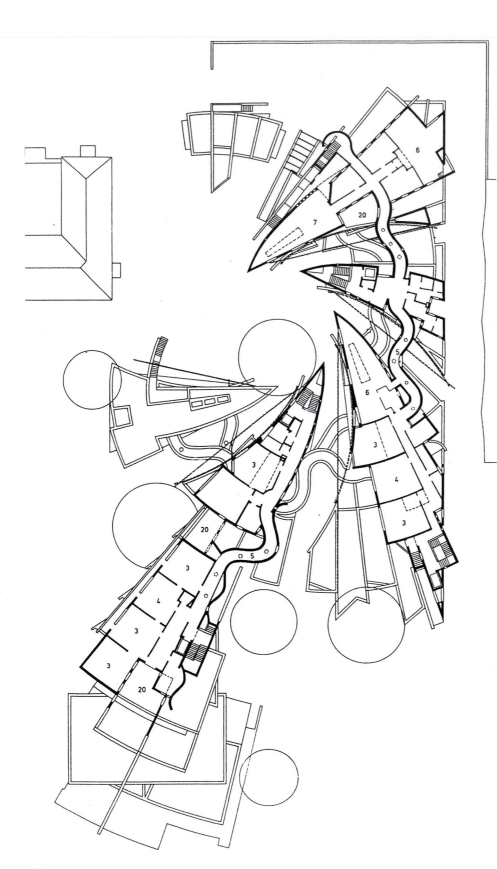

Figure CS15.7
Second floor plan.

KEY:
 1 Main entrance
 2 Secondary entrance
 3 Classroom
 4 Free time classroom
 5 Corridor
 6 Art workshop and
   laboratory room
 7 Library
 8 Conference room
 9 Administration
10 Headmaster
11 Staff room
12 Doctor's room
13 Store room
14 Mechanical room
15 Change and shower room
16 Gymnasium
17 Equipment room
18 Stands
19 Courtyard
20 Terrace
21 Play court
22 Entrance hall
23 Maintenance room
24 Auditorium and assembly
   hall
25 Gallery
26 Kitchen
27 Dining hall

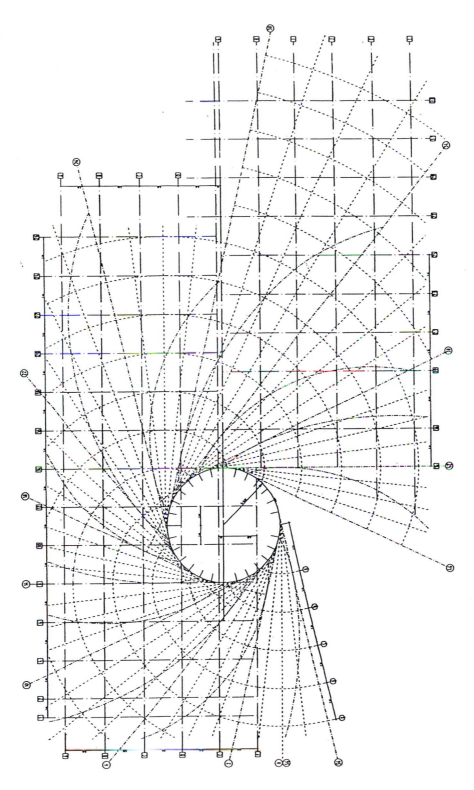

Figure CS15.8a
Geometric layout.

Figure CS15.8b
Early conceptual sketches translating the abstract idea into three dimensions.

Figure CS15.10
The geometry unfolds at the rear service side of the building where the walled city metaphor becomes even more appropriate. (Photo: © Michael Kruger.)

Figure CS15.9
View of the main entrance from the public courtyard with access doors discreetly set back behind the thick sculptural walls of the building. (Photo: © Michael Kruger.)

Figure CS15.11
A corridor on a meandering and playful route, emphasizing the sense of spatial diversity captured within the plan. However, the classroom forms are conventional (see also plate 18).

Because of the many trees on the site, the form of the school was adapted to retain the mature specimens. The rotating sunflower form of the plan focuses on to the entrance court, where all the disparate parts meet to form a semi-enclosed public space. Other more private and smaller scale courtyards have their own individual character. The structure consists of 36.5 cm thick brick load-bearing walls plastered both inside and outside. High insulation values have been ensured by the use of concrete in the floors and ceilings Cheap corrugated metal for the external cladding of corridors and other exposed links is adopted, and chunky triple-glazed timber windows.

The building almost defies categorization. Its message is highly symbolic and yet paradoxical. It is closed and secure, a fortress against a hostile world perhaps, yet its form is also playful and overtly optimistic. Given the context this is the only way to look, forwards rather than backwards, an optimistic investment in education for the new Jewish community of this once troubled city.

16   North Fort Myers High School, Florida (Additions and Renovations)

Perkins and Will

Type of project:
A specialist secondary school for 1600 students from 9th to 12th grades with curriculum emphasis on mathematics,

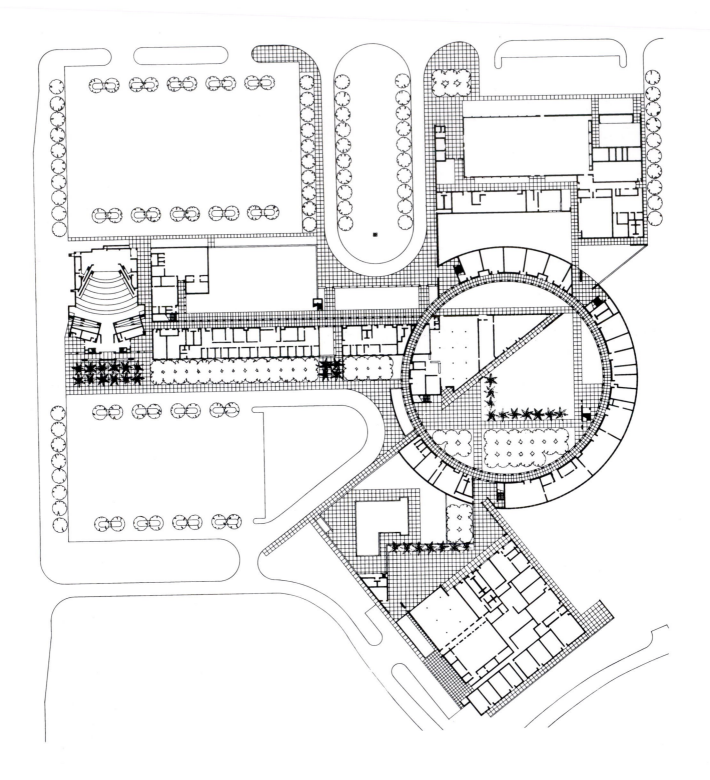

Figure CS16.1
Campus plan.

science and environmental science subjects. Sport and physical recreation facilities feature strongly and are particularly important in establishing and maintaining strong links to the community.

Client:
The School District of Lee County, Florida.

Site area:
The edge-of-city site has an area of approximately six hectares, laid out as a campus with a football stadium (including running track) with bleacher seating for 2000 spectators, a baseball stadium with bleacher seating for 500, parking for 200 students and 20 buses and a 6000 ft² environmental garden. The garden flora and fauna replicate the swamp area conditions which once dominated southern Florida.

Number of teaching spaces:
Forty-four new classrooms, twelve science laboratories, an ecology garden and an experimental garden for the exploration of native plants, the desert landscape and other ecological studies.

Type of construction:
A steel structural frame with brick cladding in several colours, beige buff and terracotta. Varying pitched metal roofs with acoustic ceilings throughout. The internal walls are either of solid rendered blockwork construction, or movable plastic laminated partitions. Solid floors are finished in ceramic tiles or resilient rubber flooring.

Special features:
Many new schools adopt a fortress-like appearance, particularly those in urban areas. Here the architects have enclosed the campus with walls and secure gates which are closed at night; however, for most of the time the school is an open campus, a city with a similar rich range of ingredients which are open and accessible throughout the day, encouraging students to be similarly open. The school takes advantage of the Florida weather which is warm to humid with all circulation taking place outside, beneath covered walkways and extended projecting roofs.

Schedule of areas:

Ground floor	12,000 m²
First floor	493 m²
Total area	16,965 m² (12,700 m² of new accommodation, 3,065 m² of renovated space, 1,200 m² of unchanged areas)
Typical classroom	79 m²
Typical science lab	157 m²
Media centre/library	1,300 m²

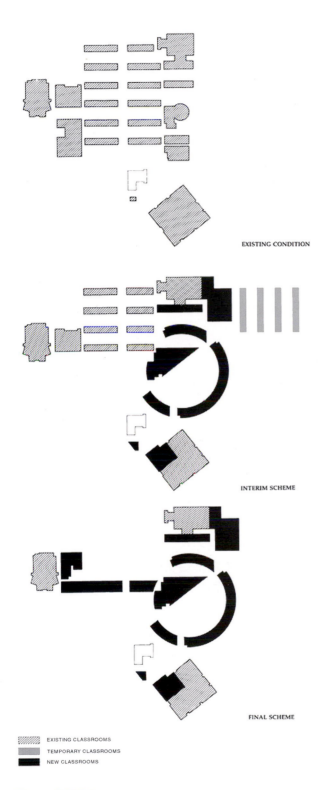

EXISTING CONDITION

INTERIM SCHEME

FINAL SCHEME

EXISTING CLASSROOMS
TEMPORARY CLASSROOMS
NEW CLASSROOMS

Figure CS16.2
Diagrammatic representation of the three-stage redevelopment process.

Summary

The original problem facing the architects was how to introduce some order into an unplanned sprawling collection of buildings spread across the site. To address this issue, they adopted a 'collage approach' superimposing new buildings onto the existing fragmented plans, retaining some and demolishing those which were not worth saving. The masterstroke was the imposition of a large-scale geometry across the site in the form of a circle and a long thin line of new accommodation. The three stages of the redevelopment are illustrated in the diagram. The circle is invaded by the arrow-headed form of a new media centre, which becomes the physical and symbolic heart of the school.

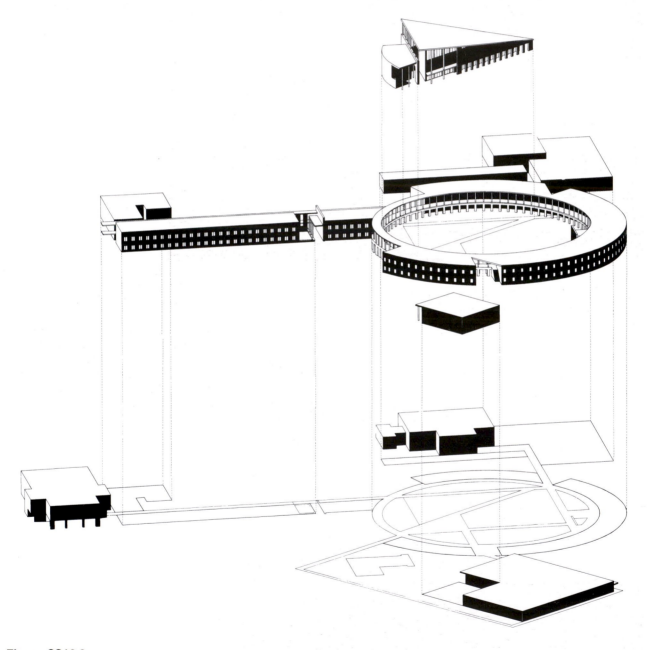

Figure CS16.3
An exploded perspective – existing buildings are knitted into the new rotunda to make the whole campus appear more integrated.

Figure CS16.4a
The media centre/library with entrance marked out by the eccentrically pointed roof. Note the subtle interplay between the structural frame and the envelope of the building to create shading in the right places.
(Photo: © Nick Merrick, Hedrich Blessing Photographers.)

Figure CS16.4b
The interior is lit by a diverse range of natural lighting sources, from high level horizontal clerestory windows to the vertical 'slot' above the entrance doors and low-level courtyard windows to provide relaxing views for the users.
(Photo: © Nick Merrick, Hedrich Blessing Photographers.)

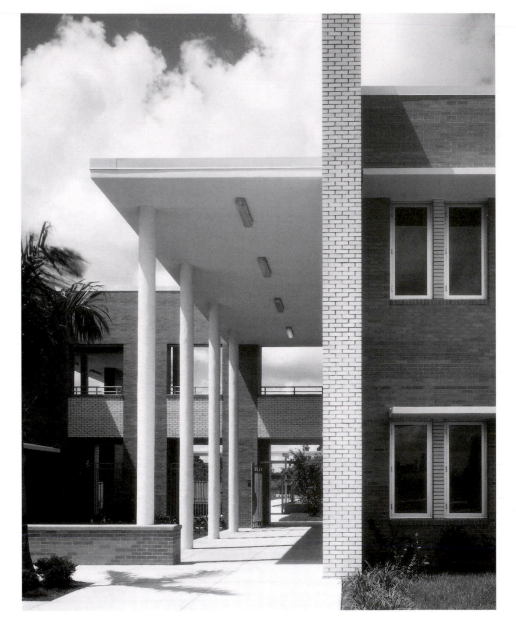

Figure CS16.5
The interplay between solid and void is a key architectural theme. Here the threshold between the sports centre and media piazza is identified by the curving wall of the rotunda articulated as a frame which maintains the enclosure without having any functional use. A limited range of brickwork is mixed to further enhance the planar integration. (Photo: © Nick Merrick, Hedrich Blessing Photographers.)

The centre houses the library, dedicated computer classrooms, and a radio/television laboratory. The enclosed courtyard becomes the new social centre of the campus, being used throughout the year. The new buildings embrace an existing auditorium and science building on the site, connecting both, and creating 'in-between' spaces for informal meetings and social events. An architecture of concrete frame and crisp metal roofing acts as a foil to the monumental aesthetic of brick columns and piers. The construction is a modifier of the hot summer sun; similarly the covered walkways allow sun penetration whilst affording some shading to the classrooms.

17   Albert Einstein Oberschule, Berlin

Stefan Scholz

Type of project:
1000 place secondary school 'Gymnasium' for 12–19-year-old students in the academic or grammar streams.

Client:
The Education Department of the Neukolln district of the City of Berlin.

214

Site area:

A total schools campus area of approximately 3 hectares includes an existing elementary school and a new sports hall. This was originally an edge-of-city site close to the East–West frontier. The original buildings were developed in 1950 to accommodate the children of emigrant families. Der Hufeisensiedlung housing developments set out by Taut and Wagner are close by. The suburban setting is complemented by mature trees and a generous landscaped car park to service both the elementary school and the new gymnasium.

Number of teaching spaces:

Within the new extension there are four physics rooms, four rooms for arts and crafts, a photographic laboratory, a crafts room for heavy construction, four rooms for music and a library.

Type of construction:

In-situ concrete frame with prefabricated floor slabs. The outer cladding is a red brick with a flat high-performance roofing membrane. Interior finishes comprise exposed concrete stairwells, brick interior walls, with granite flooring.

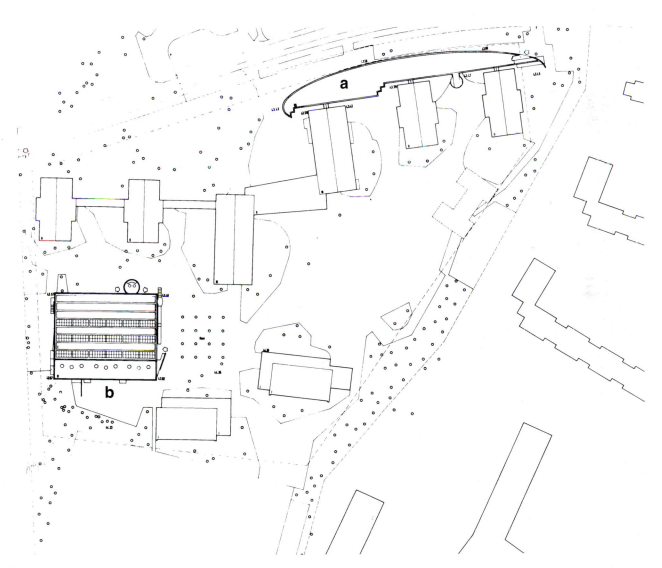

Figure CS17.1
Site plan with the new additions to the school campus: school extension (a) and sports centre (b).

Special features:
The extension is a simple three-storey 'wall' of accommodation which not only connects the three 1950s buildings together, but also protects the interior from the busy street. The external wall to the street is a gentle elliptical curve which ensures that the interior of every classroom is subtly different. The library is a two-storey volume set prominently above the entrance.

Schedule of areas:

Ground floor	1800 m²
First floor	1800 m²
Second floor	1800 m²
Total	5400 m² (new extension only)
Typical classroom	74 m²
Science laboratory	92 m²
Library	140 m²

Summary

The architect has adopted a simple organizing principle which is an elliptical red brick wall to the street enclosing the new accommodation. On approaching, the gentle curve reveals itself gradually, slightly accentuating the natural curve of the street, encouraging the visitor to move from one end of the shape to the other. At the west end the main entrance porch protrudes out from behind the brick skin. Within the building a structural grid of solid internal walls and floors establishes a rhythm along the entire length of the plan. It is an appropriate metaphor, that of ordered stability.

Inside, the connections between the old and the new parts are subtle; materials flow one into the other, the three separate 1950s blocks seamlessly attaching themselves to the new classroom wing. The palette of

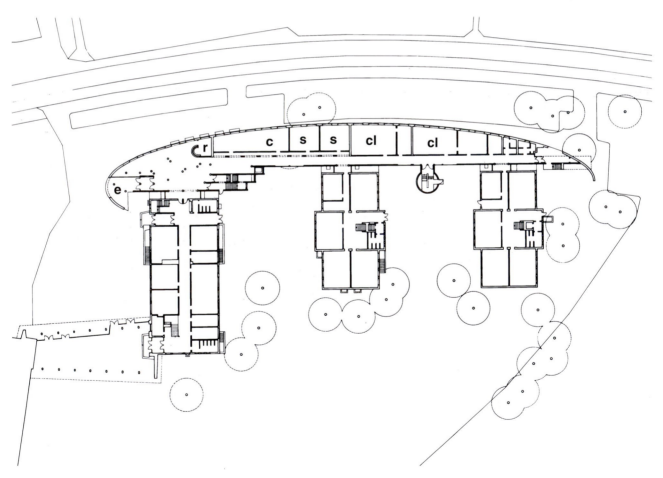

Figure CS17.2
Ground floor plan: entrance (e), reception (r), Internet café (c), classrooms (cl), seminar rooms (s).

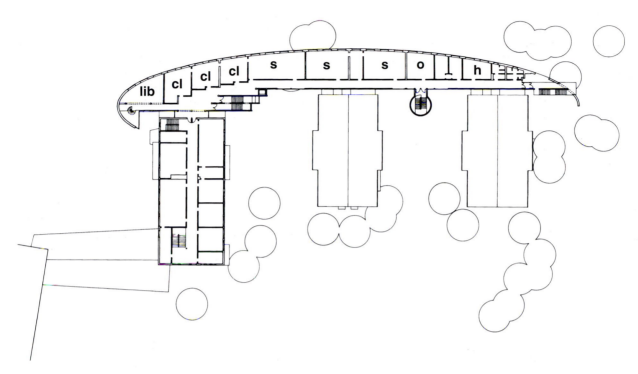

Figure CS17.3
First floor plan: library (lib), classrooms (cl), science blocks (s), office (o), headteacher (h).

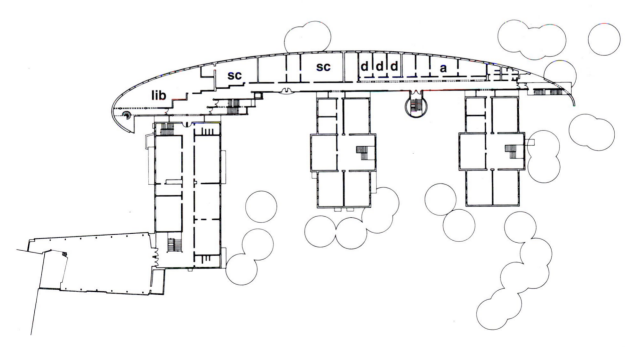

Figure CS17.4
Second floor plan: library upper level (lib), science rooms (sc), demonstration rooms (d), art suite (a).

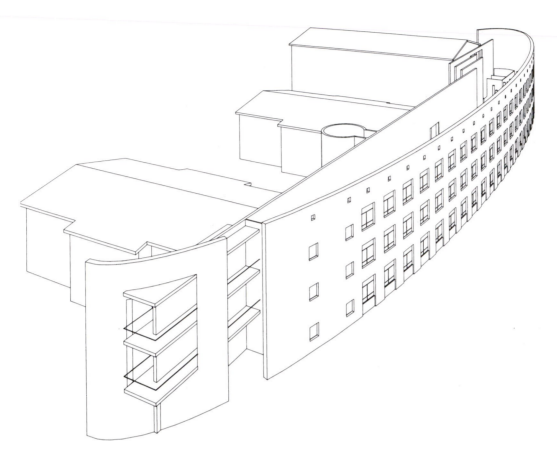

Figure CS17.5
Conceptual
perspective
showing the new
wall with existing
teaching blocks
hooked onto the
back.

Figure CS17.6
The spaces between the
existing blocks are
enclosed on one side by
the new extension to form
delightful south-facing
courtyards overlooked by
balconies and staircases.
(Photo: © R. Görner.)

Figure CS17.7
The escape staircase penetrates the wall at its eastern end, a symbolic reference to the demise of the Berlin Wall, with its social and political divisions. The new school integrates children from the former East with their Western counterparts, a difficult transformation made easier by the new environment. (Photo: © R. Görner.)

Figure CS17.8
The entrance foyer with durable finishes, exposed fair-faced concrete and brickwork for ceilings, walls and floors, an appropriate threshold between inside and outside. (Photo: © R. Görner.)

materials is limited yet creates a warm purposive atmosphere, with granite floors, in-situ concrete stairwells and light timber doors. Inside the classrooms, walls are white rendered; however, the rhythm of the grid is clearly stated, with exposed concrete beams spanning the space from the rear corridor grid to the curved external wall. It all adds up to a highly successful balance between old and new; proof perhaps that it is most difficult to be simple.

18   Barnim Gymnasium, Berlin

Stefan Scholz

Type of project:

A mixed grammar school for pupils aged 11–19 years with five classes in each year.

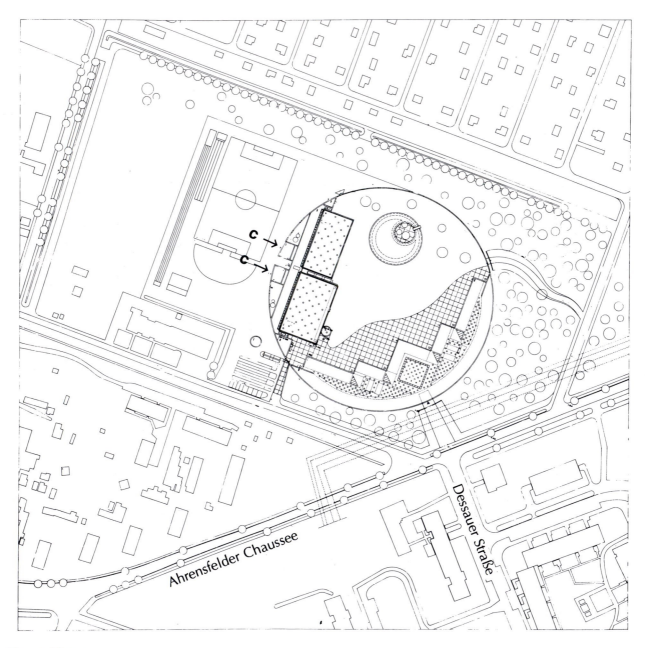

Figure CS18.1
Site plan. (c) – access to community rooms.

Client:
The Education and Building Department, City of Berlin.

Site area:
30,000 m². The site lies in the outer suburbs of the formerly communist-controlled East Berlin. Here is a fragmented landscape of monolithic social housing blocks, and to the east, sub-suburban dachas and scrubland. The overall atmosphere was one of decay and deprivation of the aesthetic senses.

Number of teaching spaces:
Forty conventional classrooms, with twenty-three science, craft and technology rooms.

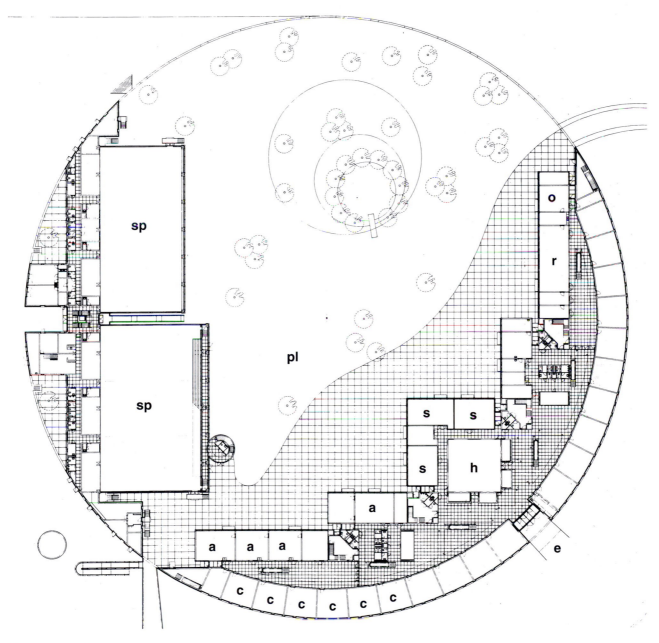

Figure CS18.2
Ground floor plan with main entrance (e), community hall (h), reception (r), office (o), science (s), art room (a), classroom (c), sports hall (sp), playground (pl).

Figure CS18.3
View from the artificial lake towards the teaching and administration block. A semi-modular construction is lightened by the use of glass block and conventional window units within the framework of the internal façades. (Photo: © Ulrich Schwarz.)

Type of construction:
In-situ concrete frame with prefabricated floor slabs. The outer cladding is a red brick with a flat high performance roofing membrane. Interior finishes comprise exposed concrete stairwells, brick interior walls, with granite flooring.

Special features:
The building, whilst urban in character, establishes a comfortable relationship with its surrounding environment. This is emphasized by the provision of minimal car parking. Unless staff have things to carry, they are expected to take public transport. Large parts of the building are prefabricated with included window, wall and floor elements. The aesthetic transcends the uniform feel typical of this approach through the adoption of a circular outer wall and a non-standard inner core. Views out to the surrounding area are carefully orchestrated to ensure that this variety is enhanced wherever possible.

Schedule of areas:

Ground floor	8000m^2
First floor	7800m^2
Total	15,800m^2 (not including the sports building)
Typical classroom	63m^2
Multi-function hall	1020m^2

Summary

Taking its cue from the earlier Albert Einstein Gymnasium, the architect has adopted a strong form to respond to the fragmented physical and social conditions surrounding the site. Accommodation is divided between two blocks comprising sports facilities and, to the southeast, academic classrooms and science laboratories. There is a multi-function assembly hall for theatre, music and drama at the heart of this block. Both parts are then circumscribed by a great circular perimeter wall, with a diameter of 160 metres. The elements of the composition sit within, disposed asymmetrically to maintain an informal relationship to this pure geometric shape.

The architect believes that it is a strong unifying architectural statement, yet one which remains partly open to the surrounding landscape and therefore democratic in spirit. Stefan Scholz also refers to it as a fortified structure, slightly raised above the ground, insulating its users against a harsh external environment. The rotunda establishes an enclosed courtyard effect, which is used as an external play space; the social world of young people is symbolically at the centre of things, with half the accommodation looking over this pleasant secure area. A small circular lake seeps out into the landscape beyond, again subtly unbalancing the natural symmetry of the form.

The permeability of the wall is emphasized by the provision of rooms which open outwards away from the central courtyard to engage with the surrounding site

Figure CS18.5
The boundary of the school is marked out by the form of the rotunda which has a symbolic presence around the open northern side, marking out the territory of the school, an interface between the formal and the informal landscape of dachas with allotments. This clarity becomes all important when viewed in three dimensions (drawing of bird's eye perspective). (Photo: © Ulrich Schwarz.)

Figure CS18.4
The external access ramp is on axis with the internal atrium to provide a visual connection. The architecture has an articulacy which is important in such a large building. This is achieved not just by the use of primary forms but also by the use of particular materials: the external façade (left) is in brick whilst the internal elevations are white-painted render to distinguish between backs and fronts; this legibility is important in this degraded urban environment of the former East Berlin. (Photo: © Ulrich Schwarz.)

areas. The accommodation sneaks out from behind the brick wall; there is a function room for hire, raised external picnic areas and external sports facilities to complement the two great sports halls. These are available to the community outside of school hours. The academic side of the building is condensed without appearing too cramped. The external two-storey walls of classrooms are clad both externally and internally in red-brick. On the internal courtyard elevations the laboratories and administrative facilities are clothed in glass blocks and white brick, a reflection of the more fluid activities taking place within.

The juxtaposition of curved and orthogonal geometries creates an interesting sequence of intermediate spaces within the teaching block. The area is covered over by a heavy concrete roof pierced with circular lanterns admitting natural light and ventilation. It is criss-crossed by galleries and staircases. With its exposed concrete finishes and long vistas, this is one of its weaker architectural moments. It appears somewhat austere at times; however, it can be said that a cool backdrop is established for the animated interactions of the students rushing between classes. Careful attention to the acoustics ensures that noise is never a problem even when the spaces are full to bursting.

Unlike many other secondary schools based on a more dispersed campus layout, this school is easy to get around with the majority of its teaching spaces enclosed within this area; travel distances are limited. Inspired by the rationalist theories of O.M. Ungers and Aldo Rossi, this is a building which is both powerful and humane. The rotunda form combined with a freer development of the plan creates an ordered tranquillity within a rich and diverse composition of internal and external spaces. Due to its completeness, later additions may be difficult to incorporate; however, for the moment, it is an appropriate and economical response to the difficult site.

19   Odenwaldschule, Frankfurt (Extension)

Peter Hübner

Type of project:
Two additional classrooms for a private residential school for pupils aged 11 to 16.

Client:
The School Reform Movement prepares pupils for both academic and manual occupations. It was set up in response to the changes brought by unification and industrialization after the First World War.

Site area:
Approximately 2.0 hectares of hilly woodland. The site chosen lies on a path between two existing villas on a steeply sloping valley side. Initially a clearing had opened up with the death of a pair of large maples. Before they could be felled one of them burst into leaf, so the architect decided to build around the living tree.

Number of teaching spaces:
Two new classrooms.

Type of construction and special features:
The chosen site determined an ingenious cantilevered construction. In order to avoid the roots, a structure was devised which could sit on two short concrete piles. In order to preserve humidity around the trunk of the tree, a form of roof drainage was devised to channel rainwater into the centre of the root system. The tree grows seemingly in harmony with the building, through the centre of the balcony.

Schedule of areas:

Classroom 1	80m².
Classroom 2	80m²
Entrance lobby	30m²

Summary

Sometimes the site for a new school can be a negative factor providing insurmountable problems. In this case it

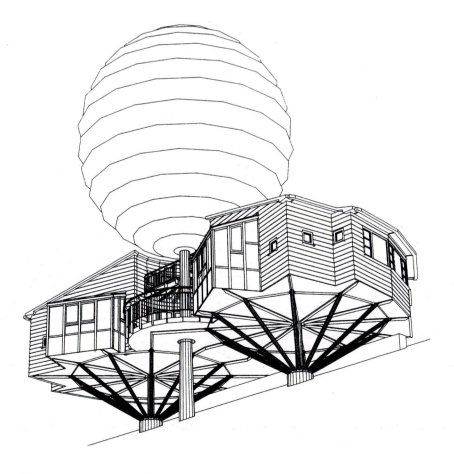

Figure CS19.1
Axonometric projection from beneath illustrates the interplay between steel and concrete structures and the tree between the two classrooms.

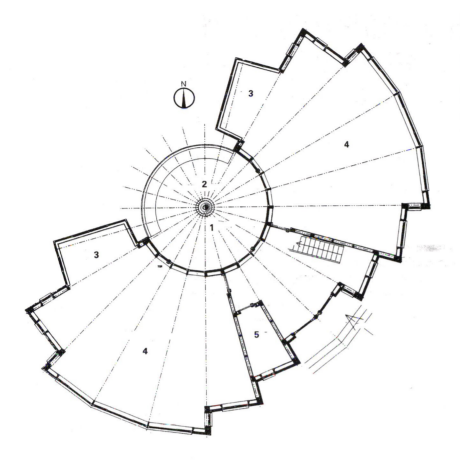

Figure CS19.2
Floor plan.

KEY:
1 Tree
2 Balcony
3 Oriel
4 Classroom
5 Lavatory

Figure CS19.3
Lower structure, concrete supports steel, supports timber.

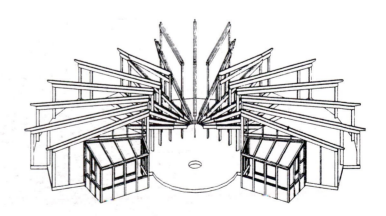

Figure CS19.4
Upper structure in timber sitting on the rigid floor plate beneath.

Figure CS19.5
The interior is a calming environment surrounded by foliage during the summer months, giving views to the valley beyond during winter. A school which fully exploits its natural setting. (Photo: © Peter Hübner.)

was fundamental in suggesting the inspiring solution. The architect and structural engineer have struggled to overcome these problems and created a building of vivid beauty which is in harmony with the educational ethos and its picturesque site.

Initially an exclusively timber building was planned. This quickly became unworkable, as the structural forces around the base of the tree were so great. The design team came up with a combined timber/steel and concrete solution. First a concrete plate was linked to two pile foundations by a radiating grid of steel struts. This was treated as a foundation upon which a traditional timber frame building was constructed, with wall and roof finishes of Alaska Cedar.

Peter Hübner is always concerned with staff and pupil participation in the construction of his buildings. Here the sophisticated structural solution limited the amount of direct participation. A three-dimensional computer system transferred the varying lengths required for the roof

beams and structural joints to enable complex geometrics to evolve. But it requires specialist contractors. Nevertheless, the extent of pupil participation enabled identification with the building to emerge, which is a lesson in itself.

20   Waldorf School, Chorweiler, Cologne

Peter Hübner

Type of project:
A Waldorf private school based on Rudolph Steiner's philosophy[1] incorporating classrooms, craft workshops and music rooms.

Client:
The Waldorf Free School, Cologne.

Site area:
12,000m². The generous site is on the edge of Cologne in a working class residential area dominated by large blocks of flats and wide traffic boulevards. The location was chosen mainly because of the cheap land.

Number of teaching spaces:
Ten conventional classrooms for academic subjects with five music rooms, six handicraft spaces and two dance/eurhythmy rooms.

Type of construction:
Reinforced concrete internal walls and floors cast in-situ with a subsidiary timber frame and timber cladding.

Special features:
The holistic nature of the Steiner ethos is seen in this centrally planned main building, which is conceived as a rose with petals and a stem. The centre of the plan is the meeting hall where parents and friends from the wider community are welcomed. The functional and aesthetic shape of the building embodies a natural organic form based on the geometric progression 5/10/20.

Schedule of areas:
Ground floor	2,200m²
First floor	2,000m²
Second floor	1,950m²
Total area	6,150m² (main school building)

Figure CS20.1
Site plan showing the school and sports building.

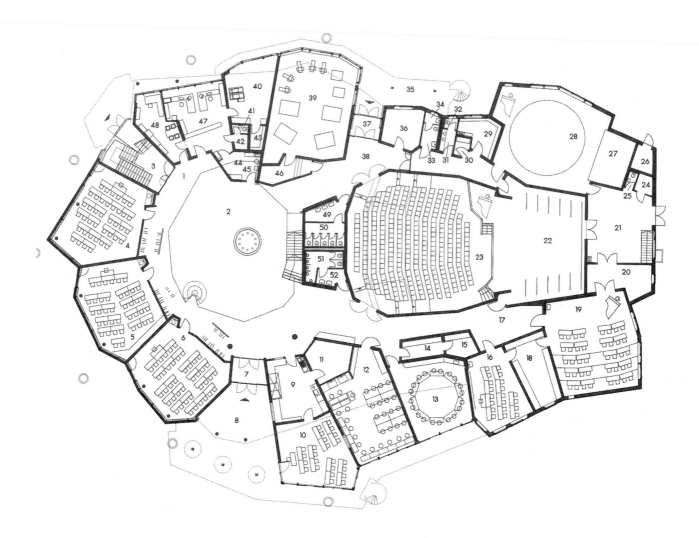

Figure CS20.2
Ground floor plan.

KEY:

1 Circulation
2 Atrium
3 Stairway
4 Classroom 3
5 Classroom 2
6 Classroom 1
7 Wind lobby
8 Open rest room
9 Housekeeping
10 Housekeeping
11 Refrigeration
12 Manual work 1
13 Manual work 2
14 Manual work suppliers

15 Costume storage
16 Orchestra, small
17 Corridor
18 Orchestra, side room
19 Orchestra
20 Orchestra, side room
21 Storage, stage
22 Small stage
23 Auditorium
24 Store
25 Stage toilets
26 Bin store
27 Altar
28 Eurythmy room
29 Eurythmy changing room
30 Eurythmy changing room
31 Ante room
32 Female toilets
33 Disabled toilets

34 Cleaner's storeroom
35 Open rest room
36 Common room
37 Wind lobby
38 Corridor
39 Manual work 3
40 Archive
41 Toilets
42 Staff room
43 Materials/store
44 Waiting area
45 Medical
46 Housekeeping
47 Administration
48 Office
49 Girls lobby
50 Girls toilet
51 Boys toilet
52 Boys lobby

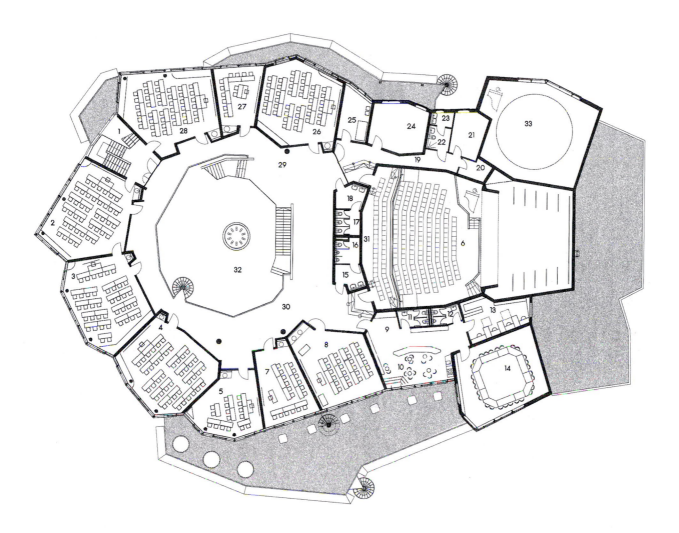

Figure CS20.3
First floor plan.

KEY:

1 Stairway
2 Classroom 6
3 Classroom 5
4 Classroom 4
5 Group room 2
6 Upper auditorium
7 Group room 3
8 Biology room
9 Cloakroom
10 Staff room
11 Ladies toilets
12 Gents toilets
13 Teachers' workroom
14 Conference room
15 Boys lobby
16 Boys toilet
17 Girls toilet
18 Girls lobby
19 Corridor
20 Store
21 Speech therapy
22 Disabled toilets
23 Cleaners' storeroom
24 Room for contemplation
25 Quiet room
26 Classroom 8
27 Group room 1
28 Classroom 7
29 Corridor
30 Corridor
31 Balcony
32 Upper part of atrium
33 Upper part of eurythmy room

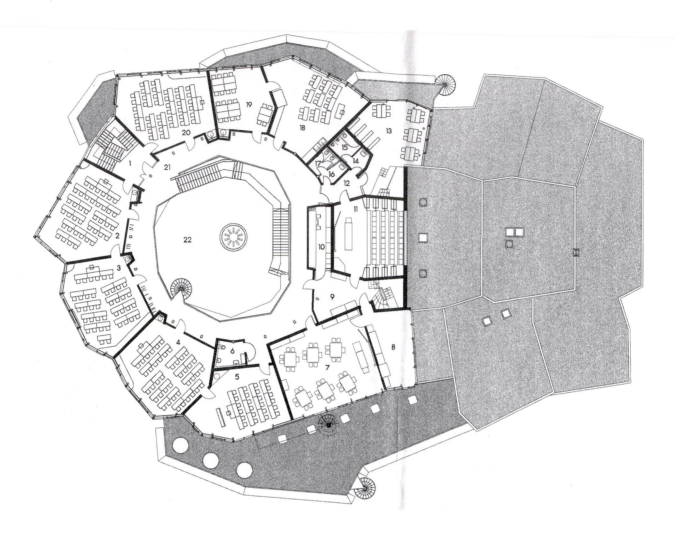

Figure CS20.4
Second floor plan.

KEY:

1 Stairway
2 Classroom 10
3 Classroom 11
4 Classroom 12
5 Classroom 13
6 Disabled toilets
7 Technology room
8 Chemistry lab
9 Physics lab
10 Biology lab
11 Performance space
12 Lobby
13 Library
14 Lobby
15 Boys toilets
16 Lobby
17 Girls toilets
18 Art room
19 Book binding/painting room
20 Classroom 9
21 Corridor
22 Atrium

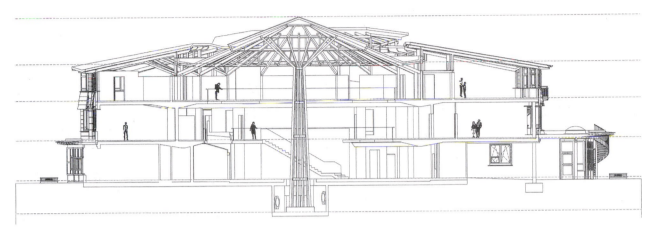

Figure CS20.5
Cross section through classrooms and entrance atrium.

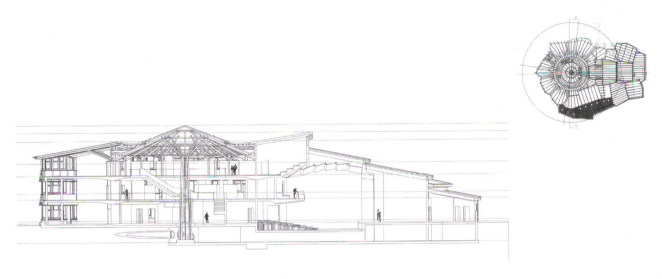

Figure CS20.6
Longitudinal section through atrium and main auditorium.

Typical classroom area	68m² (each classroom has a different shape)
Eurhythmy dance studio	115m²

Summary

The privately run Waldorf schools are popular throughout Germany. They receive some state subsidy but benefit mainly from parental contributions. In this case the finance for the building was borrowed against personal guarantees by parents. Here the contribution also included an active participation not just in the design process, but also in the construction of elements of the building itself. For example, they undertook the construction of the workshops which were added after the main sports hall was completed. It is the intention to replace the standard doors with hand-made doors produced on the premises by staff and students, to further enhance this process.

The new school comprises two buildings: the main school and the sports hall. They are located in the northern side of the site with a landscaped pathway separating the two. At the centre of each building is the largest communal area, the auditorium and sports hall. The classrooms surround this central core, ranged around the south

231

Figure CS20.7
Here the garden façades are intended to be in close proximity to the, as yet, undeveloped garden to fulfil the essential requirements of this very particular curriculum (compare with plate 23).

and east sides. The sports hall has a glazed façade which benefits from some winter solar gain.

The school building focuses inwards to a spectacular three-storey circulation space. It has a glass roof supported by a tree-like canopy of radiating timber columns. The space serves as a ventilation shaft, sucking air up as the glazing heats, to be dispelled through large rooftop vents. Air is drawn in through external ducts and is distributed through a system of underground pipes. This air can exchange heat with the mass of the earth cooling in summer and warming in winter. Further passive control features add to this sense of purposive ecology.

The only active air-handling element is a rooftop fan which extracts air from the auditorium when in peak use. The ethos is exemplified in this building for the senses. As Peter Blundell Jones states: *... the organization of a building reflects and determines social relationships ... the qualities of space and light in a classroom affect the learning of the children.*[2] This is clearly understood, and enhanced by the parents' enthusiasm and personal investment showing the extent of their concern for the education of their children.

Notes

1 Anthroposophy has been described as the wisdom of man combined with his spiritual being. Rudolph Steiner (1861–1925) established the principles for an architecture which would be the spiritual embodiment of man's relationship to nature. He sought to create a vitality of form where concave surfaces were combined with convex ones to create a natural organic system or which resembled an image of growth. This would be an embodiment of the process through which the pre-school child passes.

2 Blundell-Jones, Peter, 'Academic engagement.' *Architectural Review*, February 1999, p.42.

Figure CS20.8a
The interior atrium illustrates how large the building really is. The opening ceremony accommodated more than 1000 people with ease.

Figure CS20.8b
The architect ponders on his structure with internal planting beginning to relate to the rooftop structure.

Index

Aalto, Alvar, 2, 30
Admiral Lord Nelson Secondary School, Portsmouth, 56, 95–6, 101, 193–9
After-school requirements, 76, 82
Agassiz, BC, *see* Seabird Island School, Agassiz
Albert Einstein Oberschule, Berlin, 214–20
Aldrich, Richard, 46
Alma School, 6
Almere, *see* Bombardon School, Almere
Amsterdam, orphanage, 35, 36, 159
Analysis of function, 1, 6, 10
Anne Frank School, Papendrecht, 153–8
Anning, Angela, 44
Annual Capital Guidelines (ACG), 119
    Basic Need proposal, 120, 123
Anthroposophy, 232
Anvalankoski, *see* Tehtaanmäki Elementary School, Anvalankoski
Apollo Schools, 36, 154
Architects, selection, 126
Architecture PLB, 98, 103, 108, 115, 184
Architectuurstudio Herman Hertzberger, 153, 159
Aries, Philippe, 5
Arnold, Dr Thomas, 11
Assembly halls, 116–18

Barnard, Henry, 11
Barnim Gymnasium, Berlin, 220–3
Basic Need proposals, 120, 123
Basle, primary school, 37
Bavinck School, 28
Beard, Andy, 124
Beaudouin, Eugene, 27
Behavioural problems, 46–7
Behnisch and Behnisch, 178
Bennett, Martin, 58
Bennett, Neville, 50
Berlin, *see* Albert Einstein Oberschule; Barnim Gymnasium; Heinz Galinski School
Bijboet, Bernard, 27
Bishop, Robin, 90

Blundell Jones, Peter, 108, 131
Blunkett, David, 73
Bolles Wilson and Partner, 77, 116
Bolton, *see* Prestolea School, Bolton
Bombardon School, Almere, 159–62
Bonner Street Primary School, Hackney, 7
Bordon, *see* Woodlea Primary School, Bordon
Bottisham college, 24
Bournemouth, *see* Pokesdown Primary School, Bournemouth
Boustred, Aiden, 98
Brampton, 2000 project, Newham, 96–8
Brampton Manor Secondary School, Champions Group, 123
Briefing process, building projects, 127–9
Brighton, *see* Dharma School, Brighton
Brighton University, Department of Architecture, 51
Brown, Alan, 98
Buchanan, Peter, 93
Buckinghamshire Education Department, classroom sizes, 61
Buddhism, effect on school environment, 63
Building projects:
    briefing, 127
    design development, 73, 129–30
    development plan, 127
    financing, 74
    hand over, 130–1
    pre-contract stages, 125–7
    programme stage, 127
    safety requirements, 125
    site construction work, 130
Buildings Regulations, 125
Burkard Meyer Steiger, 93
Burlington Secondary School, 28, 29
Burnet Tait and Lorne, 28

Cambridge County Architects, 92
Canada, education system, 46
Capital project funding, 119, 122–4
Carme Piños, 189

Chicago, *see* Little Village Academy, Chicago
Children's centres, 82–4
Chorweiler, *see* Waldorf School, Chorweiler, Cologne
Christopher Place, *see* Speech and Learning Centre, Christopher Place
Churcher, Nev, 31, 90
Cité de la Muette à Drancy, school, 27–8
City Technology Colleges, *see* Specialist Schools
Clarendon School, Hampton, 122
Clark, Peter, 117
Clarke Hall, Denis, 30, 32
CLASP (Consortium of Local Authorities Special Programme), 79
Class Size Reduction Initiative, 119
Classroom:
    ideal, 50–1
    research project, 51–6
    working environment, 13, 44–5, 53–6, 58–9, 61
Cleves Primary School, Eltham, 65, 67, 85
    learning environment checklist, 70–1
Cologne, *see* Waldorf School, Chorweiler, Cologne
Community Classroom, EDG scheme, 81
Community Nursery, EDG scheme, 81–2
Community Schools (LEA), 121
Computers, use in schools, 50, 68
Construction (Design and Management) Regulations (CDM), 125
Consultants, building projects, 125–6
Corona School, Bell, Los Angeles, 68
Cottrell, Richard, 80
Cottrell and Vermeulen, 75, 122, 145
County schools funding, 74
Crestwood Secondary School, Eastleigh, 96
Croft Centre, Richmond upon Thames, 86
Crookham Junior School, 103, 104
Crowley, Mary, 79
Curry, William Burnley, 22

Darmstadt primary school, 33, 34
Dartington community, 22
De La Salle School, Liverpool, questionnaire, 53
De Stijl movement, 28, 29
Dearing Report (1994), 47
Dearing, Sir Ron, 47
Defects liability period, 130
Delft, *see* Montessori Primary School, Delft
Department for Education and Employment (DfEE):
  A & B Branch, 90, 125
  capital projects, 123
  constructional standards, 125
  funding responsibility, 120
  tendering process, 127
Design Build Finance Operate (DBFO) projects, PFI, 124
Design process, phases, 129–30
Dewey, John, 18–19, 50, 118
Dharma School, Brighton, 63
Disability Discrimination Act, 1997, 125
Discovery method, Canadian schools, 46
Dresden, *see* Saint Benno Catholic Secondary School, Dresden
Dual use schemes, PFI, 124–5
Dublin, *see* Ranelagh Multi-Denominational School, Dublin
Dudok, Willem Marinus, 28
Duiker, Jan, 27
Dunblane Primary School, Stirling, 83
Dunne, Elizabeth, 50
Dyck, James, 56

Early Excellence Centres, 83–4, 86
Eastleigh, *see* Crestwood Secondary School, Eastleigh
Ecole des Beaux Arts, 24
Edison Project, in USA, 118
Education Act, 1870, 25
Education Act, 1944, 46
Education Act, 1998, 47
Education Act (Scotland), 1872, 16
Education Action Zones, 118
Education Design Group (EDG), 81, 122
Education Reform Act, 1988, 68, 118
Educational Alternatives, in USA, 118
Edward Cullinan Architects, 103
Elementary Education Act, 1870, 11, 12
Elementary School, Morella, 189–93
Elementary school requirements, *see* primary/elementary school requirements
Eltham, *see* Cleves Primary School, Eltham
Elton Report, 1989, 114
Energy saving, 102, 103, 107–8
English teaching, 48–9

Environmental control, 106–8
Esherick House, 87
European schools, design, 27–8
Evans, Barrie, 106–7
Evans, Melanie, 51–6, 129
Expanding Nursery project, 79, 82
External space potential, 108–112

Fabritius School, 28
Facilities management schemes, PFI, 125
Factory Act, 1833, 11
Female teachers, 18
Fenoughty, Sue, 74, 112–14
Finmere Two-Class School, 66
Fisher, H A L, 18
Fisher, Thomas, 118
Fixed feature space, 6
Florida, *see* North Fort Myers High School, Florida
Foale, Peter, 126
Forest Kindergarten, Denmark, 83
Formula Capital, 119
Foundation Schools, 121
Frankfurt, *see* Greisheim-Sud; Odenwaldschule
Fréjus, *see* Lycée Polyvalent, Fréjus
Froebel, Friedrich, 10
Fry, Max, 24
Funding:
  current arrangements, 74–5
  nineteenth century, 11
  pre-school facilities, 78
  terminology, 118–20
Funding Agency for Schools (FAS), 121

Gamston, Nottingham, new school proposal, 123
Garnier, Tony, 24, 25
Geranium School, 28
Geschwister School, Lünen, 34, 57
Gibson, Sir Donald, 79
Glasgow Education Society, 16
Glasgow Infant School Society, 15
Glasgow School Board design, 17
Glastonbury Thorn First School, Milton Keynes, 59, 60, 61, 116
Goldfinger, Erno, 9, 24, 79
Good Shepherd Primary School, Nottingham, 109, 116
Grangaard, Helle, 85
Grant maintained schools, 120
  funding, 74
  see also Foundation Schools
Green architecture, 108
Greisham-Sud Kindertagestätte, Frankfurt, 116
Greisheim-Sud day-care centre, Frankfurt, 74, 77–8
Grey water systems, 108
Gropius, Walter, 24

Hadow Report, 1931, 26
Halifax, *see* Ridings Secondary School, Halifax
Hall, Edward T, 1, 6
Hallfield School, Paddington, 31, 73–4, 91
Hammersmith, *see* Larmenier School, Hammersmith
Hampshire County Architects, 90, 95, 148, 193
Hampstead, *see* King Alfred School, Hampstead
Hampton, Geoff, 43
Hart, Roger A, 38
Hatfield House (plan), 7
Haute Vallée School, Jersey, 104, 105, 108, 129, 184–8
Haverstock Associates, 88
Heathland School, school assembly, 117
Heinz Galinski School, Berlin, 200–9
Helling Street Park, London, 110–11
Heritage Park School, Peterborough, 92–3
Hertford Junior School, 44
Hertzberger, Herman, 5, 32, 36, 56
Highfield Nursery, Saltley, 87
Highfields School, Long Eaton, 26
Hillside Home School, Wisconsin, 19–20
Hilversum developments, 28
Hochi-Dattwil complex, 93
Hogarth, Chris, 80
Horne, Sandra, 50–1
Horsham, *see* Tambridge House School, Horsham
Hübner, Peter, 118
Hunstanton School, 31–2
Hygienic environment concerns, 25–6

ICT, introduction into schools, 68
Ideal classroom, 50–1
  research project, 51–6
Impington Community College, 24
Initiatives in Design, 96
Isaacs, Susan, 21

Jersey, *see* Haute Vallée School, Jersey
Jersey College Preparatory School for Girls, 103
Jersey High School for Girls, 106, 115
Jigsaw, 118
Jobson, Richard, 95, 104, 129, 185
Johnson-Marshall, Stirrat, 26
Jonson Street Board School, Stepney, 16
Joseph, Sir Keith, 47

Kahn, Louis, 87
Karl Marx Hof development, 22–3, 31
Kendall, Henry, 11, 12
Kids Unlimited, 118
King Alfred School, Hampstead, 88–90

Kompan Kindergarten, 85
Landscapes, 111, 112–15
Larmenier School, Hammersmith, 113
Lasdun, Denys, 30, 31
Lawrence, Evelyn, 22
Le Corbusier, 24, 29, 31, 75–6
Learning environment checklist, 70–1
Learning process, 50
    environment checklist, 70–1
Learning Through Landscapes (LTL),
    111–12
Lehnert, Klaus, 43
Lescaze, William, 22, 23
Light and air requirements, 31–2, 67
'Lilliput' Nursery concept, 80, 122
Liquidated damages, 130
Little Village Academy, Chicago, 172–8
Lloyd Wright, Frank, 18, 19–20
Local Education Authorities (LEAs):
    Asset Management Plan (AMP),
        123–4
    capital project control, 123
    control framework, 120–1
    funding arrangements, 74, 120
Local Management of Schools (LMS),
    120, 131
    budget management, 74, 118
Lods, Marcel, 27
London Board Schools, 10, 11
'Lunch box wall', 72, 76
Lycée Polyvalent, Fréjus, 94, 95
Lyn Kinnear Associates, 110

Mackintosh, Charles Rennie, 16–18, 19
MacMillan, Margaret, 18, 25
Male teachers, 18
Malting House School, 21–2
Martyr's Public School, Glasgow, 16
Mary McLeod Bethune Elementary
    School, Rochester NY, 67
Michael Hopkins and Partners, 61
Milton Forman, 163
Milton Keynes, see Glastonbury Thorn
    First School, Milton Keynes
Ministry of Education, 32, 65
    Architects and Buildings Branch, 26
    see also Department for Education and
        Employment
Montessori, Maria, 18
Montessori system, 21
    Primary School, Delft, 56, 57
Morella, see Elementary School, Morella
Morris, Henry, 23–4, 25
Mortimore, Peter, 42
Multi User Dungeons (MUDs), 49
Myer, Hanns, 37

Nagele community, 35
National Audit Office, school energy
    review, 108

National Curriculum:
    effect on school design, 42, 45, 48–50,
        57, 65
    effect on writing teaching, 49
    as instrument of political control, 45–7,
        69
Neutra, Richard, 68
New Deal for Schools (NDS), 119
New Earswick village, 23, 25
Newham, see Brampton, 2000 project,
    Newham
North Fort Myers High School, Florida,
    209–14
Nottingham, see Good Shepherd Primary
    School, Nottingham
Nunn, Percy, 21
Nursery schools, 75–8

Oak Lane County Day School, 22
Odenwaldschule, Frankfurt, 224–6
O'Donnell and Tuomey, 168
O'Neil, Edward, 109
Open plan/closed plan experiments, 58
Open-air schools, 25, 27–8
Owen, Robert, 15

Papendrecht, see Anne Frank School,
    Papendrecht
Parker, Barry, 23
Patkau Associates, 138
Penn, Helen, 109
Perkins and Will, 209
Perret, August, 24
Pestalozzi, Johan, 10
Peter Hübner, 224, 226
Peterborough, see Heritage Park School,
    Peterborough
Photovoltaic cells, 108
Picton, Lydia, 117
Planning supervisor, 125
Playground layout, 8
Plincke, Leaman and Browning, see
    Architecture PLB
Plowden Report (1967), 27, 44
Pokesdown Primary School,
    Bournemouth, 163–7
Portakabin system, 80–1
Portsmouth, see Admiral Lord Nelson
    Secondary School
Prairie House formula, 20
Pre-school requirements, 75–9, 84
Prefabricated construction, 9, 26
    primary schools, 79
Prestolea School, Bolton, Fantasy
    Garden, 109–10
Primary/elementary school requirements,
    88–93
Private Finance Initiative (PFI), 118,
    124–5

Procurement process, changes, 73
Prouvé, Jean, 79

Queen Anne building style, 13, 15
Queen's Inclosure First School, Cowplain,
    41, 61–2, 90

Ranelagh Multi-Denominational School,
    Dublin, 168–71
Recurrent funds, 119
Reflective architect approach, 50–1
Richmond, nursery school, 103
Richmond High School for Girls, 30
Ridings Secondary School, Halifax, 117
Rietveld, Gerrit, 155, 159
Robson, E R, 19
    board school designs, 7, 10, 11, 12–13,
        15, 16
Roof lights, 103, 104
Room identification, 6

Safety requirements, building projects,
    125
St Benedict's Infant and Nursery School,
    Small Heath, 113–14
Saint Benno Catholic Secondary School,
    Dresden, 178–83
St Crispin's Secondary Modern School,
    Wokingham, 26
Saltley, see Highfield Nursery, Saltley
Sant'Elia nursery school, Como, 27
Sawston college, 24
Scharoun, Hans, 32–4, 38, 57
School Curriculum and Assessment
    Authority, 47
School Development Plan, 119, 127
School effectiveness, key factors, 42
'School Works' (research approach), 53
Schooling, definition, 41–2
Schroeder House, Utrecht, 159
Scotland, school development, 15–18
Scotland Street School, 17, 18
Seabird Island School, Agassiz, 138–41
Seaborne and Lowe, 8, 26
Secondary school requirements, 93–8
Security concerns, 108–9
Seed Challenge Capital, 119
Sensory garden, 87
Sheffield University:
    School of Architecture, 67
    Schools Research Unit, 82–3
Sheridan, Gerry, 63, 121
Single Regeneration Budget (SRB),
    Birmingham City Council, 74
Sir Norman Foster and Partners, 94, 95
Small group activities, effect on design, 49
Small Heath, see St Benedict's Infant and
    Nursery School, Small Heath
Smith, Dianne, 96
Smithson, Alison and Peter, 31–2

Social interaction, 99
Software technology, use in schools, 49–50
Southwark Central School, 13, 14
Special Agreement (Voluntary Aided) Schools, 121
Special needs schools, 84–8
    funding, 74
Special Schools, 121
Specialist Schools, 121–2
Speech and Learning Centre, Christopher Place, 87–8, 133–7
State education system, funding, 118–20
Stefan Scholz, 214, 220
Steiner, Rudolph, 232
Stephen Hawkins Primary School, Tower Hamlets, 88
Stewart, John, 61, 116
Stiff, Mike, 82
Stow, David, 15–16
Strawberry Vale School, Victoria, 141–4
Stuttgart-Stammheim School, 108, 118
Summerson, John, 38
Suresnes school, 27–8

Tambridge House School, Horsham, 103

Tehtaanmäki Elementary School, Anvalankoski, 2–5, 30
Tendering process, building projects, 127
Terragni, Giuseppe, 27
Thomas Carlyle Infant and Junior School, Nuthall, 64, 65, 108–9
Tower Hamlets, *see* Stephen Hawkins Primary School, Tower Hamlets
Tregenza, Peter, 67
Troughton and McAslam, 87, 133

Unwin, Raymond, 23, 25
Urban environment, 10
    schools development, 10–15
    schools in Scotland, 15–18
Urwin, S E, 24

Valentine, Gill, 44
Van Eyck, Aldo, 32, 35–6, 159
Van Heyningen and Haward Architects, 89
Vermeulen, Brian, 74, 80
Victoria, BC, *see* Strawberry Vale School, Victoria
Village schools, 12, 23, 26
Villejuif, prefabricated construction, 79
Voluntary aided schools funding, 74

Waldorf School, Chorweiler, Cologne, 226–33
Waldron, John, 98, 103
Westborough Primary School, Westcliff-on-Sea, 72, 74, 75–6, 145–8
Westcliff-on-Sea, *see* Westborough Primary School, Westcliff-on-Sea
Westville Road Primary School, Hammersmith, 9
Whiteley Woods Open Air School, Sheffield, 8, 26
Whitney-Elmhirst, Leonard and Dorothy, 22
Widows, George, 26
Wilderspin, Samuel, 10
William Tyndale School, Islington, 46
Wilson, Peter, 77–8
Windham Nursery School, Richmond upon Thames, 86
Wisewood School, Sheffield, display panels, 54
Wittwer, Hans, 37
Woodlea Primary School, Bordon, 31, 90, 91, 92, 148–53

Zvi Hecker, 200